Thinking – Resisting – Reading the Political

Thinking – Resisting – Reading the Political

Thinking Resistances
Current Perspectives on Politics and Communities in the Arts, Vol. 2

Edited by
Anneka Esch-van Kan, Stephan Packard,
and Philipp Schulte

diaphanes

1. Auflage / First Edition
ISBN 978-3-03734-217-6

www.diaphanes.net

Umschlag / Cover design: Eike Dingler
Satz und Layout / Prepress: 2edit, Zürich
Druck / Printing: Druckhaus Nomos, Sinzheim

Table of Contents

Anneka Esch-van Kan, Stephan Packard, Philipp Schulte
Politics and Aesthetics: Introduction 9

I. Thinking

Stephan Packard
Introduction 19

Maria Muhle
From the *Plebs* to the *Demos*
Two Notions of Political Subjectification 25

Chantal Mouffe
Democratic Politics in the Age of Post-Fordism 43

Josef Früchtl
As If We Could Trust
Fiction and Aesthetics of the Political 53

Dieter Mersch
The Political and the Violent
On Resistances 65

Friedrich Balke
All in Good Time? Fiction and the Possibility of Historic Events 89

Jacques Rancière
Doing or Not Doing: Politics, Aesthetics, Performance 101

II. Resisting

Anneka Esch-van Kan
Introduction 121

Judith Butler
Ethical Ambivalence 127

Frank Ruda
Thinking Politics Concretely
Negation, Affirmation, and the Dialectics of Dialectics and Non-Dialectics 137

Simon Critchley
Is Utopianism Dead? 155

Jon McKenzie
Abu Ghraib and the Society of the Spectacle of the Scaffold 163

Anneka Esch-van Kan
"Torture Chicks" – Resistance and the Political in Coco Fusco's *A Room of One's Own* and *A Field Guide for Female Interrogators* 185

Andreas Hetzel
Prendre la parole
Voices of Resistance in Contemporary Theory 201

III. Reading

Anneka Esch-van Kan and Philipp Schulte
Introduction 215

Armen Avanessian
Reading Political Theories (not) Reading
Towards a Contemporary Realism of Reference 221

Wim Peeters
Contesting "the Democratic Chattering of the Letter"
Politics of Commentary in 20th Century Literature 231

Juliane Rebentisch
Realism Today
Art, Politics, and the Critique of Representation 245

Nikolaus Müller-Schöll
Plus d'un rôle
Playing Together in Contemporary Dance, Theatre, and Performance 263

Philipp Schulte
Alternative Genealogies – Critique and Style in Contemporary Performance Art 275

Stephan Packard
Why are Story Arcs Dark and Gritty?
On the Metaphysics of Seriality in *Dexter* and Kammerer 291

Gabriel Rockhill
Critical Reflections on the Ontological Illusion
Rethinking the Relation between Art and Politics 311

Contributors 325

Anneka Esch-van Kan, Stephan Packard, Philipp Schulte

Politics and Aesthetics: Introduction

"La politique s'oppose spécifiquement à la police. La police est un partage du sensible dont le principe est l'absence de vide et de supplément."[1] In the seventh of his "Ten Theses on Politics," Jacques Rancière connects politics to an interruption of the sensible order of the police. If that order is to be considered as a distribution of the sensible, consigning parts of society to their respective modes of visibility and perception, then the disruption of that order may be easily and perhaps too easily linked to an emphatic aesthetics as relating to politics' disruptive impetus. But if we relegate the resistance of rare and transient politics, as it opposes the stability and the claim to permanence of the police, to aesthetic practices and their appreciation in criticism, we could easily turn out to be closing the voids and eradicating the supplements by appropriating their resistant potential through a proper placement in museums, galleries, on the stages of theatres – or of dance festivals and academic conferences. Such a turn would, for instance, identify political action directly with artistic performance, and reduce both while ostentatiously appreciating their respective *resistant* value, as Rancière points out in his inquiry into the various kinds of "doing" involved, in this volume.[2] Instead, the first aesthetic topic of politics and police is to be found in a much more basic, and much less "modern," partition of the conditions of the possibility of sensual experience, on which the aesthetic practices of the arts can only be superposed, not as modulations but as explorations of further possibilities of perception.[3]

And yet, philosophical considerations in and of politics cannot help but refer to the aesthetics of the arts as well as of the discourses in the realm of the police, even as students, critics and scholars of the arts cannot help but be informed by their understanding of the political dimension of aesthetic interruptions and eruptions. Perhaps more importantly, resistance in the present has hardly avoided mediations of philosophy, as well as aesthetics, in its presentations, as well as its

---

1 "Politics is opposed specifically to police. Police is a distribution of the sensible, its principle being the absence of voids and supplements." (Translation S.P.) – Jacques Rancière, "Dix Thèses sur la Politique," *Aux bords du politique* (Paris: Gallimard, 1998), pp. 221–254, p. 240.

2 Pp. 101–118.

3 Compare Jacques Rancière, *Le Partage du sensible. Esthétique et politique* (Paris: La Fabrique, 2000), chapt. 1.

reflections and judgments. So there is no way to circumvent the apparently essential unease of that triad of thinking, resisting, and reading politics.

Among the voices collected here, Jon McKenzie perhaps best demonstrates the bitterness of such unease when he examines the spectacle of the scaffold re-emerging in the Abu Ghraib photography, found to be in inescapable contact with aesthetic traditions of the staged as well as the pictorial, and to retouch the appearance of sovereign power alongside the exterior significance of a brutal state of exception.[4] Clearly, any rash optimism pulling together subversive points of irony in comfortable artistic playfulness with a claim to politically relevant resistance or reflection falls short of the underlying disagreement of orders, concepts, and expectations – and threatens instead to return to that "consensus at the centre" against which Chantal Mouffe continues to warn intentions towards sincerely democratic politics.[5]

In her seminal piece on "Ethical Ambivalence," reprinted in this volume,[6] Judith Butler reflects that an apparent or merely alleged recent return to ethics might have constituted an escape from politics. The discomfort that separates once more the discursive establishment of a newly found ethics from the disconnections of an eventual reintroduction of possibilities in some ways echoes the strain of sustaining a gap, a void and potential for supplements, between reading and thinking politics. Yet even as a part of philosophy seems to some to have fled to the departments of art, theatre, or comparative literature, in a movement which might sometimes threaten the clarifying and corrective rigor of philosophical discipline, philosophy repeatedly presents itself as readings, or an emergence from readings, of thereby newly canonized literatures, performances, and arts (as Armen Avanessian points out).[7]

What shape, then, is left for a productive triangulation of philosophy, resistance, and reading? Scholars' commentary might always be said to relieve the contingency of the aesthetic text by fixing if not its meanings, then its validated effects (as Wim Peeters explores in detail)[8]; and Gabriel Rockhill's recent reconsiderations of ontological illusions between politics and art describe the "talisman complex," "according to which the politics of art amounts to a political force inherent in works of art that is supposedly capable of producing politi-

---

4 Pp. 163–183.

5 Pp. 43–51.

6 Pp. 127–136.

7 Pp. 221–230.

8 Pp. 231–243.

cal consequences through a nebulous, preternatural alchemy."[9] And yet to deny that resistance is voiced in contemporary theory is to render its appropriation of concepts incomprehensible, and to ignore the power of aesthetic re-framings and experiments in active resistance (as Simon Critchley's analyses make clear).[10] This would effectively mean discarding some of the very forms of perceptions available to their politics outside the distribution of the sensible; denying any potential of theory and art to generate forms of perception that interrupt a given distribution of the sensible, whether or not they thereby allow politics to show or to take place.

In thinking, resisting, and reading politics, there is, then, a tendency and a temptation to confuse three aspects by excluding their differences in a focus on their mutual dependencies or independent assemblies, thus arresting the very irritation of politics in a newly fixed distribution of sensibilities. As Rancière remarks in one of his most prominent readings, such a "disparition tendancielle des différences de la politique et du droit dans l'indistinction éthique définit aussi un certain présent de l'art et de la réflexion esthétique."[11] But still the readings continue. It is in this three-way tension that the efforts of the new contributions and reprints of this volume operate: Thinking – Resisting – Reading the Political.

It is here that the unease accompanying the treatment of resistant politics and their aesthetics in established aesthetic criticism may turn to the similar, but differently aligned distinction of politics and the political, as suggested by a number of approaches that are subsumed under the notion of theories of radical democracy.[12] While *la politique*'s opposition to *la police* might be said to return in the contrast of the political versus politics, it is at once possible to consider Mouffe's and Laclau's political as a meeting place of *la politique* and *la police*.[13] These distinctions converge in a difference between an ontic level of politics as an established political order, consisting of practices of government and functional distributions of the sensible, and an ontological

---

9 Pp. 311–323, here 311.

10 Pp. 155–162.

11 "The gradual disappearance of differences between politics and law in an ethical indistinctiveness also defines a certain present of art and aesthetic reflection." (Translation S.P.) – Jacques Rancière, "Le tournant éthique de l'esthétique et de la politique," *Malaise dans l'esthétique* (Paris: Galilée, 2004), pp. 143–173, p. 159.

12 See Chantal Mouffe and Ernesto Laclau, *Hegemony and Socialist Strategy. Towards a Radical Democratic Politics* (London: Verso, 1985).

13 Jacques Rancière, "Afterword / The Method of Equality: An Answer to Some Questions," *Jacques Rancière: History, Politics, Aesthetics*, ed. Gabriel Rockhill and Philipp Watts (Durham: Duke University Press, 2009), pp. 273–288, p. 287.

level, at which politics returns to its basic decidability and decisionism, oriented towards transient events, breaches and ruptures of sensible orders defining and re-defining their distributions.[14]

But if such conceptualizations of politics and the political reflect and depend upon readings of aesthetics as well as stances of resistance, how do they change when they return to re-inform readers as well as movements? When placed between the thinking and the reading of the political, in which ways do or even should acts of resistance turn into manners of resisting either politics, or even the political itself? And how can political reflections and stances justifiably inform aesthetic readings?

At this point, these questions may be phrased as a return to an age-old question of method: Which paths – pre-established or constantly reinvented – may or must research in literary criticism, theatre studies, art history, dance studies and other disciplines reflecting arts travel in analyzing its objects? The question commonly attracts special emphasis where the contemplated forms of art aspire to, or are ascribed, resistant or political qualities, be it as direct topics or as the center of exploratory orbits; be it that they evade established grids of perception and analysis systematically or erratically. Μέϑοδος is to take a certain way in order to reach a clear goal; but more recent endeavors deliberately turn away from a pre-established clarity of known goals and continue to redefine the object of analysis in its very course, accepting that to take the project seriously is to consider that the eventual goal might lack preliminary visibility, a problem exacerbated but not created by the most recent thoughts on philosophy, politics, and their distributions of the sensible. An unquestioning application of methods pursuing predetermined goals would preclude all disruptions of that distribution, while traditional enumerations of forms and functions have their own exclusions, gaps, and supplements. A *critical* practice, on the other hand, following Michel Foucault's perspective, has to enable a continuing return to questions and re-examinations of the limits of the most fixed modes of thought. As a practice, such critique "oversees a domain it would want to police and is unable to regulate."[15] And yet in the same argument, Foucault defines critique as an attitude rather than a method, as an "art of voluntary insubordination",[16] always keeping

---

14 See especially Oliver Marchart, *Post-Foundational Political Thought – Political Difference in Nancy, Lefort, Badiou and Laclau* (Edinburgh: Edinburgh University Press, 2007).

15 Michel Foucault, "What is Critique," *The Politics of Truth*, ed. Sylvere Lotringer, trans. Lysa Hochroth (Los Angeles, CA: Semiotext(e), 2007), pp. 41–81, p. 42.

16 Ibid., p. 47.

up its flexibility and evading, as a means of reflection, its own reliance on the institutions and mechanisms of power.

Our own perspectives on the questions surrounding the thinking, resisting, and reading of the political diverge. One might emphasize the need for that insubordinate flexibility (Schulte). At the same time, one might replace the safety of strict methods with a desire for equally strictly argued consequences from political theory in aesthetic theory (Packard). Or one might stress the need for a critical (meta-)reflection of one's own premises and ways of doing research – which includes the explicit consideration of the relationships and dynamics between thinking, resisting and reading the political – as an integral part of readings that attempt to trace the political in art and theory (Esch-van Kan). From different directions, we each return to the issues that started an international conference by the same title in Giessen in October 2010 and are continued in this volume: Which perspectives and methods does advanced cultural theory offer for our attempts to grasp political discourse and analyze aesthetic treatments and performances of resistance today?

It is under this general motto that the conference brought together scholars from the fields of theatre, literature, art, and media studies, from cultural theory, sociology, and philosophy, to discuss possibilities and limits of current models and attempt new approaches. Conference discussions focused on the areas of tension between reading, thinking, and resisting the political, theory, and art: In what theoretically describable forms of thought can resistance appear, and how can resistance be thought of as an object of theory? How can the political mark certain texts, and what procedures are available for a reading that is marked by an appropriate sensibility for the contents and orders of the political?

This volume – along with its companion focusing on *Dance, Politics, and Co-Immunity* – continues and expands these discussions. It aims to better understand, clearly describe and critically discuss such concepts of a political dimension in aesthetics by looking at those facets of the political that are problematized in the differing disciplines and discourses: At phenomena, that is, that depend upon their fundamental incommensurability with representations and institutions, with stable notions of political order and uninterrupted political discourse. Such interpretations distance themselves from a simple equation of political reading with an interest in politically engaged, appellative texts and literatures that support or accuse specific party politics or revolutionary programs; nor does their focus rest on purely literary treatments of categorical de- and re-differentiation in established political discourse, as they are discussed in postcolonial, gender, and minority studies among others. Rather, a first summary might confront the political as intended in our title with the incoherencies balancing the politics of coherent commonality and communicability in favor of conflicting political autonomy and enouncement.

Our point of departure was a perceived doubled deficit: The demands and possibilities of these concepts had rarely been fulfilled or even systematically considered in cultural studies. Faced with a large number of almost positivistically empirical studies focusing on particular phenomena on the one hand, and ambitioned speculative designs on the other, we found a vast array of possible links, each of which has proven itself productive, and yet each of which threatens to oversimplify the "application" of single terms and ideas taken from overarching theories by turning them into tools for highly specialized disciplines. At the same time, it is the political ambitions and presuppositions of many superficially adopted theories that seemed to be insufficiently reflected, sometimes even hardly made aware of, in such "applications".

The intention that brought together the following voices was to attack both deficits. Both, we suggest, are owed not least to the difficulties engendered by the very idea of an "application," a "use" that is in itself often foreign to the main tenets of the original discourses. Again, a naïve concept of method in the sense of established philosophy of science, or even following traditionally hermeneutical, descriptive, e.g. structuralist, and most poststructuralist approaches sometimes misrepresents theory as a toolbox, its instruments readily separated from their originating beliefs and turned to the screws and nails of otherwise unconnected objects of culture and art. But these stand in stark contrast to the central observation that political, social, conceptual conditions and artistic practices are incontrovertibly interlinked. Similarly unconvincing are those adoptions of radical theory that avoid discussing any consequences from the positions they adopt, omitting the necessary reflection of their own view of scientific and scholarly practice in contemporary cultural studies.

Directly or indirectly, each of the following contributions discusses the problematic "consequences in methodology" attributed to these theories from a number of different vantage points. During and after the conference, the interdisciplinary setup provided opportunities to productively and controversially discuss theories of various provenience and to grapple with works of art and individual analyses, examining, defending, or rejecting the possibility of a methodology informed by advanced theory.

Can there be methods for a scholarly sound reading of the political? Is the activity of dealing with always already elusive and thus doubly resistant categories at all graspable in terms of methods or techniques? And whatever the answer may be, can it in turn help us to better understand common suppositions of methodology and contribute to a productive argument on what a method is, has been, or could be today – or by what it might be replaced? Within the continuing discussion, here is a plurality of views and journeys of that tense field of inquiries.

*

Neither our conference nor this volume would have been possible without the generous organizational or financial backing of our partners: the International Centre for the Study of Culture (GCSC) as well as the Centre for Media and Interactivity, the Presidium and the Giessener Hochschulgesellschaft at Justus-Liebig-University Giessen as well as the Institute for Media Culture Studies and the French Centre at Albert-Ludwigs-University in Freiburg. Most of all, the GCSC, which hosted the original conference, counts two of the three editors among its members, and has developed into a splendid and varied place of disciplinary and interdisciplinary communication, has nourished and placed complete confidence in this project from the start. We are greatly indebted to each and every one of these institutions and the individuals that they present, and wish to offer our sincere gratitude for their tremendous trust, guidance and support. Special thanks are due to the choreographers Mette Ingvartsen, Xavier Le Roy, and Saša Asentić, whose artistic projects during the festival *Dance & Politics* accompanied our and the parallel conference on *Dance, Politics & Co-Immunity*, leaving us with important impulses for our discussions. The Kulturamt Giessen and the Hessian Theatre Academy generously supported these performances.

Our personal thanks go to Gerald Siegmund and Stefan Hölscher at the Giessen Institute for Applied Theatre Studies, who developed the parallel project on *Dance, Politics & Co-Immunity* in close collaboration. The many joint discussions on academic concepts as well as organizational issues never failed to be friendly and productive. We also feel obliged to Jörn Ahrens, who co-organized the conference, and to Wim Peeters, who actively took part in the discussions out of which the idea for this project emerged. We give profuse thanks to the hardworking student assistants who did tremendously well and became an integral part of the conference. They not only made sure things run smoothly, but videotaped all lectures and made them available online at www.mefeedia.com/channel/121241/episodes. Thanks also go to the hundreds of international scholars, students and artists who travelled to Giessen to actively take part in this event. But most of all, our gratitude is to the speakers and contributors at the conference and for this volume. It is the inspiring, sophisticated and yet ever personal co-operation of all these different institutions, disciplines, and scholars that allowed the construction of this platform for interdisciplinary and international debate. Last but not least, we give our thanks to diaphanes for publishing this volume. We sincerely hope that the perspectives, arguments and questions of this volume will reach their audience and inspire its readers to engage in the ongoing conversation.

I. Thinking

Stephan Packard

Introduction

This volume traces concepts of the political between that *politique* which interrupts the *police* order or distribution of the sensible, and that *political* which opposes *politics* in its insistence on a genuinely democratic interruption of deliberative democracy. But thinking the political is not the same as to engage in political thought, nor merely to reflect upon politics. Any intention to think the political is not least challenged to make the differences to the latter pursuits explicit: How can it conceive of the thought in political movements and events without confusing concept and realized action, and how can it at once prevent that distinction from turning into the kind of abstraction that protects all concrete political actions and inactions from any irritations or interventions, which a purely reflective philosophy threatens to stage only in name?

When the first discussions for this project began in early 2009, and our plans were still focused on a much smaller and regional, predominantly German-speaking symposium, we worked with the paronomastic title *politisches denken – widerständiges lesen*, phrases that allow at least two translations: *to think the political* no less than *political thought*, as well as *to read the resistant* and *resistant readings*. The idea was by no means original, as we soon found out: the next year, Ulrich Bröckling and Robert Feustel published a volume on *Das Politische denken*, and that volume had in fact resulted from a lecture series by the same name back in 2007 and 2008.[1] (And of course, the Yearbook *Politisches Denken* with its much broader, but less ambiguous focus on "political thought" has been around since 1991, its publishing society dating back to 1989.[2] In this unambiguous sense, the term is consistently established no later than by Hannah Arendt's essays in the 1950s, and its meaning reaches back in scope to Ancient Greece.[3]) So

---

1 Ulrich Bröckling and Robert Feustel, eds., *Das Politische denken. Zeitgenössische Positionen* (Bielefeld: transcript, 2010). The editors discuss the doubled meanings of the phrase on the very first page (p. 7). The lecture series had taken place at the Institut für Politikwissenschaft at Leipzig University.

2 Volker Gerhardt et al., eds., *Politisches Denken* (1991-). The interdisciplinary Deutsche Gesellschaft zur Erforschung des Politischen Denkens (DGEPD) co-operates with the *Conference on the Study of Political Thought* (CSPT).

3 "Our tradition of political thought had its definite beginning in the teachings of Plato and Aristotle [...]," Hannah Arendt, "Tradition and the Modern Age," *Between Past and Future* ([1954], reprint New York: Penguin, 1995), pp. 17–40, p. 17.

while we can make no claim to precedence, much less uniqueness, the revisited ambivalence expressed in such recent grammar games pinpoints a problem that is central to the understanding of recent philosophical theories concerning politics and the political. It is not first produced by the topical bent towards aesthetic criticism and practices of reading, but the very issues of accepted or transformed perception are of inevitable importance for the distinctions needed in thinking the political in modernity. For the practices of artistic interpretation and aesthetic validation become confused with those of politics in defining ways.

So if the contributions in this first section are assembled with an eye to consider concepts and processes of thought that can present – not grounds, rules, or applicable concepts, but rather – impulses, insistences, and actual interventions for the attempts to read resistance while maintaining a resistance in reading, then to that extent we might ask precisely how they distinguish *Politisches denken* and *politisches Denken*, and render political thought and thoughts about the political recognizable. It might be useful, then, to recall some of the most typical confusions that counteract clear distinctions in a context of contemporary studies in aesthetics. Confusions in this sense are not understood as mere mistakes in defining or applying abstract concepts,[4] but as concrete and observable processes, repeated shifts in thought that bring forth identifications of phenomena and adopt describable functions within discursive practice and political order. There is, for instance, an insistence on that very processuality, denying the stability of binary semiotic descriptions of texts, performances, and images no less than those of political orders, juridical systems, and governmental representation. Gilles Deleuze has traced the emergence of blind spots and voids in the course of structuralists' incessant negotiations that are the practice of structuralism's claims of already negotiated structures.[5] But even if the "principle of the absence of void and supplement" defines *la politique* for Jacques Ranciére,[6] and the reference both to Deleuze and Derrida holds true,[7] still the reintroduction of this neces-

4 Compare the concept of confusion in Gerge Spencer Brown, *Laws of Form* (reprint Portland: Cognizer, 1994), pp. 11, 18, et passim.

5 Gilles Deleuze, "A quoi reconnaît-on le structuralisme?" *Histoire de la philosophie VIII. Le XXe siècle*, ed. François Châtelet (Paris: Hachette, 1973).

6 Jacques Rancière, "Dix Thèses sur la Politique," *Aux bords du politique* (Paris: Gallimard, 1998), pp. 221–254, p. 240. Compare the introduction to this volume.

7 On Deleuze, see Jacques Rancière, *Ist Kunst widerständig* [*Si l'art résiste à quelque chose?*], ed. and trans. Frank Ruda and Jan Völker (Berlin: Merve, 2008). On Derrida, see Jacques Rancière, "The Thinking of Dissensus: Politics and Aesthetics," *Reading*

sity in structuralist analyses of any text or piece of art, increasingly conscious in more recent structuralist and in post-structuralist work, cannot identify each specific aesthetic crux with the suspension of the distribution of the sensible incorporating *la police*.

The concept of suspension and irritation itself offers another, yet different potential for confusion: As moments of aesthetic irritation or rhetorical sublimity may interrupt ordered sensibilities in intractable instances,[8] they are nevertheless the expected exception, the ascribed function in a situation defined by the social sphere from which established art emerges, while politics in this understanding would remain distinct in another sphere. The borders violated by the sublime are building blocks of the critical philosophy that denies it the structure of otherwise thinkable concepts. Negotiations on perception as style then do not elicit, but replace renegotiations of representations as power. Furthermore, by insisting on the *Ansinnen* of aesthetic judgment,[9] the foundation of that observed disruption turns into an appeal to consensus, as participants agree that the astounding fact disrupts the agreeable concepts of agreed-upon boundaries, avoiding the unreconciled and fundamentally disagreeable dissent proper to the political.

There is also a *via negativa* of the transient and rare political that appears not least as aesthetic moments of this kind eventually fail to identify political suspensions, and the order of the truly political event is then declared yet more elusive, still more unpredictable, and ever more inconceivable. Instead of discovering the political in every interesting piece of art, it is then sought in vain in any political action: Not this performance, not this image – not this demonstration, not this movement. As Alain Badiou maintains, "when Lula became the president of Brazil, it was a simple fact and not an event of historical transcendence"; and "it's clear that Obama's victory is not a political event."[10]

Not in a correction, but in an acknowledgment of productive confusions, a reversal may consider these shifts, inclusions, and exclusions of the political in other observations its very characteristic in modernity. The fascination with processuality as a representation of

---

Rancière, ed. Paul Bowman and Richard Stamp (London: Continuum, 2011), p. 1–17, esp. pp. 12–14.

8 Compare, for instance: Neil Hetz, *The End of the Line* (Columbia: Columbia University Press, 1985), esp. pp. 40–46.

9 Immanuel Kant, *Kritik der Urteilskraft*, § 29.

10 Alain Badiou, "Is the Word 'Communism' Forever Doomed?," lecture held on Nov 6, 2008, at Miduel Abreu Gallery in New York; archived at *Lacan.com* (http://www.lacan.com/essays/?page_id=323, publ. unknown, cit. August 2012).

transience in symbolic structures, the intractability of modern aesthetic judgment and the sublime, and the insistent rareness of accepted political events are then assembled as aesthetics of the political and its complications in representation. Philosophy turns political by at once returning such aporia to politics, as Rancière emphasizes,[11] as well as by recognizing it as it appears in the discourses of politics, art, and elsewhere, precisely because its seemingly arbitrary reproduction participates in the political's transience. The contributions in this section not only lead on to the careful observation of emphatic affirmations of the political in resistance, and to considerations of the consequences from these concepts of the political for reading resistances, but place these eventual connections as the vanishing points of their arguments.

The first two contributions refer to and reinterpret the concepts of *politique* and the *political* respectively. Maria Muhle reconsiders the tradition and departure of Rancière from Foucauldian discourse analysis, recapitulating the basic concepts of *politics* and *police* in her examination of the *plebs* and the *demos* as terms and concepts between these thinkers. To think the political as a politics of the supplement returned to the voidless police is to acknowledge the precondition for the latter's rupture, and to render it distinguishable. Across that rupture, the *demos* is that which is at once the whole and its part, and the defining moment of those that lack a part in the whole. Its aesthetic involves a "quasi-mimetic capacity,"[12] to which Foucault's treatment of the *plebs* as an aspect of the infamous can be considered precursory. This leads to what is probably the central, certainly the most persistent question of thinking the political: How can resistance be thought within systems, if those systems double as the objects of resistance? As Foucault places the resistance of the *plebs* within the relations of power from which it emerges, the mimesis that familiarizes resistance at its most dangerous with the shape of the resisted comes into focus.

Chantal Mouffe's "Democratic Politics in the Age of Post-Fordism," reprinted in this volume, turns the definition of the political as ontologically opposing politics to the issue of its rareness: Is the disappearance of radical adversity progressive, and is it total? Contrasting the Frankfurt school to the autonomist Marxism emerging in the 1960s, Mouffe's seminal argument centers on the parallel and co-extensive shift from Fordian production to a "post-Fordism" as a reaction to new resistances. From the perspective of a theory of hegemony, the cultural inertia of the consensus, she reintroduces basic concepts of her radical

---

11 Jacques Rancière, *La Mésentente. Politique et Philosophie* (Paris: Galilée, 1995), p. 9.
12 P. 38.

democratic theory, at once acknowledging and pleading for genuinely antagonistic practice informing continued transformations.

If the similarities and precise differences between the two traditions of thinking the political taken up in this volume are thus presented and productively recast, the following two essays open up the controversy about their very preconditions. Demonstrating the reliance on a consensus in ascribing aesthetic as well as moral and political judgments, Josef Früchtl defends the mode of the consensual *as if*, a fiction that allows, as he argues, not only for the stability of political discourses negotiating controversy, but also for the mimetic assumption of equality essential to any radically democratic resistance. Früchtl thus repositions Rancière, but also reconsiders how Habermas' theory of truth within speech acts turns into a decisively political point of view, moving him closer to Lyotard's description of the *différend*. Just as the *différend* needs to be understood by the differing parties, for Habermas dissent requires the possibility of agreeing to disagree, starkly opposed to the radical disagreement of a Rancièrian *mésentente.* And yet Früchtl sees the same basic potential for consensus at the very heart of the "aesthetic community" that may recognize the claim to equality in resistance movements as well as the exception of the aesthetic experience.

Dieter Mersch re-examines the possibilities for the political within a language theory organized towards speech acts with quite different results. Arguing from a broad semiotic perspective, Mersch emphasizes the divisions in every performative act. Far from accepting their reconciliation by a consensus accepted for its epistemological as well as discursive necessity, he points out the "the key dissociation and thus anomie or anarchy of the performative"[13]: There is a violence immanent to performance and any signification, which introduces discordant *katastrophé* as an inevitable element of the very *conditio humana*, culminating in a diabolical and a tragic potential for politics in each human action, which is not ultimately closed off nor enabled by the fiction of consensual understanding, but on the contrary remains an incessant threat to teleologically understood and conceived action.

From this controversially tense field of thinking the political, how does the observation of resistance become conceivable? The final two contributions specify this for two differently circumscribed fields. Friedrich Balke discusses the fiction and the possibility of historic events, contrasting the envelopment of all exceptions in the impossibility of historical deviance as claimed in the exemplary mode of the

13 P. 72–73.

Annales-school with the role of the heretic that can only be defended against such appeals to homogeneous and hegemonic periodization. The fiction is here unambiguously located in the archive, and the many small fictions that archives employ to close their gaps and render their descriptions continuous are exposed. Opposition to these practices is found in the insistence on the event as evidenced in the series of repetitions in Borges' *Menard's Quijote*, which reiterates the seemingly exact same sentence as written by Cervantes and showcases how utterly unalike the repetition becomes, and how it reimagines its original in a newly heretical interpretation that transgresses the apparent consensus of either period.

Concluding this section, Jacques Rancière once more re-examines the problem of performance situated at the very heart of the concept of action, turned here to an inquiry into the "activation" so often sought in political movements, and ascribed to politically engaging arts. Considering the imagery of early 20th century film, Rancière connects the issue of action to the distinction of a "natural" and a "mechanical" man or agent: The depiction and dissection of bodies and movements in posters and cinematic sequences. The interruption here focuses on "the gap between functionality and play,"[14] which is reflected and reshaped in several artistic renditions of dance, movement, and corporality. It is in this mode of analysis that the aesthetic becomes neither a stand-in nor an instigator of the political, but rather the political and its aporias are returned to politics precisely through the consideration of the aporetical claim to activity and activation in performance. The thus reactivated ambivalence of thinking the political returns at a similar juncture for the essays at the beginning of the following section.

---

14 P. 116.

Maria Muhle

From the *Plebs* to the *Demos* Two Notions of Political Subjectification

> Dans son principe, comme dans son origine historique, la représentation est le contraire de la démocratie. La démocratie est fondée sur l'idée d'une compétence égale de tous. Et son mode normal de désignation est le tirage au sort, tel qu'il se pratiquait à Athènes, afin d'empêcher l'accaparement du pouvoir par ceux qui le désirent. La représentation, elle, est un principe oligarchique: ceux qui sont ainsi associés au pouvoir représentent non pas une population mais le statut ou la compétence qui fondent leur autorité sur cette population: la naissance, la richesse, le savoir ou autres.
> (Jacques Rancière, "L'élection, ce n'est pas la démocratie," *Nouvel Observateur*, April 18th, 2012.)

In a recent interview, published only a few days before the first round (*premier tour*) of the French presidential elections on April 22, 2012, Jacques Rancière exposes his understanding of politics. He theorizes politics through the opposition between "representation" (or representational democracy) as an oligarchical principle, and another notion of democracy as founded on the assumption of the equal capacity of anyone and everyone, and functioning in the mode of the "drawing of lots". While the oligarchical principle presupposes a *specific* capacity that gives access to power, such as birth, wealth or knowledge, the truly democratic principle presupposes the negation of *any* specific capacity and the affirmation or enactment of a fundamental equality: "Politics only exists through the bringing off of the equality of anyone and everyone in a vacuous freedom of a part of the community that deregulates any count of parts."[1]

In the following, I would like to take a closer look at this opposition between representation and democratic indifference. Rancière relates this to the Platonic partition between the harmonious order of the common, where every party and body of the common is attributed its specific part (lot) and acts in consequence, and the negation of that distribution by the excessive power of the poets to do several things at once. It is this excessive power that Rancière rephrases in the notion of the literary excess and/or the homonymic capacity of words that blur the specific and specifying logic of the police. I will thus expose,

1 Jacques Rancière, *The Disagreement* (Minneapolis: The University of Minnesota Press, 1999), p. 61.

in the first part of this text, the opposition between politics and police in order to understand the central function of the figure of the people – the *demos* – for Rancièrian politics.

In the second part, I would like to confront this notion of the *demos* that Rancière presents as a non-sociological category designating "those who have no part" to another political but non-sociological entity – the notion of the *plebs*, as Michel Foucault outlines it in the interview "Powers and Strategies" with Rancière published in 1977 in *Révoltes Logiques*.[2] The idea behind this confrontation would be to interrogate the link between the Foucauldian notion of power and Rancière's reformulation of the opposition between politics and police. One might think of it as the resuming of Foucault's critical analysis through Rancière's notion of politics as a possibility to reconfigure the relation between the common and its partition. The subtext of this proposition is the often-made reproach to Foucault that his notion of politics is purely negative, and that he does not allow for a *positive* notion of politics. Or, put differently, that resistance to power is not possible in his theoretical mind-set, since power is everywhere and every relation is already a power relation, since there is no outside to power. Even though I would claim that this reproach is far too simplistic, it is true that Foucault, at least in his major works, describes resistance in a very reductive and rather unclear way as the capacity "to counter the grips of power with the claims of bodies, pleasures, and knowledges, in their multiplicity and their possibility of resistance."[3] From here a straight line is often drawn to Foucault's turn to the subject (or to the self) in the last two volumes of the *History of Sexuality*, where the practices of the self are understood as an individualistic possibility of resistance. In opposition to this almost canonical reading of Foucault, I would like to ask if it is possible to understand the introduction of the notion of the *plebs*, in the interview with Rancière, and the extrapolation of the plebeian logic in several interviews and articles mostly related to the *dossier* Pierre Rivière and his work about the Groupe d'Information sur les prisons (G.I.P), as a precursor or premonitory element of Rancière's notion of the *demos*.

---

2 Michel Foucault, "Powers and Strategies" (1977), *Power/Knowledge*, ed. Colin Gordon (New York: Pantheon Books, 1980), pp. 134–145; see also Michel Foucault, "Social Work, Social Control, and Normalization: Roundtable discussion with Michel Foucault," *Reading Foucault For Social Work*, ed. A. Chambon, A. Irving, and L. Epstein (New York: Columbia University Press, 1999), pp. 83–97.

3 Michel Foucault, *The History of Sexuality. An Introduction* (New York: Random House, 1978), p. 157.

Politics and Police

Rancière's political theory moves between two conceptual complexes: the reformulation of the opposition between police and politics on the one hand, and the conceptualisation of the fundamental aesthetics of politics through the notion of the distribution of the sensible (*le partage du sensible*) on the other. Rancière formulates the first complex, the opposition between police and politics, in *The Disagreement* and takes it up, among others, in his "Ten theses on politics," first given as a lecture in 1996 at the Istituto Gramsci in Bologna. The notion of politics that Rancière considers is, first of all, confronted to and differentiated from the kind of interpretation of politics that someone in the line of Hannah Arendt would propose – i.e. politics understood as an interaction of free political subjects, capable of free actions, in a free public space. On the contrary, it is Rancière's formulation of the notion of *police* that relies on such a model of politics, since the police encompasses those mechanisms and operations: Rancière locates all the operations that are normally thought of as specifically political, such as the formation of and the agreement upon a type of community, the organisation of powers, the distribution of the places and functions, and the legitimization of that distribution, in the realm of the *police*.

The police therefore is "not a social function but a symbolic constitution of the social" that Rancière opposes to the common understanding of police: "The essence of police lies neither in repression nor even in control over the living. Its essence lies in a certain way of dividing up the sensible."[4] The operations of the police, like the operations of politics, are essentially linked to *a visibility or invisibility of the bodies in the common space*. Or, as he says in *The Disagreement:* "Policing is not so much the 'disciplining' of bodies as a rule governing their appearing, a configuration of *occupations* and the properties of the spaces where these occupations are distributed."[5] The police determines a

---

4 Jacques Rancière, "Ten Theses on Politics," *Dissensus* (London/New York: Continuum, 2010), pp. 27–52, p. 36.

5 Rancière, *The Disagreement*, p. 29. Samuel A. Chambers insists on the fact that Rancière, who seldom quotes any other thinkers, when introducing the notion of the police refers to Foucault's analysis of the "petty police" as a "more general order that arranges that tangible reality in which bodies are distributed in community" (Rancière, *The Disagreement*, p. 28). He emphasizes that Rancière's notion of the police thus already functions within Foucault's notion of governmental power relations because, as Chambers states: "'police order' designates not only phenomena much more general than the 'petty police' but also irreducible to simple domination or inequality." Samuel A. Chambers, "The Politics of the Police: from Neoliberal-

specific order of the visible and the sayable, in which some activities are visible while others are not, in which some words are perceived as discourse and others only perceived as noise: *Police* embodies a "logic of inequality" that determines the roles, activities and appearances in relation to specific capacities or qualities, such as birth, wealth, knowledge. *Politics*, on the contrary, emerges when this logic of inequality is confronted with a logic of equality, i.e. with an activity that interrupts the harmonious distribution of places, spaces and activities and redistributes them. Politics thus does not make the invisible visible but rather enacts the fundamental fact that nothing is naturally invisible, that invisibility is always produced by others and does not exist as a natural condition. In the same way, it does not transform noise into discourse but demonstrates that the opposition between noise and discourse is part of the police logic of inequality.

Consequently, both police and politics are defined by Rancière in terms of their way of partitioning the sensible space – and this is the second complex in Rancière's political thought –, which means dividing the common into different shares and distributing these shares in a specific way. The partition of the sensible neither always belongs to the realm of politics nor to the realm of police, but describes the way in which the individuals, their occupation, and their appearance relate to each other. In his interview on *The Distribution of the Sensible*, in which Rancière further explores some of the more provocative theses of *The Disagreement* (especially those related to the aesthetics of politics and the distribution of the sensible), he gives the following definition of what he means by the expression "distribution of the sensible":

> The distribution of the sensible reveals who can have a share in what is common to the community based on what they do and on the time and space in which this activity is performed. Having a particular 'occupation' thereby determines the ability or inability to take charge of what is common to the community; it defines what is visible or not in a common space, endowed with a common language, etc. There is thus an 'aesthetics' at the core of politics [...].[6]

---

ism to Anarchism, and Back to Democracy," *Reading Rancière*, ed. Paul Bowman and Richard Stamp (London: Continuum, 2011), pp. 18–43, pp. 22–23. On this point, see also Friedrich Balke, "Zwischen Polizei und Politik. Eine Genealogie des ästhetischen Regimes," *Das Politische und die Politik*, ed. Thomas Bedorf and Kurt Röttgers (Frankfurt/M.: Suhrkamp, 2010), p. 207–234, pp. 214–216.

6 Jacques Rancière, "The Distribution of the Sensible," *The Politics of Aesthetics*, trans. Gabriel Rockhill (London: Continuum, 2004), pp. 7–45, p. 13.

Consequently, the realm of the police is defined by the fact that every body or individual or class is attributed a specific occupation, which at the same time determines their degree of participation in the common. Whereas the wealthy men, as in the classical Aristotelian model, have the leisure and time to discuss the issues of the *polis*, the state, the worker is busy maintaining the community physically, i.e. he is in charge of the survival of the community and has simply no time to participate in its configuration.

Thus, a redistribution of the sensible is political, as Rancière explains, not only insofar as it makes an individual body or group of bodies appear, but inasmuch as this appearance relates to the whole of the community and fundamentally redistributes the established partitions, therefore underscoring the constructedness of the so-called natural order of things.

Politics of the Supplement

Rancière distinguishes two principles that grant the qualification to rule within the realm of police: the order of *filiation* or the power of birth on the one hand, and the order of activities in a society or the power of *wealth* on the other. The conventional historico-political progress leads from a society ruled by the power of birth – monarchy – to a society ruled by the power of wealth – capitalism –, where everyone occupies the position for which he or she has received their qualification. The characteristic of this kind of order is not so much its authoritarian structure, but the *specific way* in which the logic of the police has to count the parties and the parts of a community, which consists in counting "real parts only – actual groups defined by differences in birth, and by the different functions, places, and interests that make up the social body *to the exclusion of every supplement*."[7] This last apposition, surprisingly not translated in the first English version of the *Thesis* published in *Theory & Event* in 2001, is the central piece of Rancière's understanding of politics, inasmuch as it points to the very moment where the logic of politics can hook into the police logic, i.e. to that very place and time at which the derailment or the disturbance, the misguidance or misdirection of the normal or *harmonious* order of things becomes possible.

---

7 Rancière, "Ten Theses on Politics," p. 34 (emphasis mine).

> Politics exist insofar as the people is not identified with a race or a population, nor the poor with a particular disadvantaged sector, nor the proletariat with a group of industrial workers, etc., but insofar as these latter are identified with subjects that inscribe, in the form of a supplement to every count of the parts of society, a specific figure of the count of the uncounted or of the part of those without part. That this part exists is the very stake of politics itself.[8]

The existence of a supplement constitutes the very possibility of rupture with the logic of the police understood as an operator of a harmonious distribution of the sensible: because it dislocates or displaces this *normal* distribution, i.e. a distribution between the people, their occupations and their space of visibility that is called harmonious insofar as there is nothing left over, no void, no supplement. It is a distribution of the common in which every kind of person, may they be rich or poor, old or young, male or female, have their occupation and correspondingly occupy *his or her* place. In opposition to this logic of the police, the logic of politics, i.e. the logic of equality, is a different way of counting the parts of the community, which counts *in addition* to the empirical or real parts counted by the police, "a part of those without part" (*la part des sans-parts*). This part of those without part is the part of the *demos*, the people, that is not identified with a sociological, economical or racial category (it is neither a specific race, a specific economical or sociological class, nor the working class, nor the immigrants), and embodies the power of misguiding the *harmonic* distribution of the parts. Or, in Rancière's words: "The essence of politics consists in disturbing this [harmonious] arrangement by supplementing it with a part of those without part, identified with the whole of the community."[9]

The "choice of God"

The *demos*, or people, is a symbolic operator, an "artifice," a "supplementary existence that inscribes the count of the unaccounted for, or part of those who have no part – that is, in the last instance, the equality of speaking beings without which inequality itself is inconceivable."[10] To understand how this operation is possible, I would like to retrace the short genealogy of the notion of *demos*, whose origin Rancière

8 Ibid., p. 35.
9 Ibid., p. 36.
10 Ibid., p. 33.

follows back to Aristotle: For Aristotle, *demos* is not the name of the community as a whole – as in democracy – but the name of a part of the community; the *demos*, like the *aristoi* and the *oligoi*, is a part of the community that has a specific qualification or title: While "virtue" is the entitlement of the *aristoi* to rule, and "wealth" that of the *oligoi*, "freedom" is the paradoxical title of the *demos*.

That freedom of the *demos* is paradoxical insofar as it is intrinsically linked to a likewise paradoxical notion of equality essentially different from the liberal notion that understands equality as a balance of rights and duties. This freedom, even though it is part of the logic of the *arche*, i.e. of the police distribution between the positions and the qualifications, undermines it from the inside by actualizing the specific kind of equality to which it is linked: An indeterminate equality or, better, an equality alluded to by the indeterminacy that Plato discusses in the *Laws* as the seventh qualification for ruling, i.e. "the choice of god" or the "drawing of lots." Democracy, for Plato, and he obviously means this as a critique, is characterised by "the complete absence of any entitlement to govern."[11]

Rancière thus agrees with Plato that democracy, the power of the *demos*, refers "to the fact that those who rule are those whose only commonality is that they have no entitlement to govern."[12] But he inverts the orientation of the Platonic argument when he situates politics in the encounter of the logic of inequality of the *arche*, i.e. the logic of seniority, birth, wealth, virtue, and knowledge, with the "logic of equality," understood as the pure indeterminacy of positions, functions and qualifications that relies on the paradoxical freedom of the people or *demos* that Plato had defined as the greatest danger to a harmonious politics.

In consequence, the Rancièrian understanding of politics operates two fundamental dislocations: Rancière underscores the central importance of the *demos*, the people, in the political constellation, but as a *non-sociological entity*, i.e. without being identified as the revolutionary subject in a traditional way; and consequently he attributes a specific logic to the *demos* that he localizes in the fact that it passes from naming a part of the community – the poor – to naming the *whole* of the community – the people. It is, by *homonymy*, both: the part and the whole at once. And this homonymy – and not the simple access to speech – is what Rancière calls upon in order to define *politics*: "The modern political animal is first a literary animal, caught in the circuit of

11 Ibid., p. 31.
12 Ibid., p. 32.

a literariness that undoes the relationships between the order of words and the order of bodies that determine the place of each."[13]

Homonymy…

The name of a part of the community, the *demos*, is defined as the part that has no part in the common, and yet in virtue of this paradoxical qualification, which is the qualification to have no qualification, becomes the name of the community as a whole – democracy: "The people exists only as a rupture with the logic of *arkhê*, a rupture of the logic of commencement/commandment. […] The people is the supplement that disjoins the population from itself, by suspending all logics of legitimate domination."[14] – This disjuncture of something, in this case the population, from itself can also be understood as the literary *dédoublement*, the homonymic strategy of blurring a specific relationship between things and words, or between the population or part of the population and its role.

What politics must do is to make the existence of this supplement, i.e. of the void, or of the excess, possible. While the order of the police tries to negate the void by filling up every symbolic spot of the common space and assigning a qualification and space to every class or group, politics only exist within the dynamic that makes this supplement possible: Politics is not always *there*, but is *produced by the claim* of the part of those who have no part.

The Aristotelian freedom of the *demos* is hence the trigger of the Rancièrian politics – though not in its traditional conception, adopted by Arendt, according to which the *demos* is in charge of, and limited to, the biological survival of the *polis*, i.e. "of the metabolism of society," as Arendt puts it, borrowing Marx's words. On the contrary, Rancière shows how the freedom of the *demos* is far more paradoxical than Aristotle assumed, because it has the capacity to blur the harmonious distribution of the shares and titles: The indetermined freedom of the people incarnates the fact, which is at the same time the scandal of democracy, that any of the mute, working, uncultivated bodies in their radical indifference has the possibility to take part in the common affairs. This freedom undermines the dominant equation of wealth and power which it should have supported, as it makes it possible for the *demos* to *claim* its part in the common, which is denied to him by

---

13 Rancière, *The Disagreement*, p. 37.

14 Ibid., p. 33.

both the arithmetical equality of the rich and the geometrical equality of the virtuous:

> For freedom – which is merely the position of those who have absolutely no other, no merit, no wealth – is counted at the same time as being common virtue. It allows the *demos* (that is, the actual gathering of men of no position, these men whom Aristotle tells us "had no part in anything") to identify with the whole of the community through homonymy.[15]

By virtue of the wrong that is done to the *demos* in the name of those whose qualities have the natural effect of throwing it back into the inexistence of those who have no part, the *demos* consequently identifies itself – by homonymy – with the totality of the community, since it cannot be identified with one of its parts. This is why, Rancière continues, the *demos* does not found a specific form of politics, democracy, *but politics in general*, or put differently, it is why democracy is not a specific regime but *the* regime of politics: "Democracy is the very institution of politics itself – of its subjects and of the form of its relationship."[16] Politics is hence the disruption of the arithmetical logic of the rich that distributes the parts in the common following the order of wealth. But politics is at the same time the disruption of the geometrical equality that distributes the parts of the common following the qualifications of the different classes and developing a natural order: Because the *demos*, by claiming a part that the power of wealth had not foreseen for them, by claiming its part-taking in the common and thus by disturbing the arithmetical logic, elevates its empty title, freedom, to the common of the community, and, by doing so, founds a fundamental miscount in the geometrical distribution of the parts.

Thus the platonic project, the replacement of the arithmetical equality of exchange by the natural or divine order of geometrical proportions, in which every part of the community gets its part and establishes true harmony, is interrupted by the emergence of a third equality: The freedom as the qualification to have no qualification, "the equality of anyone at all with anyone else: in other words, in the final analysis, the absence of *arkhê*, the sheer contingency of any social order."[17] This equality of anything with anything, the arbitrary or indifferent equality, blurs the partition and distribution of the tasks and positions in the *polis*, where the guardian guards, the philosopher governs, and the worker labours. In the *Republic*, Plato calls this equality the "confu-

15 Ibid., p. 9.

16 Rancière, "Ten Theses on Politics," p. 32.

17 Rancière, *The Disagreement*, p. 15.

sion of activities," the *polypragmosyne*, the simple fact of doing many things, *too* many things, which equals *anything*. Because the natural order in Plato's *Republic* relies on the fact that everyone pursues the activity to which he is entitled, everyone carries his share of the common, and nothing is left unattended. This notion of equality hence explains why the disturbance of the harmonious distribution of the activities by the *demos* equals the decline of a specific distribution of the sensible: Because the *demos*, whose only qualification is to have no qualification, by claiming its share in the common, puts into practice a certain form of "double function" – it actualizes the homonymic quality of its name by identifying with two things at once: the part of those who have no part, and the totality of community. The *demos* can fulfil *its* activity in the common, which is to work, and at the same time participate in the common, in its ruling, and in the configuration of its laws. And this kind of double function, of *dédoublement* or of literary indeterminacy, is by definition the end of a well-ordained Platonic state.

This is one of Rancière's most interesting points regarding politics, as well as regarding pedagogical, aesthetical, and literary reflections: The constitution of a specific unspecific category which is neither sociological nor historical, but in a way structural in the constitution of politics. The *demos* challenges a distribution of the sensible and makes politics possible. Because politics is not determined by genuine objects or questions, politics only happens in a conflict, or *dissensus*, with the unequal logic of the police to which it opposes a logic of equality, which is at the same time a logic of the arbitrary or the indifferent. Equality is not the *aim* of politics, but its axiomatic foundation and means of confronting two voices as well as two partitions of the common world. Politics exist in this *dissensus*: "Politics exists wherever the count of parts and parties of society is disturbed by the inscription of a part of those who have no part."[18]

…, not Ideology

This disturbance is thus enacted by Rancière's figure of the *demos* and its fundamental political gesture, its taking the podium, speaking up, and talking, using words and not noises, as exemplified by the adventure of Menenius Agrippa and the plebeians on the Aventine. And it relies on what Rancière calls, in his afterword to the recently repub-

---

18 Ibid., p. 123.

lished anthology *La parole ouvrière*, "the equality of intelligences that remains the most intemperate thought that one can nourish on social order."[19] In *The Disagreement*, Rancière refers to this gesture as a figure of subjectification that opposes the police gesture of identification. Here, he puts forward the idea that homonymy – also fundamentally a notion of dis-identification – founds *dissensus*: Rancière presents the category of *class* (like the *demos* or the people) as the example of a homonymy partaken by the logic of the police and the logic of politics: The first understands the class as a group of people linked by their origins or their activities, which gives them a specific rank or status. Class is thus in the best case a group of professionals, the class of the printers or the hat makers, as Rancière recalls, or, in the worst case, a caste. But within the political logic, a class is something very different: It is "an operator of conflict, a name for counting the uncounted, a mode of subjectification superimposed on the reality of all social groups."[20] The *demos* in Athens, but also the proletariat to which the bourgeois Blanqui claims to belong when asked about his "profession" in court, are classes in the political sense, i.e. positions with the capacity of declassifying the social classes.

This difference between class and class, people and people can be read in two ways: a meta-political way unveils the "ideological" gap between the form (such as the declarations of rights or the battle for representation) and those who have to fill these forms (such as the social movements, the working class, ...), and from there concludes the impossibility of the egalitarian form. This difference is the one Giorgio Agamben points out in his article "What Is a People?," when he says: "What we call people was actually not a unitary subject but rather a dialectical oscillation between two opposite poles: on the one hand the *People* as a whole and as an integral body politic and, on the other hand, the people as a subset and fragmentary multiplicity of needy and excluded bodies."[21] The critique of the ideological interpretation of politics continuously points at this double meaning of People as the sovereign people of a nation-state and of people as the *plebs*, *le menu peuple*, the hard-working excluded bodies, and pinpoints its ideological functioning in society. But it is also the gap between citizen and man, highlighted by Marx in *The Jewish Question*, adopted by Arendt in *The Origins of Totalitarianism*, and radicalized by Agamben in his notion of bare life as the radicalization of the figure of the stateless and

---

19 Jacques Rancière, *La parole ouvrière* (Paris: La Fabrique, 2007).

20 Rancière, *The Disagreement*, p. 83.

21 Giorgio Agamben, "What Is a People?," *Means without ends: Notes on Politics* (Minneapolis: The University of Minnesota Press, 2000), p. 29–36, p. 31.

nationless human being, that constitutes a meta-political interpretation of this opposition, since it denounces the disruption of an identification, i.e. it tries to close the "interval between identities, be these identities determined by social relations or juridical categories."[22]

But the "subject of politics" is defined by this very interval:

> The worker (industrial or otherwise) as political subject is the one who separates himself from his assignation to the non-political, private world that these terms imply. Political subjects exist in the interval between different names of subjects.[23]

To the meta-political distinction, Rancière thus opposes a *political* interpretation of the gap between man and citizen that does not consider its emphasis as a scandal that has to be denounced, but as the first condition for politics: "There is politics from the moment there exists the sphere of appearance of a subject, *the people,* whose particular attribute is to be different from itself, internally divided."[24] In this case, the written declarations of the rights of men are more than empty forms that are denied by its impossible content: "They are an effective mode of appearance of the people, the minimum of equality that is inscribed in the field of common experience."[25] The political issue therefore is not to denounce this appearance as an appearance, but on the contrary to *confirm appearances*:

> Wherever the part of those who have no part is inscribed, however fragile and fleeting these inscriptions may be, a sphere of appearance of the *demos* is created, an element of the *kratos,* the power of the people, exists. The problem is to extend the sphere of this materialization, to maximize this power.[26]

---

22 Jacques Rancière, *Hatred of Democracy* (London/New York: Verso, 2006), p. 59. See for a discussion of Arendt's and Agamben's critique of the rights of men: Rancière, *Hatred of Democracy*, pp. 58–60 as well as Jacques Rancière, "Who is the Subject of Rights of Men?," *Dissensus*: pp. 62–75.

23 Rancière, *Hatred of Democracy*, p. 59.

24 Rancière, *The Disagreement*, p. 87.

25 Ibid., p. 88. In *Hatred of Democracy* and "Who is the Subject of Rights of Men?," Rancière discusses this materialization further, referring to Olympe de Gouge's Declaration of the Rights of Women from 1791 and its claim that if "women were entitled to go to the scaffold, then they were also entitled to go to the assembly" and therefore to vote. Rancière, "Who is the Subject of Rights of Men?," p. 68.

26 Rancière, *The Disagreement*, p. 88.

Politics is about interpreting in "the theatrical sense of the word," as Rancière puts it, "the gap between a place where the *demos* exists and a place where it does not, where there are only populations, individuals, employers and employees, heads of households and spouses, and so on."[27] Politics has to establish a relationship where there is no relationship, it has *to stage* that missing link. But this link is not established by the sovereign people and its representatives, nor by the working people and its becoming conscious; it is the work of a third people that operates with different names and links a specific litigation to the count of the unaccounted for.[28] Consequently, this third people is not constituted by specific political subjects, since in politics

> subjects do not have consistent bodies; they are fluctuating performers who have their moments, places, occurrences, and the peculiar role of inventing *arguments* and *demonstrations* – in the double, logical and aesthetic, senses of the terms – to bring the nonrelationship into relationship and give place to the nonplace.[29]

The meta-political (or ideological) appearances are thus opposed by these forms of *materialization*; the game of appearance and its negation, i.e. the construction and deconstruction or unveiling of ideologies is opposed by the political practice of the *as if* that is concerned with the forms of materialization of the people, *demos*, proletariat... – And materialization means the confirmation, the enactment or enforcement of *appearances as material operators*. It is in this sense that Rancière speaks of an aesthetics of politics insofar as the production of a dissensus is intrinsically linked to the aesthetic power of words to signify in excess, i.e. to their homonymic nature of designating two things at once (which is analogous to Plato's nightmare of the artist doing several things at once without having the authorizing knowledge to do

---

27 Ibid., p. 89.

28 As Rancière shows, *proletariat* has been one of the names of this third people, which is the name of the "universalizing subject of wrong" (Ibid.: 89) that has functioned as the political mode of subjectivation: "The proletariat are neither manual workers nor the labor classes. They are the class of the uncounted that only exists in the very declaration in which they are counted as those of no account. The name *proletarian* defines neither a set of properties (manual labor, industrial labor, destitution, etc.) that would be shared equally by a multitude of individuals nor a collective body, embodying a principle, of which those individuals would be members. It is part of a process of subjectification identical to the process of expounding a wrong. 'Proletarian' subjectification defines a subject of wrong – by superimposition in relation to the multitude of workers." Ibid., p. 38.

29 Ibid., p. 88.

them). The people, *demos,* or proletariat is thus not a sociological, but an aesthetic-political entity of the *as if* that has the capacity to identify itself with nothing, or with the whole of the community at once.

Demos and Plebs

The political gesture of the *demos* can consequently be described as a quasi-mimetic capacity, just as Rancière has outlined it in his account of the revolt of the *plebs* on the Aventine: In reaction to the order established by the patricians that simply negates the plebeians' access to the logos and considers them "beings of no ac/count," the plebeians establish another order, "by constituting themselves not as warriors equal to other warriors, but as speaking beings sharing the same properties as those who deny them these. They thereby execute a series of speech acts that *mimic* those of the patricians."[30]

This description of the paradoxical force of a mimetic approach to power that gives way to a redistribution of the sensible resonates with yet another account of an imitation of the strategies of power that produces an unintended subversion: In "Lives of Infamous Men," it is with respect to the internment records and *lettres de cachet* of the 17th and 18th century that Foucault recalls that the birth of this immense possibility for discourse relied on the mimicry which the letters enacted toward the official discourse of the monarch, whose attention had to be drawn to the account of the miserable lives and commonplaces of the "little people". As Foucault writes: "They [the 'king's orders'] were solicited for some obscure family trouble, *as if* it involved a great crime meriting the sovereign's wrath: rejected or abused spouses, a squandered fortune, conflicts of interest, disobedient young people, knavery or carousing, and all the little disorders of conduct."[31] And it is

---

30 Ibid., p. 24 (emphasis mine). This quasi-mimetic strategy is a strategy of dis-identification, or as Rancière also puts it, an anti-representative mimesis that plays a central role in his political aesthetics when he claims that the aesthetical revolution consists in the rupture with the representative regime of the arts that gives way to the aesthetic regime, and whose original moment is 19th century realism. I therefore would propose to call this anti-representationalist realism an aesthetic realism. See Maria Muhle, "Realism, Dis-Identification and the Image," *Everything is in Everything: Between Intellectual Emancipation and Aesthetic Education*, ed. Jason E. Smith and Annette Weisser (Pasadena: Art Center Graduate Press, 2012).

31 Michel Foucault, "Lives of Infamous Men," *Power: the Essential Works of Foucault*, vol. 3 (New York: The New Press. 2001), p. 157–175, p. 167 (emphasis mine).

this "encounter with power," whose beam of light illuminated the infamous lives for a moment and "snatched them from the darkness":

> The power that watched these lives, that pursued them, that lent its attention, if only for a moment, to their complaints and their little racket, and marked them with its claw was what gave rise to the few words about them that will remain for us – either because someone decided to appeal to it in order to denounce, complain, solicit, entreat, or because he chose to intervene and in a few words to judge and decide. All those lives destined to pass beneath any discourse and disappear without ever having been told were able to leave traces – brief, incisive, often enigmatic – only at the point of their instantaneous contact with power.[32]

It is in this context of the infamous, the dossier Rivière, but also the work related to the G.I.P., that a notion takes shape that never found its way into Foucault's "great books," but nevertheless occupies an important position, as I would like to claim, in his thought: the notion of the *plebs*, that in some way can be thought of as a pendant, or even precursory notion, of Rancière's understanding of the *demos*. While the notion of the *plebs* seems to be subsumed by the notion of the infamous in this text, it is addressed explicitly in the interview of the same year, 1977, quoted above, which Rancière did with Foucault for his recently founded magazine *Les révoltes logiques*. Here, Foucault discusses the phenomenon of the infamous, which he had also called elsewhere *les classes dangereuses*, the dangerous classes, by name of the *plebs*, as "the permanent, ever silent target for apparatuses of power."[33] But while the relation of the infamous to power strategies is explicitly described as mimetic, the relation between the plebeian resistance and power is only implicitly so, since resistance *takes on the form of power*: resistance "exists all the more by being in the same place as power; hence, *like* power, resistance is multiple and can be integrated in global strategies."[34]

As it is for Rancière, the *plebs* for Foucault is not a sociological reality – the *plebs* does not exist as such, but there is always "a certain plebeian quality or aspect (*'de la' plèbe*)": "There is indeed always something in the social body, in classes, groups and individuals themselves, which in some sense escapes relations of power, something which is by no means a more or less docile or reactive primal matter, but rather

32 Ibid., p. 161.
33 Foucault, "Powers and Strategies," p. 137.
34 Ibid., p. 142 (emphasis mine).

a centrifugal movement, an inverse energy, a discharge."[35] The *plebs* is in the bodies and the souls, in the proletariat and the bourgeoisie, but always different, changeable. It is therefore not the impossible *outside* of power relations, but their *limit*, their flipside, their *contrecoup*. The *plebs* reacts to power with a movement to clear itself from power. At the same time, this *contrecoup* challenges power and initiates the spiral of power and resistance.

Hence, Rancière addresses this dynamic by questioning the absolutization of power, which is always already there, engaged in this endless movement of action and reaction, and abstaining from posing the question to what and to whom it is instrumental or valuable. Foucault answers very briefly to this critique by the plurality and modifiability of power relations that interconnect with local and global strategies. He thus follows the conceptualization of the notion of power that he had laid out *in extenso* in the first volume of *History of Sexuality*, published a year earlier: Power is not to be thought of in terms of a binary opposition between the dominating and dominated, but as a heterogeneous, multiple, malleable net of power relations. While in *History of Sexuality* he had limited the conceptualization of resistance to rather nebulous claims about the power of resistance "of bodies, pleasures, and knowledges," in this interview, Foucault seems to turn to a more concrete understanding of resistance that is spelled out in a Rancièrian way *avant la lettre*: He thus returns to the affirmation that there is no outside of power, that one is always already "trapped" within power, and that there are no margins to break out of the global power relations. At the same time, this closure of power relations does not entail the impossibility of resistance, on the contrary: "there are no relations of power without resistances; the latter are all the more real and effective because they are formed right at the point where relations of power are exercised; resistance to power does not have to come from elsewhere to be real, nor is it inexorably frustrated through being the compatriot of power."[36]

---

35 Ibid., p. 138.

36 Ibid., p. 142. In her "Attempt to think the Plebeian," Isabell Lorey proposes an analysis of Rancière's interview with Foucault that she then refers to Titus Livius' account of the struggles between plebeians and patricians on the Aventine, that would become the central example of Rancière's *Disagreement*. She also insists on the entanglement between resistance and power put forward by Foucault in the interview. Following Virno, she states that what plebeian struggles do is to "change the contexts in which a problem emerges as a problem, rather than choosing one or another solution already offered. They change the assemblage of power and multiply the power relationships." For Lorey, the Plebeian "always signifies an immanent refusal, that is why it is productive. The plebeian is the capacity to productively

The resisting *plebs* is thus a paradoxical subject that blurs the power relations from the inside by adopting their same mechanisms, strategies, and energies, and without stating a purity of the political outside power relations. And it shares these dynamics with the Rancièrian *demos* as the "third people" that is not constituted by specific political subjects, but rather represents the "universalizing subject of wrong." Consequently, and if we would like to establish a genealogy of the Rancièrian political project, we could claim that while his notion of the police concurs with what Foucault understands under the notion of power – be it sovereign, disciplinary, or governemental power –, Rancière's notion of politics finds its antecedent in the very conceptualization that Foucault proposes of the notion of the *plebs*. Which, as a conclusion, makes necessary a double reconsideration: In the first place, Foucault proposes, with the notion of *plebs*, to think resistance to power relations from *within* these very power relations, from the intimate core of power and through a quasi-mimetic strategy – and without running the risk of being neutralized through these interactions; in the second place, the notion of the *plebs* is a great resource to understand Rancière's notion of politics as a quasi-mimetic impulse, that does not oppose different fields or subjects, but that re-arranges existing elements in a different, new, non-representationalist or non-naturalist way.[37]

---

refuse power relations and elude them in this way, whereby the assemblage of power permanently changes and one or the other constraining mode of governing vanishes." Isabell Lorey, "Attempt to Think the Plebeian. Exodus and Constituting as Critique" (http://eipcp.net/transversal/0808/lorey/en; pub. April 2008, cit. May 13th 2012).

37 In a recent book, Alain Brossat has proposed a very interesting reading of the notion of the *plebs* in Foucault's thinking by focusing on its lack of access to the spoken or written word. Contrary to Rancière's theorization of a *prise de parole*, a "moment of equalization through the word," Brossat claims that the *plebs* relates not globally to the unaccounted for, but more specifically to those who lost their words – who are ultimately barred and excluded from the community of the word. For Brossat, the paradigmatic figure of the plebeian that has literally lost his language is Melville's Billy Budd, when he undergoes the radically unjust and violent treatment through his superior Claggart, that leads to an explosion of violence on Billy's side and to Claggart's subsequent death. As Brossat claims, these purely plebeian moments, in which the language has been co-opted by the ruling class and only exists on the side of the masters, are not graspable with Rancière's notion of politics that relies on the emancipation through the word. On the contrary, they give way to explosive and violent outbursts. See Alain Brossat, *Plebs Invicta* (Berlin: August Verlag, 2012), pp. 127–130.

Chantal Mouffe

Democratic Politics in the Age of Post-Fordism[1]

In recent years we have witnessed an incredible acceleration in the process of commodification in the field of culture. With the development of the culture industries, the worst nightmares of Horkheimer and Adorno seem to have been realized. Indeed, some theorists claim that, through our dependence on the entertainments corporations, we have become totally subjugated to the control of capital and that we cannot even imagine modes of resistances. Aesthetics, they say, has been so completely harnessed towards the development of a hedonistic culture that there is no space left for a subversive experience – not even in art.

Were this to be true, we would have to conclude that there is no alternative to the present post-political world. The current hegemonic form of neoliberal globalization would constitute our only horizon and we would have to abandon the hope of fostering the agonistic democracy that I have been advocating in my work. To be sure, there are those who would rejoice at such a prospect because they see the present situation as a cause for celebration. In their view, the post-political consensus indicates that, with the disappearance of the adversarial model of politics, democracy has become more mature and that antagonisms have been overcome.

I disagree with such a view and I consider that a well-functioning democracy requires a confrontation of democratic political positions. If passions cannot be mobilized by traditional democratic parties because they privilege a "consensus at the centre," those passions tend to find other outlets, in diverse fundamentalist movements, around particularistic demands or non-negotiable moral issues. When a society lacks a dynamic democratic life with a real confrontation among a diversity of real alternatives, the terrain is laid for other forms of identifications of an ethnic, religious, or nationalist nature, and this leads to the emergence of antagonisms that cannot be managed by the democratic process. In my recent work I have, for instance, tried to show how the post-political consensus which characterizes most advanced liberal-democratic societies is at the origin of the growing success of rightwing populist parties. They are often the only ones who challenge the "there is no alternative" dogma proclaimed by the traditional par-

---

1 This essay first appeared in *Open* 16, "The Art Biennial as a Global Phenomenon" (2009): pp. 32–40.

ties and attempt to mobilize passions against what they present as the uncaring "establishment," composed of elitist bureaucrats who do not listen to the voice of the people and ignore its real concerns.

Such an evolution clearly represents a threat for democracy, and a central aim of my reflection has been to bring to the fore the dangers of post-politics and the urgency of revitalizing democracy thanks to the proliferation of a variety of agonistic public spaces. To visualize how an agonistic democracy can be brought about, it is necessary to grasp the challenge facing democratic politics, and this requires an adequate understanding of the terrain in which we have to act. We need, for instance, to understand the nature of the transition that advanced industrial societies have undergone since the last decades of the twentieth century. This transition has had important consequences in the field of artistic and cultural practices, which is why I have decided to centre my intervention on this topic.

A great number of theorists coming from a variety of theoretical perspectives agree that advanced industrial societies have, at the end of the last century, witnessed a transition which they present, either as a move from industrial to post-industrial society, from Fordism to post-Fordism, or from a disciplinary society to a society of control. I have chosen to concentrate on the Fordism to post-Fordism approach because it is the most influential one. However, I would like to note that those approaches are not necessarily incompatible and might even be combined. Each is inscribed in a specific intellectual tradition and it emphasizes a particular aspect of the transition.

From Fordism to Post-Fordism

To apprehend what is at stake in the transition from Fordism to post-Fordism, it is useful to examine the differences between the approaches influenced by the critical theory of Adorno and Horkheimer and those who are influenced by the Italian autonomist tradition. Their main disagreement lies in the role that the culture industry has played in the transformations of capitalism. It is well known that Adorno and Horkheimer saw the development of the culture industry as the moment when the Fordist mode of production finally managed to enter the field of culture. They see this evolution as a further stage in the process of commodification and subjugation of society to the requisites of capitalist production. For Paolo Virno and some other post-Operaist theorists, on the contrary, the culture industry played an important role in the process of transition between Fordism and post-Fordism because it is there that new practices of production emerged which led to the overcoming of Fordism. The space granted to the informal, the unexpected and the unplanned, which for Horkheimer and Adorno were uninfluential remnants of the past, are for Virno anticipatory omens. With the development of immaterial labour they began to play an increasingly important role, and that opened the way for new forms of social relations. In advanced capitalism, says Virno, the labour process has become performative and it mobilizes the most universal requisites of the species: perception, language, memory, and feelings. Contemporary production is virtuosic, and productive labour in its totality appropriates the special characteristics of the performing artist. According to him, the culture industry is in fact the matrix of post-Fordism.

Theorists influenced by the autonomist tradition concord on the fact that the transition from Fordism to post-Fordism needs to be understood, not as dictated by the logic of the development of capitalist forces of production, but as reaction to the new practices of resistances of the workers. Disagreements exist, however, among them concerning the political consequences of this transition. Although many of them use the notion of "multitude" to refer to the new type of political agent characteristic of the current period, they do not envisage its future in the same way. Some, like Hardt and Negri, celebrate in the multitude the emergence of a new revolutionary subject which will necessarily bring down the new form of domination embodied in empire. Incorporating, although not always in a faithful way, some of the analyses of Foucault and Deleuze, they assert that the end of the disciplinary regime that was exercised over bodies in enclosed spaces like schools, factories and asylums, and its replacement by the procedures of control linked to the growth of networks, is leading to a new type of governance which opens the way to more autonomous and independent forms of subjectivity. With the expansion of new forms of cooperative communication and the invention of new communicative forms of life, those subjectivities can express themselves freely, and they will contribute to the formation of a new set of social relations that will finally replace the capitalist system.

Paolo Virno, while agreeing on the potential for new forms of life, is not so sanguine about the future. He sees the growth of the multitude as an ambivalent phenomenon, and he also acknowledges the new forms of subjection and precarization which are typical of the post-Fordist stage.[2] It is true that people are not as passive as before, but it is because they have now become active actors of their own precariza-

---

2 Paolo Virno, *A Grammar of the Multitude* (New York: Semiotext(e), 2004).

tion. So instead of seeing in the generalization of immaterial labour a type of spontaneous communism like Hardt and Negri, Virno tends to see post-Fordism as "a manifestation of the communism of capital."

Despite their differences, there is something, however, that all those thinkers have in common: their conviction that it is necessary to relinquish the conception of radical politics aimed at "taking power" in order to control the institutions of the state. They claim that one should ignore the existing power structures, and dedicate oneself to constructing alternative social forms outside the state power network as well as the existing institutions. Virno asserts that it is in the refusal to work and the different forms of exodus and disobedience that one should locate any possibility of emancipation. Any majoritarian model of society, organized around a state, has to be rejected and replaced by another model of organization of the multitude which is deemed to be more universal. It has the form of a unity provided by common places of the mind, cognitive-linguistic habits and the general intellect.

A Hegemonic Approach

While agreeing on the necessity to acknowledge the fundamental transformations in the mode of regulation of capitalism represented by the transition to post-Fordism, I think that we should envisage this transition from the point of view of the theory of hegemony. I recognize the importance of not seeing the transformations undergone by our societies as the mere consequence of technological progresses and on bringing to the fore their political dimension. As social philosopher André Gorz, among others, has pointed out, they should be understood as a move by capital to provide what was a fundamentally political answer to the crisis of governability of the 1970s. Many factors have contributed to this transition, and it is important to grasp the complexity of its dynamics.

My problem with Operaist and post-Operaist views is that, by putting the emphasis on the workers' struggles, they tend to see this transition as if it was exclusively moved by one single logic, the workers' resistances to the process of exploitation forcing the capitalists to reorganize the process of production, and to move to the post-Fordist era of immaterial labour. According to them, capitalism can only be reactive, and contrary to Deleuze and Guattari, they refuse to accept the creative role played by both capital and the working class. What they deny is in fact the role played in this transition by the hegemonic struggle.

To clarify what I understand by hegemonic struggle, let me introduce some basic tenets of my theoretical framework. According to the approach that I am advocating and which has been developed in *Hegemony and Socialist Strategy* written jointly with Ernesto Laclau, two key concepts are necessary to grasp the nature of the political: "antagonism" and "hegemony".[3] On the one side, it is necessary to acknowledge the dimension of the political as the ever present possibility of antagonism, and this requires, on the other side, coming to terms with the lack of a final ground and the indecisiveness that pervades every order. This means recognizing the hegemonic nature of every kind of social order and envisaging society as the product of a series of practices whose aim is to establish order in a context of contingency. The practices of articulation through which a given order is created and the meaning of social institutions fixed are what we call "hegemonic practices". Every order is the temporary and precarious articulation of contingent practices. Things could always have been otherwise and every order is predicated on the exclusion of other possibilities. It is always the expression of a particular structure of power relations. What is at a given moment accepted as the "natural order," with the common sense that accompanies it, is the result of sedimented hegemonic practices; it is never the manifestation of a deeper objectivity outside of the practices that bring it into being. Every hegemonic order is susceptible to being challenged by counter-hegemonic practices which attempt to disarticulate it to install another form of hegemony.

I would like to suggest that in order to introduce the hegemonic dimension in the transition between Fordism and post-Fordism, we can find interesting insights in the interpretation of this transition put forward by Luc Boltanski and Eve Chiapello. In their book *The New Spirit of Capitalism*, they bring to light the role played by what they call "artistic critique" in the transformation undergone by capitalism in the last decades of the twentieth century.[4] They show how the demands of autonomy of the new movements of the 1960s have been harnessed in the development of the post-Fordist networked economy and transformed into new forms of control. The aesthetic strategies of the counterculture: the search for authenticity, the ideal of self-management, the antihierarchical exigency, are now used to promote the conditions required by the current mode of capitalist regulation, replacing the disciplinary framework characteristic of the Fordist period. Today, artistic and cultural production play a central role in the process of capital

---

3 Ernesto Laclau and Chantal Mouffe, *Hegemony and Socialist Strategy: Towards a Radical Democratic Politics* (London/New York: Verso, 2001).
4 Luc Boltanski and Eve Chiapello, *The New Spirit of Capitalism* (London/New York: Verso, 2006).

valorisation, and artistic critique has become an important element of capitalist productivity through "neo-management".

From my point of view, what is interesting in this approach is that it reveals that a crucial dimension of the transition was a process of discursive rearticulation of existing elements. This is what makes it possible to understand it in terms of a hegemonic struggle. To be sure, Boltanski and Chiapello do not use this vocabulary, but theirs is a clear example of what Gramsci calls "hegemony through neutralization" or "passive revolution" to refer to situations where demands which challenge an established hegemonic order are recuperated by the existing system, by satisfying them in a way that neutralizes their subversive potential. To envisage the transition from Fordism to post-Fordism in such a mode helps us to understand it as a hegemonic move by capital to re-establish its leading role and to reassert its legitimacy.

By adding to the analysis offered by *The New Spirit of Capitalism*, the undeniable role played in this transition by workers' resistances, we can arrive at a more complex understanding of the forces at play in the emergence of the current neoliberal hegemony. This hegemony is the result of a set of political interventions in a complex field of economic, legal and ideological forces. It is a discursive construction that articulates in a very specific manner a manifold of practices, discourses and language-games of very different nature. Through a process of sedimentation, the political origin of those contingent practices has been erased, and they have become naturalized. Neoliberal practices and institutions appear as the outcome of natural processes, and the forms of identification that they have produced have crystallized into identities which are taken for granted. This is how the "common sense" which constitutes the framework for what is considered as possible and desirable has been established.

To challenge neoliberalism it is therefore vital to transform this framework, and this requires the production of new subjectivities capable of subverting the existing hegemony. Today's capitalism relies increasingly on semiotic techniques in order to create the modes of subjectivation which are necessary for its reproduction. In modern production, the control of the souls (Foucault) plays a strategic role in governing affects and passions. The forms of exploitation characteristic of the times when manual labour was dominant have been replaced by new ones which require the constant creation of new needs and an incessant desire for the acquisition of goods. Hence the crucial role played by advertising in our consumer societies. It is the construction of the very identity of the consumer which is at stake in the techniques of advertising. Those techniques are not limited to promoting specific products, but aim at producing fantasy worlds with which the consumers of goods will identify. Indeed, nowadays to buy something is to enter into a specific world, to become part of an imagined community. To maintain its hegemony, the neoliberal system needs to permanently mobilize people's desires and shape their identities. This is why the cultural terrain now occupies such a strategic place. To be sure, the realm of culture has always played an important role in hegemonic politics, but in the times of post-Fordist production this role has become absolutely crucial. A counter-hegemonic politics should therefore engage with this terrain, so as to foster other forms of identification.

Counter-Hegemonic Struggle and Agonistic Practices

Now that I have presented the main lines of the hegemonic approach to the transition from Fordism to post-Fordism, I would like to make some considerations concerning the construction of counter-hegemonic practices. It is clear that, once social reality is envisaged in terms of hegemonic practices, the process of social critique characteristic of radical politics cannot consist, as in the view advocated by the post-Operaist theorists to whom I referred earlier, in withdrawing from the existing institutions but, on the contrary, must engage with them so as to disarticulate the existing discourses and practices through which the current hegemony is established and reproduced. Such a counter-hegemonic struggle cannot merely consist of separating the different elements whose discursive articulation is at the origin of those practices and institutions. The second moment, the moment of re-articulation, is crucial. Otherwise we would encounter a chaotic situation of pure dissemination, leaving the door open for attempts of re-articulation by non-progressive forces. Indeed, we have many historical examples of situations in which the crisis of the dominant order led to rightwing solutions.

It is also important not to envisage this struggle as the displacement of a supposedly false consciousness that would reveal the true reality. Such a perspective is completely at odds with the anti-essentialist premises of the theory of hegemony which rejects the very idea of a "true consciousness" and asserts that identities are always the result of processes of identification. It is through insertion in a manifold of practices, discourses, and language-games that specific forms of individualities are constructed. According to the hegemonic approach, social reality is discursively constructed, and the political has a primary structuring role because social relations are ultimately contingent; any prevailing articulation results from an antagonistic confrontation whose outcome is not decided in advance. What is therefore needed is a strategy whose objective is, through a set of counter-hegemonic interventions, to disarticulate the existing hegemony and to establish a more democratic one thanks to a process of re-articulation of new and old elements into different configurations of power. This is why the transformation of political identities cannot consist of a rationalist appeal to the true interest of the subject, but of its insertion into practices that will mobilize its affects towards the disarticulation of the framework in which the process of identification is taking place, thereby opening the way for other forms of identification.

I would like to stress that to construct oppositional identities it is not enough to simply foster a process of "de-identification" or "deindividualization". The second move, the moment of "re-identification," of "re-individualization," is decisive. To insist only on the first move is in fact to remain trapped in a problematic which postulates that the negative moment is sufficient, on its own, to bring about something positive, as if new subjectivities were already there, ready to emerge when the weight of the dominant ideology is lifted. Such a view, which unfortunately informs many forms of critical art, fails to come to terms with the nature of the hegemonic struggle and the complex process of construction of identities.

That the critique and disarticulation of the existing hegemony needs to be accompanied by a process of re-articulation is something that is missed by all approaches in terms of reification or false consciousness that think that the critique of ideology is sufficient to bring about a new order, free from oppression and power. It is also missed, albeit in a different way, by the theorists of the multitude who believe that its oppositional consciousness does not require political articulation. This leads them to evacuate what I take to be the crucial question for a radical democratic politics: how to establish a "chain of equivalence" among the different democratic struggles. Those struggles do not automatically converge, and they might often conflict with each other. The aim of a radical democratic politics should be to provide surfaces of inscription where their diverse demands can be articulated around a "collective will" (Gramsci). I am convinced that cultural and artistic practices could play an important role in the agonistic struggle because they are a privileged terrain for the construction of new subjectivities. Think, for instance, of the success of feminist artistic practices in undermining the hegemonic order by revealing how the construction of images contributed to the construction and reproduction of oppressive social norms and by offering alternative views. To revitalize democracy in our post-political societies, what is urgently needed is to foster the multiplication of agonistic public spaces where everything that the dominant consensus tends to obscure and obliterate can be brought to light and challenged. This can be done in a multiplicity of ways, but the thought that I want to share with you is that radical politics can only be successful when it is envisaged in the mode of a "war of position" aimed at transforming the existing institutions and the creation of a new hegemony.

Josef Früchtl

As If We Could Trust Fiction and Aesthetics of the Political

Fiction: A Short Story

I would like to begin with a short story. And in doing so, I draw upon an experienced German story-teller and philosopher (who, by the way, is very well known in Giessen). It is a short story, but a fundamental one – as is the tradition with philosophy –, and it goes like this[1]:

For a long time, philosophy needed fiction, roughly speaking, only when figments of the imagination were called for. Sometimes this would be for arbitrarily combined characteristics (such as those which make up the creatures found in fables, like centaurs or unicorns), and sometimes for a self-contradictory non-entity (like a square circle or a wooden iron). For Immanuel Kant, a non-entity (*nihil negativum*, *Unding*) was located right at the bottom of the "scale of nothing," meaning as it did a term which cancels itself out, a term in opposition not only to reality, but also to possibility. In contrast, a thought-entity (*ens rationis*, *Gedankending*) may also be a "mere invention" or "fiction," as Kant stated, but at least one which is possible. The opposite concept to fiction was thus initially that of reality. A fiction is not real but possible. As the concept of reality gradually merged with the one of truth (something is true if it really complies in a certain manner), especially under the omnipotent influence of Christianity, the concept of fiction, secondly, assumed a mantle of negativity, of deceit and delusion. According to this view, fictions were deceptive in a formal sense, in that they veiled their status of fabrication. When Christian religion had to relinquish its power over science and philosophy at the end of the 18th century, however, one reaction to this development was the crystallisation of an additional, a third interpretation of fiction, believing it to be beyond the alternative between true and false, able to stand up in its own right. Evidence of this interpretation can be found in science and art equally. In the former, fiction achieved validity as a hypothesis, as a statement principally capable of being true,

1 Compare Odo Marquard, "Kunst als Antifiktion – Versuch über den Weg der Wirklichkeit ins Fiktive," *Aesthetica und Anaesthetica. Philosophische Überlegungen* (Paderborn: Schöningh, 1989), pp. 82–99; Karlheinz Stierle, "Fiktion," *Ästhetische Grundbegriffe*, vol. 2, ed. Karlheinz Barck et.al. (Stuttgart/Weimar: Metzler, 2001), pp. 380–428; on Kant, compare Immanuel Kant, *Critique of Pure Reason*, B 348–9.

but not (yet) proven true. In the latter, fiction – that world created in literature, drama, paintings, and opera – was viewed as facilitating an area of truth, as expansively presenting metaphors and images which were potential candidates for the truth. A fourth interpretation of the concept of fiction which emerged was that of self-reference. Here fiction refers to itself, in other words it does not attempt to conceal the fact that it is imaginary, fabricated, created. In so doing, it can itself stake a certain claim to truth (and not just facilitate a potential truth). This can also be found as a rudimentary concept in the work of Kant, before it was tackled explicitly by Georg Wilhelm Friedrich Hegel.[2] The following generation, led by Friedrich Nietzsche, was to witness the unfolding of the last chapter in the history of fiction, at least for the time being: its "fundamentalisation." What for millennia had been known as the truth now became a "lie in an extramoral sense," a kind of self-delusion without which the human species could not survive. Truth had now become a necessary and fruitful fiction. The explicit link to Kant led on to a *Philosophy of As If.*[3] Hans Vaihinger, its author, emphasised the productive, heuristic function of fiction in the sciences. A final and prominent place within this short story is awarded to Jürgen Habermas' discourse theory. Its counterfactual assumptions and idealising suppositions were once again to lend a validity to the concept of necessary fiction in terms of truth theory.

So ends the short story. If one asks oneself why the European history of the arts should have led to such a fundamentalisation of the fictitious, then, bearing in mind Hans Blumenberg's *The Legitimacy of the Modern Age* (*Die Legitimität der Neuzeit*), one might venture the following major theory: "The eschatological destruction of the world is the trauma *post Christum natum et mortuum* that the here and now is seeking to counteract by living, and that philosophy is seeking to counteract by thinking." Ultimately, fiction helps. Fiction permits a "counter-eschatological reinstatement" of the world in an *as if* mode.[4]

---

2 On Hegel, compare G. W. F. Hegel, *Aesthetics: Lectures on Fine Art, vol I,* trans. T. M. Knox (New York: Oxford University Press, 1975), p. 9: The "pure appearance of art has the advantage that it points through and beyond itself," that it "does not present itself as deceptive." On Kant, compare Immanuel Kant, *Critique of Judgment,* § 51: In contrast to the orator, "the poet promises little and announces a mere play with Ideas."

3 Vaihinger's *Die Philosophie des Als Ob. System der theoretischen, praktischen und religiösen Fiktionen der Menschheit auf Grund eines idealistischen Positivismus. Mit einem Anhang über Kant und Nietzsche* was written in the years 1876–1878 and published only in 1911. There is a new edition by Esther von Krosigk (Saarbrücken: VDM, 2007).

4 Marquard, "Kunst als Antifiktion," p. 87.

As implied, this is a very daring theory. There is, after all, a broad philosophical consensus that a major destruction of the world, a destruction of trust in the world, has been with us at least since the subject-based philosophy of Modernity. This loss of trust is the result of a radical epistemological and ontological dualism. If the connection between thought and spatially extended things, between the *res cogitans* and the *res extensa*, can only be guaranteed through the metaphysical-religious authority of God, then without God's help the subject can be certain of itself, but not of the world.

This is, then, our starting position: an ontological loss of trust, coupled with a fundamental, possibly complementary function of the fictitious in the sense of *as if*. I would now like to relocate the position of Jacques Rancière. This not only immediately lends our theme a political aspect, but also and ultimately leads us to a concept which has stood in relaxed opposition to the familiar habit of suspicion, mistrust and demasking for two hundred years: the concept of trust. Before we go any further, we need to rehabilitate the concept of consensus and communitisation. Kant's analysis of aesthetic judgement in its *as if* structure provides us with the necessary framework. Accordingly, the political becomes a sphere in which a (utopian-anticipatory) demeanour is feigned. In addition, however, the *as if* structure is characteristic of the further context of the action itself. The *as if* structure, as a description of fiction, is thus in an aesthetic, political, and everyday context at the same time a description of trust: it is simultaneously uncertain and fundamental.

The Consensual and the Dissensual

Just how fundamental the status of fiction for contemporary philosophy actually is, can, as I inferred earlier, be ascertained prominently for the theory of truth linked to the name of Habermas and to the concept of consensus, a concept which – from the standpoint of recent demasking theorists – has become severely discredited. It should be noted that, while Habermas introduces the concept of consensus within the framework of a theory of truth, to a certain extent it is also socially and politically relevant, for to Habermas, as a successor of Kant and Hegel, Modernity appears to be characterised, amongst other things, by the inevitable pressure of the discursive, of justified utterances to the effect of yes or no, in other words: of the exchange of arguments and changing points of view. But such an exchange would make no sense were it not to take place on common ground, on shared convictions, and were it not to lead to a result shared by all participants. In a real case, such a result can of course be dissent. There then exists (at the meta-level) a consensus concerning the fact that (at the factual level) there is no consensus.

In contrast, for more than half a century now the philosophy of dissent has untiringly stressed that at the very root not only of politics, but also of language itself as we use it, a conflict is present which cannot be appropriately resolved. A rule of judgement which could be applied to both sides of the conflict, to two different ways of thinking, is missing. In the style of Kant's analysis of the sublime, Jean-François Lyotard coined the term *différend*. It soon becomes obvious that Lyotard himself requires a contrasting term, or rather a contrasting image, namely that of an archipelago, a cluster of islands, in which each island stands for a heterogeneous method of discourse. They can be connected by a ship-owner or an admiral, in other words the capacity for judgement. This connection should consist in nothing other than a continual repetition of the statement that the methods of discourse are heterogeneous and cannot be connected. And yet, the way to refute this is glaringly obvious: the statement itself presupposes that the person uttering it has always already made the connection. Thus a différend cannot occur until the two conflicting parties, for Kant they are imagination and reason, acknowledge their conflicting claims, in other words comprehend each other. According to Lyotard, "it is patently necessary that the parties 'understand' one another for their différend."[5]

This short reminder seems necessary to me because, like so many other theorists in the French-language field of discourse, Rancière joins in enthusiastically with the philosophy of dissent and difference, immune to the formal and fictitious sense of the concept of consensus. He does point out that the concept of the différend must not be confused with that of "political disagreement" (*mésentente*), and to me that seems justified insofar as Lyotard's focus on language stands in opposition to Rancière's focus on perception theory, aesthetics, history, and sociology. "Disagreement is less concerned with arguing than with what can be argued," it concerns the "tangible presentation" of the

---

5 Jean-François Lyotard, *Die Analytik des Erhabenen. Kant-Lektionen* (Munich: Fink, 1994), p. 142; see also Jean-François Lyotard, *Le Différend* (Paris: Les Éditions de Minuit, 1983), p. 9, pp. 189–191; Manfred Frank, *Die Grenzen der Verständigung* (Frankfurt/M.: Suhrkamp, 1988), pp. 77–79; Wolfgang Welsch, *Vernunft. Die zeitgenössische Vernunftkritik und das Konzept der transversalen Vernunft* (Frankfurt/M.: Suhrkamp, 1995), pp. 328–330.

object of the dispute.[6] But even for Rancière, "consensus democracy" means that "idyllic" state in which the "dispute" and thus politics has disappeared behind the "regime of opinion" and "right." Rancière also calls this "postdemocracy."[7] However, it is important to be clear about the fact that an essential part, even half, of this postdemocratic consensus is based on feeling. According to Rancière, consensus democracy is the bringing together of "the *one* of the law and the *one* of feeling," the bringing together of the "power to agree and to enter into contracts" with the "power to consent."[8] It thus at the same time somehow brings together two "great figures" of political philosophy: so-called "archipolitics" for which Plato provided the model (the republic as the community of the *ethos*); and the modern, contractualistic variant of "parapolitics". The bad reputation held by the concept of consensus is thus due not to the semantics of the Habermas-Frankfurt School, which includes it in the concept of discourse, i.e. the argumentative, mutual problematisation of claims to truth, but rather to a combination of the Modern principle of power and contract assigned to Thomas Hobbes and the Ancient principle of ethos assigned to Plato. Consensus is bad because it makes the law of cohabitation a matter of contractual exchange as well as a matter of feeling.

Aesthetic Community and As If

For Rancière, however, the matter is not dismissed this simply. For he refers at a crucial point in his own concept of politics to the idea of an *aesthetic community*. Moreover, he does so within the framework not only of his concept of politics, but also of his concept of aesthetics. In the Modern age, the so-called "aesthetic regime," art for him is a "visualisation which communitises the ideas." He believes that spreading ideas "to the common people" in this way is the "oldest programme of aesthetics," which is, of course, a reference to the so-called *Oldest Systematic Programme of German Idealism*, in which, in the mid-1790s, Friedrich Wilhelm Joseph Schelling, Friedrich Hölderlin,

---

6 Jacques Rancière, *Disagreement. Politics and Philosophy* (Minneapolis: University of Minnesota Press, 1995), p. xii; see also p. 50.

7 Rancière, *Disagreement*, pp. 95, 101–102. – In contrast, the concept of post-democracy is constructed politologically in Colin Crouch's *Post-Democracy* (Oxford: Polity Press, 2004). He refers to the constellation of civil apathy, PR orchestration, and back room politics.

8 Rancière, *Disagreement*, pp. 120–121; on "archi-" and "para-politics" see also pp. 61–64.

and Hegel presumably wrote down their Kantian thoughts impetuously and thus in a very non-Kantian manner.[9] Kant also provides some key words for Rancière. Even though, on the one hand, the latter holds fast to the idealistic-romantic project of the aesthetic generalisation of ideas, in other words to the project of the New Mythology, as it is called in the *Systematic Programme*, on the other hand he states that truly "democratic politics" is based on a "practice of the *as if*," one "that opens up an aesthetic community, in Kantian fashion, a community that demands the consent of the very person who does not acknowledge it."[10]

Kant actually does analyse the argumentative logics of aesthetic judgement as a logic of the *as if*.[11] Accordingly, one "must believe that one has reason to expect a similar delight from everyone." In other words, one "believes" oneself to have a "universal voice." An aesthetic judgement is an "imputation" or a "request" (in German: *Ansinnen*) to everybody to "agree" (and maybe the English words "to consent" and "to acclaim" are closer to the German word *zustimmen*, in which you can hear the noun *Stimme*, meaning "voice"). This agreement takes place not on the basis of concepts, but plainly and simply through the agreement itself, through confirmation by others. On the one hand, an aesthetic judgement is accordingly based on hypothetical agreement because, like the political judgement, it is formulated *as if* consensus were (in principle) possible. But, on the other hand, it is also based on actual agreement, for according to Kant's conviction there are no concepts, no soundness of reasons which one can resort to,[12] leaving only

---

9 Jacques Rancière, "Die Geschichtlichkeit des Films," *Die Gegenwart der Vergangenheit. Dokumentarfilm, Fernsehen und Geschichte*, eds. Eva Hohenberger and Judith Keilbach (Berlin: Vorwerk 8, 2003): pp. 230–246, p. 240; on the *Oldest Systematic Programme*, compare Walter Jaeschke, *Hegel-Handbuch. Leben-Werk-Wirkung* (Stuttgart/Weimar: Metzler, 2003), pp. 76–80.

10 Rancière, *Disagreement*, p. 90. – One should not forget that Deleuze, as well, speaks of the "emancipation of dissonance, the discordant accord" as "the great discovery" of the *Critique of Judgment*, including the aesthetics of the Beautiful and the Sublime. Compare Gilles Deleuze, *Essays. Critical and Clinical*, trans. D. W. Smith and M. A. Greco (Minneapolis: University of Minnesota Press, 1997), p. 35.

11 Compare on the following citations paragraphs 6, 7, 8, as well as 19 & 20 from Kant's *Critique of Judgement*.

12 Compare Cristina Lafont, "Law, Normativity and Legitimacy: Can Kantian Constructivism be Fruitful for Legal Theory?," *New Essays on the Normativity of Law*, eds. Stefano Bertea and George Pavlakos (Oxford: Hart Publishing, 2011), pp. 229–245. Hypothetical agreement is central to the Kantianism of Rawls, Habermas, and Scanlon. The connection could be a Kantian statement such as that in "On the common saying: this may be true in theory, but it does not apply in practice." The "original contract" which political philosophy has been drawing upon since Hobbes,

the option of saying that an object is beautiful and awaiting the agreement or disagreement of one's conversational partner. Neither partner can provide sound reasons. If the two fail to agree in their judgements, each must then examine his or her judgement to see whether it might not be based on subjective preferences after all. In this sense, Kant's statement is also interpreted as "soliciting" agreement. This solicitation cannot be verbose, but only deictic, indicative, and inviting, along the lines of: look or listen again! Can't you see, can't you hear what I mean: that the object is beautiful? And Kant ultimately calls the general voice a "common sense" based on "feeling" which is the "effect" of the "free play" of our cognitive and imaginative "power."

On the basis of this play of oppositional powers – and it is impossible to stress too often that they are strictly oppositional, for the one does precisely what the other does not want – it is possible to speak of the aesthetic *as if* it were a conceptually "substantiated fact." In an aesthetic judgement we maintain something which we cannot prove, but do so as if we could prove it. That's the point of an aesthetic judgement. For what we maintain has a felt concomitant claim to general validity "accrued from" the endless interaction between understanding and imagination.

Following Friedrich Schiller's interpretation, Rancière declares this aesthetic act to be the leading example of a political utopia, while to a certain extent remaining loyal to its Kantian origins. In political terms, one demands a right aesthetically by acting as if this right were already a reality, in other words by proclaiming its fictitious status to be that of reality. A prominent example of this are women's rights in the context of the French Revolution. According to Rancière, women could "demonstrate," or prove through public actions, two things: firstly, "that the rights owing to them by virtue of the Declaration of Human Rights were denied them," and, secondly, "that they possessed the rights which the Constitution omitted to grant them."[13] Following on from Rancière, we may observe that, provided it does not merely accept whatever is given at the time, whatever is perceived and said,

---

is accordingly "a *mere idea* of reason, but one which undoubtedly has a (practical) reality," namely to oblige the legislator to formulate and implement laws in such a way that they "*could have* originated" from the overall will of the people, and to see each citizen "*as if*" he had agreed to that will. Immanuel Kant, *Werkausgabe*, vol. X, ed. Wilhelm Weischedel (Frankfurt/M.: Suhrkamp, 1977), p. 153. In contrast, Lafont argues in favour of separating democratic agreement from hypothetical agreement.

13 Jacques Rancière, "Who Is the Subject of the Rights of Man?," *The South Atlantic Quarterly*, Vol. 103, Nr. 2/3 (2004): pp. 297–310, p. 304.

politics is dependent on the *as if* mode of acting, on feigning something as real which is not (yet) real, on maintaining that something is proven when it is not proven and may even be unprovable. To this extent, politics shares an essential element with aesthetics, namely the aesthetics which were the provenance of Kant. To be sure, politics has one essential element which is far removed from aesthetics: the element of equality. Indeed, according to Rancière, politics "only" exists through the principle of equality.[14] At this juncture one would be justified, as Oliver Marchart does, in criticising the "emancipatory apriorism" which Rancière shares with Alain Badiou. "Politics is a politics of equality, *ergo* emancipatory – or it is not politics." This is so unconvincing in empirical terms that Rancière can only state it "axiomatically."[15] Generally speaking, an axiom is a principle which is neither capable of nor requires proof. In this context, however, or so one would like to think, it definitely would require proof. Whether or not it would also be capable of being proven, is another question. And precisely because it is located in the grey area of an assertion which cannot be proven, yet appears as if it could be proven, the principle of equality is, in my eyes, itself a fiction in the sense stated. Only when these two principles come together, the principle of the aesthetically acquired *as if* and that of equality (which in turn is based on an *as if* structure), in other words only when one comprehends it as Kantian fiction, does politics follow the formula, in the normative sense, of acting in a certain practical situation *as if* those who did not count in this situation were already accounted for.

In a certain respect, aesthetic communitisation acquires an anti-romantic accent here. I am convinced that prominent, fairly recent, French-language philosophy pursues the romantic metaphysics of a primacy of the unutterable and the non-identical, and that, in political terms, especially for that tradition which started in the late 1970s with Philippe Lacoue-Labarthe's and Jean-Luc Nancy's *L'Absolu littéraire*,[16] one needs to speak not of a "Left Heideggerianism," but of a Left *Romanticism*, albeit with the pertinent familiar danger of an essentialisation of the political.[17] And yet I am also convinced that for Rancière

---

14 Rancière, *Disagreement*, p. 33.

15 Oliver Marchart, *Die politische Differenz. Zum Denken des Politischen bei Nancy, Lefort, Badiou, Laclau und Agamben* (Berlin: Suhrkamp, 2010), p. 183.

16 Philippe Lacoue-Labarthe and Jean-Luc Nancy, *L'Absolu littéraire*, Paris: Editions du Seuil, 1978.

17 Compare Josef Früchtl, "Auf ein Neues. – Ästhetik und Politik. Und dazwischen das Spiel. Angestoßen durch Jacques Rancière," *Deutsche Zeitschrift für Philosophie*, Year 55 (2007): pp. 209–219; critically, Drehli Robnik, *Film ohne Grund. Filmtheorie,*

the issue is far more tense, and thus conceived of in a more balanced way. Accordingly, art in the 20th century, and especially film, is not a harmonising sensualisation of ideas to serve the people, but the sensualisation and thus communitisation of a "confrontation," of a "contradiction of two worlds." The consensus consists in the dissensual; the disparity is the link. New protagonists are forcing their way, more or less violently, onto the "common stage" of politics. The only thing the protagonists have in common - why "only"? - is then that fundamental quarrel about whether or not they have anything in common, whether there is anything "between" them which links them, apart from the quarrel.[18]

Two Statements

I would like to conclude my short deliberations on the link between fiction, aesthetics, and politics with two statements.

(1) In Rancière's case, the political is a sphere in which the fictitious is proclaimed to be reality, namely the sphere in which one acts as if

---

Postpolitik und Dissens bei Jacques Rancière (Vienna/Berlin: Turia + Kant, 2010), pp. 75–76; on political philosophy in France since the 1980s, compare Thomas Bedorf, "Das Politische und die Politik. Konturen einer Differenz," *Das Politische und die Politik*, ed. Thomas Bedorf and Kurt Röttgers, (Berlin: Suhrkamp, 2010): pp. 13–37, pp. 13–15; on the concept of Left Heideggerianism compare Marchart, *Die politische Differenz*, pp. 59–60; the harsh criticism from Micha Brumlik ("voluntarism," "decisionism," "irrationalism," ultimately fascistic "in core and structure") applies far more to Badiou and Žižek than to Rancière, compare Micha Brumlik, "Neoleninismus in der Postdemokratie," *Blätter für deutsche und internationale Politik*, 55.8 (2010): pp. 105–116, p. 115.

18 Rancière, *Disagreement*, pp. 26–27. Robnik believes, in contrast, in a need to turn Rancière against Rancière, since the latter, in his emphasis on the communitising power of art, especially film, seems to leave out the dissensual dimension of politics which he develops in another context (compare Robnik, *Film ohne Grund*, pp. 21–22.). I can only mention here that my theoretical beliefs follow the line Hannah Arendt has developed with her political reading of Kant's aesthetics; compare Hannah Arendt, *Lectures on Kant's Political Philosophy* (Chicago: The University of Chicago Press, 1982); compare as well Seyla Benhabib, "Models of public space: Hannah Arendt, the liberal tradition, and Jürgen Habermas," *Habermas and the Public Sphere*, ed. Craig Calhoun (Cambridge, MA: MIT Press, 1992), pp. 73–98; Susan Bickford, *The dissonance of democracy. Listenting, conflict and citizenship* (Ithaca: Cornell University Press, 1996); Kennan Ferguson, *The Politics of Judgment. Aesthetics, Identity, and Political Theory* (Lanham/Maryland: Lexington Books, 1999). From a different, namely Heideggerian angle, Nancy's emphasis on "co-existence" and "co-appearance" can be added; compare Jean-Luc Nancy, *Etre singulier pluriel* (Paris: Éditions Galilée, 1996).

certain rights, certain normative characteristics, were real. Translated into the language of Kant, it is a sphere in which one asserts something one cannot prove *as if* one could prove it. In the case of politics, the object of that assertion is a right. This distinguishes politics from aesthetics. But what links the two is that the assertion is characterised in general by an *as if* structure and in particular by a structure of community, bringing together unity and separation, the consensual and the dissensual.

However, the *as if* structure is not only a feature of aesthetic and political judgement and action (in each case requiring a separate further differentiation). In a specific sense, it can also presumably be demonstrated for moral action.[19] In a peculiar way, it is also characteristic of action itself. All actions have an inherent fictitious element. Because it is never totally calculable, because uncertainties will always remain, an action initially has to feign success in order, then, to become reality. All actors have to act as if their actions were calculable; otherwise they would not act at all. And in the context of politics and aesthetics, a specific term is interesting here, namely that of "parasocial interaction," in which one person first feigns a social relationship to another person in order, then, to form it: a fiction with real consequences. A prime example is our dealings with stars on the TV or cinema screen or our dealings with strangers, in other words people who appear on our life stage without really belonging to it (in space/time, thus ontologically, or socially).[20]

(2) Thus in a *general* fashion, the *as if* structure characterises the fictitious element in everyday, political or aesthetic judgements and actions. For the *aesthetic* sphere against a Kantian background, however, something else is characteristic, namely an element of hope and trust. Without making this connection explicitly, and without speaking of trust explicitly, Kant in my opinion does refer to it when he says: "Beautiful things announce that human beings fit into the world." ("Die schönen Dinge zeigen an, dass der Mensch in die Welt passe.")[21]

---

19 Kant's postulates of pure practical reason thus also seem to be fictions conducive to action. We then have to act as if God existed; otherwise we cannot be sure that, through the morally imperative action, a good outcome will ensue (compare Marquard, "Kunst als Antifiktion," p. 85).

20 Compare Harald Wenzel, *Die Abenteuer der Kommunikation. Echtzeitmassenmedien und der Handlungsraum der Hochmoderne* (Weilerswist: Velbrück, 2001), pp. 11, 19–20; Josef Früchtl, "George Clooney, Brad Pitt und ich, oder die schöne Illusion des Vertrauens," *Zeitschrift für Ästhetik und Allgemeine Kunstwissenschaft*, 54. 2 (2009): pp. 273–282.

21 Reflexion 1820a, cited in Birgit Recki, *Ästhetik der Sitten. Die Affinität von ästhetischem Gefühl und praktischer Vernunft bei Kant* (Frankfurt/M.: Klostermann,

They announce in the sense that an advertisement or a short newspaper article announces something, or that a symptom announces the onset of a disease. They tell us something briefly, point out something that will happen or has already happened, but leave space for different interpretations and concretions. In the Kantian context, they announce that we fit into the world ontologically-epistemologically and ethically-politically. This means that the "gulf" existing, firstly, between our capacity for knowledge and the things around us and, secondly, between the realm of nature and freedom, the realm of causal determination and action, is not unbridgeable, that, in brief, our knowledge and actions make sense. An aesthetic experience can give us back our hope and trust in the world because, in its playful structure, its exciting balance of images and concepts, it awakens a feeling of agreement/correspondence/consonance/consensus which invites one also to conclude such an agreement between the self and the world. The idea of hope and trust, then, is nothing more, but also nothing less than an attitude of *as if*.

Summing up, I would like to maintain that rethinking politics, i.e. acting collectively under normative ideas, requires the acknowledgment of *consensus*, above all if we wish to rethink politics in a Kantian context, as is also the case for Rancière. At the same time, it requires taking the *as if* structure as a central structure of political action and community. Since the structure of *as if* is not specific to the political alone, it is required to work out the *specificity* of diverse *as if* structures. And the specificity of the *aesthetic* structure of *as if* lies, among other things, in the fact that it permits ethical hope and ontological trust.

2001), p. 135. Recki argues in favour of the theory that Kant's famous third philosophical question: "What may I hope?" (besides the questions: "What can I know?" and "What should I do?") also finds an answer in the *Critique of Judgement*; see also Odo Marquard, "Kant und die Wende zur Ästhetik," *Aesthetica und Anaesthetica*, pp. 28–30.

Dieter Mersch

The Political and the Violent
On Resistances

Politics and the Political

This essay explores *the political*, in particular that which we might call the vanishing of the political. We should first be aware that the terms *politics* and *the political* are polysemous and their applications are many. Politics as praxis can be used against the political as a discursive principle or attitude and, vice versa, the political as an ethos or universal category of "being-with" (Nancy) can be opposed to politics. If we take *politics* to mean the organization of societies and their futures, including institutional systems and the handling of conflicts, *the political* addresses firstly the human state of *being political*; our existence as *zoon politikon*, which has always placed us in a space of "dispute" (Lyotard), dissent or "disagreement" (Rancière). At the same time, the political denotes that discursivity in which the reasons for the structuring orders of the social are experienced as divided and posited in conflict (*Aus-einander-setzungen*). The political thus also designates the necessity of forming and structuring the social, as well as the *dispositif* of its legitimacy and rejection, which always accompany it. We are thus dealing in two ways with measures that are as practical as they are theoretical, that equally produce and reflect upon the social. However, it is not the discursive alone which is most important – that *discursivity of discourse* which builds upon the classic political dichotomization between freedom and the lack thereof, justice and injustice, law and violence, etc. – but rather the *practical* which establishes and enforces the differences within the social. Nor should we fail to mention that the differences that pervade discourses of the political are on the one hand themselves the effects of practices which in turn can be described as such, just as on the other hand discourses *are* practices, situated in the space of politics and the political. The problem of talking about the political is therefore that it both has the power to create society to a certain extent – to order it and to quash it – and at the same time denotes reflections on this power, in which it is justified or criticized – and the two terms cannot simply be separated.

The intricate situation results thus from the political referring to both a practice of creation and a practice of theory or reflection, which, as a practice, is part of the political in which it intervenes. Every criticism of social conditions or the political systems which they uphold is itself already a political action, participating in the power structure, even and especially when suppressed or prohibited. There is thus no extrapolitical terrain, no apolitical discourse, no conflict about the political which transpires in a special philosophical space outside of that which the term denotes. This by no means should imply that the political nature of these practices is so unavoidable that we are locked into them as in a cage.[1] Politics and the political are rather complementary like the two sides of a mirror, which is not accidentally the cardinal metaphor of reflection; but – like with every mirror – they distort reflection and only make some aspects visible while highlighting selected details that otherwise would have remained hidden. This also means that we must see politics and the political to a certain extent as universal categories. Just as there is no beyond to social systems, there is no beyond to the political – the structure and organizational forms of the social necessitate politics and the political. It is this circumstance that makes the reciprocal clarification and understanding of their relationship so difficult; the question of the politics of discourse and the discursivization of politics, not to mention the politicalness of the question of the political, which always intervenes unreasonably in political relations and dares to criticize them.

However, in order to begin somewhere, I choose the *polis* as the paradigmatic stage on which all these questions play – on the etymological level as well. The *polis* already includes the symbolic question of the *politiké*, the *politeia*, and the problem of thinking about the source of these structures, their *arché* or foundation and legitimacy. The terms *politics* and *the political* thus both deal in equal measure with the *body politic* and its realization, whether in the form of different political systems and their specific instruments – or media –, such as laws, the public sphere, means of negotiation, relations to the outside world, etc., or in the form of the formulation of general principles which go before, and which, according to Martin Heidegger's reconstruction of early Greek philosophy, were of course situated in the *physis*.[2] It is also of note that all of these questions are directly connected to *ethos*, or were and still are touched upon in discussions on ethics – in particular all questions of justice and a just order and, correspondingly, laws such as the ones introduced in the Greek city-states

---

1 On this see, for example, Ulrich Bröckling and Robert Feustel, eds., *Das Politische denken. Zeitgenössische Positionen*, 2nd ed. (Bielefeld: transcript, 2010).

2 See in particular Martin Heidegger's many studies of the "first beginning," esp.: *Contributions to Philosophy (Of the Event)*, trans. Richard Rojcewicz and Daniela Vallega-Neu (Bloomington: Indiana University Press, 1989); also *The Event*, trans. Richard Rojcewicz (Bloomington: Indiana University Press, forthcoming).

after the overthrow of tyranny in the 6th century BCE. At the same time, these questions are contextually tied to *episteme*, knowledge and its philosophical justification which is taken on the one hand from an *other* – namely a natural ontology –, without asking whether this is a transferable category; and on the other hand from the *phronesis* of practical intelligence meant to guide governance and its tactics. The aim is not to justify the order and specific organizational structures of the *polis*, but rather to ensure strategies of exchange such as the long-term transmission of tradition and its protection through a way of life. The latter necessitates in particular the temporalization of the varying respective beings and the shaping of their relationship to one another. Differences between desires and order must be balanced and this balance must be preserved or withstood, whereby the former took the form of a kind of spatialization of participation (*methexis*), which invented the *polis* as a whole, as a unified organism.[3] This inventory makes the origins of the different terms and their particular perspectives clear, as well as the solutions they intend to offer and the extent to which clarifying them is in turn connected to questions of metaphysics, of life, and of relations between creatures, as well as the extent to which they are permeated by freedom and violence.

Performativity and the Political

The great philosophical systems of antiquity of course offered ambivalent answers to these questions. They either started with a sweeping idea from which they extrapolated the particular or, in contrast, took a particular case as given in order to develop concrete solutions from this case. One of the advantages of the Aristotelian *politeia* over the Platonic, especially the *Nicomachean Ethics* as a foundation of the political, is that it searches for practical philosophy in *praxis* and action rather than by formulating general ideals and forcing these upon the creation of community. The basis of the political thus leads to individual human practices and their mode of existence. These do not subordinate themselves *per se* to the authority of higher institutions, laws or constitutions, but rather follow from them. If praxis comes from action, this also implies that the political must be thought of as something which belongs to the human being so absolutely that it defines the person and his options, not the other way around. The

3 On the diverse organic metaphors in political theory and practice see Thomas Frank et al., *Der fiktive Staat. Konstruktionen des politischen Körpers in der Geschichte Europas* (Frankfurt/M: Fischer, 2007).

central realization of the Aristotelian *politeia* is that man is, as the famous definition states, "*zoon logon echon zoon politikon,*"[4] a political being by nature who is forced to live in community while its concurrent access to *logos* allows it to give community political meaning. Being *in nature* thus already means being political or becoming part of a community; however, the political is in itself not a natural given, but rather the product of *logos* and thus dependent upon realization, upon the Reason of rational meaning.

If we stay in an Aristotelian mode and take the practical as our starting point, we are immediately confronted – and this is the crux of the matter – with the dual meaning or ambiguity of the term *to act*. This ambiguity is linked to the category of the performative. The political is not simply about connecting praxis to *logos* to make the *polis* possible, but praxis itself contains an element which is always able to disturb or undermine *logos* – its performativity. The concept of performativity therefore becomes relevant to the question of the political. However it is important to say that the performative dimension is not added to praxis as if it were a second, additional element. Rather performativity is intrinsically linked to the practical as its form of execution or enactment and the manner in which it is posited, the two cannot be separated. The performative however suffers no rationalization – it must be differentiated from meaning and from the intelligibility of the intention.[5] This is what makes the concept so interesting with regard to the political, because it shows that there is an element within each action which resists "politicization," as the subordination to and control by the political. Put another way, we are dealing with an "an-archic" moment, something which sets a limit to jurisprudence and is able to destabilize or explode its order.

And in fact this intuitive idea accompanies theories of the performative from the very beginning, even if they did not deal with it explicitly. On the contrary, the category of performativity has been studied with an eye towards its ability to form identities and to rationalize, and in connection with intentionality and authorship. However, actions

---

4 Aristotle, *Politics*, trans. Carnes Lord (Chicago: University of Chicago Press, 1985); Aristotle, *Nicomachean Ethics*, trans. Joe Sachs (Newburyport, Mass: Focus Publishing, 2002), 1162 a.

5 On this see my diverse attempts to delineate this concept beyond the classical definitions: Dieter Mersch, "Kommunikative Identitäten und performative Differenzen. Einige Bemerkungen zu Habermas' Theorie der kommunikativen Rationalität," *Preproceedings of the 20th International Wittgenstein-Symposium* (Kirchberg: 1997), p. 621–628; Dieter Mersch, "Ereignis und Respons. Elemente einer Theorie des Performativen," *Performativität und Praxis*, ed. Jens Kertscher and Dieter Mersch (Munich: Fink, 2003), p. 69–94.

can be divided not only into *actiones* and *passiones* - proper actions and experiences -, but all praxis has a duplicitous character, as is expressed by aspects of the *symbolic* and the *performative*. On the one hand, actions accomplish something akin to setting aims and goals to which they give a meaning and which distinguish them within a field of other practices, separate or connected. As aims and goals, actions can in principle be guided or subordinated. On the other hand, they are themselves something that *intervenes* in the field, causing things to happen or changing them - even as an act of strengthening or rejection. In other words, practices can always be read in two ways - as *symbolic praxes* which can be coopted by power, which always participate in the symbolic; and as *situated in the real*, which from the outset does not follow any rules, but rather lays something down, situates or asserts itself to bring something into the world which was not there before.

Jürgen Habermas famously described this in reference to communication, albeit in another context, as the "performative-propositional dual structure of speech acts."[6] This takes into account that a sentence, the declaration as an act, must take the form of an assertion, a promise, a threat, etc. From this we can extrapolate a series of far-reaching effects on the rationality of communication as well as on the constitution of the social and the normativity of the political and its legitimacy.[7] Public debates are bound to the form of discussion and its rules, but the question remains open whether there is such a thing as general or "universal pragmatic" rules of communication. We are thus confronted with a rationalization of the politicization of the political which is both procedural and a matter of discourse theory, whereby *discourse* must be understood as the reflective form of interactions that take the form of argumentations. This explanation of the performative, first applied only to linguistic philosophy, can be expanded to include actions in general, so that spoken and practical situations are fundamentally analogous. It is not Habermas' theory of democracy, a philosophy of the political grounded in communicative practices, which is decisive to an exploration of these questions, but rather his insight into linguistic practices: that the practical and the performative belong together and are directly interlinked, an insight which is in principle applicable to all practices and their performative contours. Habermas

6 Jürgen Habermas, "Vorbereitende Bemerkungen zu einer Theorie der kommunikativen Kompetenz," Jürgen Habermas and Niklas Luhmann, *Theorie der Gesellschaft oder Sozialtechnologie* (Frankfurt/M: Suhrkamp, 1971), p. 101–141.

7 See Jürgen Habermas, *The Theory of Communicative Action, vol. 1 and 2*, trans. Thomas MacCarthy (Boston, Mass.: Beacon, 1985).

built in particular on the linguistic philosophy of John L. Austin and John Searle, who, however, traced the performativity of spoken utterances to an *intentio*, which they connected directly to an auctorial speaker/subject and its intention.[8] Concurrently, the performative points towards a *will to posit*: I *intend* to claim something or to doubt it, make a promise or express a feeling, rather than being unaware of my motives or reasons for doing something by saying something, or of completing an act in doing. The duplicity between the symbolic and the performative mentioned above is thus one-sidedly ascribed to the subjectivity of the subject, and any analysis of the speech act, and thus also of any performativity, is tied to the logic of intentionality. More than anyone, to Searle's great annoyance, Jacques Derrida pointed out in "Signature, Event, Context" and later in *Limited Inc.* that to each act belongs the moment of its *happening* as well as the *event* of its execution, which are at least capable of divorcing the act and the event from their intention.[9] The duplicity of the symbolic and the performative is thus crossed by a second duplicity which has largely been ignored by speech act theories as well as theories of action and interaction. It is the *duplicity of the performative itself*, namely between an "act of positioning" and the "irreversibility" which follows from it.[10] For it should not be forgotten that the situating of the performative in reality, its impact and intervention *within* a situation causes reactions to and interactions with other actions, which in turn unleash their own, irreproducible powers. It is telling that analytical theories of speech and actions regularly leave out such interlinkages and do not make them an object of study,[11] or at best relegate them to the field of perlocutionary, secondary effects.

---

8 John Langshaw Austin, *How to do Things with Words*, 2nd. ed. (Oxford: Oxford University Press, 1975); John R. Searle, *Speech Acts. An essay in the philosophy of language* (Cambridge: Cambridge University Press, 1969).

9 Jacques Derrida, "Signature, Event, Context," *A Derrida Reader*, ed. Peggy Kamuf (New York: Columbia University Press, 1991), p. 80–112; also Jacques Derrida, *Limited Inc.* trans. Jeffrey Mehlmann and Samuel Weber (Evanston: Northwestern University Press, 1988). John Searle, in his answer to Derrida, continues to insist on the primacy of intention: "There is no getting away from intentionality, because a meaningful sentence is just a standing possibility of the corresponding (intentional) speech act," John R. Searle, "Reiterating the Differences. A Reply to Derrida", *Glyph* 1 (1997): p. 198–208, p. 202.

10 See Dieter Mersch "Das Ereignis der Setzung," *Performativität und Ereignis*, ed. Erika Fischer-Lichte, Christian Horn, and Matthias Warstat (Tübingen/Basel: Francke, 2002), p. 41–56.

11 This also applies to Donald Davidson's action theory. See his essays translated and compiled in *Handlung und Ereignis* (Frankfurt/M: Suhrkamp, 1985).

In contrast, we can assume that there is little difference between the illocutionary and the perlocutionary, even that the perlocutionary, as the medial form of praxis, is the *true heart of the performative.*[12] This is necessarily so, for the idea of the performative is that *through* an act something is brought into reality, a world of its own is created, as it were – at the beginning of the social is the act, which situates the fact. The *through* is important; it points towards an act of *mediation* that brings together the concepts of the medium and the performative. I would like to take a discursive detour here to reveal the explosive nature of this thought; for the *per* in perlocution makes it much closer to the *per* in performative than to illocution. In *per,* the true mediality of an act is expressed. If Austin in contrast differentiates between illocution and perlocution by stating that the illocutionary act constitutes meaning "in saying" whereas perlocution induces something "by saying" (through),[13] the latter proves to be analogous to the phrase "by means of," which, similar to mediation, describes a figure of immanence, located *in* the world. If we change linguistic camps and go to the Latin and Greek, *through* – by means of – can be translated as *per* or *dia* respectively, prefixes of composites such as *dialogoi* (to read from), *diaphane* (shining through), *diheiresis* (cutting through), *diagrammata* (to draw through), and others in which *dia* is meant actively and denotes a mediated process. In other words, *the performative and mediality cannot be separated*[14] – and to the extent that mediation takes place through language or through an act, we are in the arena of the concept of the performative which in the process of *locution* becomes *per-locution.* Performativity is characterized by an elementary division or differentiality, because perlocution diffuses meaning and can turn a statement into an insult or criticism into obeisance. In this way, the specific mediality of speech is revealed – or to put it more pointedly: *The mediality of the performative which is manifest in the perlocutionary participates not in the logic of identity, but in a logic of difference.*

---

12 See in particular Dieter Mersch, "Performativität und Ereignis. Überlegungen zur Revision des Performanz-Konzeptes der Sprache," *Rhetorik. Figuration und Performanz, Schriftreihe Germanistische Symposien, Berichtband 25*, ed. Jürgen Fohrmann (Stuttgart-Weimar: Metzler, 2004), p. 502–535.

13 Austin, *How to do Things with Words*, pp. 121–132.

14 On this delineation of mediality see Dieter Mersch "Meta/Dia. Zwei unterschiedliche Zugänge zum Medialen," *Zeitschrift für Medien- und Kulturforschung, vol. 2* (2010): p. 185–208.

Both, John Searle and Jürgen Habermas – and this is important to my argument – tried to ignore or even obliterate this difference as well as the constitutional ambiguity of that which can be called the act and its effect. For if an act creates a fact, it seems irrelevant whether the creation is an effect of the act or the effect of the effect of an act, because the act as act can only be analyzed retrospectively on the basis of its consequences. Embedded in a sequence of actions, at the site of their creation they are literally diverted. In contrast, the discursive maneuver of subjectification seems clear: If our starting point is the intentional, the "principle of expressibility"[15] as well as the fundamental conventionality of actions or their tendency to follow rules, then every speaker or actor stands for that which he says or does and can in turn, as in the case of libel, calumny, or false promises, be made accountable for his speech or actions. John Searle – like John L. Austin or later Karl-Otto Apel and Jürgen Habermas – further promotes belief in the stability of a subject in control of its self. This subject becomes the basis of their social theory, which presumes the existence of a certain legal structure that the political can build upon. We, however, are interested in those consequences which take place in practical events and which are not just *occasional* coincidences or casual side effects, for example when dialogic mishaps occur – what Austin calls "infelicities" or "misfires"[16] –, or when an action veers off course because of the convergence of numerous intentions which cannot be controlled. These effects are not sporadic anomalies. Rather, they are the core of the mediation of the practical and, as they are eventful, they stem from its systemic indetermination and inaccessibility. Most interesting are the moments in which both – intentionality and non-intentionality – become intertwined and create fractures or contradictions, where the splits and layers in the process of communication or interaction proliferate to such an extent that promises and deception or violence and recognition become so intertwined as to be indistinguishable. In short, while illocutions are what they say and thus call up figures of identification because they – following the "principle of expressibility" – are always already connected to the subject and his intentions, perlocutions and the performances thereof imply the enforcement of differentiations which mediate social situations from the inside just as much as they erode or disassociate these situations.

Thus if we take as our starting point neither the political as an ordering and situating of laws from the perspective of the practical, nor the responsibility of acting as the basis of the social, but rather the key

15 Searle, *Speech Acts*, pp. 19–21.
16 Austin, *How to do Things with Words*, pp. 14–18.

dissociation and thus anomie or anarchy of the performative, then we attempt to add an element to thinking about the politicalness of the political and its models of power and structures of freedom which from the very beginning counters or resists these thoughts. We thus start with an ambiguity which is inherent to the simple act and its "scene": For the singular act does not exist, but it is only ever "situations"[17] which interweave the complexities of actions with contingencies, and of which we simultaneously try to show that they precede the political and that they are built upon a series of fundamental paradoxes, which, from the start, irritate the classical concept of politics. I shall return to this in greater detail below. For the time being it is sufficient to note that in this way something is inscribed into the necessity of the political which both precedes and complicates the possibility of community, of the *polis*. By thus posing the question of the constitution of human collectives, we reach a layer before communities, on which they are founded without being constituted and which bring to them a genuine inconsistency or "not being at home" (*Unbehaustheit*). This also means that if the political consists firstly of creating community and its organizations, or making available the media or *dispositif* necessary to its creation and initialization (for no collective preexists as an independent entity or organizes itself, even if, following Aristotle and the political philosophies founded on his work, people must have always come together in groups and from this point on assert themselves as people in the sense of *humanitas*), nevertheless from the very beginning there is an element situated in human action which continuously undermines this production or renders it precarious. This can also be understood as follows: human beings act, but they must first be made, in their relationships to one another and to their others, to react to one another and to act with one another, if a community is to be formed. That act itself, its *actio* and *passio*, contains an element founded neither in freedom nor in desire, an element which literally and chronically "disorients" this action. As this is the case, we must also describe the political and the site thereof somewhat differently: not only as the creation of community (*polis*) through the *dispositif* of collectivization, but as the power of the limitation and control of the performative itself, which inscribes a non-correspondence or discordance into the political. Thus there can be no concept of the political which is not contradictory: it is made up of both the conditions and requirements necessary to the constitution of society, as well as the conditionals of

---

17 The term *situation* refers to the political theory of Jean-Paul Sartre, *Critique of Dialectical Reason. Vol. 1*, New Edition, trans. Quintin Hoare (New York/London: Verso Books, 2010).

interpersonal relations and their connections or "engagements". Their very production implies their restrictions, and thus forms of resistance which stem from the performative elements themselves. Only then do questions of justice and its *separation* arise, questions of dissemination or, following Jacques Rancière, its systems of distribution and division.[18] The latter rest upon the former, not vice versa.

Positing Violence

To summarize our ideas on the performative up to this point, we can say that through the performative, a specific dialectic or dispersion is set into force which links it intrinsically to what can for now be termed *immanent violence*. It is virtually unavoidable. The concept of violence I am using here – or of power – is not a moral one; it is a violent force immanent to the performative which at the same time circulates within actions without being situated in a specific place or having a particular addressee. The term *violence* in a certain sense cross-references Searle's "illocutionary force"[19] or the Classical rhetorical term *peithein*, the persuasive force of language.[20] It describes the linguistic power of persuasion, which can be connected to the concept of performative violence, because *power* and *force* are unthinkable without violence. All three terms correlate to one another, because every human action contains the possibility of violence, as long as it posit or assert itself within a "situation" – a field of contexts, coincidences, and decisions which necessarily disturb it. As an act, it imposes itself on the Other and on that which came before by taking its place, partially transforming it, overwriting or suppressing it, while also limiting alternatives. Every practical instantiation or positioning is inscribed with a moment of principle asymmetry or non-reciprocity. It consumes, interrupts or divides the performative scene and delimits its opportunities, while shifting, reversing or obliterating others. To *posit* something means to make it manifest, and through this to prejudge every further step in time. Whether as continuation, break or refusal – all require an

18 See Jacques Rancière, *Disagreement. Politics and Philosophy*, trans. Julie Rose (Minneapolis: University of Minnesota Press, 1999); and Jacques Rancière, *The Politics of Aesthetics*, trans. Gabriel Rockhill, (London/New York: Continuum, 2006), esp. "The Distribution of the Sensible," pp. 7–10.

19 See John Searle and Daniel Vanderveken, *Foundations of Illocutionary Logic* (Cambridge: Cambridge University Press, 1985), pp. 1, 7–9, 20–21.

20 See Andreas Hetzel, *Die Wirksamkeit der Rede. Zur Aktualität der klassischen Rhetorik für die moderne Sprachphilosophie* (Bielefeld: Transcript, 2010).

act of fundamental positing which in and of itself already includes self-affirmation. What is more, every action, by positing itself, must suffer the consequences without being able to reverse them. At best effects can be diverted or corrected, but only at the price of a further act which cannot undo that which the first act unleashed. This brings about new consequences – sometimes a series of further actions which themselves cannot avoid following their own logic and dictating their own distinctive conditions, etc. Furthermore, every action is passive endurance (*Erleidnis*) in that it can only refer to a previous situation or scene, with all its concomitant capricious and opaque qualities. This scene determines the act, delimits its scope, and defines its possibilities. No action can escape the shadow of its past, which has given it immutable conditions that are immediately transcended and abandoned. In short, the human situation and its praxis, which first summons and simultaneously dismantles the political, is characterized by an elemental temporalization which contains a paradoxical constellation even while wrestling with this paradox. One must therefore, if one takes the practical as a starting point for the examination of questions of the political, assume an inherent distortion or contradiction which colors the performative scene from the beginning without immediately subjecting it to ethical considerations or disciplinary measures.

The result is that violence, or rather the discord, the overthrow, or *katastrophé* are intrinsic elements of the *conditio humana*. They are fundamental parts of being human and of human social reality and in fact permeate every human articulation, every symbolic form, even every term and concept that we posit in the world or impose upon reality and ascribe to the Other, the creature with the mark of Cain and the experience of violence. This applies even to the concept of Reason, which Habermas explicitly set in opposition to violence. "My wish is to show," he contributed to a debate, "that discourse is not subject to arbitrariness, but that we live within a social order which really only allows two mechanisms for solving conflicts of action: Violence or rational communication [*Verständigung*]."[21] We can counter this argument, for even rational discourse – limiting ourselves to philosophical argumentation or agreement in the emphatic form of consensus and political rapprochement – is intertwined with violence; and not only because of the superiority which in this way is ascribed to the supposed "unconstrained constraint of the better argument,"[22] but exactly

---

21 Jürgen Habermas, "Diskussionsbeitrag," *Transzendentalphilosophische Normenbegründungen*, ed. Willi Oelmüller (Paderborn: UTB, 1978), p. 114.

22 Habermas, "Vorbereitende Bemerkungen zu einer Theorie der kommunikativen Kompetenz," p. 137.

through the gesture of limitation, of exclusion with which the discursive element is placed before all other forms of expression and given absolute priority. Paying attention to such gestures of exclusion or positing differences already means addressing a dimension of the performative which in this case, by positing rationality as the *only legitimate means of fighting and the sole form of solving conflicts*, reveals its own immanent violence: a violence that duplicates itself by positing itself as absolute to the same extent to which it denies that it *itself* is violent.

We thus touch on a further point: performative events not only contain an internal paradox that is always able to turn reason into unreason, and truth into lies, or justice into injustice, but rather they continuously shift and overturn the situation or scene of the performative, so that we must assume an event of incessant differentiation. No meaning can ever be stable or reliable – this is the core tenet of *différance* with which Jacques Derrida confronted hermeneutics and the varying systems of structuralism as well as their reliance on the reconstructability of symbolic orders. We are now becoming aware of the same effect in the area of the practical; even in the form of the most inflexible norm or its social containment through fixed codices or conventions, because its release and its eventfulness are owed to what might be called a principle of performative *différance* – a concept that does not really aid its "deconstruction," but rather acts as a metaphor for the possibility of infinite shifts and turns or uses and abuses within the practical. It should be stressed that these turns caused by uses (Ver-wendungen) and these uses as 'turns' (Wendungen)[23] do not occur because they were intended. Rather, every action turns at the site of the scene, and is thus at once diverted, placed beyond the actor's control. Speaking, acting, creating or resisting thus always also mean doing or saying something else – because from the start the conditions of the scene have already been changed. Seen in this way, each performative act thus undergoes a continuous transformation because, as regards the scene, they are subject to an alterity which is not so much the alterity of the Others, but rather a diversion or distortion and estrangement that consists of the fact that we can never determine where an action or a speech act has already gone or will shift itself to. The power or force of the performative, that which we have identified as its specific violence, is not necessarily subject to this estrangement, rather it creates it anew in every moment.

---

23 In German, this suggests a paronomasia: "diese Verwendungen aus Ver-wendungen und Verwendungen als Wendungen."

We therefore do not own ourselves – neither our actions nor their meanings or consequences. Rather we are owned by a force, a violence, which continuously subverts our common praxis and, with us, is always making trouble. It turns against the best intentions, pushes them into their opposite, inverts their aims or disperses them in impenetrable directions.[24] In fact, our ruminations aim to decipher this diversion, distortion, or estrangement as an indication of a genuinely tragic moment within the human condition. The term *tragic*, which we here mark as almost vital to existence, addresses the inescapable violence which happens to us although we do not intend it and which we therefore also cannot rule or control. It is similar to the paradoxical nature of the human condition which encroaches on the paradoxicality of all cultural formations. There is no praxis characterized by counter-finalities. For this reason, the scene of both the performative and the political, and every act of positing social relationships, are close to tragedy, because the performative *différance* operating behind the actors' backs continually confuses or disturbs their actions or even dooms them to failure. This is exactly what the old idea of *diabolé* or *diábolos* meant to express, literally to throw through, a counter-concept to *symbolon*, the symbolic or "thrown together" – the guarantee for meaning. Its calamitous force, the foundation of which is unidentifiable, shows itself mostly in the momentum of the turn towards immediate violence. This phenomenon is well-known in daily life – the decision that veers into chaos, the proposal that becomes intrusive, the innocent aid that causes humiliation, and the gift which, the moment it is accepted, turns into a burden that cannot be reciprocated. It is not man who – speaking anthropologically – is made of crooked wood, as Immanuel Kant put it,[25] rather we are confronted with the fragility or instability of the social. Continuously and against our will, an Other appears which "intervenes," uncannily and insubordinately, mocking the illusion of sovereignty and our attempts at unanimity – to the extent that the religions of antiquity as well as their Manichean and Christian successors did not hesitate to see in this the workings of a diabolical principle. Ethics of antiquity, rooted in tragedy, were oriented towards the fact that there is no stable, non-paradoxical reference point that can

24 As related to processes of understanding and communicating, see a similar argumentation in Dieter Mersch, *Posthermeneutik* (Berlin: Akademie, 2010).

25 Immanuel Kant, "Idea for a Universal History with Cosmopolitan Intent," trans. Thomas M. Greene and H. Hudson, *German Essays on History*, ed. Rolf Sältzer (New York: Continuum, 1991), p. 8.

act as a solid ground or foundation and on which any kind of "truth" or objective law might rest. We waver, thrown upon subversion and contingency. For this reason ethics knows no universal principle, but, at best, the case, the singularity. This is particularly true for all ethical categories that are relevant to social contexts, which relate to the praxis of human relationships, such as trust, loyalty and belief – categories that precede every written law or normative sanctioning.

This means that being or existing in the practical implies that we posit that over which we have no control, just as we are permanently exposed and susceptible to it. If we earlier coupled the concept of the performative with *positing*, we must now place *exposure* as an equal partner at its side, in the sense of exposition, to the extent that exposure always simultaneously contains elements of a break and the violence of exposure. To act means to expose oneself both in the active and in the passive sense; it means presenting oneself, displaying oneself and at the same time imposing oneself and exercising power through the manifestation of a presence. In the same way to expose oneself means to be vulnerable to the attacks and the arbitrariness of others, not to know what the effects of an action will be and how it will assert itself within the situation or scene, only to become "perverted" bit by bit with every new step. Human existence is possible only in connection with others, and every participation or taking part also includes a parting or a difference and also needs an elementary responsiveness,[26] which, to a certain extent, must always already include others, before *I*, my practice or the "economy" of my desires, can exist. Just so, I am equally dependent upon the Others and their practices, their benevolence or their violence, which I meet with, which attack me, which provoke my response. In turn my reactions themselves posit, intervene, pervert, and thus differentiate, they are accepting or rejecting and thus themselves exclude or are potentially violent.

This can also be expressed as follows: Performativity, with its genuinely triple act of positioning, exposing, and transposing, also includes a moment of injustice or guilt, which was already reflected by the saying of Anaximander: "Where the source of things is, to that place they must also pass away, according to necessity, for they must pay penance and be judged for their injustices, in accordance with the ordinance of time."[27] This saying's depth does not lie in its invocation

---

26 On the figure of responsiveness see in particular Bernhard Waldenfels, *Antwortregister* (Frankfurt/M: Suhrkamp, 2007); and Dieter Mersch, *Was sich zeigt. Materialität, Präsenz, Ereignis* (Munich: Fink: 2002) and Mersch, *Posthermeneutik.*
27 As interpreted by Friedrich Nietzsche, *Philosophy in the Tragic Age of the Greeks*, trans. Marianne Cowan (Washington, D.C.: Regnery Publishing Inc., 1998), p. 45.

of a fateful cycle of becoming and decaying, but in the connection of becoming and injustice. That which is, or that which we create and make, is owed to an original illegitimacy which can only be mended by its transience – we will come back to this below. Similarly, Walter Benjamin noted that "guilt" is the "highest category of world history."[28] There is no intervention, no technical correction of a fault, no production or revolutionary act which does not carry a trace of violence on which its ethical volatility can ignite. Admittedly, it is impossible to change anything or to have an impact without intervening, crossing borders, and leaving the past behind; but there is also no transformation without deformation, no metamorphosis without disfigurement. These prove the uncanniness of the diabolical discussed above, which, recusant and tenacious, lodges itself into the work of realization only to oppose both knowledge and reflection. This is why it is haunted by the tragic which we are discussing here and which means that every project, every admonition or design of an *actio* is also a disenfranchisement. The human condition only exists because of this disenfranchisement, which counters the idea of political justice. This is the reason why the phenomenon of "violence" is found only in the human realm, because humans are inextricably bound to the inhuman, whereby the political – the focus of this study – is made up of the always futile sites of equalization and reconciliation. It is an answer to the ineluctability of violence – or power –, which it counters with violence or power of its own. We shall return to this below as well.

The Paradox in the Political

This means that the perspective of the performative makes violence ubiquitous, both as an element of *actio*, its irreversible positing in reality, and in relation to the *passio* – the vulnerability or passive exposure (*Widerfahrung*) to situational events that never become a whole or allow themselves to be subsumed under our practical aims and plans. This makes it sound as if, in light of the inevitability of violence, we should generally refrain from ever doing anything and opening ourselves to the world or to others. But not only is the conclusion

---

On this see also Martin Heidegger "Anaximander's Sayings," *Off the Beaten Track*, trans. Julian Young and Kenneth Haynes (Cambridge: Cambridge University Press, 2002), pp. 242–281.

28 Walter Benjamin, "Zur Geschichtsphilosophie, Historik und Politik," *Gesammelte Schriften, vol. VI*, ed. Rolf Tiedemann and Hermann Schweppenhäuser (Frankfurt/M: Suhrkamp, 1991), pp. 90–108, p. 92. (Trans. here Laura Radosh)

unavoidable, so too is its avoidance. If we consciously try not to act, whenever we stop, are silent, or retreat, we are still acting in relation to the world and others. Practical asceticism cannot escape that which I have tried to reveal as the fundamental tragedy of humanity. The *tragic* connotes that – the Greek word describes the insolvability of the conflicts relating to the practical and the violence thereof; just as the truthfulness of tragic consciousness lies in its mythical and ritual performance. And in fact Greek tragedy derives its volatility and its topics from unsparing descriptions of the human condition as a permanent unfolding and refolding of the performative scene, which in every moment is about to unleash the countering powers of destruction. The political is its blueprint and its counter-reaction. It refuses to accept these powers. This explains the restlessness of politics, its overexertion shortly before the fall. Sophocles' *Antigone* – alongside many other works[29] – can be taken as exemplary for this state, which can also be read as an enactment of the conflict between, on the one hand, individual desire and its incalculable effects – which can be neither controlled nor traced – and the order of law on the other hand, which attempts to rein in this force and domesticate it. One could say that the political comes "in between" the tragic performative, it interrupts it, sets caesura in actions and subsumes them under its sovereign dominion. Resolving the paradoxical does not promise *catharsis* or reconciliation within the human condition – rather it forms its fundamental problem.

With this realization, the question arises as to the constitution of social orders as a political problem. At stake here, in the words of Jean-Paul Sartre, is the problem of "fusion" or "groups-in-fusion,"[30] those spontaneous associations or gatherings that carry the power of bundling, connection or possible cooperation. We should keep in mind that production would not be productive, and no communication or play could exist, without this concatenation of practices and without the bond of cooperation and its intrinsic commitments. The question of politics and the political is thus directly connected to this, for the political defines the conditions under which bonds can be created; it makes them possible despite the severances or differences engendered by the practical. The scene of the performative has been seen to be unavoidably permeated by violence; nevertheless it demands this vio-

---

29 See in particular Judith Butler, *Excitable Speech. A Politics of the Performative* (New York: Routledge, 1997).

30 Jean-Paul Sartre, *Critique of Dialectical Reason, Bd. 2*, trans. Quentin Hoare (London/New York: Verso, 2006) esp. pp. 173–176. See also Dorothea Wildenburg, *Jean-Paul Sartre* (Frankfurt/M: Campus, 2004), pp. 123–125.

lence be banned, delimited or inhibited, as is expressed in the plethora of social frameworks, laws, customs, norms, and rules of etiquette which in turn always tend to become repressive. Convening en masse at the site of the scene, they are also an indication of how many barriers and borders are necessary to tame the elementary paradoxicality of the practical and its intrinsic "anomie." One may therefore doubt the spontaneity of cooperative movements, of which Sartre believes the taking of the Bastille was exemplary, and in which the masses are moved only by the thought of ending their impossible social conditions. Social conditions must in this case be so impossible that they also end the performative dispersal; and in coming together, a political will must be articulated that is able to create another form of community. In contrast, the performative and its ambiguity, its violence or tendency to excess and especially to uncontrollability is first formed or *joined* under duress: joined in the sense of affiliated, subsumed, or continued. It marks the site of coming together, which Heidegger has in another context given the equally political denotation "assembly."[31] In this same essay, Heidegger deals with the question of "jointure," albeit in the context of the thing that "presences the presencing," the "between" to which "the jointure must belong."[32] The theme of joining thus replaces the question of the synthesis which, following Kant, imagination and understanding must undergo in theoretical questions, but which takes on a different shape in questions of the practical. We may have the same problem, namely how an "assembly" can be achieved, but political theories usually trace this back to voluntary actions meant to bring freedom and order into harmony. In contrast, in the problem of joining the link between the performative and its dispersals – the "between" which both connects and divides it – we do not see assembled beings, but rather the imperious manifestation of order.[33] It is therefore a *joining* which attempts to jump over the divide of the performative *différance*. One could therefore say that the foundation of the political is a continuous struggle against the anomies and anarchies of the practical by means of the tools of limitation and repression, which obsessively attempt to join their jointure. Its preferred forms are dominion, regulation, subservience, and, above all, the law as the basic form of the political – but these are not its only forms.

---

31 Heidegger, "Anaximander's Sayings," p. 266.

32 Ibid., p. 267.

33 See also Christoph Tholen, *Die Zäsur der Medien, Kulturpolitische Konturen* (Frankfurt/M: Suhrkamp, 2006).

From this follows that the joining in question tries to pacify the interstice, the violence, and the literal alien-ation of the performative, in particular through the rule of law as a principle of order and formation. The constitution of the political in Greek antiquity – the source of political discourse and its philosophical reasoning – therefore begins with the problem of *nomoi*, laws, as the structuring of the practical in the *polis*. The law (*Gesetz*) thus marks the positing (*Setzung*) sanctioned by writing, which in turn limits the positings and therefore the divisions of the performative and in this way joins an order, the seeds of whose inversion are sown in its ascertainment. Politics is based on the formation of structures, as represented by their respective historically conditioned orders which have become powerful, but can only hold and try to temporalize their position by continuing and enlivening the violence they are perpetually attempting to hide. Since antiquity, the metaphor of the body politic has grown; the living organism whose *organs* or *members* come together as a unified whole and must collaborate as sub-systems with specific functions. The violence at its middle, or mediality, is thus masked as a natural phenomenon. In short, the image is a corpus of identity which subsumes the performative *différance* under a forced totalization.[34] It confronts the singular powers by taming and delimiting the productivity of division and subsuming it under the regulation of order to the extent that it creates a *secondary violence*. This secondary violence and the measure to which it accrues power – and concomitantly, legitimation – is nothing other than the law to which the anarchies and anomies of the performative are subsumed, and by which they are permanently consumed.

Commandment and Law

Other types of *joining* besides the figure of the political delineated above include the ethical with its system of traditional norms, values, and virtues, and the religious: in the original meaning of *religio*, or binding, meaning not only the covenant with God, but also the covenant between people. One must also add the aesthetic, or at least certain forms of the aesthetic, because art is not necessarily a tool of subversion, but rather develops its own visual or artistic means of binding linked to ethics. In this way we are confronted with different levels of *assembly* or coming together, just as all these figures correspond with one another and, together with the political, form a

34 See Susanne Lüdemann, *Metaphern der Gesellschaft, Studien zum soziologischen und politischen Imaginären* (Munich: Fink, 2004).

knot that is difficult to untie. Far from having thus formed figures of a political theology, my interest is in the localization of the particular character of the political; its localization *between* the performative and the asociality latent in the social which it aims to master, at the price of continuing violence. This also holds true for both ethics and religion, each in their own way. For while the political acts at the site of the attempt to manage differences by means of law and hegemony, the religious community, at least in its Christian makeup – as Giorgio Agamben has recently shown in a study of monastic law – gives itself a law for life which it merges with the form of life (*forma vivendi*).[35] Emmanuel Lévinas, in his essays on the Talmud, makes a similar study of the concept of obedience.[36] However, obedience does not mean blindly following, as in the case of the early Greek local aristocrats who later became the tyrants.[37] Instead, obedience – as Heidegger has also noted of *Gehorsam* – stems literally from *oboedire,* to listen to, and thus expresses a precondition of communication as does *religio* – the social bond as a holy bond or binding in God: Obeying the divine and obeying the Other to whom we are bound. Thus Lévinas writes in "Revelation in the Jewish Tradition": "Commandment [...] constitutes the first movement in the direction of human understanding; and, of itself, is the beginning of language."[38] Language, as the transmitter of sociality, is preceded not by law, but by the Commandment, a *gift*. Commandment and law cannot be separated from one another – the former is not necessarily political, but is first and foremost literally a *given*, through the inalienable gift of the absolute to which life aspires to adhere, whereas the latter belongs to the political sphere and reacts to the ambiguity of the practical with regulatory disambiguation. Whosoever, as Lévinas continues in an interpretation of a Talmudic Midrash, adheres to the law is higher than he who does not.[39] To act outside of the commandment is not to be free, but to remain stuck in the anarchy of the performative. The enactment of a commandment in contrast demands abandon. The commandment thus denotes a defrayal of the task of overcoming, jumping over, or surmounting practical "anarchies," and thus first makes alterity or, more precisely, a relationship

---

35 Giorgio Agamben, *Höchste Armut. Ordensregel und Lebensform,* trans. Andreas Hiepko (Frankfurt/M: Fischer, 2012).

36 Emmanuel Lévinas, *Beyond the Verse. Talmudic Readings and Lectures,* trans. Gary D. Mole (London/New York: Continuum, 2007).

37 See Jean-Pierre Vernant, *Myth and Society in Ancient Greece,* trans. Janet Lloyd (New York: Zone Books, 1996).

38 Lévinas, *Beyond the Verse.* p.141.

39 Ibid., p. 77.

to others possible. This can perhaps be better understood as "response-ability," or responsiveness and responsibility.

However, seen in this way, the innate obligatory character of the commandment remains chronically underdetermined. It is based on a form of relationship which for its part is brought about by performatives and is neither guaranteed by a norm, the law and its order, nor by "obedience" as a form of life, but rather – in the true meaning of the word – always *obeys* the Other or tries to satisfy the Other and the site of the Other. The delineations which reduce the anomies of the performative are thus always in the preceding presence of the Other, which comes before the opportunity to act and thus the opportunity for the political. We are, we must agree with Lévinas, no longer under the reign of the precarious *right* of positioning, of suppression or supplanting. Instead, the focus is on overriding this right to replace it with the commandment which one has embraced within one's own life. It limits, qua life, the "animal energies," as Lévinas says, and subsumes them under true *response-ability*,[40] because it places the positing of one's own praxis under the primacy of the Other and neutralizes its violent power: "Man is the rupture of being which produces the act of giving, only giving with one's hands full rather than bringing struggle and plunder."[41] But this is only true when he displays his humanity in the "face of the other," which carries signs of the "trace of God."[42]

Accordingly, in the past two or three decades, alternatives have been proposed to the classical concept of the political, based on varying terminologies and discourses – for example ideas on an "ethics of the gift", or a "politics of friendship", as well as the idea of hospitality, and similar concepts.[43] These theories all make use of *pre*-political arguments and deal with community before politics and its laws – a space from which the political and its categories could be newly delimited. Such conceptual efforts strive to solve the same problem of joining and balance, but without resorting to using the concept of justice or sanctioning the political through the instantiation of a structure. In fact, Lévinas expressly says that the commandment and its ethics are older and more binding than the political, which, without a relation to the Other, is founded only on concepts of rule or the tenets of natural law or the laws of reason. However, we must disagree with Lévinas in

---

40 Ibid., p. 58.

41 Ibid., p. 142.

42 Emmanuel Lévinas, "The Trace of the Other," trans. A. Lingis, *Deconstruction in Context*, ed. Mark Taylor (Chicago: University of Chicago Press, 1986), p.345–359.

43 See in particular Jacques Derrida, *The Politics of Friendship*, trans. George Collins (New York/London: Verso Books, 2006).

that this does not make the category of the political obsolete. Rather the site of the political is shifted to a different space, whether earlier or later, and the political is positioned at a site which is, to a certain extent, in opposition to religion and not affected by it. And in truth, the significant concepts of the political – at least in its European form – are drawn from varying concepts of justice that try to master social hierarchies and the violence of the practical by calling upon *equality* or *freedom*. They attempt in particular to neutralize the differences and asymmetries of the performative so that the political is involved with the *constitution* and the contouring of interstices, those gaps which literally tear participants asunder, and whose "media" of equalization are law and order, be they arbitrarily enacted or legitimized by a community. One could say that the arena and actions of the political are located at exactly this fault line, this dislocation (*Verwerfung*) which has haunted the social scene from the beginning; while the actions of the ethical and the religious attempt to save intersubjective commitments by means of belief, trust, *forgiveness* (Vladimir Jankelevitch), etc. They always display a reciprocal structure and are rooted in the *relationship to others* and their *intrinsic alterity*, even before they appear on the performative scenes and are confronted with the latter's "anarchy."

Politics and Resistance

If we compare these ideas with the concepts of justice still found in the dominant political theories of John Rawls or Jürgen Habermas, we can immediately see the shortcomings of the latter – and also the futility of any political philosophy founded on Reason. In contrast to theological reasoning, which places the idea of binding or relationship before the order of the political and the idea of justice, political teachings on justice, from *Isonomia* to Liberalism, use varying rationales, but all end in postulates which skip over the true question of the form of the relationship – *the relationship to the Other, to creatures, to things.*[44] These are instead treated only formally. The concept of justice is also of course a concept of relationships, but it deals first and foremost, especially in the European tradition, with the *form* of this relationship. This is particularly true for law and jurisdiction, which judge mostly

44 One of very few alternative approaches can be found in the work of Michael Serres and Bruno Latour. On the ethics of nature see also Gernot Boehme, *Natürlich Natur. Über Natur im Zeitalter technischer Reproduzierbarkeit* (Frankfurt/M: Suhrkamp, 1992).

using formal criteria. Individual singular cases and singularities resist the rules, break rank, remain incompatible. Accordingly, the concept of justice shrinks to procedural principles such as the reciprocity of interests – sometimes written out on the basis of ideas on economic distribution[45] – whereby Habermas, for his part, relies completely on the process of discursive negotiation. His design therefore produces a meta-theory at best, which is lacking in bindingness because its obligation and the sociality it creates through "discursive praxis" can hardly be guaranteed, and because its concept of performance is drawn solely from illocutionarity. This, as I have intimated above, assumes both that action and meaning are identical, and gives primacy to *intentio*, which links the practical *situation* to subjective responsibility, while precluding the principle of responsiveness. In this way it denies the performative *différance* which forms the reason for division and violence in the social arena. Instead, Habermas locates the social obligation of practice within language itself and thus misses what we have called the event of the *joining*. The performative is not the foundation of the social, rather within it lurks the unconsidered abyss of incessant disruption which continuously separates that which binds the two. Reference and rift intersect: by leveling their chiasmus and rejecting its dialectic, he at the same time downplays and obscures the power or force rooted in the performative.

From this it follows that in the end Habermas does not answer or perhaps even pose the true question of the political, just as our deliberations suggest that the riddle of the *jointure* has no proper place in classical political theories. Instead, in the presence of the political we are always also confronted with the absence of that which makes it possible: the absent text of a force of law, which tries to bundle and condense the performative elements, to subsume them under that normative force which is supposed to constitute the social, but does not itself have the power to own it; or which go astray because the *jointure* or binding force of its normativity is extortionist, not inviting. The regimes of jurisdiction therefore have to derive their energies elsewhere, they cannot stem from that which constitutes the social, but are from the start founded on a form of repressive production which in turn lacks any grounding, in the literal sense of the ground, or any

---

45 For an early discussion of this question see Ludwig von Mises, *Liberalism*, trans. Ralpf Raico (Irvington on Hudson: The Foundation for Economic Education, 2002 [1927]); see also Friedrich August von Hayek, *Law, Legislation, and Liberty, 3 vol.* (Chicago: Chicago University Press, 1978 and 1981); Robert Nozick, *Anarchy, State, and Utopia*, (Oxford: Oxford University Press, 1992); and for a general discussion Otfried Höffe, *Gerechtigkeit* (Munich: Beck, 2004).

jointure. That which aims to reconcile and balance the anomie of the performative – its *an-archies* – at the same moment interrupts this reconciliation; for ἀναρχία does not only mean without rulers and, in the connection of *alpha privativum* with αρχία, i.e. the ground or source, a lack of a beginning or origin, but also the *unjoinability of the practical* – that which cannot in the literal sense be brought together through order, law or another form of norming or limiting. The "anarchistical" hence , would be resistance itself, the insubordinate or literal counter-acting which refuses any integration just as it undermines the commandment, the gift and the hospitality, and repeatedly disperses the social.

I would like to note that the terms chosen and the thoughts behind them should not be read in the tradition of discourses on political theology, nor in the manner in which Giorgio Agamben has recently used the Pauline *oikos* or *oikonomia* to counter political theology.[46] Rather, my interest is solely in revealing an elementary contradiction inherent to the performative, its chiasmus between positing, violence, and irreversibility, as well as the anomie and rift that opens "on the scene," between the practical and its diversion or trans-position, and their chronic wound, which first poses the actual question of the political. The thesis is that any politics which roots in the principles of justice is beholden to an original incurable injustice, because it itself is not founded on a power or force that can be balanced or kept in check. This is the crux of the problem of the political; that it feeds parasitically on the same power or force that it attempts to battle by grafting it onto another violence and another power or force. It answers violence with violence, but in such a way that this cycle always begins anew. This is particularly true for juridical law: it creates a general norm and by thus confronting the anarchy of the performative also, in another manner, participates in it. The law thus seems to be fundamentally illegitimate, it denies its own right just as justice is always without rights, because the law which it speaks is always outside any juridical principle, but rather first legitimates it. Accordingly, there is no way to control these forces rationally, rather they act as unjust measures of an order that continually bears its disorder anew. This is why *diké* and *adikía*, as Heidegger understood it, belong together.[47] What is more, the dis-joint lurks as an abyss within the joint, for there is no just reasoning for justice, just as little as there is a commandment or gift which does not

---

46 Giorgio Agamben, *The Kingdom and the Glory. For a Theological Genealogy of Economy and Government*, trans. Lorenzo Chiesa (Stanford: Stanford University Press, 2011).

47 See Heidegger, "Anaximander's Sayings," pp. 248–251.

always already anticipate its conversion or undermine the possibilities of trading.

The political orders themselves prove to be – literally – anomic. By revealing their intrinsic illegitimacy at the site of violence, as an open reference to that which they claim to govern, they at the same time become a constant source of strife and resistance, and thus a site of perpetual objection. This, analogous to the famous Freudian phrase of the "unease in culture", could be called the "unease in the political." It offers cause for permanent revolt. Its resistance stems from its structure as another violent force that will never be able to override or tame the former, just as the former remains equally contradictory and insolent. Therefore no political system or law is forever, no commandment is eternal, because all always also participate in provocation through their own "insubordination" of resistance. No law – as the structural foundation of the political – and no commandment – the structural foundation of religion – and no gift – the structural foundation of exchange – can thus have an unparadoxical relationship to the social. They rein in the ambiguity of the performative on the basis of a further ambiguity which they cannot escape, and it is exactly this paradox that creates within itself continuous and unavoidable subversion.

(*Translated by Laura Radosh*)

Friedrich Balke

All in Good Time? Fiction and the Possibility of Historic Events

I. Good time

Should historiography beat history - social, cultural, or even media histories - into shapes that fit a principle determining the possibility or impossibility of objects, mentalities and events? To deal with this question, I refer to Jacques Rancière's considerations presented in his 1997 lecture titled "The Trouble with Ana."[1] Rancière first developed the same argument in his 1992 book *The Names of History*.[2] To me, this is still one of his most interesting books, productive as it is for the histories of cultures and sciences, even though it does not yet deal with *aesthetic regimes* or *disagreement* (*mésentente*). My own thoughts on the matter touch upon the question of the political in so far as they concern the relation between names or words and the places or "spaces" in which they appear. For as Rancière pointed out later in *Disagreement*, "Political activity is whatever shifts a body from the place assigned to it or changes a place's destination. It makes visible what had no business being seen, and makes heard as discourse what was once only heard as noise."[3] Even before politics engages intentions, interests, needs, goals, and aims, it displaces or "undoes the perceptible divisions."[4]

Historians and sociologists disagree, of course. Whatever happens, to them, has its own space and its own time: *All in good time*, as they say. Both the chronical and the epochal perception of time depend upon this normative principle, a kind of "police" in Rancière's terms, of the "good time": That everything happens in its own time (and in its own place) demonstrates the good morality of that time, the good morality of history as a whole. In the 20th century, a new history or *nouvelle histoire* emerges in France to connect this orderly time to a specific

---

1 Jacques Rancière, "The Trouble with Ana," *Vom Nutzen und Nachteil historischer Vergleiche. Der Fall Bonn – Weimar*, ed. Friedrich Balke and Benno Wagner (Frankfurt/M./New York: Campus, 1997), pp. 35–49.

2 Jacques Rancière, *The Names of History. On the Politics of Knowledge* (Minneapolis: University of Minnesota Press, 1994).

3 Jacques Rancière, *Disagreement. Politics and Philosophy* (Minneapolis: University of Minnesota Press, 1999), p. 30.

4 Ibid.

conception of space: A space that functions as the sum of all those forces that retard, relativize, and functionalize the event, not only pluralizing the times of history, but relegating to a background the hectic rhythms at its surface, favoring instead the so-called *longue durée* with its series and periods that reach beyond generations and epochs. The geographicalization of history and the "territorialization of meaning"[5] are supposed to guarantee that any word that is spoken and defiantly hurled against an existing power cannot reveal anything beyond the specific worldview or "social interest" of those who utter it.

Rancière renews the question of heresy in a sense that is at once scholarly and political. His question is the very question of the political: Whether there is an alternative to the practice of the inquisitor, who professionally persecutes heresy, and that of the historian, who makes heresy disappear by means that are no less strict, albeit less cruel. The following passage from the *Names of History* demonstrates the perspective from which the question of a (political) resistance as an epistemological category may be raised:

> The inquisitor removes heresy by exterminating it – he marks it, locks it up, he kills it. The historian, on the contrary, surpresses it by giving it roots. He removes it, as it were retrospectively, from the inquisitorial condemnation by giving it the color of the earth and the stones, by rendering it indiscernible from its place. In this way the fundamental relation between the history of mentalities and heresy becomes evident. The historian of mentalities doesn't encounter heresy as a particular section of his territory. He encounters it as the identity of the condition of possibility and the condition of impossibility of such a territory.[6]

II. Suspicions of Fictionality

Lucien Febvre, one of the founders of the *Annales*-school, called anachronism "the worst of all sins"[7] – in the preface to a book treating the *Problem of Unbelief in the Sixteenth Century* through the case of Rabelais. The subtitle, by which Febvre anticipates his solution to that problem, speaks of *The Religion of Rabelais*, a phrase by which he opposes all those who put Rabelais to "trial for atheism and anti-Christian sentiment,"[8] and

5 Rancière, *The Names of History*, p. 66.

6 Ibid., pp. 73–74.

7 Lucien Febvre, *The Problem of Unbelief in the Sixteenth Century. The Religion of Rabelais* (Cambridge/London: Harvard University Press, 1982), p. 5.

8 Ibid., p. 5.

who face him as judges, but not as historians. As opposed to the court of law that identifies offenders and assigns punishments, Febvre sees the task of historians as determining the very historic possibility of an action or fact. In this case: whether it could even historically be the case that Rabelais was an unbeliever. Febvre wants to replace the juridical question: *Is it true* with the question: *Was it possible*,[9] or at least prioritize the latter before the former. "Let us take up the record again and look at it carefully."[10] For even if the files contain testimonies of what today would indubitably count as unbelief, everything hinges upon withholding judgement while we question the – transcendental – conditions of the possibility of unbelief in Rabelais' time.

For Rabelais' time, Febvre is confident that the people of the 16th century – "as opposed to our time, in which one might make a choice for or against Christianity" – had "no choice":

> Whether one wanted to or not, whether one clearly understood or not, one found oneself immersed from birth in a bath of Christianity from which one did not emerge even at death [...]. From birth to death stretched a long chain of ceremonies, traditions, customs, and observances, all of them Christian or Christianized, and they bound a man inspite of himself, held him captive even if he claimed to be free. And first and foremost they pressed him on his private life.[11]

The rhetoric of Febvre's text is conspicuous. Historical present tense and paratactical phrases that describe everyday actions as the eternal return of the same are dominant:

> A child was born, and it is living. It was carried without delay to the church and baptized while bells rang which themselves had been solemnly baptized by the bishop, anointed with holy oil, and sentenced with frankincense and myrrh, and were not rung on secular occasions.[12]

> Birth and death. Between these two extremes everything a man did in the normal course of life was marked with the stamp of religion. A man ate, and religion surrounded his food with rules, rituals, and prohibitions.[13]

---

9 Ibid., p. 16.
10 Ibid., p. 17.
11 Febvre, *The Problem of Unbelief*, p. 336.
12 Ibid., pp. 336–337.
13 Ibid., p. 340.

Religion, in short, controls the life, the thoughts and the feelings of men from the large to the small. It is, as one might say with Marcel Mauss, a *fait social total*, a total social fact. "What about public life?" Febvre asks, only to immediately answer: "Is it necessary to remind ourselves how saturated with Christianity the state still was – in nature, spirit and structure?"[14] What was true of church bells was also true of the king "heading France": both were "anointed with holy oil."[15] To sum up Febvre's argument throughout the 500 pages of his book, he "orchestrates the time of Rabelais as a time that took from him the possibility of unbelief."[16] Rabelais was no unbeliever, because he could not have been an unbeliever – no matter whether the statements offered by archives and files, in other words, by everything that is written and documented, fulfil the theological and juridical criteria for heresy. Lucien Febvre's colleague historian Marc Bloch summarizes the analytics of historiographical impossibility in one sentence: "Men bear greater resemblance to their time than to their parents." Thus, to be an unbeliever in Rabelais' time can only mean "not to belong to one's own time, that is, not to exist."[17]

Now the 16th century with its confessional schisms and wars for truth is far from an era of (universally shared) belief. The *Annales*-historian accounts for this by treating the (public) manifestation of unbelief and heterodoxy as a privilege of scholars: Only those who treat clerical dogma by means of their professional intellectual skills, by using and misusing theological concepts, by affirming existing or creating new statements, may violate that dogma with intent. Only scholars *know* what they do and only they do (new or surprising) things with words. By using words, or by saying something, we do something, as Austin and speech act theory have taught us; but from Austin's judicial point of view, doing things with words also implies the possibility of what he calls an "unhappy functioning of a performative."[18] Speaking also implies the possibility to "sin against"[19] the rules that determine our performative utterances. Yet, the great majority of the people in 16th century Europe, as Febvre sees it, is unable to *sin* against the rules that determine their religious speech and thought. They are condemned to *live* in the truth of belief without *knowing* that truth, that is, without

14 Ibid., p. 347.
15 Ibid., p. 348.
16 Rancière, "Trouble," p. 41.
17 Ibid., p. 43.
18 John L. Austin, *How to do things with words* (Cambridge: Harvard University Press, 2001), p. 14.
19 Ibid., p. 15.

ever unfolding their belief in terms of truth or falsehood. From Febvre's point of view one might argue that the common people, illiterate as they are, exist in a certain sense outside the space of literature, outside a discourse bound to books and letters, to *littera*. Thus the people exist outside of fiction. Michel de Certeau has pointed out that occidental historiography is "at war with fiction,"[20] which does not mean that it aspires to say the truth, but that it derives its own *raison d'être* from its continuous and never-ending correction of errors, which it takes to be the errors of fables: "From this perspective, fiction is that part of a culture which historiography institutes as error, in order to demarcate its own realm."[21]

For the historians of the *Annales*-school, who take fictitious histories to court with a special fervor, and with mainly quantitative statistical methods, the people appear only in their function as a representation of the factual, taken as a specific notion that limits possible events. The "common people" can never be wrong (will never even want to be wrong) with regards to the historical truth that they embody. Regarding the rhetorical structure of Febvre's depiction of the people's belief or the impossibility of their unbelief, we find that his sentences are short, and that they bear only, if any, the most minimal temporal markers, forcing Rabelais' time onto the reader as an absolute present tense, "which to escape is impossible, unless one does not belong to one's own time, that is to say, unless one does not exist."[22] Febvre, I would argue, submits historiographical discourse to the *registry*. The registry is a media technique that forecloses the option that anything might exist that is not inscribed in it. Registries transform what is said into what is given. The transformation of history into a scientific discipline promoted by the *Annales*-school consists in a rigorous (and yet impossible) deletion of all literary operations, and the conversion of historical accounts into such a registry. A registry: narrative no more, literature's end.

The Spanish registries of passengers, which Bernhard Siegert analyzes in *Papiere und Passagiere* (*Papers and Passengers*),[23] are of great significance for the problem of historiographical anachronism, because it is here, at the very heart of the 16th century and its allegedly characteristic impossibility of unbelief, and at the very heart of the registry

---

20 Michel de Certeau, *Theoretische Fiktionen: Geschichte und Psychoanalyse* (Vienna: Turia and Kant, 2006), p. 33.

21 Ibid.

22 Rancière, "Trouble," p. 42.

23 Bernhard Siegert, *Papiere und Passagiere. Schreibakte auf der Schwelle zwischen Spanien und Amerika* (Munich: Fink, 2006), p. 77.

and its transformation of everything told to the state authorities into indubitable data, that the "plague" of fiction and a generalized "suspicion of fictionality" breaks out. Who will guarantee that the data conserved in these registries, forcibly collected from subjects willing to leave their country, "correspond to anything in the real"?[24] The *Annales* and Lucien Febvre cannot help but submit their writing to the registry's (fictitious) truth effect, situating the mode of historiographical discourse strictly outside the order of the literary – understood as a technique of assigning events to subjects and not reducing them to social or anthropological functions –, while remaining unable to exclude all suspicion that the historiographical registry is – if not the place of systematic lies and deceits – at least the place of the unreliability of its sources.

III. Fiction in the Archive

Nowadays, few people will doubt that history operates in the medium of fictions, even before it is *written* and organized in narratives by professional historians. The decisive finding here is not that even Clio, remembering and contemplating the past, is a poet's muse, but that the material in the documents as used by historians, as found in archives, is often already organised und structured in a fictitious way. Natalie Zemon Davis, to give an example, has examined the practice of French appeals for juridical pardons.[25] She traces the ways by which convicted felons escaped the gallow. Those convicted felons had to retell the story that led to their deed, from their subjective point of view and with all rhetorical means available. Their attempt was to reach the king with so-called *lettres de rémission*, circumventing the courts that had long condemned the perpetrators. The telling original American title of Zemon Davis' treatise is *Fiction in the Archives*. What interests me here is the status and the effects of this archival fiction. The fiction embedding the specific literary strategy of the *lettres de rémission* does not, as one might assume, refer to the miracle of royal pardon, but rather to the discursive process itself by which the *subjective* truth of the petitioner – against all determinations in court – acquired the strength to initiate a paradoxical *alliance* with the royal source of all

24 Ibid.

25 Natalie Zemon Davis, *Fictions in the Archive. Pardon Tales and their Tellers in Sixteenth-Century France* (Stanford: Stanford University Press, 1987), p. 2.

state authority, who pardons the convicted criminal, and by doing so, suspends a legitimate judgement of the monarchic bureaucracy.[26]

Returning to the case of emigrants for the Spanish colonies overseas, we find again a model that served to extend the reach of state power into the everyday life of ordinary people. This was achieved by the royal bureaucracy's request for those who were ready for emigration to first tell their story to the questioning authorities, to explain their reasons for leaving the country, and to produce a witness that would testify to all the information they provided about their origin, their family background, and most of all their Catholic beliefs. Only on the basis of transforming oneself into an object of royal knowledge would an individual of 16th century Spain be granted legitimate status as a subject to the royal state power, which was in turn a precondition for the licence to cross the Atlantic. For it was only things and humans previously registered that were allowed to leave the old world, having been transformed into legitimate objects of a state-sanctioned transfer between continents.[27] Subjects are matters of state, which also means by reverse that people are forced to identify and subjectify themselves, as long as states and a state-related literature exist. Although the state's institutions receive their knowledge from subjective sources, they are eager to delete all traces of narration and literature, all indications of the instances that are involved in administering the process of the state's inquiry. Once all linguistic traces of such instances have been erased, the written can appear as the truth itself.

IV. Original repetition: Don Quijote

One of Jorge Luis Borges' stories – found in his *Ficciones* first published in 1941 – treats the problems of the historiographical assignment of each word to its place, its *topos*, in a fundamental manner. The territorialization of sense "removes the possibility that any spoken word would ever be vain."[28] It is no coincidence that the founders of the *nouvelle histoire* are concerned so deeply with the issue of religious dissidence, as we have seen. For it is heresy that precisely demarcates the borderline case of a discourse, or a mere utterance; that disturbs the coherence of word and place, or to put it more accurately: of word, place, and time. It might be defined as an "excess of speech,"[29] or

---

26 Davis, *Fictions*, pp. 17–21.
27 See Siegert, *Papiere und Passagiere*, pp. 27–62.
28 Rancière, *The Names of History*, pp. 66–67.
29 Ibid., p. 67.

as a fiction. Heresy, Rancière remarks in *The Names of History*, is "a piece of metal or language that can't be ajoined to any other, a motherless child, a voice separated from the body, a body separated from the place."[30] It is precisely this curious mother-child-relation that reappears in a central sentence in Borges' tale of "Pierre Menard, the author of *Quijote*," written in 1939. Its topic is a case of excessive anachronism, drawing the most extreme consequences from that worst of all sins, against which the *nouvelle histoire* mobilizes all its scholarly pathos. Once more: According to this view, nothing may exist unless its time allows for its possibility. Borges' tale opposes that view throughout, and even in its title, it asks for a historical impossibility: Can somebody be the author of a text if he or she is evidently not its creator? While this is categorically excluded for literary texts, bound as they have been since the mid-18th century to a specific singularity called ingeniousness and to the institution of authorship, it is a different matter for discourses that may continue to exist without an author function, although they do receive social appreciation and offer themselves up for unlimited repetition (think of rumors, the Bible, cooking recipes, or instruction manuals).

At first, Borges' title seems to be no more than a joke or a simple lie, for the (fictitious) Pierre Menard is definitely not the author of *Don Quijote*; as we have all learned in school, or know from books of literary history, a man from 17th century Spain by the name of Miguel de Cervantes Saavedra is. Pierre Menard, a fictitious novelist from the 20th century, cannot by any means have authored a book from 1605 to 1615, unless he received an, say, intra-literary authorization as a quasi-author from Cervantes. But the name of somebody called Pierre Menard is not mentioned once throughout the novel. And yet Borges, referring to nothing but the "scant authority" of his narrator, makes just that claim, the claim that Menard does, in a certain way, re-author the text of *Don Quijote*. Menard's ambition is not to write one of those "parasitic books that set Christ on a boulevard, Hamlet on La Canebière or Don Quijote on Wall Street": The narrator condemns these popular versions of a modernized or modernizing repetition:

> Like every man of taste, Menard abominated those pointless travesties, which, Menard would say, were good for nothing but occasioning a plebeian delight in anachronism or (worse yet) captivating us with the elementary notion that all times and places are the same or are different.[31]

---

30 Ibid., p. 68.

31 Jorge Luis Borges, "Pierre Menard, Author of the *Quijote*," *Collected Fictions*, ed. & trans. Andrew Hurley (New York: Viking Press, 1998), p. 88–95, pp. 90–91.

Menard's project is described as follows:

> Pierre Menard did not want to compose *another* Quijote, which surely is easy enough – he wanted to compose *the* Quijote. Nor, surely, need one be obliged to note that his goal was never a mechanical transcription of the original; he had no intention to *copying* it. His admirable ambition was to produce a number of pages which coincided – word for word and line for line – with those of Miguel de Cervantes.[32]

What might it mean to remove a novel, or even just one sentence, from its historical place, and to write it again, word by word, but without copying or transcribing it? Menard's project combines an ultimate fidelity to the novel (which is supposed to be Cervantes' work and literary property) with an ultimate will for its usurpation. Menard wants to do nothing less than to literally "re-write" the Quijote, and in doing so, to expropriate its original author and bestow the text unto himself. The result of this arduous work of many years, albeit eventually indistinguishable from a mere transcription of the novel, is yet supposed to be something utterly different to the kind of product that results from a mere act of *mindless* copying. Menard does not insert the act of repetition into the work in its visible form (his ambition is not to produce new episodes in some kind of Cervantes-like style), but in the invisible process of its production, by assimilating himself to the cultural and intellectual conditions that formed Cervantes: "Initially, Menard's method was to be relatively simple. Learn Spanish, return to Catholicism, fight against the Moor or the Turk, forget the history of Europe from 1602 to 1918 – *be* Miguel de Cervantes."[33] But Menard discards this method as "too easy," for although he wants to "produce" the sentences of the novel over again, he does not want to do so "in dependence" to the person who wrote it in the early 17th century. Menard wants his novel to be read "as if Menard had con ceived it."[34] That is why the text as repeated by Menard appears to be the same as the original; and yet is a completely different discourse. To say it in Febvre's logic: Menard wants to show that the *Quijote* can be removed from its own time, which made it possible; that it can be produced anew, under completely different historical conditions, and that the same sentences, repeated in this manner, can begin to carry utterly new meanings. Historical time, as powerful as it may be, can

---

32 Borges, "Quijote," p. 91.
33 Ibid., 91.
34 Ibid., 92.

not enclose a cultural object and assimilate it to the point where it becomes impossible and inconceivable outside its confines. An object, event, or trait can only exist, claims Febvre, if they belong to their own time, if their time allows for their existence. Menard is here to prove the opposite, not by modernizing Cervantes' novel, nor by transferring it to our time, but by endowing the original sequence of letters with a new discursive stature through a modification of its mode of enunciation. At its heart, Borges' tale is an exemplary discourse analysis by literary means, referring literary speech to "the different modalities of enunciation, instead of referring to *the* synthesis or *the* unifying function of *a* subject."[35]

This is why the narrator can value the – fragmentary – result of Menard's life-long efforts so highly: "The Cervantes text and the Menard text are verbally identical, but the second is almost infinitely richer."[36] It is infinitely richer because the same sentence opens up a completely new space of meanings or referents under the conditions of its re-writing, more than three centuries after its publication by Cervantes:

> Composing the *Quijote* in the early seventeenth century was a reasonable, necessary, perhaps even inevitable undertaking; in the early twentieth, it is virtually impossible. Not for nothing have three hundred years elapsed, freighted with the most complex events. Among those events, to mention but one, is the *Quijote* itself.[37]

If the narrator attests a higher degree of subtlety to Menard's *Quijote*, he does so because the novel calls upon a quite different cluster of associated utterances in Menard's cultural situation. From the perspective of discourse analysis, statements such as "The Earth is round," or "Species evolve," do not constitute the same enunciation before and after Copernicus or Darwin, even though it is the same letters and words that are combined to form these different enunciations. What transforms the repetition of the same verbal phrase into historically distinct statements is their embeddedness into their own respective epistemological fields, as well as their relations to other claims, demonstrations, and observations. Borges' tale concerns the weight of this kind of discursive materiality, for it is not the material element of

35 Michel Foucault, *Archaeology of Knowledge* (London: Routledge Classics, 2005), p. 60.
36 Borges, "Quijote," p. 94.
37 Ibid., p. 93.

a concrete copy, its datability, the moment when and the place where it was produced, that guarantees the identity of a statement.

Borges quotes an example for this discursive difference which is validated by the identity of the sentences written by Cervantes and by Menard. It is one sentence from the 9th chapter of the first part of *Quijote*, in which history is named – the *mother of truth*, "rival of time, depository of deeds, witness of the past, exemplar and adviser to the present, and the future's counselor." "Written in the seventeenth century," the narrator explains, "this catalog of attributes [...] is a mere rhetorical praise of history."[38] But in Menard, who repeats the sentence unchanged, the thought is "staggering," because he, "a contemporary of William James," defines history "not as a *delving into* reality but as the very *fount* of reality": "Historical truth, for Menard, is not 'what happened'; it is what we *believe* happened."[39] To Menard, history is no longer a collection of examples, it has transformed into a collective singular, an unresistable force penetrating every aspect of reality and providing the only access to true knowledge about our own condition. It is easy to see that Menard's new conception of the corresponding phrase in Cervantes is at once the credo of the scientific revolution performed by the *nouvelle histoire*, as it elevates history to the rank of the "mother of truth." Febvre's friend, the historian Marc Bloch, claimed, as we have seen, that "men bear greater resemblance to their time than to their parents," and thus clearly anchored the truth of history in some kind of genealogical similarity and stable descent. Yet, as much as the program of the *nouvelle histoire* and the techniques of historical analyses that it deploys doubtlessly emerge from the 20th century, its historical truth could have been *literally* uttered even in the year 1605. As the narrator eventually concludes: "Menard has (perhaps unwittingly) enriched the slow and rudimentary art of reading by means of a new technique – the technique of deliberate anachronism and fallacious attribution."[40]

Finally: "Why the Quijote? my reader may ask."[41] Is it a coincidence that Borges tells us about this excessive poetical mimesis, in which an author's work takes possession of his late successor, with *Don Quijote* as his example? On *Quijote*, Michel Foucault writes in *Les choses et les mots*: "Like a sign, a long, thin graphism, a letter that has just escaped from the open pages of a book. His whole being is nothing but

---

38 Ibid., p. 94.
39 Ibid.
40 Ibid., p. 95.
41 Ibid., p. 92.

language, text, printed pages, stories that have already been written down."[42] And he continues:

> The book is not so much his [Don Quixote's] existence as his duty. He is constantly obliged to consult it in order to know what to do or say, and what signs he should give himself and others to show that he really is of the same nature as the text from which he springs. The chivalric romances have provided once and for all a written prescription for his adventures.[43]

We understand now the calculation by which Borges chose the *Don Quijote*: For what the books demand from the knight of the sad face as he reads them and they take possession of him, is what Cervantes' book demands from Pierre Menard. The novel itself rests upon Cervantes' fictitious translation of a fictitious Arabic manuscript. One of the three chapters recreated by Menard, the 9th chapter of the first part, tells the story of the fictitious discovery of the manuscript and the production of its translation. Menard, the new author of the *Quijote*, appears himself as no more than a long meager graphism, sacrificing his whole physical and literary existence to the task of repeating an oeuvre in absolute fidelity to each letter, and by this operation producing at the same time an utmost, yet unperceivable difference to what the original meaning of his master copy might have been. Cervantes' novel is already situated in that outer space defined by the sum of all the discourses that repeat a historically obsolete chivalrous way of life. As Foucault writes: "Don Quijote reads the world in order to prove his books."[44] Pierre Menard, Borges' fictitious hero and new author of the *Quijote*, reads Cervantes' novel in order to prove it to be that book which reveals repeatability, and the production of difference through repetition, at the origin of modern literature that is so closely connected to the novel.

---

42 Michel Foucault, *The Order of Things. An archeology of the human sciences* (London/New York: Routledge Classics, 2005), p. 51.
43 Ibid., pp. 51–52.
44 Ibid., p. 52.

Jacques Rancière

Doing or Not Doing
Politics, Aesthetics, Performance

I must make a preliminary statement to avoid a possible misunderstanding of my title. I am not going to speak about the art of performance, viewed as a specific art. The art that we have been used to name *performance* for a few decades is in fact the offspring of a wider idea of the performance of art – the "performance of art" meaning both the completion of its specific operations and its role in the distribution of social activities and collective energy. Therefore the remarks that I will present about *performance* belong to a wider investigation. They belong to the project of a genealogy of the categories that we use to perceive and conceptualize the relationships between art, aesthetics, and politics. That investigation is based on a hypothesis formulated in my book *The Politics of Aesthetics*:

> The arts only ever lend to projects of domination or emancipation what they are able to lend to them, that is to say, quite simply, what they have in common with them: bodily positions and movements, functions of speech, the parcelling out of the visible and the invisible.

So the question is not about the effects that an artistic performance can produce on political practice. It is about the very sense of action, community, freedom, or equality carried out by the positions and movements of the bodies and by the mode of their visibility.

The whole problem might lie in the seemingly simple notion of action. Becoming *active* is a typical demand of political art, and it has continuously been opposed both to the purely verbal and imaginary performance of words and to the passivity of the spectator. This demand has readily been equated with a certain idea of *Modern art*, thought of as the passage from the paradigm of *representation* to that of a *direct performance*. But action is not the mere fact of doing something. It is a certain way of doing which expresses a certain way of being. It is a specific relation between a way of moving and a regime of meaning within which that movement can be identified. In my terms, action is a category in the distribution of the sensible. Therefore the becoming-political of art is not a question of becoming active, it is a question of the very sense of action, its place and function in the distribution of the sensible. This is what I will try to show by examining two ways of framing the issue of movement and action: a philosophical one, dating back to Ancient Philosophy, and a visual one, dating back to 20th century revolutionary art.

In Aristotle's *Poetics*, the tragic plot is defined as an arrangement of actions according to necessity or verisimilitude. This arrangement of actions can be compared, Aristotle says, to a beautiful animal in which all parts are in harmony. This model of the poetic plot as a harmonious body determines two oppositions. Firstly, poetry is opposed to history. History just tells the facts as they happened; poetry tells how they could have happened; it constructs a causal plot. Next, it is opposed to the spectacle, i.e. to the performance on stage. The spectacle is *psychagogic*, says Aristotle. It is an excitement for the souls. But that excitement is far removed from art and poetry. The true pleasure of the play is the one produced by the *peripeteia* and the recognition which are the soul of the plot.

It is clear that those distinctions are also social distinctions. There are people whose story can be described as an arrangement of actions and people whose life is only a succession of facts. The latter are the same whose coarse souls are excited by the spectacle, while the former can enjoy the pleasure of the plot. The ground for those distinctions is spelled out in the eighth book of Aristotle's *Politics*, in which the philosopher examines which arts – meaning which knowledges and techniques – must be learnt by the free citizen. The criterion for the selection is simple: what does this or that art make him do with his body? There are at least four reasons to exclude the teaching of an art from the education of the free citizen: if it provokes an excessive tension of the body, if it demands a high level of technical skill, if it is too strictly committed to usefulness, and if it can be practiced as a salaried job. All those arts are mechanical in two senses: firstly, they are not made for the sake of their own perfection, they are means for something else; secondly, they are suitable for *mechanical men*, men who are only dealing with means: means of performing a useful task and means of earning their living. Such arts automatically deform the body of those who practice them; they turn them into bodies of artisans, into non-free bodies.

This distinction between the activity of the free man and that of the mechanical man is a hierarchy in *inactivity* too. What is the activity which is suitable for the life of leisure, asks Aristotle? Leisure is not rest. It is the state in which there is no need to do something for the sake of another thing. This is the privilege of the free man. The kind of cultivation that belongs to leisure cannot be play. Play entails the idea of relaxation, a slowdown of tension in opposition to the tension required by work. Play then is the form of enjoyment suitable for the

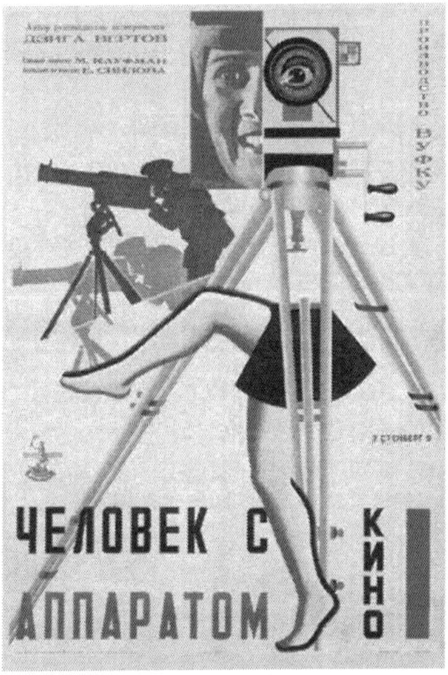

Fig. 1: Man with a Movie Camera. Film poster, designed by Vladimir and Georgy Stenbergs (1929).

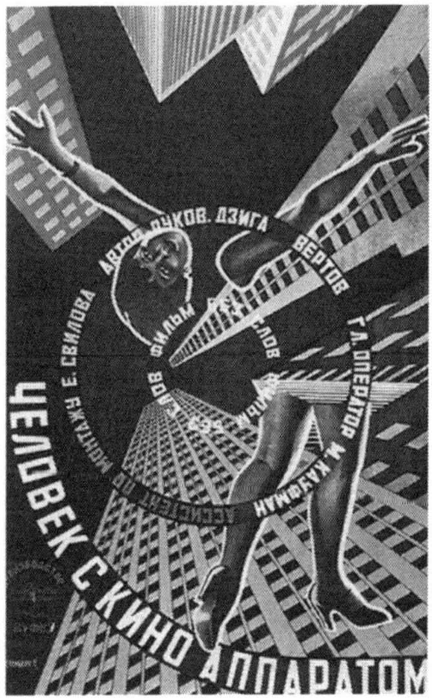

Fig. 2: Man with a Movie Camera. Film poster (1929).

mechanical man who needs a release to restore his bodily capacity. Action and inaction are thus forms of the distribution of the sensible that entail an implacable separation between two forms of life. That which sustains the order of representation is not only a canon of poetic rules. It is a whole hierarchical distribution of relationships between ways of being and ways of doing.

Let us now move from Greek philosophy to the Soviet Revolution. Here are two posters designed in 1928 by the Soviet artists Vladimir and Georgii Stenberg (the Stenberg brothers) for Dziga Vertov's film, *Man with a movie camera* – an emblematic film of course, since the three words – man, movement, and apparatus – that compose its title sound like a whole aesthetic and political program, identifying the performance of the new man with an art that makes the production of movement and the production of a new form of visibility one and the same performance. This is what is epitomized in the couple of the dancer and the camera. This couple is substituted for the one that could be expected, the one that usually appears on posters advertising films: the couple of a man and a woman whose stories of love and hate, joy and pain are proposed to spectators as an incitement to share in their emotions. Instead, the posters show us the elements that constitute the film and the way in which they are linked together. This means that the film is not the representation of an action. It is an action. It is not destined to provoke terror and pity. It is destined to shape a new sense of action and community. And the posters don't advertise the film. They contribute to the construction of the new sensorium to which the film belongs. They do so in two complementary ways, an analytic one and a synthetic one. The first poster shows us the elements constituting the film as an assemblage of pairs: the camera and the tripod; the mechanical eye and a human eye; the legs of the tripod and the legs of a dancing woman; the curve of the legs and the curve made by the silhouette of the cameraman bent over his machine; the silhouette and its shadow; the visual fragments and the assemblage of words. The second one shows us, as it were, the machine at work: the body is moving, at least a body consisting in one head and four limbs, a body constructed by the movement that it performs in a space structured by low angle shots of skyscrapers on a black background. In this space the parts of the body and the letters giving the title of the film and the names of the filmmaker, cameraman, and editing assistant are combined so as to suggest at once the lens of a camera and the propeller of a plane cleaving through the air, and making the film itself a vehicle launched into a new world and a new life.

The posters construct a sensorium whose main characteristic is homogeneity. Words, visible forms, and bodily movements are woven into the same fabric. Words are no more opposed to action. They are forms and those forms describe, in their space, a dynamic spiral in tune with the movements of the dancer. The same goes for seeing. Seeing can no more be equated with the passivity of the spectator or the coarseness of the artisan eager for spectacles. Seeing is an action that the attitude of the cameraman makes us perceive as similar to that of the soldier bent over his machine-gun. The machine for seeing is a machine which produces movement. The fusion of seeing, speaking, and doing appears to hinge on a specific linkage: the linkage between the body and the machine. On the first poster, the female face has a mechanical eye, and the camera a human eye. On the second one, the body of the dancer is fragmented like the cogs of a machine, but this very fragmentation contributes to the Dionysian energy of the dance. The graphic forms, the movements of the living body, and the pieces of the machine are carried together in a space where everything is moving, everything is action, and all actions are homogeneous.

The poster appears thus as the visual manifesto of an art that has become entirely active. That art parts with the logic of action conceived as the logic of the plot telling a story and of the expressive performance of actors making the spectators share the feelings and emotions of the characters. It is no more representation but direct performance. By the same token, it is the manifesto for a new society where there is no more any hierarchy between men of ends and men of means, men of leisure and men of work and rest, any opposition between the gestures of the mechanic and the movements of the free man – who has become a free woman: only one and the same collective movement which is a joint performance of men and machines. Everything is action, everything is dance.

This is what the designers show us in the language of forms. Now the point is about this language itself. There are two oddities about the image of the dancer. Firstly, though she expresses an ecstatic vitality, she nevertheless lacks what seems to be the condition for dancing. Her body is not a true body, I mean a body made by the articulation of a head, a trunk, and four limbs. On the first poster, we have a half-body; on the second, the body has no trunk. Next, the space is not a space for real dancing. The chequered ground on which the woman is supposed to dance is turned into a skyscraper, so that her dance becomes a flight or a fall seen from a reverse angle. The equivalence of the ground and the sky, the up and the down denies the depth of the three-dimensional stage on which dancing bodies are used to draw their figures. So the acting body is not a body and the space is no space for action.

It can be objected that it is a poster and that the stylization of the forms is paramount in the art of the poster in which the visual message prevails over the accuracy of the representation. This is quite true, but the question bounces back: why did the art of the poster play such an important role in the transformations of art practice and in the politics of art between the end of the 19th century and the 1930s. The answer – quite opposite to the fairy tale about the autonomisation of art and its commitment to its own medium – is that, in the art of the poster, the transformation of the canons of art was directly linked to a certain use, which was not so much to sell this or that object as it was to construct the sensorium of coexistence between those objects and the viewers, to construct a scene of the visible and the doable. This is what accounts for the strong commitment of Soviet artists that came from *non objective painting* to the art of the poster.

These posters are a good example, and from this point of view we can understand the two oddities. The dancing woman is in fact a combination of two bodies. The first one is an ecstatic body, symbolizing an adhesion to a holistic impulse of modern life. It is not incidental then that this "woman" with her short hair, her ring and her high-heeled shoes looks more like an American free woman than a Soviet activist. The second one is a mechanical body, a fragmented body. It obeys a rule of fragmentation and combination of the fragments which is the rule commanding the practice of film montage just as in Taylorised work and Leninist strategy. On the one hand, the dancing machine is the immediate identity of work and leisure. On the other hand, it is a splinted body. The ecstatic body and the mechanical body remain separate. That separation entails the dissociation of the model of the organic body. In order to liberate life, the "beautiful animal" has to be split into two bodies.

The same goes for space. The space of the performance breaks away from the normal representation of the third dimension on a bi-dimensional plane. The main feature of that space is obliqueness. It is also a typical feature among Soviet avant-garde artists; and the diagonal had been theorized by El Lissitzky as the spatial configuration suited to the new communist age in the same way as the sphere was to the classical order and the vertical to the gothic; it constructs an egalitarian space which has abolished the very hierarchy of high and low, and an infinite space which can no more be embraced within the categories of our order: the infinite universe of the new life.

The posters construct this new body and a new space which, at the same time, are an impossible body and an impossible space. They have to do so because the "direct performance" of the bodies must be symbolized. It cannot at the same time achieve the unification of art and life, and tell us that it achieves it. The physical performance needs to be supplemented by a semiological performance that shows what it does without being able to tell that it is what it does. The semiological performance is the construction of a specific fabric, an aesthetic fabric, in which the meaning of the physical performance of the mechanical dancing body is explained – at the cost of presenting an impossible body and an impossible movement. This construction entails the combination of several types of bodies and several paradigms of performance. It entails a complex set of relations between bodily movements, visual forms and modes of speech. It is only within this complex set that the anti-representative aesthetic revolution can be understood and that its political implications can be grasped.

To understand that complexity and its political implications, a genealogical inquiry is necessary. This inquiry leads us back to the middle of the 18th century, to a moment when the logic of the representative regime was at once at its climax and on the verge of its collapse. On the one hand, the logic of action had been perfectly completed, since the idea of the *arrangement of actions* exactly matched a hierarchical logic of characters and situations, prescribing what kind of events could happen to this or that character, and what kind of feelings and language they should use, in accordance with their dignity. Moreover, this double logic of coherence in action and suitability of expression had been extended from poetry to visual arts that were judged according to their capacity to represent actions. In parallel, dance had been codified at the court of Louis XIV. Dance was not considered a fine art. It was a form of entertainment. But entertainment had its hierarchy too, and this is why it had been codified as a set of noble attitudes, virtuoso movements, and refined figures, expressing the excellence of aristocratic life, the excellence of the life of those men of action who were also men of leisure. Nevertheless, in the space of a dozen years, the representative edifice was shattered in several ways. The interesting point is that the first attack was an overturning of its own principles. The most significant example of that overturning is offered by the book of the French choreographer Jean-Georges Noverre, *Letters on Dance and Ballets*, a very influential book, first published in 1760. Noverre exactly overturned the Aristotelian opposition. The *aristocratic* ballet is a merely mechanical thing, he said, since it is a merely physical performance. It tells no story, it conveys no emotions, it only speaks to the eyes. In order to become art, dance has to speak to the soul. It has to become pantomime, to create a language of mimicry and gestures, telling stories and expressing the situations and feelings of characters that look like those one can meet in real life and in all conditions. This is also why any subject is good and the dancers and choreographer must study all sorts of movements, notably the movements of the workmen in the workshops, the peasants in the fields, or the crowds in the streets or the markets.

In that way the opposition was overturned: "mechanical" now meant "having its end in itself." Noverre's reform of the ballet could then meet a project of reform of dramatic action that had been formulated a few years before by Denis Diderot in his *Conversations on the Natural Son*. Diderot criticized the two main aspects of the theatrical convention: the contrived cleverness of the plots with their *coups de théâtre* to which he opposed the reality of situations in ordinary life; the conventions of noble language to which he counter-posed the variety of tones, smothered cries, interruptions, silences, and the multifarious gestures and attitudes which express the truth of the feelings, the intensity of emotions, and the multiplicity of their quasi-imperceptible variations in real life. The convention of theatrical *action* and the conventional tones and attitudes of the actor had to be replaced by a language of the body, a language of corporeal signs.

The keyword of that critique was the word *expression*. The mechanics of the plot and those of the noble gestures and contrived attitudes had to be replaced by a unique art of the performing body: the art of expression. We know how loudly the idea of the expressive body has resonated in performing arts and in the idea of life becoming art. One of the inventors of modern dance, Rudolf Laban, held Noverre to be a "visionary" because, in his *action ballet*, "the whole range of human passions had found its expression." But Laban could pay homage to Noverre only at the cost of radically transforming the idea of expression. The language of the body opposed by Diderot and Noverre to the representative action still is a mimetic language, a language of motivated signs. It supposes a correspondence between the feelings of the souls and the traits, gestures, and attitudes able to express it. Such a language of the body claimed to be heir to the ancient Roman pantomime, but its visual model was much more a pictorial one, which Diderot found epitomized in the paintings of Jean-Baptiste Greuze, with the intensity of diverse emotions expressed by each character on the canvas. This also means that the stage of *expression* was wavering between two opposite spaces: the domestic stage where the members of the family express their emotions, regardless of the spectator, and the big theatre of the people, intended to revive the Greek tradition of the theatre as the assembly of the people opened to the deployment of the great emotions.

So expression could only take on its whole potential by being freed from the semiological model of the language of signs. This required that the movements of the body be separated from the significations with which they had been associated. Paradoxical as it may seem, that dissociation required a pause in movement and a default in expression. It required a form of disruption of the representative model more discrete but probably more influential in the long run.

Four years after Noverre's *Letters on Dance and Ballets*, Johann Joachim Winckelmann published his *History of Art in Antiquity*. His polemics went in exactly the opposite direction, since that expressivity which had meant the progress of liveliness in art to the reformers of dance and theatre was a sign of decadence to him. This is the reason why he has sometimes been considered as the reactionary champion of neo-classicist sculpture. Such a criticism pays little attention to the paradox of that so-called *classicism*: in Winckelmann's view, the most perfect achievement of Antique sculpture is embodied in the crippled statue of a Hercules who has neither a head nor limbs. Such perfection contradicts the representative model of plastic beauty. Accordingly, it contradicts the representative privilege of action conceived as the exact adjustment of parts in a whole, the act of a willing head commanding the action of the limbs. Winckelmann's Hercules is an inactive Hercules, welcomed among the Olympic Gods after the end of his works. He is only pondering his past deeds, but, as he has no head for pondering, his thought is only expressed by the curve of his back and the muscles of the torso whose forms are "engulfed by one another" in a continuous movement similar to the indifferent rise and fall of the waves. This in-different "rise and fall" of the wavelike muscles entails a new idea of movement: an idea of movement which neutralizes the very opposition of movement and rest. That identity of movement and stillness received a name: it is a free movement, a movement which is not fettered by the obligation to perform actions or express emotions. This implies a new idea of the body, of its life and of its movement, that 20th century dancers and performers will set out to revive by looking at Greek vases or sculptures. What makes the body alive is no longer the organic link of action in which limbs obey a head; nor is it the language of the expressive body translating thoughts and emotions into gestures and attitudes. The *free movement* is a movement that has no end in the two senses of the word: first, it never begins, nor does it ever end. Next, it has no goal. If we stress the first meaning, we will define the free movement as rhythm – a notion which in fact played a major part in the modern conception of the performing body. It was notably formulated by Isadora Duncan as the endless generation of movement from movement. As she puts it: "Every movement, even in repose, contains the quality of fecundity, possesses the power to give birth to another movement." Accordingly, rhythm is the breath that continuously moves all through the body and is present in the same way in any part. This is why any fragment can express the impulse of the whole: a form of expression that does no longer obey the semiological model.

The expressive body could break the mimetic frame only through the model of the immobile movement that disconnected bodily attitudes from the model of the language of signs. Now what the *free* movement of the muscles/waves provides is not only a paradigm of movement, it is also a paradigm of freedom. The wavelike movement of the muscles expresses the acme of Greek art, which is also the acme of Greek freedom, Winckelmann affirmed. He was totally wrong, as far as the date of the statue is concerned. But that is of secondary importance. That connection between *free movement* and political freedom was an implicit answer to the biggest challenge that art lovers had to face at that time. Not long ago, Jean-Jacques Rousseau had launched his devastating polemic about the effects of art. Theatre teaches nothing, he said. The taste for the theatre and the cultivation of the arts always goes along with the decrease of popular freedom. This is why he opposed to the false lessons of morality of the theatre the collective energy given to the Spartan citizens by their songs and dances, or the sense of community conveyed by the Swiss popular festivals. Winckelmann's interpretation of Greek art was an implicit answer to Rousseau: the free movement of the statue is the expression of Greek freedom just as the distortions of Baroque sculpture are the expression of despotism.

Thirty years later Friedrich Schiller made the idea of the *freedom* expressed by the statue both more explicit and more problematic, as he turned the identity of movement and immobility into an identity of action and inaction. What he called the play-drive is not so much a specific type of movement as it is a specific form of experience: a form of experience in which the subject is no longer determined to enact a specific capacity in order to respond to a specific impulse, need or interest, as it happens in the ordinary forms of experience. Aesthetic freedom or play is the experience of a capacity of indetermination, which is properly an experience of humanity as such: the experience of a capacity which can be shared by anybody as it dismisses the hierarchical oppositions that structured both action and inaction. That which shines on the face of the Greek deity, Schiller says, is idleness, the absence of any care and will. Now those attributes of the deity are in reality the attributes of the free people who commissioned the work of the sculptor. They are the characteristics of aesthetic experience in which the usual hierarchies of sensible experience are suspended. Aesthetic freedom is freedom from the power of will, and notably from the will to use art in order to produce effects on individuals and collectives. In that sense, play can be seen as the notion founding both a new idea of art and a new idea of the individual and collective art of living.

So there are at least three paradigms for thinking the passage from *representation* to *direct performance* and the way in which art may become life: expression, rhythm, and play. All of them challenge the old representative order. All of them oppose to the conventions of representation and to the mechanical forms of domination a paradigm of life and movement which is a paradigm of freedom and equality. This is why they plaid a large role in the endeavours to turn the practice of art into a direct performance of community. But each of them also has something disturbing about it, something disturbing for the idea of political action and of the political community. Expression wavers between two models: on the one hand, the language of nature that finds its achievement in the domestic space from which the spectator is excluded; on the other hand, the theatre of the people giving way to the multiplication of emotion by blurring the separation between the actors and the spectators. 20th century dramatists and choreographers will set out to reconcile those two notions, a reconciliation which supposes that expression be dissociated from its semiological model. This is certainly what is provided by the paradigm of free movement or rhythm. And the paradigm of the rhythmic community will play an important role in the times of Émile Jaques-Dalcroze, Duncan, or

Laban. But it will do so at the cost of calling into question the logic of action seen as the pursuit of certain ends through definite means. Laban emphasizes this discrepancy when he sums up the discovery made by Duncan:

> Movement considered hitherto – at least in our civilization – as the servant of Man employed to achieve an extraneous practical purpose was brought to life as an independent power creating states of mind frequently stronger than man's will. This was quite a disconcerting discovery at a time when extraneous achievements through will-power seemed to be the paramount objective of human striving.[1]

It is still worse with play. Play as defined by Schiller is the very identity of action and inaction, the state in which there is "no force to contend with force." And Schiller strongly makes the point that art creates a new individual and collective capacity on the condition that it gives up the pretence of giving to the souls any definite trend. Play is, he says, the basis of a new art of life for individuals and communities. But play also is the state in which any trace of volition has disappeared, any idea of purposeful organisation of life has vanished.

Those models of performance thus seem to be not well suited to become the models of a revolutionary strategy of transformation for the world. But things can be put the other way round. Communism and revolution themselves were marked by the tension between the representative and the aesthetic model. As viewed by the young Karl Marx, the "human revolution" is an anti-representative revolution which puts an end to the law of alienation that separated the human subject from its essential forces. By the same token it puts an end to the logic that separates the means from the end and leisure from work. In that sense it is an aesthetic revolution, it is the weaving of a new sensible fabric of the common. Now that undivided community has to be made possible by a historical process. But this process itself can be conceived in two ways: on the one hand, there is the strategic – or the representative – model: revolutionary action is the arrangement of actions leading to the disruption of the existing order; on the other hand, there is the aesthetic plot: the development of the productive forces breaks through the limits of the capitalist system within which they have been generated. Of course, Marxist science purported to join the two logics: the science of the development of production was set up as the basis for the strategy of the conquest of power and

---

1 Rudolf von Laban, *Modern Educational Dance* (London: MacDonald and Evans, 1948), p. 6.

the organisation of the new society. Strategic action is based on the development of life. But this supposes that life has an orientation. The great optimistic narratives of the end of the 19th century contend that science demonstrates this orientation. But they are bitten from the inside by a new suspicion, the suspicion that life wants nothing and leads nowhere. This is the secret that literature, for its part, claims in the open. From Stendhal and Balzac to Dostoyevsky, Tolstoï and Ibsen, it does not stop representing the failure of the strategic view of the world, the failure to give an orientation to the movement of life. Behind the idea of the scientific adaptation of strategic action to the movement of life, there was the divorce between two ideas of communism and the unavowed feeling that this movement may lead nowhere and that the will to change life does not rely on any objective process. This is why scientific rigor had to reverse itself, to affirm itself as the mere necessity of the violent break that imposes a direction to the endless movement of productive life.

It is this inner discrepancy of the revolutionary model which created the gaps and intervals within which artists, and notably artists dealing with the arts of movement, could propose their own paradigms of action and community: figures of the active communist subject, more active and more dynamic than the empirical agents of social transformation; ways of shaping a communist sensorium, ahead of the slow move of strategic action aimed at creating the material conditions of a new society.

This is the point where a multiplicity of combinations of the triad expression, rhythm, and play could come in. This is, for instance, what the posters by the Stenberg brothers construct: a sense of action in which there is no opposition between the ends and the means of communism; the free movement of the dancer here and now is already the manifestation of the new communist sensorium in which the bodies and the machines share the same rhythm. The posters show the union as natural and unproblematic. But we know that this is not so. How can the "free movement" of the dancer coincide with what was the enemy against which the paradigms of expression, rhythm, and play had been shaped, i.e. their mechanism?

There are different ways of conceiving the principle of the coincidence. The first one can be summarized in one word: functionality. In that view, art becomes a form of life to the extent that its forms have the same kind of rationality as the forms of economic and social life and that its products and performances enact the same principle as the one which determines the efficiency of the machines and that of the working bodies. Man and machine, the making of art and the constitution of a new community are united by the same principle:

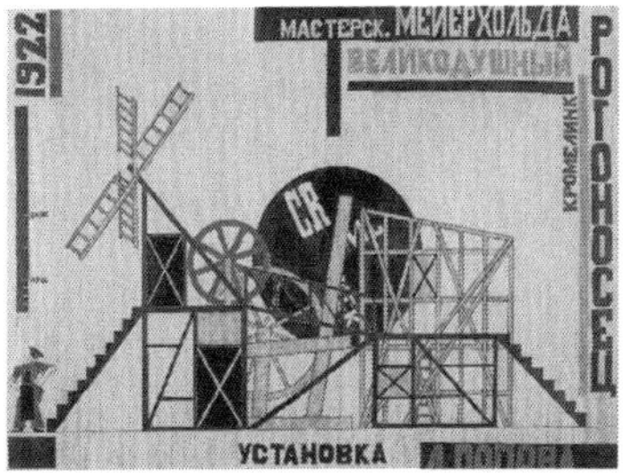

Fig. 3: Popova's Machine. Poster.

the definition of a series of elementary operations that maximize the efficiency of the machine and that of human gestures. This is the ideal that is summed up by Wsewolod E. Meyerhold in a text from 1922, *The Actor of the Future and Biomechanics*, that sets the problem in the terms of social engineering. Art in a socialist country can no longer be thought of as a form of entertainment within a society where labour and rest are separated. It is a social activity that has to help workmen in their work and not to entertain them. The work of the actor must be considered as a "production necessary for the good organisation of the labour of all citizens." Now to perform this task for the benefit of the workers the actor has to adopt movements that maximize the efficiency of his own work. He has to acquire the qualities of the good worker trained at the Taylorist school: the elimination of useless, non-productive gestures; the rhythm and the exact awareness of his centre of gravity. He must train his body so that it can obey the instructions within the shortest delays and reach the level of excitability that determines the efficiency of his performance.

Obviously, it is dubious whether the woman on the poster fulfils such conditions of efficiency. But the point is that it is dubious whether Meyerhold's shows themselves fulfil them. What is offered to the spectators of his most famous mise-en-scène, devoted to Fernand Crommelynck's play *The Magnanimous Cuckold*, is not so much the functionality of Taylorist work as it is the demonstration of a "machine-for-acting" with stairs, slides, ladders, revolving doors, chutes, and other apparatuses allowing the "actors" to transform themselves into gymnasts and turn the play into a series of acrobatic and burlesque exercises. Between the modernist artistic dream of a physical performance replacing the old system of expression and the social Taylorist dream of an exact calculation of efficient gestures, the coincidence is only apparent. The model of the new theatrical performance is not the Taylorist worker adapted to his machine. It is the acrobat who cares for no efficiency extraneous to his performance. Or it is the new mime,

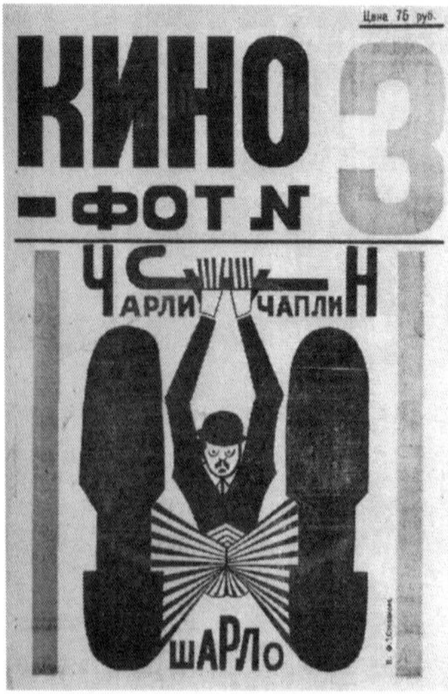

Fig. 4: Cover of the Kino-Phot Magazine. Designed by Varvara Stepanova.

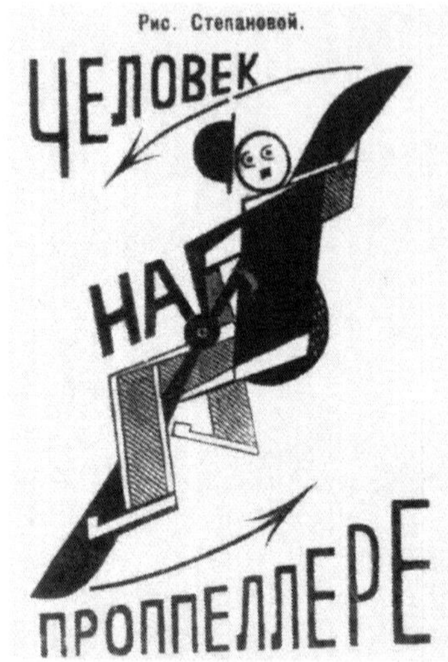

Fig. 5: Kino-Phot Magazine. Drawing by Varvara Stepanova.

the mechanical mime whose gestures don't imitate the efficiency of the machines but their endless repetitive and meaningless movement. When we look at the propeller composed on the poster by the members of the dancer and the words, we can't help but think of the figure that epitomizes artistic modernity for Soviet avant-garde artists fond of virtuoso performance and social efficiency: Charlie Chaplin, the actor who affirms that the cinematographic stage is the stage on which "the laws of movement reign supreme." The conversion of the social figure of the tramp into a precise nervous machine is the model proclaimed by almost all Soviet artists. In a special issue of the magazine Kino-Phot, devoted to Chaplin, there is a significant series of drawings made by Varvara Stepanova. The drawings illustrate sentences from an article by Stepanova's husband, Alexander Rodtchenko, opposing the concrete actions of Charlot to the gestures of actors performing characters. But more important is the very dynamic of the series. The first drawings and the very cover of the issue represent the awkward limping gait of the tramp falling on all fours (image 4). But as the series moves on, the clumsy gestures of the clown are turned into the perfect movements of a plane's propeller and of the technician operating it (images 5 and 6). The point is that the perfect transformation of the clumsy tramp into an efficient machine shows us its flip side as

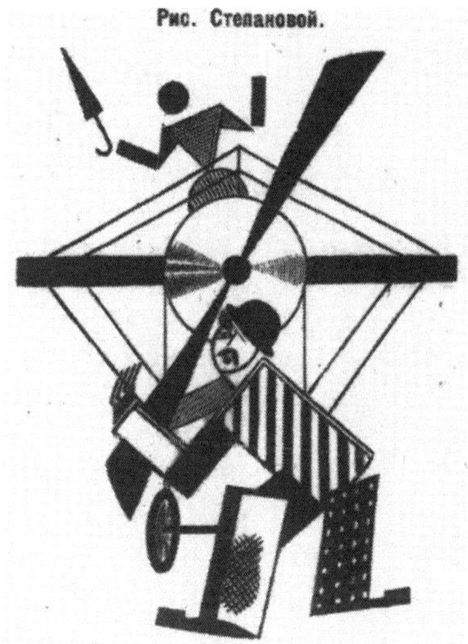

Fig. 6: Kino-Phot Magazine.
Drawing by Varvara Stepanova.

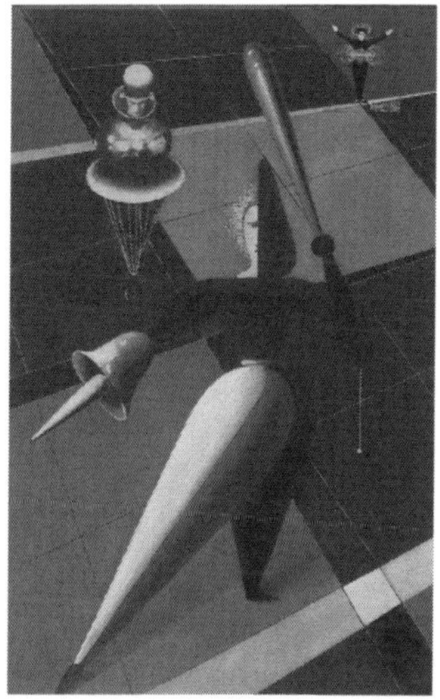

Fig. 7: Study for the "Triadic Ballet".
Oskar Schlemmer (ca. 1924).

well: the perfection of the body-machine of the clown is the conflation of two mechanisms: an efficient one and an automatic, endless, inefficient one. What Charlot symbolizes is not the efficiency of the new world of efficient machines and Taylorised gestures; it is the equivalence of the functional mechanical movements with the nonsensical automatisms. His gestures are not actions, but the demonstration of an identity of action and inaction, an identity whose proper name, since the time of Schiller, has been play.

Play comes in to disjoin the dreamed identity between the free movement of the communist body and the rationality of Taylorised work. At the same time as the Stenberg brothers illustrate the dream of an exact mechanical performance, replacing the old theatrical ritual by hybridizing on a plane surface the parts of a woman's body and the parts of an optic machine, Oskar Schlemmer designs the figures of his triadic ballet. He designs them in the *Bauhaus*, an institution which had been devoted to creating a new form of artistic practice, producing no more works of art but the *living machine* adapted to the dwellers of a new world, characterized by the rationalization of the setting and of all the furniture and accessories of everyday life. The figures of the ballet, however, seem very far from that project of rationalisation. The heavy geometric costumes that Schlemmer invents for the dancers are the exact opposite of any idea of liberating the free flow of movement. On the other hand, this is not a mechanical ballet. Between the spring of life and the cogwheels of the machine, Schlemmer thinks that a mediation has to be found: the mediation of artifice. Artifice is the technical artefact created by human hands and machines. But it is also the manifestation of the human taste for play, appearance, and masquerade. The ballets of the *Bauhaus* symbolize the harmony between the functional forms invented by science and technology, and the non-functional human taste for play and appearance. That harmony must be play, because there is no common rhythm unifying the performances of the dancers, the functioning of the machines, and the breath of universal life. The synthesis has to be symbolized on that theatrical stage that once had epitomized old bourgeois art for the new engineer-artists. Furthermore, it has to be symbolized by dancing bodies whose technological perfection amounts to the impossibility of free movement.

It transpires as though the ecstatic body of the dancer on the poster had been designed with the explicit purpose of denying this gap between functionality and play. Instead, it affirms a free movement of the body in tune with the movement of a machine. But it is the film itself that becomes thus the test for the verification of that harmony. The film embodies a vision of the performance of art that rejects any stage of representation. There are only facts, only actions: those same actions that are performed everyday in the streets, the shops, the factories, the offices, the stadiums, or the workers' clubs. Filming thus is not a way of representing those actions. It is an action that creates a link between all those actions and organizes them into a "film-thing" which is itself part of the construction of the new life. Its main operation consists in rendering all of them equal. This means three things: first, making them equally important; next, fragmenting them into very short pieces; and finally, editing them according to an accelerated rhythm. The machine of the operator and that of the editor make all those fragmented activities the expression of a new collective life characterized by the acceleration of movements and their instantaneous connection. In such a way the assembly line in the factory and the wipe given by a shoe-shiner in the street, the work of the miner and the doing of nails in a beauty parlour are represented as equivalent manifestations of energy. This overall connection has one condition. The condition is that each of those actions be disconnected from its own temporality, disconnected from the ends that it pursues. The detractors of Vertov had already made this point about his earlier films: his machines might compose an impressive symphony of movement, but nobody knew how they functioned and what they produced. This is the point. Vertov does not "represent" communism as the result of a planned organization and hierarchy of tasks. He creates communism as the common rhythm of all activities. Now this common rhythm supposes that the performance of the body shares the same characteristic: unwillingness. Cinema redeems all movements from their dependency upon specific wills. Thus it proposes a form of communism that escapes the dilemmas of communist strategies by overturning the secret of the aimlessness of life. Communism is the endless movement through which life expresses nothing but its equal intensity. The space of the poster and the time of the film are the space and time of aesthetic play.

This is what is illustrated by the last part of the film in which we meet again the dancer and the tripod as we see the film being projected in a theatre. Those sequences show us two opposite performances of the machine: there is the performance of the telephone exchange which appears time and again as a refrain in the film. That performance is the metaphor of the filmic action as an interconnection of actions. But the condition of that interconnection is that all the actions are split up into fragments, appearing and disappearing at the same speed as the plugging and unplugging in the telephone exchange. This is why, in the episode of the screening in the theatre, the tripod and the camera present us with a very different image of the machine: they are turned into automatons, bowing to the audience before demonstrating their tricks. On the one hand, the cameraman is only the employee of the telephone exchange that connects every activity with all other activities. On the other hand, he is the magician that turns all of them into tricks. Hence the two accusations levelled against Vertov: the accusation of formalism on the one hand, and that of pantheism or "Whitmanism" on the other hand. But both amount to the same. What is common to the free body and to the machine is that they do not pursue any end. What is common to the Whitmanian or Duncanian rhythm and to "formalist" play is that both make will and unwillingness equivalent. The direct performance of art becoming action and life is a play. As is well known, the builders of "true" or "effective" communism rejected that "playful" or "pantheistic" communism and asked artists to give up the pretension of constructing the sensible forms of the new community. What they had to do was to serve the strategy of the party by representing the life and problems of the real people and by recreating workers.

The art of movement appeared to suit exactly the dream of the becoming-political of art, which means the immediate identity between the aesthetic constitution of the community and its political constitution. The layout of the poster and the montage of the film set out to achieve that dream by making all movements homogeneous in a common sensory fabric. But that homogeneity only exists in the space of play. There is no aesthetic constitution of the community. What *aesthetics* means is much more than the collapse of any principle of homogeneity. It is the equivalence of movement and rest, action and inaction. It is the equivalence of the machine that serves the projects of will and the mechanical, involuntary movement. It is the suspension of the normal relationship between ends and means, causes and effects. That suspension creates a specific fabric which cannot coincide with the economic and social fabric of the community and which appears split into two forms. On the one hand, there are the forms of modern dance and performance aimed at expressing the still unknown powers inhabiting the bodies and souls of individuals and communities; on the other hand, there is the art of the moving image which is the new art emblematising the progress of technology. The poster and the film want to make them coincide. Instead, they bear witness to the impossibility of that coincidence. The *cinematism* of the camera devours that of the bodies. Cinema "writes" the movement, it writes the poem of the cinematic community; it wants to equate this poem with the living performance of the community. But the writing of the movement on the screen does what writing does in general. Like literature, it divides; it transforms bodies into quasi-bodies or into shadows. The art of the machine remains an art of shadows just as literature remains an art of words.

This is why we should receive with some suspicion the accusation levelled against the art of the moving image. The art of the shadows has sometimes been accused of complicity with the totalitarian powers of the 20th century. This reproach is in line with the old Platonic idea that people are subjected because, as spectators, they are manipulated by the machine of illusion that makes them see shadows. It is also in line with the idea that the big totalitarian parades were the implementation of the aesthetic utopia. But the art of the shadows is much more the art that splits the glorious body of the people from the inside. That division is at work in the theatre where Vertov shows us the spectators laughing at the spectacle of the frantic acceleration of their daily activities. They play with the idea that those activities are the implementation of the communist idea. They play with the great promise and with the non-fulfilment of the promise, or its fulfilment as a play in the theatre at the end of the day. The artist wants to achieve the aesthetic promise of the new community, but what he does instead is to foster the capacity to deal with the promise, its non-fulfilment, and the horizon of expectation opened by both the promise and its non-fulfilment.

II. Resisting

Anneka Esch-van Kan

Introduction

As the violence of "real socialism" has turned many revolutionaries from the promises of socialist utopias, and experiments of communal living and leadership have continued to fail, it has become unfashionable to speak of one's aspiration to change the world, to imagine a better, peaceful, or more just future: As Jacques Rancière points out, the intention to change the world towards greater justice is no longer that well regarded.[1] Calls for revolution are greeted with ridicule, and the adherence to a utopian mindset is belittled and devalued as the naïve belief of a handful of left-behind starry-eyed idealists. Of course, this has not put an end to activism or a pluralism of social groupings that pursue defined goals and often act on a local scale, but it did put an end to the *grand narratives*[2] of former times and evoke a paralyzing crisis in leftist thinking.

Poststructuralist theories served as a welcome safe haven by offering a way of thinking that challenges thetic and binary reasoning. A way of thinking, that is, that allows reflection upon the paradoxes and sore points of revolutionary movements and practices, while offering a fresh perspective on the complexities of a globalized world. Poststructuralist philosophy has led to significant insights about the general possibility of resistance: namely, that if there is no outside of power, it is only ever possible, but thus necessary, to attack a system from within; that if language plays an important part in the construction of hierarchical orders, it therefore needs to be challenged itself; and that if it is desirable to avoid grand theories, we must favor a tentative and decidedly meta-reflexive way of expression. Poststructuralist scholarship has then met no less hostility, and fallen under suspicion of opening a fundamentally apolitical, and in many respects all too abstract, perspective.

---

1 "Es ist nicht mehr sonderlich gut angesehen, die Welt ändern zu wollen, um sie gerechter zu machen." – Jacques Rancière, *Ist Kunst widerständig*, ed. and trans. Frank Ruda and Jan Völker (Berlin: Merve, 2008), p. 8. The original lecture, *Si l'art résiste à quelque chose?*, presented at the Quinto Simpósio internacional de filosofia – *Nietzsche et Deleuze. Arte e resisténcia*, in Fortaleza, Brazil, 2004, is not available in a published version.

2 Jean-François Lyotard, *La Condition postmoderne: Rapport sur le savoir* (Paris: Éditions de Minuit, 1979).

This supposed lack of a decidedly political attitude has been answered, on the one hand, by the concept of an "ontological difference"[3] in various theories of radical democracy; and on the other hand, by the invocation of an "ethical turn" based on the assumption of a shared humanity and insisting on the idea of justice as the subjection of everyone to the human rights as declared in the Geneva Conventions. To conceive of the political as an ontological dimension underlying the concrete manifestations of politics allows understanding philosophical writing and scholarly practices as resistant, while advocates of the "ethical turn" call for much more concrete interventions and positions in and towards contemporary areas of conflict.

Most of the contributions assembled in this section share a certain kind of skepticism towards the so-called "ethical turn,"[4] but in different ways adopt double-edged perspectives that often include a partial return to the seemingly out-dated modes of revolutionary thought. The essays echo the voices of many academics, such as performance scholar Jill Dolan, who has claimed – fully aware of the risks of her argument – that it is necessary to hold on to the hope that the world might – even if only gradually – change in certain respects.[5] Her notion of "utopian performatives" very obviously links to the Deleuzian notion of a "people to come"[6] and Derrida's concept of a "democracy to come,"[7] and in this sense parallels many of the following arguments. Even though there might be no utopian place for us to arrive at, even though there might not be real justice, the way to that non-existent place itself, and the demand for a more just world, can become the goal. The questioned or demanded necessity to keep on trying to resist – despite most likely (partial) failure – offers one joint perspective on the articles of this section.

---

3 Oliver Marchart, *Post-Foundational Political Thought – Political Difference in Nancy, Lefort, Badiou, and Laclau* (Edinburgh: Edinburgh University Press, 2007).

4 This strongly applies to Judith Butler's and Simon Crichtley's contributions in this section. For an extensive critique of the "ethical turn" also see: Jacques Rancière, "Le tournant éthique de l'esthétique et de la politique," *Malaise dans l'esthétique* (Paris: Galilée, 2004), p. 143–173.

5 Jill Dolan, *Utopia in Performance: Finding Hope at the Theater* (Ann Arbor: The University of Michigan Press, 2005).

6 Gilles Deleuze, *Essays critical and clinical* (Minneapolis: University of Minnesota Press, 1997), p. 4.

7 Jacques Derrida, "The Last of the Rogue States: The 'Democracy to Come,' Opening in Two Turns," *South Atlantic Quarterly* 103:2/3 (Spring/Summer 2004): p. 323–341; Jacques Derrida, *Rogues: Two Essays on Reason*, trans. Pascale-Anne Brault and Michael Naas (Stanford: Stanford University Press, 2005).

How then is resistance possible under contemporary conditions? How do resistant practices relate to theories of radical democracy? Which tactics could be employed to resist a hegemonic power or a given distribution of the sensible? How could art relate to the ways of thinking resistance, and what might be resistant practices in art, preparing not least an adequate awareness of resistance in its readings? Is it – and how is it – possible to break through the confines of language? And is it possible to theorize and live by a non-violent ethics?

In her strongly performative essay on her "Ethical Ambivalence," reprinted in this volume, Judith Butler continues her search for precisely such an "ethics of non-violence." She "maps" her resistance against the so-called ethical turn in the humanities, holds on to her argument that "the return to ethics has constituted an escape from politics,"[8] and emphasizes the violence at the heart of any ethical demand. Her central idea is that – especially after the de-Man affair brought deconstruction into disrepute by linking it to a national socialist mindset – it is of paramount importance to show how deconstruction could relate to "responsibility, resistance, and antifascist ethics."[9] Keeping an inquiring, non-thetic and very personal tone, Butler offers a virtuoso deconstructive reading of Friedrich Nietzsche by confronting his position with the ethical perspective of Emmanuel Levinas. Qualifying her outright rejection of ethics as moralizing, and as a ground for practices that ignore their own violence and righteousness, Butler suggests a possibility for a non-violent ethics that remains resistant in its constitutive inclusion of the critique of ethics itself, and the challenge to its very value.

Frank Ruda proposes a very different direction for resistant philosophy by returning to, re-examining, and dialectically rehabilitating the dialectics of grand revolutionary theory, even by pointing out the dialectic relation between these abstractions and the practices of their realizations. Taking cues from Alain Badiou's turn to a mathematical Platonism in an event-oriented ontology, his ambitious argument follows the structure of the three logical forms of negation to differentiate that relation, ultimately pleading for multiple negations in dealing with the doubled temptation of faithfulness to revolution, and its opposite. Thus by overcoming and re-framing the thought of the seemingly still contemporary 20th century, a 21st century becomes conceivable.

Simon Critchley, on the contrary, takes a clear stance against the future in "Is Utopianism Dead?" He combines Butler's consciously tentative mode of writing with Ruda's decidedly thetic call for concreteness,

---

8 P. 127.
9 P. 130.

and mixes both with more than a dash of polemics. Far from being a mere stylistic choice, this combination of different voices and attitudes marks the central point of Critchley's reflections on and suggestions for practices of resistance. He too starts from clear statements about the contemporary condition: "We are living through a long-1960s"; "most of us are passive nihilists and cynics"; and the disillusioned and defeated retreats from politics and resistance imply the assumption that "[h]umanity is a plague."[10] Next, however, Critchley challenges the absoluteness of such consequences drawn from the failures of the utopian experiments of the 1960s. While his exemplary analyses of and references to contemporary art and revolutionary practices seem to feed the wide-spread skepticism towards utopian endeavors, Critchley concludes by emphasizing the necessity to confront past and current experiments in a critical but non-pejorative way. He pleads for the persistence of a certain "utopian impulse," which is less directed at a future that is to be improved, but rather understands that "[t]he future of radical, creative thought is its past."[11] While the polemic nature of some statements exposes the untenability of a rigorous cynicism that seems to have turned into a common stance, the decisive formulation of strong theses confronted with the tentative mode of a never completely fading "perhaps" suggests a mode of writing and resistance that could build on the past without falling short of the theoretical premises and complexities of our time.

Just as Critchley argues that there hardly seems to be a good alternative to a careful return to a utopian impulse, Jon McKenzie holds the view that it is "unavoidable" to accept the risks that one might fail to resist and eventually perpetuate violence in one's writing or art. In his 2009 essay on "Abu Ghraib and the Society of the Spectacle of the Scaffold," reprinted in this volume, he insists on the necessity to critically engage with the scandalous pictures of torture and prisoner abuses, and think through those practices and their consequences. McKenzie focuses on two anachronisms: following Judith Butler's argument in *Precarious Life*,[12] he argues that the torture scandals reveal a "reemergence of sovereign power" that is assigned to investigators and other military personnel; and combining Foucault and Debord, he concludes that the exhibition and staging of torture points to "the reemergence of the spectacle of the scaffold." Using "theatricality as a way to ana-

---

10 P. 155.

11 P. 162.

12 Judith Butler, "Indefinite Detention," *Precarious Life: The Power of Mourning and Violence* (London/New York: Verso, 2004), p. 50–100.

lyze the techniques of America's torture machine,"[13] his close reading of a sequence of pictures of prisoner M-----, who was later given the name "Shit-Boy" by the guards, reveals how closely practices of torture relate to performance. McKenzie particularly stresses the importance of the "temporal and processual dimension" and traces the construction of the character of "Shit-Boy," and the invention of this trope. This allows McKenzie to bring awareness not only to the violence performed and represented, but also to the "violence of representation itself." Connecting his argument to the central theses of his influential book *Perform – or Else. From Discipline to Performance*,[14] he suggests that the way torture has been used in Abu Ghraib closely relates or might even "come to define [...] the global formation of power/knowledge," which with reference to Deleuze and Guattari's *A Thousand Plateaus* he calls "performance stratum."[15]

Continuing McKenzie's reflections on the recent torture scandals in American prison camps, I turn to performance artist/scholar Coco Fusco's series of theatrical and filmic responses to the specific role of female interrogators (2005–2008). Avoiding the snares of ethical arguments, Fusco sidesteps the question whether torture is legitimate, asking instead how torture could be defined; and shifts the perspective from the victims to the perpetrators. With an all-female group of artists and scholars, Fusco took part in a boot camp designed for non-military persons who desire to be trained in interrogation techniques, entered into a dialogue with the instructors, and developed a film, a street as well as a lecture performance, and a book out of her experiences and in-depth research. In "'Torture Chicks' – Resistance and the Political in Coco Fusco's *A Room of One's Own* and *A Field Guide for Female Interrogators*," I try to vindicate the view that the plurality of interlinked forms of artistic expressions are fundamental for the resistant potential of Fusco's artistic work and emphasize how it relates to an inextricable triangulation of thinking – resisting – reading the political. I argue that Fusco's confrontation of debates on the legitimacy and definition of torture with feminist struggles against female exploitation and stereotypes can be considered in terms of Lyotard's *différend*,[16] and that Fusco's entire project and her tactics closely relate to contem-

---

13 P. 168.

14 Jon McKenzie, *Perform – Or Else: From Discipline to Performance* (London/New York: Routledge, 2001).

15 P. 163.

16 Jean-François Lyotard, *The Differend: Phrases in Dispute*, trans. Georges Van Den Abbeele (Minneapolis: University of Minnesota Press, 1988). [*Le Différend* (Paris: Éditions de Minuit, 1983)].

porary thoughts on the political. Finally, I claim that Fusco's artistic practices are closely connected to more general shifts in the thinking of resistance and political art. The confrontation of art, research, and philosophy in (resistant) artistic practices then proves itself productive and allows utopian impulses to subsist that otherwise might be devalued as flawed or naive.

In performance and theater studies, the search for a resistant potential of art often coincides with a certain wariness towards language and an emphasis on performativity. In his essay on "*Prendre la parole*: Voices of Resistance in Contemporary Theory," Andreas Hetzel turns his hand to questioning how philosophy, as a practice inevitably bound to language, can think and itself perform a "counter-hegemonic or resistant speech" that goes "beyond the 'one' language we know." How is it possible to resist the "one" language in language, in speech? Starting from classical rhetorics, Hetzel argues that language should not be understood as a "precondition" but as a "result" of speech. He then introduces three rhetorical figures that build on this very assumption and indeed seem to allow a repeated redrawing of "the limits of languages": Jacques Derrida's and Judith Butler's notion of *translation*, which triggered the "translational turn" in the thinking of culture and challenges the stability of languages based on their fundamental dependence on a general translatability into other languages; Jacques Rancière's concept of "seizing the word [*prendre la parole*]" that insists "on the possibility of inventing a paradoxical language" of those who are supposedly outside of language but in spite of that seize the word; and Butler's notion of *catachrestic resignification*, "which critically appropriates or recodes a given ascription of identity."[17] Conclusively, Hetzel reasons that all three resistant figures of speech are strongly associated with a Rancièrian notion of "politics" in that they interrupt a given distribution of the sensible and "redefine the field of the sayable through their utterances."[18] In this sense, the rhetorical figures that Hetzel describes offer ways how scholarly writing can in and of itself become a resistant and political practice, even while turning to the traditional systems and concepts of reading that are further explored in the third section.

---

17 All quotes in this paragraph are – if not indicated otherwise – from p. 201.
18 P. 212.

Judith Butler

Ethical Ambivalence[1]

I do not have much to say about why there is a return to ethics, if there is one, in recent years, except to say that I have for the most part resisted this return, and that what I have to offer is something like a map of this resistance and its partial overcoming which I hope will be useful for more than biographical purposes. I've worried that the return to ethics has constituted an escape from politics, and I've also worried that it has meant a certain heightening of moralism and this has made me cry out, as Nietzsche cried out about Hegel, "Bad air! Bad air!" I suppose that looking for a space in which to breathe is not the highest ethical aspiration, but it is there, etymologically embedded in aspiration itself, and does seem to constitute something of a precondition for any viable, that is, livable, ethical reflection.

I began my philosophical career within the context of a Jewish education, one that took the ethical dilemmas posed by the mass extermination of the Jews during World War II, including members of my own family, to set the scene for the thinking of ethicality as such. The question endlessly posed, implicitly and explicitly, is what you would have done in those circumstances, whether you would have kept the alliance, whether you would have broken the alliance, whether you would have stayed brave and fierce and agreed to die, whether you would have become cowardly, sold out, tried to live, and betrayed others in the process. The questions posed were rather stark, and it seemed as if they were posed not merely about a hypothetical past action, but of present and future actions as well: Will you live in the mode of that alliance? Will you live in the mode of that betrayal, and will you be desecrating the dead by your actions, will you be killing them again? No, worse, you are, by your present action, effectively killing them again. It was unclear whether any sort of significant action could be dislodged from this framework, and whether any action could be dissociated from the ethical itself: the effect on action was generally paralysis or guilt with occasional moments of hallucinatory heroism.

We know this particular form of ethical thinking from Woody Allen films, the humor of Richard Lewis, and others. And, despite its gravity, or rather because of it, I can barely restrain myself from driving the logic into the sometimes hilarious extremes it achieves in the U.S.

---

1 First published in Marjorie Garber, Beatrice Hanssen and Rebecca L. Walkowitz, eds., *The Turn to Ethics* (New York: Routledge, 2000), p. 15–28.

context (Did you brush your teeth? Are you betraying the Jews?) but I will try not to – and not only from fear of enacting that desecration again. It was with reluctance that I agreed to read Nietzsche, and generally disdained him through most of my undergraduate years at Yale, until a friend of mine brought me to Paul de Man's class on *Beyond Good and Evil* and I found myself at once compelled and repelled. As I read further, I saw in Nietzsche a profound critique of the psychic violence performed by impossible and relentless ethical demands, the kind that takes whatever force of life-affirmation that might be available and turns it back upon itself, spawning from that negative reflexivity the panoply of psychic phenomena called "bad conscience," "guilt," and even "the soul." I read Nietzsche's *On the Genealogy of Morals* with difficulty, since what I wanted most from it was his critique of slave morality, and what I hated most in it was his persistent association of slave morality with the Jews and Judaism. It was as if the moment of the text that offered me some release from the hyperethical framework that I derived from a postwar Jewish education was the very one that threatened to implicate me in an alliance with an anti-Semitic text. The bind seemed almost airtight: to go against the hyperethicality of Judaism, I could go with Nietzsche, but to go with Nietzsche meant to go against Judaism, and this was unacceptable. If only he had left the anti-Semitic remarks aside, if only we could read him in such a way that those remarks really didn't matter!

I read since the age of fourteen a series of Jewish thinkers and writers, and if I am to be honest, I probably know more about them than I know about anything written in queer theory today. They included Maimonides, Spinoza, Buber, Benjamin, Arendt, and Scholem, and especially the work and letters of Kafka, whose ethical dilemmas impressed me as no less than sublime. But I clearly turned away from pursuing Jewish studies formally for fear, no doubt, that somewhere in those texts the crushing force of the unappeasable law would be upon me again. And I was drawn toward those kinds of readings that suspended the law, exposed its illegibility, its internal limits and contradictions, and even found Jewish authorization for those kinds of readings. I was also compelled to show that this kind of reading did not paralyze ethical or political action, to show that the law might be critically interrogated and mobilized at once.

Sometime in the last ten years I read some Levinas and found upon my first reading a hyperbolic instance of this superegoic law. I read, for instance, about the demand that is imposed upon me by the face of the Other, a demand that is "before all language and mimicry," a face that is *not* a representation, a demand that is *not* open to interpretation.

I am as it were ordered from the outside, traumatically commanded, without interiorizing by representation and concepts the authority that commands me, without asking myself: what then is he to me? where does he get his right to command?[2]

What would it mean to obey such a demand, to acquiesce to such a demand when no critical evaluation of the demand could be made? Would such an acquiescence be any more or less uncritical and unthinking than an acquiescence to an ungrounded authoritarian law? How would one distinguish between a fascist demand and one which somehow affirms the ethical bonds between humans that Levinas understands as constitutive of the ethical subject?[3]

For the Levinas of *Otherwise than Being*, the reverse question seems to be paramount: Given that we reflect ethically on the principles and norms that guide our relations to others, are we not, prior to any such reflection, already in relation to others such that that reflection becomes possible – an ethical relation that is, as it were, prior to all reflection? For Levinas, the Other is not always or exclusively elsewhere; it makes its demand on me, but it is also of me: it is the constitutive relation of this subject to the ethical, one that both constitutes and divides the subject from the start. For Levinas, this splitting of the subject, foundationally, by the Other establishes this non unitary subject as the basis for ethical responsibility.

This subject is, moreover, from the start split by the wound of the Other (not simply the wounds that the Other performs, but a wound that the Other somehow is, prior to any action). The task of this fundamentally wounded subject is to take responsibility for the very other who, in Levinas' terms, "persecutes" that self. That Other delivers the command to take responsibility for the persecution that the Other inflicts. In effect, I do not take responsibility for the Other who wounds me after the wound has appeared. My openness to the Other is what

2 Emmanuel Levinas, *Otherwise than Being or Beyond Essence*, trans. Alphonso Lingis (Boston: Kluwer, 1978), p. 87.

3 The ethical relation is that of a passivity beyond passivity, one that escapes from the binary opposition of passive and active; it is an "effacement," a "bad conscience," a primordial exposure to the Other, to the face of the Other, to the demand that is made by the face of the Other. "To have to respond to [the Other's] right to be – not by reference to the abstraction of some anonymous law, some juridical entity, but in fear of the Other. My 'in the world' [alluding to Heidegger], my 'place in the sun': my at homeness, have they not been the usurpation of the places belonging to the other man already oppressed and starved by me?" Emmanuel Levinas, "Bad Conscience and the Inexorable," *Face to Face with Levinas*, ed. Richard A. Cohen (Albany: State University of New York Press, 1986), p. 38.

allows for the wound and what also at the same time commands that I take responsibility for that Other.

When I first encountered this position, I ran in the opposite direction, understanding it as a valorization of self-sacrifice that would make excellent material for a Nietzschean psychological critique. This was clearly the will turned back upon itself, the reflexive rerouting of the *conatus* against its own strength, possibility for affirmation, and desire, a position that quite literally called into question self-preservation as the basis for ethical reflection. As an exercise, I would ask my students to take the above lines from Levinas and compare them with Nietzsche's from *On the Genealogy of Morals*:

> Hostility, cruelty, joy in persecuting, in attacking, in change, in destruction-all turned against the possessors of such instincts: *that* is the origin of the 'bad conscience.' The man who, from lack of external enemies and resistances and forcibly confined to the oppressive narrowness and punctiliousness of custom, impatiently lacerated, persecuted, gnawed at, assaulted, and maltreated himself: [...] this deprived creature, racked with homesickness for the wild, who had to turn himself into an adventure, a torture chamber, an uncertain and dangerous wilderness – this fool, this yearning and desperate prisoner became the inventor of the 'bad conscience.'[4]

Thus, it was with some wryness that I became aware of the sudden and enthusiastic turn to Levinas among the deconstructively minded after the Paul de Man affair broke into the public press. If the popular conclusion drawn from de Man's wartime writings was that something in that mode of deconstruction leads to Nazi sympathizing, then perhaps there is a way to show that deconstruction is on the side of the Jews, that it can be made to serve an ethical demand that would put deconstruction on the side of responsibility, resistance, and antifascist ethics. My sense was that it made no sense to rush to a slave morality to avert the charge of fascism, and that there had to be some other way to navigate these alternatives besides heaping reaction formation upon reaction formation.

I don't know whether I have arrived at an alternative, or whether that is what I propose to offer you in the final pages of this paper. But I

---

4 Friedrich Nietzsche, *On the Genealogy of Morals*, trans. Walter Kaufmann (New York: Random House, 1967), p. 85. In German: "Die Feindschaft, die Grausamkeit, die Lust an der Verfolgung, am Überfall, am Wechsel, an der Zerstörung – alles das gegen die Inhaber solcher Instinkte sich wendend: *das* ist der Ursprung des 'schlechten Gewissens.'" *Werke in drei Bänden*, vol. 2 (Munich: Carl Hanser Verlag, 1966), p. 799.

have come to think that the opposition that I saw between Levinas and Nietzsche was, perhaps, not quite as stark as I thought. I was going to write about the consonant meanings of "yielding" in Levinas, and "undergoing" in Nietzsche, but I am only able to clear the ground for a future reflection on the topic. I would like to point to two moments, instead, in which the subordinated becomes identified with the subordinator and where this identification is not simply an identification with the oppressor, but appears to be a paradoxical basis for a different order of commonality that puts the distinction between subordinator and subordinated into a useful crisis.

In the first essay of *On the Genealogy of Morals*, Nietzsche introduces the noble to us as someone with the capacity to forget; the noble has "no memory for insults" and his forgetfulness is clearly the condition of his capacity to exercise his will. (As he elaborates in the second essay, forgetfulness makes room for new experience, nourishes the "nobler" faculties, and keeps us from being preoccupied with what has happened to us.[5]) The slave and the man of ressentiment, we are told, remember every insult perfectly, and develop a clear memory in the service of vengefulness.

Nietzsche then starts the second essay by introducing the animal who is bred with the right to make promises, and this animal turns out to be the noble in new form. What is paradoxical, and Nietzsche marks this, is that to make a promise means to have a memory, indeed, to have a continuous memory that lasts through time. If I say that I promise at one time, then my promise fails to remain a promise if, at another time, I forget what it is I have said. A promise is the sustained memory of an utterance, a memory that becomes instilled in the will, so that I not only say what it is I promise to do, but I also do precisely what I said I would do. The temporality of the utterance must, in the case of the promise, exceed the time and occasion of its enunciation. The linguistic deed of promising is "discharged" into the nonlinguistic deed precisely by virtue of this memory that becomes the resolution of the will.

Thus, this animal who requires forgetting also breeds in itself a capacity *to make and sustain a memory*. Forgetfulness is thus "abrogated" – Nietzsche's term – in those cases in which the need to sustain a memory of a promise emerges. He will tell us that within slave morality, a mnemonics of the will is prepared, that a memory is *burned* into the will, and that this burning is not only violent, but bloody (thus, Nietzsche's famous quip that Kant's categorical imperative is steeped

5 Nietzsche, *On the Genealogy of Morals*, pp. 58–59.

in blood). The way in which this memory is burned in the will, however, is precisely through a reflexive venting of the will against itself. In other words, morality for the one within slave morality requires a self-inflicted violence. But is this actually different from the kind of memory of the will that the noble crafts for himself?

At the moment in which the noble seeks to have a memory, a continuous memory through time, is the noble acting like those who belong to the sphere of ressentiment? Can the noble keep his promise without *remembering an injury*, even if the injury that he remembers is one that he inflicts on himself?

The result of this self-infliction is a continuous and trustworthy will:

> [...] between the original "I will," "I shall do this" and the actual discharge of the will, its *act*, a world of strange new things, circumstances, even acts of will may be interposed without breaking this long chain of will.[6]

The will of the promising animal is one that is extended through time, figured as "a long chain of will," suggesting that there are different interlocking links of the will which remain unbroken by new things and circumstances or other acts of will. Whatever it is I promise, I do. And I renew that promise in different circumstances, and keep that promise *despite all circumstances*.

Of course, the figure of a chain with discontinuous links is an odd one to stand for this putatively "continuous" will. Indeed, pages later, Nietzsche reinvokes the figure of the chain to support a contradictory conclusion. Writing of the law, he argues that it makes no sense to determine the function of the law in terms of the origins of the law, the original reasons why the law was made, the original purposes it sought to serve.[7] As a social convention, the meanings and purposes of law change through time, they come to take on purposes that were never intended for them, and they no longer serve the original purposes for which they were devised. Nietzsche writes,

> the cause of the origin of a thing and its eventual utility, its actual employment and place in a system of purposes, lie worlds apart; whatever exists,

---

6 Ibid., p. 58. In German: "[...] so daß zwischen das ursprüngliche 'ich will', 'ich werde tun' und die eigentliche Entladung des Willens, seinen *Akt*, unbedenklich eine Welt von neuen fremden Dingen, Umständen, selbst Willensakten dazwischengelegt werden darf, ohne daß diese lange Kette des Willens springt" (Nietzsche, *Werke in drei Bänden*, p. 800).

7 Nietzsche, *On the Genealogy of Morals*, p. 77.

having somehow come into being, is again and again reinterpreted to new ends, taken over, transformed, and redirected by some power superior to it; all events in the organic world are a subduing, a *becoming master*, and all subduing and becoming master involves a fresh interpretation, an adaptation through which any previous "meaning" and "purpose" are necessarily obscured [...].[8]

What happens if we return to the question of the status of the promise, if we understand the promise as one of the conventions that Nietzsche mentions above? Can it be said that the cause and origin of a promise lie worlds apart, if promising is understood as a custom, and its eventual utility, its actual employment and place in a system of purposes are in no necessary way linked to the act of promising itself? What does promising become if it is understood as one way to exercise a superior power, in Nietzsche's view, to reinterpret the promise to new ends, take it over, transform and redirect it? Or are we to conclude that promising as a customary act cannot exercise or manifest this superior power?

According to the above quotation, it seems that the "masterful" and "noble" thing to do is precisely to *revise* the meaning and purpose of a thing, an organ, or a custom according to new circumstances. And this power to reinterpret a convention to new ends not only requires becoming forgetful about the past, but characterizes the noble exercise of will.

The quotation continues:

the entire history of a "thing," an organ, a custom can in this way be a continuous *sign-chain* [Zeichenkette] of ever new interpretations and adaptations [suggesting an adaptation to new circumstances] whose causes do not even have to be related to one another but, on the contrary, in some cases succeed and alternate with one another in a purely chance fashion.[9]

---

8 Ibid.; in German: "[...] die Ursache der Entstehung eines Dinges und dessen schließliche Nützlichkeit, dessen tatsächliche Verwendung und Einordnung in ein System von Zwecken *toto coelo* auseinander liegen; daß etwas Vorhandenes, irgendwie Zustande/Gekommenes immer wieder von einer ihm überlegnen Macht auf neue Absichten ausgelegt, neu in Beschlag genommen, zu einem neuen Nutzen umgebildet und umgerichtet wird; daß alles Geschehen in der organischen Welt ein Überwältigen, Herr-werden und daß wiederum alles Überwältigen und Herr-werden ein Neu-Interpretieren, ein Zurechtmachen ist, bei dem der bisherige 'Sinn' und 'Zweck' notwendig verdunkelt oder ganz ausgelöscht werden muß" (Nietzsche, *Werke in drei Bänden*, pp. 817–818.).

9 Nietzsche, *On the Genealogy of Morals*, p. 77.

This second use of the "chain" (*Kette*) seems to reverse the first, figuring the will as a chain of signs, a long sign-chain of the will, that indicates its uneven history. When the text makes this shift, the will, still called noble, not only adapts to new circumstances, but endows its customary utterances, including promises, with new meaning, divorcing it from its original and animating intention. Indeed, therefore, to be a noble is precisely *not* to keep one's promise regardless of circumstance.

But here Nietzsche wants the noble to elude the self-terrorizing practice of the slave at the same time that he elevates the promise as the right and entitlement of the noble. What remains unclear, however, is whether the promise can be kept without some measure of self-terrorization. Nietzsche proposes that "something of the terror that formerly attended all promises, pledges, and vows on earth is still effective."[10] If the noble's promise does not elude that terror, is it a result of a certain self-terrorization, a terrorization of the will? And if so, is the conscience that is said to belong to the noble any different from the conscience that is said to belong to the slave? Can the noble, in other words, forget his terror and still sustain his promise?

The promise in Nietzsche seems to arise, then, from a necessary self-affliction, a terrorizing which was originally directed against the other which now preserves the Other, one might say in a Kleinian vein, precisely through a certain kind of sustainable damage to the self. Levinas' explanation clearly differs insofar as the wound is not to be understood as the reflexive form that aggression toward the Other takes, but constitutes something of the primary violence that marks our vulnerable, passive, and necessary relation to that Other. Indeed, for Levinas, the "I" is split from the start precisely by this yielding to the Other which is its primary mode of being and its irreducible relationality. Nietzsche's noble at first appears as an individuated figure, distinct from the slave, but are these figures actually distinct from one another? Indeed, does the one figure interrupt the other in much the same way that the Levinasian subject is fundamentally interrupted by its Other? Is Nietzsche's wounded relation to the promise which is, after all, invariably a promise to the Other any different from Levinas' wounded relation to alterity?

Just as, for Nietzsche, the injury to and by the other is "burned in the will," so Levinas writes that "The Other is in me and in the midst of my very identification."[11] The Levinasian subject, we might say, also bears no grudges, assumes responsibility without ressentiment:

---

10 Ibid., p. 61.

11 Ibid., p. 125.

"In suffering *by* the fault of the Other dawns suffering *for* the fault of Others." Indeed, this self is "accused by the Other to the point of persecution" and this very persecution implies a responsibility for the persecutor.[12] Thus, to be persecuted and to be accused for this subject are that for which one takes responsibility: "[...] the position of the subject [...] is [...] a substitution by a hostage expiating for the violence of the persecution itself."[13] Importantly, there is no self prior to its persecution by the Other. It is that persecution that establishes the Other at the heart of the self, and establishes that "heart" as an ethical relation of responsibility. To claim the self-identity of the subject is thus an act of irresponsibility, an effort to close off one's fundamental vulnerability to the Other, the primary accusation that the Other bears. This is "an accusation I cannot answer, but for which I cannot decline responsibility."[14] This primary responsibility for the persecutor establishes the basis for ethical responsibility.

Levinas dedicated *Otherwise than Being* "to the memory of those who were closest among the six million assassinated by the National Socialists, and of the millions and millions of all confessions and all nations, victims of the same hatred of the other (*la même haine de l'autre homme*], the same anti-Semitism." And just when it appears that Levinas has installed the Jew as the paradigm of all victimization, he warns on the next page against Zionist persecution, citing the precautionary words of Pascal: "'That is my place in the sun.' That is how the usurpation of the whole world began."[15] And if it were not enough that the Jew figured here is *both* victim and persecutor, Levinas cites from Ezekiel the direct address of a God who bears the same double status, requiring violence and repentance at once: "if a righteous man turn from his righteousness [...] his blood will I require at your hands," and then, "pass through the city – through Jerusalem – and set a mark upon the foreheads of the men who sigh and cry for all the abominations that are done in the midst of it." But then, of course, God commits an abomination himself, instructing another man to follow the man he just instructed: "pass through the city after him and slay without mercy or pity. Old men, young men and maidens, little children and women –

12 Ibid., p. 126.

13 Ibid., p. 127.

14 "Accusation, en ce sens persécutrice, à laquelle le persécuté ne peut pas répondre – ou plus exactement – accusation à laquelle je ne peux répondre – mais dont je ne peux décliner la responsibilité." Emmanuel Levinas, *Autrement qu'être ou au-delà de l'essence*, 2nd edition (The Hague: M. Nijhoff, 1978), p. 127.

15 "Voilà le commencement et l'image de l'usurpation de toute la terre." Ibid., p. 202.

strike them all dead! But touch no one on whom is the mark. And begin at my sanctuary!" Thus, God endeavors to save from destruction those who bemoan the abominations, but he commits an abomination precisely in the act of providing salvation. Thus, God cannot condemn abomination without that condemnation becoming an abomination itself. Even with God, good and evil are less than distinct.

The subject who might seek to become righteous according to the ways of such a God will be one who is not only accused and persecuted from the start, but one who is also accusing and persecuting. In this view, there is no innocence, only the navigations of ambivalence, since it seems to be impossible to be persecuted without at once being or becoming the persecutor as well. What remains to be considered is how this scene of ethical inversion nevertheless leads to a responsibility that is, by definition it seems, constantly confounded by self-preservation and its attendant aggressions. If there is no becoming ethical save through a certain violence, then how are we to gauge the value of such an ethics? Is it the only mode for ethics, and what becomes of an ethics of nonviolence? And how often does the violence of ethics, seen most clearly when in the act of righteous denunciation,[16] pose the question of the value of the ethical relation itself? Certain kinds of values, such as generosity and forgiveness, may only be possible through a suspension of this mode of ethicality and, indeed, by calling into question the value of ethics itself.

Levinas recognizes that it is not always possible to live or love well under such conditions. He refers to this primary ethical relation to alterity as "breathless," as if the Other is what is breathed in and preserved within the hollow of the self, as if this very preservation puts the life of the ethical subject at risk. I don't know whether air that is not exhaled comes close to becoming "bad air," but certainly the ethical bearing in this instance degrades the biological conditions of life. Given that the Levinasian subject also rehearses an "insomniac vigilance" in relation to the Other, it may still be necessary to continue to call for "good air" and to find a place for the value of self-preservation, if one wants, for instance, to breathe and to sleep.

---

16 See various acts of moral denunciation of late delivered against critical theorists working with the resources of the continental philosophical tradition.

Frank Ruda

Thinking Politics Concretely Negation, Affirmation, and the Dialectics of Dialectics and Non-Dialectics

"For me… politics is always at a distance from the established order and comfort and relates to them by perpetually questioning them." (Samira Marzuk)[1]

Introduction: The Crisis of Negation and the Need to Renew Materialist Dialectics

One of the most interesting claims concerning contemporary forms of politics and resistance, at least in my understanding, was articulated by a French militant organization formerly called "organization politique,"[2] now called "contre le mauvais gouvernement, les volontaires d'une politique à la distance de l'état"[3]; and it takes the following form: The 21st century has not yet begun.[4] What this claim addresses is that when it comes to political resistance, or more generally to political action, we are still thinking in the terms of the 20th century. What were those terms? This becomes intelligible if one considers the victorious forms of resistance, or more adequately, of revolution that took place in the 20th century. Consider for example the Leninist model of political action and resistance to the dominant (imperialist) mode of oppression[5]: It was a party-based model of organizing collective political

1 Samira Marzuk, "La politique est une parole qui se prend," *Le Journal politique* 10 (2005): p. 12. (Translation F.R.)

2 For this, see also Peter Hallward's interesting interview with Alain Badiou in: Alain Badiou, *Ethics. An Essay on the Understanding of Evil* (London/New York: Verso, 2001), pp. 95–144. Also see their self-description and declarations (http://web.archive.org/web/20071016140303/http://orgapoli.net/spip.php?rubrique14, publ. 01/2007, cit. 04/2012).

3 Compare (http://journalpolitique.blogspot.com, publ. 04/2009, cit. 04/2012). Concerning this name – which itself contains the most crucial axioms and political stances of the group – let me just briefly quote one of their comments: "We have found a new word, an important word, a word which concerns the whole world; everyone can decide if this politics is good, is true, is useful and if it helps, if it allows to think, to act and to be involved." See also their internet site cited above.

4 Re-arcticulated in: Alain Badiou, "Le 21e siècle. Entretien avec Elie During," (http://www.ciepfc.fr/spip.php?article57, publ. 12/2008, cit. 04/2012).

5 For the following reconstruction also see: Frank Ruda and Jan Völker, "Was heißt es, ein Marxist in der Philosophie zu sein?," Alain Badiou, *Ist Politik denkbar?*, trans.

action, and the central aim of the party was to take state power. So the political framework within which Lenin was thinking and acting was one wherein the central issue was victory, and this very issue was defined in terms of taking power – taking power only to transform the state from within, into a non-state, into the famous dictatorship of the proletariat that would eventually lead to the state as such withering away. In consequence, this victory was only possible if the mode of organization itself was a military one, able to confront the dominant forces, the dominant powers of imperialism – that is to say: also military and police forces – on its own terrain, i.e. the state. The central question that Lenin attempted to answer was therefore: how can we be victorious, how can we win the war?[6] This is why the organization had to be a military one, employing violent means where necessary in order to counter the system. This question is clearly inherited from the Paris Commune.[7] The underlying logic of the theme of revolution, that is to say a victorious insurrection taking power was therefore what, in somewhat Althusserian or more precisely Badiousian terms, one can call an expressive dialectics.[8]

Following the famous scheme that Lenin formulated, this model of an expressive dialectics designates that masses are divided into classes, that classes are organized by parties, and that parties are led by leaders.[9] So the avant-garde of the party, that is to say, the profes-

---

Frank Ruda and Jan Völker (Berlin: Merve, 2010), pp.135–165.

6 What sort of problematic consequences were implied by this conception of political action as an expansion of war within the intra-statist realm – for example, in terms of defining and dealing with the adversary (after the revolution) – can be seen in: Alain Badiou, *The Communist Idea and the Question of Terror* (Typescript).

7 For an impressive history of the Paris Commune, see: Prosper Olivier Lissagaray, *The History of the Paris Commune of 1871* (London/New York: Verso, 2012). An analysis of the Commune can also be found in: Alain Badiou, "The Paris Commune: A Political Declaration on Politics," *The Communist Hypothesis* (London/New York: Verso, 2010), pp. 168–228.

8 See: Alain Badiou, "Politics: A Non-Expressive Dialectics, "*Beyond Potentialities? Politics between the Possible and the Impossible*, ed. Mark Potocnik, Frank Ruda, and Jan Völker (Zurich: diaphanes, 2011), pp. 13–22; Louis Althusser and Etienne Balibar, *Reading Capital* (London: NLB, 1975), p. 17.

9 This formula can be found in: Vladimir I. Lenin, "Left-Wing Communism: an Infantile Disorder," *Collected Works*, Vol. 31, April-December 1920 (Moscow: Progress Publishers, 1966), pp. 17–118. It reads in Lenin's words as follows: "It is common knowledge that the masses are divided into classes, that the masses can be contrasted with classes only by contrasting the vast majority in general… - classes are led by political parties; that political parties, as a general rule, are run by more or less stable groups composed of the most authoritative, influential and experienced members, who are elected to the most responsible positions, and are called leaders.

sional revolutionary leaders, had to express the contradiction immanent to the masses due to their organization into classes. What this whole conception is based upon is a very powerful interpretation of what abstract and determinate negation is. There is an abstract negation inherent to the social organization of masses into classes,[10] i.e. class struggle; this negation that articulates itself in the form of domination of one class over the other can be overcome if it and what it fundamentally relies upon, i.e. the use of violent force of the military and ideological power of the state apparatuses, is itself determinately negated. Resistance could only be victorious if it was conceived of in terms of determinately negating the present abstract negation of the domination of one class over another. Now, this model of thinking resistance and resistant political action – in terms of a state revolution organized by a centralized party – encountered fundamental obstacles that it was unable to overcome. To conceive of emancipatory political action, resistance or revolution within the constellation power-state-party was indeed victorious when it came to taking power, but it was not when it came to the exercise of power. This can be seen in the fundamental failures of the final outcomes of the October Revolution, but also in many respects that are different but formally comparable in the Cultural Revolution.[11] The centralized party that had taken power came with a tendency towards (immanently capitalist) bureaucratization, a tendency that the Trotskyites, quite adequately, called state-terrorism,[12] and the Maoists themselves called reformism.[13] This is why today the word revolution is completely obscure.[14] No one knows

All this is elementary. All this is clear and simple" (Ibid., p. 38). For this see also: Sylvain Lazarus, "Lenin and the Party, 1902 – November 1917," *Lenin Reloaded: Toward a Politics of Truth,* ed. Sebastian Budgen, Stathis Kouvelakis, and Slavoj Žižek (Durham: Duke University Press, 2007), pp. 255–268.

10 This can also be rendered in the following way. According to the bourgeoisie, the proletariat is the complete negation, that is to say: abstract negation of all that defines an ordinary existence in the bourgeois world. It is thus a non-existence.

11 Compare Alain Badiou, "The Communist Idea and the Question of Terror"; Alain Badiou, "The Cultural Revolution: The Last Revolution?," *The Communist Hypothesis* (London/New York: Verso, 2010), pp. 101–167.

12 Compare Leon Trotsky, *Terrorism and Communism: A Reply to Karl Kautsky* (London/New York: Verso, 2007).

13 Compare Mao Ze Dong, "The Situation and the Task in the Anti-Japanese War After the Fall of Shanghai and Taiyuan," *Mao's Road to Power: Revolutionary Writings 1912–1949,*Vol. 6: August 1937–1938 (New York: Sharpe, 2004), pp. 148–156. For detailed analyses of the different stages of the Cultural Revolution, one cannot but refer to the passionate work of Alessandro Russo.

14 For a more extensive elaboration of this diagnosis, see my: "Remembering the Impossible. For a Meta-Critical Anamnesis of Communism," *The Idea of Communism*

what it could mean. The revolutionary idea, as can be seen for example in the adaptation it received under Stalin – although in a certain sense one might argue that Stalin already took a reactive and defensive position against the universalist core of Leninist politics[15] – this very revolutionary idea was swallowed by what Hegel once called a logic of suspicion[16] that described the general state of things.

One can see in Stalin a literally perverse universalism: if the October Revolution was supposed to address everyone, under Stalin it is precisely anyone that was suspected of being a counter-revolutionary. Now, all these are moments that indicate that the model of the party with all its implications (victoriously resistant insurrection, taking state power, etc.) is saturated today.[17] The central point for addressing the question of political resistance today is thus, it seems to me, to give an answer to the question of how to conceive and how to invent a non-military discipline and new forms of organization that are detached, or rather: subtracted from power, from the party, and (first and foremost) from the state. This is both a political and a philosophical task. Why should this in any plausible way also be rendered as a task of contemporary philosophical thinking? Because as I pointed out, the 20th century model of revolution as presented in Lenin relied upon a specific expressive dialectics which included an interpretation of how determinate negation has to be thought and put into practice when it comes to concrete political action. With the saturation of the (power-)state-party model, what Badiou called a "crisis of negation"[18] necessarily also emerges. If negation is the central category of any Hegelian, but also post-Hegelian – for example, Marxian – dialectics

---

2. The New York Conference, ed. Slavoj Žižek (London/New York: Verso, 2013, forthcoming).

15 The best analysis of Stalinist Russia can be found in: J. Arch Getty, Oleg V. Naumov, *The Road to Terror: Stalin and the Self-Destruction of the Bolsheviks, 1932–1939* (Yale: Yale University Press, 2010). For a broader contextualization of the Stalinist "perversion" of the Leninist model, see: Slavoj Žižek, *Did Somebody say Totalitarianism? Five Interventions into the (Mis)Use of a Notion* (London/New York: Verso, 2002); Alain Badiou, *Metapolitics* (London/New York: Verso, 2005), pp. 68–77.

16 For a detailed account of this Hegelian characterization of the French Revolution and its actuality, see the impressive book: Rebecca Comay, *Mourning Sickness: Hegel and the French Revolution* (Stanford: Stanford University Press, 2011). An abridged analysis can also be found in: Frank Ruda, *Hegel's Rabble. An Investigation into Hegel's Philosophy of Right* (London/New York: Continuum, 2011), pp. 143–145.

17 On the notion of "Saturation," see my entry on it in: Steve Corcoran, ed., *The Badiou Dictionary* (Oxford: OUP, forthcoming).

18 Compare "The Crisis of Negation: An Interview with Alain Badiou," (http://continentcontinent.cc/index.php/continent/article/viewArticle/65, publ. 08/2009, cit. 04/2012).

and today the task is to find new means of political organization and a new popular discipline, one can claim that one essential task is to re-think negation, to re-think dialectics. What is needed is to re-think negation and dialectics in such a manner as not to remain within the schemes of the 20th century when it comes to conceiving political resistance, or – more broadly – conceiving any concrete political action. Today, thus, the following holds: Re-thinking dialectics is needed to think politics concretely; and concretely means to be able to take into account the experiences of the 20th century and the knowledge that the means employed in it are saturated, and also to start thinking what emancipatory politics can be here and now, that is to say: what forms of organization and discipline can be invented without falling into the deadlocks, avoiding the impasses of the last century. Or to put it in Freudian terms: one should repeat, remember and work through dialectics.[19] And this means: to repeat, remember and work-through its central category, the category of negation. Only in this way might we be able to exit the 20th century and let the 21st century finally begin.

Working through Negation, or: From One to Multiple Negations

Working-through dialectics is in a certain sense a repetition of the gesture that Marx himself introduced in the 1840s.[20] One may say that he reworked Hegelian dialectics and especially the concept of negation – think for example of his famous definition of the proletariat as negation of everything that the bourgeoisie includes in its definition of a human being.[21] Therefore we seem to be in a comparable situation. Working through dialectics means repeating Marx. But how can one repeat him today? How to repeat the Marxian gesture of working-through negation? This is to say: How can one develop a contemporary understanding – capable of including the knowledge that the former model of political action is saturated – of what negation is? My thesis is that one

19 And this is also to say: This repetition, remembering, and working through, has to be done by politics *and* philosophy. For the Freudian formula, see: Sigmund Freud, "Remembering, Repeating, Working Through (Further Recommendations on the Technique of Psycho-Analysis II)," *Standard Edition of the Complete Psychological Works of Sigmund Freud, Vol. XII (1911–1913): The Case of Schreber, Papers on Technique and Other Works* (London: The Hogarth Press, 1986), pp. 145–156.

20 I have elaborated how to conceive of contemporary attempts to work-through Marx in: Frank Ruda, "Remembering, Repeating, Working-Through Marx. Badiou, Žižek and The Actualization of Marxism," *Revue Internationale de Philosophie* (2012).

21 For this see: Frank Ruda, "Humanism, or: Life living Life," *Filozofski Vestnik*, Vol. XX, No. 2 (2009): pp. 175–193.

can find essential means for this task in the oeuvre of Alain Badiou. In an important article, Badiou distinguishes three forms of negation, whose relationship allows taking first steps to a renewal of materialist dialectics.[22] The first form of negation that he introduces is the classical one that can be found in Aristotelian *Metaphysics*. Aristotle develops a crucial framework for thinking negation. For he shows that thinking in general is determined by three principles: 1. The *principle of identity* that signifies that any proposition is equivalent to itself, i.e. to its truth content. 2. The *principle of contradiction* that signifies that it is impossible that in the same context the proposition P and the proposition non-P can be true at the same time. 3. The *principle of excluded middle* that signifies that for a proposition P holds that it is either true or false – either P is true or non-P is true. The power of negation in this Aristotelian model is structured in a twofold way: First there is a *power of exclusion* inherent to negation: the proposition P excludes the validity of the proposition non-P. Secondly there is a *power of a forced decision* inherent to it: Either P or non-P is valid, there is no third option. *For classical negation never holds that "yes" and "no" are valid at the same time and in turn it always holds that either "yes" or "no" is valid.* The classical negation is what Badiou calls "the core of classical logic."[23] But as one can easily see, there are more than just the classical forms of negation. Even remaining within the framework of these three Aristotelian principles, other logical combinations can be derived that introduce different forms of negation:

Negation is only *classical* when it follows the principle of contradiction and the principle of excluded middle. One can also think of a form of negation that only follows the principle of contradiction, but not the principle of the excluded middle; then one can think of a negation that only follows the principle of the excluded middle but not the principle of contradiction; and finally one can think of a negation that follows neither of these two principles. This last form of negation loses all power of negation because it neither prescribes a decision nor does it exclude anything – this form of negation knows negation only as itself negated.[24]

---

22 Alain Badiou, "The Three Negations," *Cardozo Law Review* 29:5 (2008): pp. 1877–1883. The most crucial parts of the subsequent argument I derive from this article, although an elaboration of the following logical distinctions can already be found in: Alain Badiou, *Logics of Worlds. Being and Event, 2* (London/New York: Continuum, 2009), pp. 183–185 and 189–190. The famous distinction between "democratic materialism" and a "materialist dialectics" was first developed in this book.

23 Badiou, "The Three Negations," p. 1878.

24 It is Slavoj Žižek who has argued in a personal conversation that it is precisely this fourth form of negation which is – contrary to the Badiousian argument – the most powerful and effective. It would describe the operation of negation that is proper to

The second form of negation, only following the principle of contradiction but not of excluded middle, is what Badiou calls the *intuitionist logic of negation*; the third, only following the principle of excluded middle but not of contradiction he calls *paraconsistent*. As he puts it:

> In fact the potency of negation is weaker and weaker when you go from one to three. [...] In intuitionist logic, the negation of P excludes P itself, but not some other possibilities which are in fact somewhere between P and non-P. In paraconsistent logic, the negation of P excludes that sort of space between P and non-P, but not P itself. So P is not suppressed by its negation.[25]

It is important to note that for Badiou the classical logic of negation corresponds to the discourse of ontology.[26] For his definition of being qua being – from his, i.e. from a set theoretical perspective, being is discursively presented as a multiplicity of multiplicities, whose consistency is only guaranteed by the void, the empty set –, the principle of extensionality is fundamental[27]: This means that an element of a set belongs to the set or does not belong to it. Either P (the element belongs to the set) is true or it is false, there is no third option. Any difference between two multiplicities – or two sets – thus follows from the fact – and only from the fact – that some element of one set is not an element of the other.[28] If one accepts the Badiousian framework[29]

---

the actions of the proletariat, as the proletariat can only negate the bourgeois world which produces it, by self-negating itself. One can already see traces of this in his quarrel with Badiou over the role of the "negation of negation" in Mao. Compare Mao, *De la pratique et de la contradiction. Avec une lettre d'Alain Badiou et la réponse de Slavoj Žižek* (Paris: La Fabrique, 2008). My following remarks attempt to show that what Žižek is rightly aiming at can be rendered in even more precise terms when considering the relation between the three forms of negation I will develop subsequently.

25 Badiou, "The Three Negations," p. 1879.

26 I cannot develop the defense of this argument here. For a detailed reconstruction, see: Frank Ruda, "Exiting the Woods. Cartesianism for the 21st Century (to come)," *Monokl, Reflections on Alain Badiou* (Istanbul 2012).

27Compare Alain Badiou, *Being and Event* (London/New York: Continuum, 2005).

28 This is precisely what the principle of extensionality means. There is no presumed givenness of the elements that all share a common trait or attribute. Rather, elements are contingently collected into the unity of a set, and sets only differ due to the elements they contain – and not due to attributes that all the gathered elements share. The latter presupposition is what defines the intensional conception of set theory.

29 This is not an idiosyncratic preference. It can be demonstrated that the link of ontology and classical logic is the only consistent way of treating certain paradoxes of the One and the Multiple that occur within any ontology – may it consider itself to be political or not.

this means that any form of negation that complies with the principle of contradiction and of excluded middle is not only classical but also ontological.

Yet, if classical negation is ontological, what is the status of the intuitionist logic of negation? The Badiousian answer is that such logic is the logic of appearance.[30] The ontological determination of what a multiplicity is can be distinguished from how it appears, with which intensity, in which guise: for example, if it appears in the shadows or in the brightest (or in a red) light. Although one can show that the intuitionist logic of negation is grounded in the classical one – because something cannot appear absolutely in a world and with maximal intensity and at the same time not appear in it – it is not true that within the realm of appearances one has to decide between P and non-P. A multiplicity cannot appear and not appear or exist and not exist at the same time, but it can appear or exist in multiple ways and forms or intensities. There is a multiplicity of third possibilities. The multiple "A" can appear more or less intense than "non-A," or vice versa. Therefore the principle of contradiction is valid, but not the principle of excluded middle – "A" can appear as "B" between the absolute appearance "A" and the absolute non-appearance "non-A". "A" can appear in between the maximum and the minimum of appearance. This form of negation is therefore not only intuitionist, but also linked to the discourse of appearance: to phenomenology.

To finally come to the third form of negation, the paraconsistent one – following the principle of excluded middle but not of contradiction –, one has to introduce, besides ontology and phenomenology, that which Badiou calls an event.[31] An event is logically related to being as well as to appearance. One can therefore ask: 1. What sort of multiplicity does an event name (ontologically)? 2. How does an event appear (phenomenally)? 1. An event is a contradictory multiplicity whose definition is to belong to itself – it has the property that axiomatically is prohibited (following the axiomatization of Zermelo-Fraenkel[32]) for any other multiple (or set).[33] This means that *on the level of ontology, an event is neither classical* – because it does not

---

30 For this in general, see: Badiou, *Logics of Worlds*.

31 For the most succinct formulations of the notion of the event, the reader is here once again referred back to Badiou's main works, *Being and Event* and *Logics of Worlds*.

32 A good reconstruction of the axiomatization of mathematics can be found in: Shaughan Lavine, *Understanding the Infinite* (Harvard: Harvard University Press, 1998).

33 For this also see: Badiou, *Being and Event*, pp. 201–254.

comply with the principle of contradiction – *nor intuitionist*. It is from this perspective that it can be called *paraconsistent*. But one has to be more precise here, because an event might be in itself nothing but paraconsistent but the definition it finds in Badiou contains another central point: it is nothing but the ensemble of the consequences it will have produced. An event is measured only by the consequences it is able to generate and can therefore only be thought in the linkage of being and appearances.[34] Because if the event, lest it turn into some miraculous intervention, is itself nothing substantial, one has to claim that the only thing that appears are its consequences. 2. How does an event appear? Here, two answers have to be given: On the one hand, the event is phenomenally the identity of appearance and disappearance. It is the "vanishing mediator"[35] that appears to be paraconsistent, but this does not change the fact that one can only decide what it will have been if one considers whether it produced concrete consequences (within a given historical situation) or not. Therefore its (ontologically) paraconsistent form necessitates a decision. When it is not clear whether something happened or not, a decision is needed. This decision can only take the form of a "yes" or a "no," but never the form of a "yes and no" at the same time. Therefore an event conjures the classical form of negation; it demands the power of exclusion and the power of decision. If an event is nothing but the ensemble of the consequences that it yields, one can claim that these consequences are only measured by the fact that one either said "yes" or "no" to the forced choice that it necessitates; and it is also measured by what (immediately) follows from this yes or no, from the acceptance of the choice or the indifference towards it. Therefore an event is in a certain sense *diagonal towards the classical, intuitionist and paraconsistent* form of negation.[36] But what does that mean?

One can start by stating that an event designates a sudden change of the laws that regulate the realm of appearance. Something that seemed impossible now appears in the form of a previously unthinkable possibility. Therefore an event is not directly the creation of "something" new, rather the creation of a new possibility, of a formerly non-existent

34 Badiou, *Logics of Worlds*, pp. 355–380.

35 Fredric Jameson, "The Vanishing Mediator. Narrative Structure in Max Weber," *New German Critique* 1 (1973): pp. 52–89.

36 Another way of formulating this would be: An event is that which links the three forms of negation together – the vanishing mediator without which there is simply no relation between them.

possibility.[37] If it were only the creation of something new, it would mainly be destructive,[38] but in this way it also enables the integration of something old into the construction of something new that unfolds the consequences of this new possibility.[39] But the question is precisely how far-reaching the change is which this new possibility produces. The greatest change that an event can inaugurate is the transformation of something that does not appear in a world – for example, assume that "non-A" does not appear in it – into something that appears in a world – for example, "A" yet appears. Or to put it differently: an event is what is capable of transforming the appearance of the workers that "are nothing," as the *Internationale* has it, – i.e. that do not appear at all in the world – in such a way that they become "all" – i.e. appear maximally[40]; and it is that which thereby changes the historically specific logic of appearance. This transformation is evental; it is followed and constituted by true actions of resistance and follows the classical logic. Why? Because the workers that did not appear before, now appear maximally. At the same time, the consequences of the event

---

37 This is why an event is what Badiou calls a "supplement" to being. Although this might sound Derridean, with Badiou it is clear that this supplement has to be conceived of in a so-called *subtractive way*. This simply means the following: If for example in mathematics we subtract something (we write 3–2 = X), we in some sense add something to what is given. But the mode in which we subtractively supplement that which is given implies that the "something" we add to the given is not a positive supplement. In a precise and simple sense, the subtractive supplement implies a disappearance (the "-2" in the example supplements the "3" but is only qualified by the disappearance – of the "2" – that is indicated by the minus, the very symbol constituting the supplement). Or in Badiou's words: "If a truth cannot come from the given (*une donation*), it is because it originates in a disappearance. This original disappearance, which came, for the time of a flash, to supplement the situation, and which is not localized within the latter except insofar as nothing of it subsists, and which insists *in truth* precisely insofar as it cannot be repeated as presence – this is what I call an 'event'." Alain Badiou, "Truth: Forcing and the Unnameable," *Conditions* (London/New York: Continuum, 2008), pp. 129–144, p. 132.

38 This is in some sense what the early Badiou would have claimed, insisting that change occurs when "something" – a force – is placed in a historical setting and comes to re-determine itself by destructing the determination it received by the space of places it was put in. Compare Alain Badiou, *Theory of the Subject* (London/New York: Continuum, 2009).

39 Thus the "new" also includes a renewed organization of the old. As Žižek once put it: "The only way to grasp the true novelty of the New is to analyze the world through the lenses of what is an 'eternal' in the old." Compare Slavoj Žižek, *First as Tragedy, then as Farce* (London/New York: Verso, 2009), p. 6.

40 Compare Badiou, *Logics of Worlds*, pp. 391–393. For a short version of this also see: Alain Badiou, *Second Manifesto for Philosophy* (Cambridge/Malden: Polity, 2011).

have to be thought through from the perspective of the two other logics, the intuitionist and the paraconsistent one. Either the consequences of the event are classical: "non-A" appears instead of "A"; or intuitionist: "non-A" appears as "B," which does not replace the appearance of "A" by the appearance of "non-A" (the workers appear, but this appearance does not generate a new formation of the laws of appearance, rather it inaugurates a reform or modification of these laws). Or else, finally, the consequences of the event are paraconsistent. In this case the fundamental framework of appearance is respected, the distinction of "A" and "non-A" is not touched at all. The paraconsistent form of transformation leads to the fact that it remains unclear if a transformation of the frame and of the laws of appearance happened or not. From the perspective of the world, everything remains the same, the event and the non-event are identical and the consequences are null.[41] Evental consequences, as one can summarize, can either be classical, intuitionist, or paraconsistent.

If any world of appearance is organized intuitionistically, any real political action must follow the classical logic of negation, and pseudo-actions clearly follow the logic of paraconsistent negation. But once again, one needs to be more precise here: My claim is that true political action has to be organized classically and mobilizes the double power of negation – of exclusion and forced decision –; which also implies that one needs to take into account that the consequences of the exclusive decision develop in an intuitionistically regulated world, in which multiple ways and alternatives of their materialization are possible: there are multiple third options of how evental consequences might appear. This step is necessary to avoid the false belief that one single "yes" or one single "no" could be sufficient to build the ground for all consequences.[42] In fact they have to be – and they are always – unfolded in infinitely many nuances within the realm of appearances.[43] And it has to be noted

41 Paraconsistent consequences of an event are thus indistinguishable from no consequences at all. In some sense this indistinguishability of the event and the non-event is a result of the pure – and neurotic-fetishist – insistence on the possibility of a choice. This insistence is precisely – as Descartes already argued – the lowest form of freedom. The author is preparing a systematic investigation of these questions under the provisional title: "Indifference and Repetition. Descartes, Hegel, Plato."

42 In some sense, this assumption is precisely what I would define as the essence of *dogmatism*.

43 This does not only hold for political action. To take a different example: Although the elaborated formal conception of the emergence of true change can also render intelligible how to conceive of a love encounter, each love encounter yields radically different appearances of consequences. Any practice of love can be described in these terms, although any concrete love practice appears to be fully different from

that an event – due to the fact that it appears within the phenomenal world in the form of a classical negation – is not shared by everyone. Not everyone affirms that something happened, not everyone answers the forced choice with a "yes" – some remained indifferent to the event of the October Revolution, for example.[44] One needs to think a relation between the three logics because *the ontologically paraconsistent event appears as classical negation* – something has happened or hasn't happened, and there is not third option – *within an intuitionist framework*, in which a multiplicity of consequences are possible, and at the same time there is a (paraconsistent) opposition to it/them, for not everyone shares the initial "yes" as answer to the forced choice. Also, within the procedure of unfolding the consequences –which Badiou calls fidelity[45] – there is always a temptation to transform the "yes or no" into a "yes and no." "Yes," something has happened; but "no," I do not have to draw consequences from it. This is the paradigmatic form of the *paraconsistent temptation*, or to put it differently: this is the *logic of seduction*.[46] Against it, one has to constantly perpetuate the power of exclusion and forced decision to not abate the ongoing unfolding of consequences. There has to be a continually perpetuated "yes" – this is also why the only imperative of an ethics of truth is "Continue!"[47] – which constantly, albeit taking place inside a world, subtracts from all differences – national, local, gender specific ones, etc. – that seem to be fundamental and essential in and for the world. True political action is the concrete articulation within a world, taking multiple different shapes, of a *constantly perpetuated classicism*, of the permanence of exclusion and forced decision against paraconsistent temptations.

It is precisely this relation between the three negations – the three logics of negation – that presents the matrix of a new dialectical conception (of political action). It is *dialectical* in as much as it is a relation of different types of negations that are its motor; and at the same time, it is *materialist* because it considers the concrete consequences produced by the relations of the negations. But this matrix, to the extent to which I presented it, arguably contains only the objective side of

---

any other (from the employed terms of endearment to the music the loving couple listens to, etc.).

44 This is precisely the origin of what Badiou calls the reactionary and the obscure subject. Compare Badiou, *Logics of Worlds*, pp. 54–61.

45 Compare Badiou, *Being and Event*, pp. 201–264. See also Frank Ruda, "Von der Treue als subtraktiver Institution," *Ereignis und Institution. Anknüpfungen an Alain Badiou*, ed. Gernot Kamecke and Henning Teschke (Tübingen: Narr, 2008), p. 69–96.

46 This is also what Mannoni called the fetishist disavowal. Compare Octave Mannoni, *Freud: The Theory of the Unconscious* (London: NLB, 1971).

47 Compare Badiou, *Ethics*, pp. 52.

a renewed materialist dialectics. It is also imperative to consider its subjective side.

From Objective to Subjective Materialist Dialectics, or: From Negation to Determinate Affirmation

To recapitulate: *The ontologically paraconsistent event appears in the form of classical negation, in the realm of the phenomenal that is organized following the intuitionist logic, and its consequences, albeit taking multiple different concrete forms, are either paraconsistent or classical.* Now the central question is: How does the procedure of unfolding the consequences of an event start, and how is it perpetuated? I already indicated that it can only start with a "yes," with an affirmation of the forced decision that the event introduces. So the event first subtracts from all the differences of appearance, or better: it condenses them into one point, into the choice between a "yes," something happened and I have to draw consequences from it, or a "no," nothing happened.[48] Subtraction then means to insist on the primacy of the principle of contradiction over the principle of excluded middle, which is not valid in intuitionism. The event therefore is no event without its subjective affirmation initially inaugurating the procedure of fidelity. The event is the vanishing mediator, the clinamen that marks a breaking-in, an emergence of something[49] that can only gain consistency through a primary "yes," which then is perpetuated and repeated constantly – without knowing any constitutive and immanent limitation to its continuity.

---

48 This is why an event implies three different maneuvers: An operation of intensification, an operation of contraction and an operation of localization. Compare Alain Badiou, *Le Réveil de l'Histoire. Circonstances, 6* (Paris: Lignes, 2011), pp. 104–106.

49 Throughout this treatise, I leave aside one crucial question: Where can an event take place? This question of localization is essential to fully develop the concrete levels of the dialectical matrix I am elaborating here. As this implies three things – 1. a detailed reconstruction of what Badiou calls an "evental site" (Compare Badiou, *Being and Event*, pp. 173–190; Badiou, *Logics of Worlds*, pp. 355–396), which could lead into a renewal of "political places"; 2. a systematic reading of how presentation and representation relate to one another (ontologically), an argument for the fact that representation is never abolishable, and an answer to the question how the presentation and representation relate to the (phenomenological) distinction between existence and inexistence; and 3. a systematic connection of these two layers with the overall dialectical conception I developed here – for reasons of space I leave this crucial topic for another time and place.

The event is itself nothing objective as such, but can only be(come) what it will have been through the subjective intervention(s) that first start(s) with what I would like to call a *determinate affirmation*,[50] the "yes" to a concretely determined choice. But at the same time, one "yes," one determinate affirmation, is never enough. Although it already changes the situation – it makes something appear which did not appear before. For example, in love the evental encounter does not itself produce anything but the possibility of a "yes" to a choice that allows to draw consequences from it, and only these consequences produce something that did not appear before: a loving couple which is the "subjective body,"[51] the objective materialization and incorporation of the consequences of the evental encounter; and as everyone knows: this immediately changes the concrete situation. But this is also why the "yes" has to be repeated in the situation that already changed because of the first "yes" – to stay within the example: the appearance of a couple is related to questions of organization in a very concrete manner, where to go for a holiday, how to spend time together, should one move in together or not, etc. *The subjective determinate affirmation has to be apt to sustain the "yes,"* to sustain classicism facing the world that changes fundamentally through the consequences that are already unfolded in it – and how that is to be done is not foreseeable or deducible. This is also why one – once involved in the unfolding of evental consequences – is never done with being involved. The "yes" has to be (repeatedly) sustained, although it is unforeseeable how. Only in this way can the contingent emergence of a new possibility retroactively gain consistency. Or to put it differently, it may be gained only via the consequences that are unfolded step by step, or – more precisely – "point by point,"[52] i.e. through the continuity of "yes." Only in this way can an event retroactively be considered as that which it will have been, or as one might also put it: Only in this way can an event gain objectivity. The objective side of the renewed materialist dialectics thus fully depends on the subjective determinate affirmation and its continual re-iteration and vice versa.[53]

---

50 I here read Badiou's argument against the background of Hegel's logic of negation. Badiou's worked-through conception of dialectics in my reading thus attempts to replace the primacy of determinate negation with, on the one hand, a complex network of relations between different types of negation, and on the other, with a conception of (subjective) determinate affirmation.

51 Badiou, *Logics of Worlds*, pp. 449–476.

52 For the theory of the points, compare ibid, pp. 397–424.

53 In some sense, one could claim that the paradoxical self-belonging of the event is repeated within the realm of consequences as mutual self-belonging of the objective and subjective side of this dialectical conception. That which emerges as the very

Objective is only what will have been objective by the retroactive effect of the consequences that are nothing but the sustained classicism of subjective determinate affirmation in a changing world, that changes precisely due to the effects of these determinate affirmations, which at the same time rely on the (newly emerged) possibility of a forced choice. One can also say that the constant upholding of the subjective determinate affirmation of the emergence of the retroactively objective classical negation inside the intuitionist framework and against any paraconsistent temptation is a dialectical development that always – this is precisely what retroactivity means – relies upon something that is not itself dialectically deducible. If the consequences that change the world are engendered by something – an event – which itself is nothing but what it will have generated, to not fall back into the pure intuitionist framework (which also was the framework of Hegel and thus in a certain sense of expressive dialectics), one has to insist upon the following claim: *materialist dialectics, in order to remain materialist, has to introduce something that cannot be deduced dialectically* – for in any other way, the event would be substantialized. For materialist dialectics not to fall back into the historically specific (political) shortcomings of (Hegelian and Marxist versions of) expressive dialectics, it has to be understood as a procedure of unfolding consequences, a procedure of attempting to cope with something that, by retroactivity, logically lies before it, is and will always be logically prior to it. *For materialist dialectics not to totalize dialectics* – and therefore hypostasize only one form of negation,[54] for example, the intuitionist one – *it has to be a dialectics of dialectics* (drawing of consequences) *and non-dialectics* (the contingent emergence of a new possibility). Contemporary materialist dialectics should be conceived of in terms of this linkage which I call a *dialectics of dialectics and non-dialectics.*[55]

---

condition of possibility of a new free and forced choice (i.e. the event) is precisely nothing but its consequences (i.e. the event). This is to say: through the perpetuated iteration of determinate affirmations can the consequences of an event be unfolded through which the event becomes an event, although these consequences are grounded in nothing but the contingent emergence of the possibility of a determinate affirmation which, again, is the event.

54 The danger to which I am referring here can also be articulated in the following way: Hypostatizing one form of negation is hypostatizing the One over the multiple. This is something Badiou's whole oeuvre stands against.

55 One important additional remark: Against the formula above, one might raise the objection that the link of dialectics and the non-dialectical could itself also be rendered as non-dialectical. Although I do not have the space to develop a clear-cut systematical answer here, I want to insist on the following: if one refrains from articulating the link of these two levels in a dialectical manner, one ends up with a

To Conclude Polemically
On a Contemporary Paraconsistent Temptation

There is an infamous sentence that can be found in a text called "Marxism and Insurrection," written 1917 and published 1921 by Lenin, and it says: "It is impossible to remain faithful to the revolution" – to that for which the signifier "Marxism"[56] in his conviction essentially stood– "unless insurrection is treated as an art."[57] Under the circumstances of 1917, this sentence seems fully legitimate. One has, as Mao famously put it, always the right to rebel against reactionaries, and this is because troubles, rebellions, are, as he has it elsewhere, an excellent thing.[58] After what I developed so far, one can say that this sentence, today, has to receive a different, renewed interpretation.[59] To render it in a first and provisory version one might be able to say: If art, following a definition by Badiou, is that which gives a form to what previously did not receive a form,[60] one should relate to resistance or insurrection precisely in the sense that we consider it an art: an art of giving a form, a new form to that which right now does not have a form. This is, as I pointed out already, a task at once political

---

dualist, vitalist or procedural ontology (in some sense, these positions have more in common than usually perceived). To put it shortly: Either one claims that "there is the dialectical *and* there is the non-dialectical," and thus posits a two-layer ontology which cannot properly explain their relation (= dualism); or one claims that "there is the dialectical, and there will have been the non-dialectical prior to the dialectical, but only accessible after its emergence" and thus posits – via the logic of retroactivity – a fundamental non-relationality between the two elements involved. My conviction is – and I will demonstrate this in greater detail in the near future – that the only materialist stance has to start from the latter axiom. Or to put it differently yet again: If one does not insist on the possibility of thinking that which retroactively precedes thought as that which can only be thought as being unthinkable, one ends up with one or another version of Aristotelianism (= Idealism).

56 I have investigated the relation of Lenin to the signifier "Marx" and "Marxism" elsewhere. Compare Frank Ruda, "Was ist ein Marxist? Lenins Wiederherstellung der Wahrheit des Namens," *Namen. Benennung, Verehrung, Wirkung (1850–1930)*, ed. Tatjana Petzer, Sylvia Sasse, Franziska Thun-Hohenstein, and Sandro Zanetti (Berlin: Kadmos, 2009), pp. 225–242.

57 Vladimir I. Lenin, "Marxism and Insurrection. A Letter to the Central Committee of the R.S.D.L.P.(B.)," *Collected Works*, Vol. 26 (Moscow: Progress Publishers, 1972), p. 27.

58 More precisely, Mao's phrase goes: There is great disorder under heaven – the situation is excellent.

59 I have presented a first reading of this Leninist idea in: Frank Ruda, "Lenin und das Glück," *Happy Days. Lebenswissen nach Cavell*, ed. Kathrin Thiele and Katrin Trüstedt (Munich: Fink, 2010), pp. 100–106.

60 Compare Badiou, *Logics of Worlds*, pp. 16–20.

and philosophical. It is political, because insurrection cannot be but political; it is philosophical, in as much as one needs to step out of the expressive dialectical schema and its specific deadlocks. Without the necessary linkage of the three forms of negation we will lack the concreteness in (philosophically) thinking politics – one can easily see why this is the case for any philosophy of the political which stipulates a fundamental bond, even a bond of separation, or by the way in which any form of non-dialectical thinking, such as Foucault's endless reworking of the immanent linkage of power and resistance, ends up in pure historicism.[61]

One has therefore to account for the historical specificity of the concrete experiences of the 20th century. It is a task that involves the invention of a new form of organization; a new popular discipline; a renewal of materialist dialectics as dialectics of dialectics and non-dialectics. This is what one can learn from art.[62] Fulfilling this task might once again render a possible (political) *orientation* (for action and resistance) in times of disorientation.[63] If we are still thinking – at least *if* we are thinking – in terms of the 20th century, this means there is a fundamental – historical and timely – disorientation at work. Even *if* we still think, we do not yet think as contemporaries of our time – our time being the time of the saturation of all the political categories of the 20th century. However, one can start from a simple idea: if all that what is, is not necessary – even if it allegedly be or seem so – (and this is in a very primitive way nothing but a negative and abstract indication), there is something else that can be thought as being possible. If we are not all forever doomed to remain within (political, subjective) disorientation, one can insist upon the following: There can be an orientation, there can be a 21st century. But to defend this hypothesis, one has to severely attack all the symptoms of disorientation. And one of the most significant symptoms is the mixing, or – to put it in Lacanian terms – the suturing of domains that should not be sutured. The most prominent suture today, at least in my understanding, is the suture of politics to art. As if any gallery visit in Berlin, Giessen, Munich or wherever could be compared to concrete experiences made, for example within the struggle for liberation in Palestine.

The claim to the contrary is, euphemistically put, highly blind for concrete differences. To redraw the distinction between art and poli-

---

61 See my: Frank Ruda, "Back to the Factory. A Plea for a Renewal of Concrete Analysis of Concrete Situations," *Beyond Potentialities?*, pp. 39–54.

62 Compare Alain Badiou, "The Courage of Obscurantism", *The Symptom 11* (http://www.lacan.com/symptom11/?p=163, publ. 02/2010, cit. 08/2012).

63 Ibid.

tics thus seems to be a fundamental task of contemporary thinking of any new form of politics. Thus the contemporary position should start from two claims: 1. Yes, politics and art today are related when it comes to questions of forming the unformed. 2. No, they are not related because art is not, never was and never will be politics. The amalgamation of art and politics is one of the contemporary – and this is to say: structural – symptoms of disorientation. And it is necessary to overcome it by drawing radical distinctions, lines of demarcations between different fields of practice. Otherwise, we precisely lose the (historical) specificity and (historically determined) concreteness of their situations. An imperative against disorientation can thus be: De-suture what needs to be de-sutured! If the word "communism" stood within history for at least three things[64] – (1) the hypothesis that a politics of non-domination is possible, that introduces (2) an equality of anyone to anyone, and overcomes (3) the dreadful division of labor by introducing a polymorphous, or to speak with Badiou, a generic[65] conception of labor, then Lenin's sentence can be given the following form today: "One cannot remain faithful to what the word communism stood for and will forever stand for, unless it is treated as an art." And this means that one has to come up with a form of that which has not yet received a form, the communist hypothesis. One essential task is to give a new guise, a new articulation, and a new concrete existence to the as yet unformed emancipatory hypothesis of a politics of non-domination, the hypothesis of equality of anyone with anyone, and the hypothesis that the separation inherent to the organization of the working sphere can be overcome. This is again a philosophical task on the one hand, which is to say: one has to rethink what a materialist dialectics might look like, how negation can be thought; and it is also an imminently political task, which demands concrete experiences and experiments in local situations, not in galleries. These experiments need to be as much separated from that from which dialectical thinking must also remain separated: the state. Both have to remain at a distance from the state. Therefore, to conclude, one maxim that might be valid today is: Stop dancing politics and start thinking it concretely.

---

64 Badiou, "Le courage du présent".

65 The idea of renaming the polymorphous labor category of Marx in Badiousian terms "generic labor," I introduced together with Jan Völker in: Frank Ruda and Jan Völker, "Théses sur une morale provisoire communiste," *L'idée du Communisme 2*, ed. Alain Badiou and Slavoj Žižek (Paris: Lignes, 2011), pp. 215–237. The systematic elaboration of what such a conception of labor nowadays entails is still to come.

Simon Critchley

Is Utopianism Dead?

We are living through a long anti-1960s. The various anti-capitalist experiments in communal living and collective existence that defined that period seem to us either quaintly passé, laughably unrealistic or dangerously misguided. Having grown up and thrown off such seemingly childish ways, we now think we know better than to try and bring heaven crashing down to earth and construct concrete utopias. To that extent, despite our occasional and transient enthusiasms and Obamaisms, we are all political realists; indeed most of us are passive nihilists and cynics. This is why we still require a belief in something like original sin, namely that there is something ontologically defective about what it means to be human. The Judaeo-Christian conception of original sin finds its modern analogues in Freud's variation on the Schopenhauerian disjunction between desire and civilization, Heidegger's ideas of facticity and fallenness and the Hobbesian anthropology that drives Carl Schmitt's defense of authoritarianism and dictatorship, which has seduced significant sectors of the Left hungry for what they see as *Realpolitik*. Without the conviction that the human condition is essentially flawed and dangerously rapacious, we would have no way of justifying our disappointment and nothing gives us a greater thrill than satiating our sense of exhaustion and ennui by polishing the bars of our prison cell by reading a little John Gray. Gray represents a very persuasive Darwinian variant on the idea of original sin: it is the theory of evolution that explains the fact that we are *homo rapiens*. Nothing can be done about it. Humanity is a plague.

It is indeed true that those utopian political movements of the 1960s, like the Situationist International, where an echo of utopian Millenarian movements like the Heresy of the Free Spirit could be heard, led to various forms of disillusionment, disintegration and, in extreme cases, disaster. Experiments in the collective ownership of property or in communal living based on sexual freedom without the repressive institution of the family, or indeed R.D. Laing's experimental communal asylums with no distinction between the so-called mad and the sane seem like distant whimsical cultural memories captured in dog-eared, yellowed paperbacks and grainy, poor quality film. As a child of punk, economic collapse and the widespread social violence in the United Kingdom in the late 1970s, it is a world that I have always struggled to understand. Perhaps such communal experiments were too pure and overfull of righteous conviction. Perhaps they were, in a word, too *moralistic* to ever endure. Perhaps such experiments were doomed because of what we might call a *politics of abstraction*, in the sense of being overly attached to an idea at the expense of a frontal denial of reality. Perhaps, indeed.

At their most extreme, say in the activities of the Weather Underground, the Red Army Faction and the Red Brigades in the 1970s, the moral certitude of the closed and pure community becomes fatally linked to redemptive, cleansing violence. Terror becomes the means to bring about the end of virtue. Such is the logic of Jacobinism. The death of individuals is but a speck on the vast heroic canvas of the class struggle. This culminated in a heroic politics of violence where acts of abduction, kidnapping, hijacking and assassination were justified through an attachment to a set of ideas. As a character in Jean-Luc Godard's *Notre Musique* remarks, "to kill a human being in order to defend an idea is not to defend an idea, it is to kill a human being."[1]

Perhaps such groups were too attached to the idea of immediacy, the propaganda of the violent deed as the impatient attempt to storm the heavens. Perhaps such experiments lacked an understanding of politics as a constant and concrete process of *mediation*. That is, the mediation between a subjective ethical commitment based on a general principle, for example the equality of all, friendship or, in my parlance, an infinite ethical demand, and the experience of local organization that builds fronts and alliances between disparate groups with often conflicting sets of interests, what Gramsci called the activity of "hegemony." By definition, such a process of mediation is never pure and never complete.

Are these utopian experiments in community dead or do they live on in some form? I'd like to make two suggestions for areas where this utopian impulse might live on, two experiments, if you will: one from contemporary art, one from contemporary radical politics and the two areas can be interestingly linked. Indeed, if a tendency marks our time, then it is the increasing difficulty in separating forms of collaborative art from experimental politics.

Perhaps such utopian experiments in community live on in the institutionally sanctioned spaces of the contemporary art world. One thinks of projects like *L'Association des Temps Libérés* (1995), or *Utopia Station* (2003) and many other examples gathered together in a retrospective show at the Guggenheim Museum in New York in Fall 2008,

---

1 *Notre Musique* 2004, J.-L. Godard (dir.) (France/Switzerland: Avventura Films, Péripheria Suisse, France 3 Cinéma et al).

Theanyspacewhatever.[2] In the work of artists like Philippe Parreno and Liam Gillick or curators like Hans-Ulrich Obrist and Maria Lind, there is a deeply felt Situationist nostalgia for ideas of collectivity, action, self-management, collaboration and indeed the idea of the group as such. In such art practice, which Nicolas Bourriaud has successfully branded as "relational," art is the acting out of a situation in order to see if, in Obrist's words, "something like a collective intelligence might exist."[3] As Gillick notes, "maybe it would be better if we worked in groups of three."[4] So much contemporary art and politics is obsessed with the figure of the group and of work as collaboration, perhaps all the way to the refusal of work and the cultivation of anonymity.

Of course, the problem with such contemporary utopian art experiments is twofold: on the one hand, they are only enabled and legitimated through the cultural institutions of the art world and thus utterly enmeshed in the circuits of commodification and spectacle that they seek to subvert; and, on the other hand, the dominant mode for approaching an experience of the communal is through the strategy of *reenactment*. One doesn't engage in a bank heist, one reenacts Patty Hearst's adventures with the Symbionese Liberation Army in a warehouse in Brooklyn, or whatever. Situationist *détournement* is replayed as obsessively planned reenactment. The category of reenactment has become hegemonic in contemporary art, specifically as a way of thinking the relation between art and politics (perhaps radical politics has also become reenactment). Fascinating as I find such experiments and the work of the artists involved, one suspects what we might call a "mannerist Situationism," where the old problem of recuperation does not even apply because such art is completely co-opted by the socio-economic system which provides its life-blood.

To turn to politics, perhaps we witnessed another communal experiment with the events in France surrounding the arrest and detention of the so-called "Tarnac Nine" on November 11, 2008 and the work of groups that go under different names: Tiqqun, The Invisible Committee, The Imaginary Party.[5] As part of Nicolas Sarkozy's reactionary

---

2 See the documentation collected in *Theanyspacewhatever* (New York: Guggenheim Museum, 2008).

3 H.-U. Obrist, "In Conversation with Raoul Vaneigem," *E-Flux Journal* (http://www.e-flux.com/journal/view/62, publ. May 2009, cit. 01/14/2012).

4 Liam Gillick, "Maybe it Would be Better if We Worked in Groups of Three?," *E-Flux Journal* (www.e-flux.com/journal/view/35, publ. February 2009, cit. 01/14/2012).

5 For more information see "Tarnac 9" (http://tarnac9.wordpress.com, publ. 2010, cit. 01/14/2012). See also the commentary by Alberto Toscano, "The War Against Pre-Terrorism: The Tarnac 9 and The Coming Insurrection," *Radical Philosophy* (http://www.radicalphilosophy.com, publ. March/April 2009, cit. 01/14/2012).

politics of fear – itself based on an overwhelming fear of disorder and desire to erase definitively the memory of 1968 – a number of activists who had been formerly associated with Tiqqun were arrested in rural, central France by a force of 150 anti-terrorist police, helicopters and attendant media. They were living communally in the small village of Tarnac in the Corrèze district of the Massif Central. Apparently a number of the group's members had bought a small farmhouse and ran a cooperative grocery store and were engaged in such dangerous activities as running a local film club, planting carrots and delivering food to the elderly. With surprising juridical imagination, they were charged with "pre-terrorism," an accusation linked to acts of sabotage on France's TGV rail system.

The basis for this thought-crime was a passage from a book from 2007 called *L'insurrection qui vient.*[6] It is a wonderfully dystopian diagnosis of contemporary society – seven circles of hell in seven chapters – and a compelling strategy to resist it. The final pages of *L'insurrection* advocate acts of sabotage against the transport networks of "the social machine" and ask the question, "How could a TGV line or an electrical network be rendered useless?"[7] Two of the alleged pre-terrorists, Julien Coupat and Yldune Lévy, were detained in jail and charged with "a terrorist undertaking" that carried a prison sentence of 20 years. The last of the group to be held in custody, Coupat, was released without being prosecuted on May 28 2009, although bail of 16,000 Euros was levied and Coupat was forbidden to travel outside the greater Parisian area.[8] Fresh arrests were made in connection with the Tarnac affair late in 2009.[9] Such is the repressive and reactionary force of the state, just in case anyone had forgotten. As the authors of *L'insurrection* remind us, "Governing has never been anything but pushing back by a thousand subterfuges the moment when the crowd will hang you."[10]

L'insurrection qui vient has powerful echoes of the Situationist International. Yet – revealingly – the Hegelian-Marxism of Debord's analysis of the spectacle and commodification is replaced with very strong echoes of Agamben, in particular the question of community in Agam-

---

6 *L'insurrection qui vient* (Paris: La Fabrique, 2007); trans. anonymously as *The Coming Insurrection* (Los Angeles: Semiotexte[e], 2009).

7 *L'insurrection qui vient*, p. 101.

8 "Tarnac9" (http://tarnac9.wordpress.com/2009/05/29/julien-coupat-released, publ. 05/29/2012, cit.01/14/2012).

9 "Tarnac9" (http://tarnac9.wordpress.com/2009/12/05/statement-from-the-tarnac-ten, publ. 12/05/2009, cit. 01/14/2011).

10 *L'insurrection qui vient*, p. 83.

ben as what would survive the separation of law and life.[11] Everything turns here on an understanding of the relation between law and life and the possibility of a nonrelation between those two terms. If law is essentially violence, which in the age of bio-politics taps deeper and deeper into the reservoir of life, then the separation of law and life is the space of what Agamben calls politics. It is what leads to his anomic misreading of Paul.

The authorship of *L'insurrection* is attributed to *La Comité Invisible* and the insurrectional strategy of the group turns around the question of invisibility. It is a question of "learning how to become imperceptible," of regaining "the taste for anonymity" and not exposing and losing oneself in the order of visibility, which is always controlled by the police and the state. The authors of *L'insurrection* argue for the proliferation *of* zones of opacity, anonymous spaces where communes might be formed. The book ends with the slogan, "All power to the communes" *("Tout le pouvoir aux communes")*. In a nod to Maurice Blanchot, these communes are described as "inoperative" or "*désœuvrée*," as refusing the capitalist tyranny of work. In a related text simply entitled *Call*, they seek to establish, "a series of foci of desertion, of secession poles, of rallying points. For the runaways. For those who leave. A set of places to take shelter from the control of a civilization that is headed for the abyss."[12]

A strategy of sabotage, blockade and what is called "the human strike" is proposed in order to weaken still further our doomed civilization. As the Tiqqun group write in a 1999 text called "Oh Good, the War!": "Abandon ship. Not because it's sinking, but to make it sink." Or again: "When a civilization is ruined, one declares it bankrupt. One does not tidy up in a home falling off a cliff."[13] An opposition between the city and the country is constantly reiterated, and it is clear that the construction of zones of opacity is better suited to rural life than the policed space of surveillance of the modern metropolis. The city is much better suited to what we might call "designer resistance," where people wear Ramones t-shirts and sit in coffee shops saying, "capitalism sucks," before going back to their jobs as graphic designers.

---

11 The obvious connection here is between *The Coming Insurrection* and Giorgio Agamben's *The Coming Community*, trans. Michael Hardt (Minneapolis: University of Minnesota Press, 1993).

12 See *Call*, http://bloom0101.org/call.pdf (cit. 01/14/2012), p. 57. *Call* was an earlier text by The Invisible Committee circulated anonymously in 2004.

13 In *Politics is not a Banana* (The Institute for Experimental Freedom, 2009), pp. 156 & 162.

L'insurrection is a compelling, exhilarating, funny and deeply lyrical text that sets off all sorts of historical echoes with movements like the Free Spirit and the Franciscan Spirituals in the Middle Ages, through to the proto-anarchist Diggers in the English Revolution and different strands of 19th Century utopian communism. We should note the emphasis on secrecy, invisibility and itinerancy, on small-scale communal experiments in living, on the politicization of poverty which recalls medieval practices of mendicancy and the refusal of work. What is at stake is the affirmation of a life no longer exhausted by work and cowed by law and the police.

This double program of sabotage, on the one hand, and secession from civilization, on the other, risks, I think, remaining trapped within the politics of abstraction identified above. In this fascinatingly creative *reenactment* of the Situationist gesture – which is why I stressed the connection with contemporary art practice – what is missing is a thinking of political mediation where groups like the Invisible Committee would be able to link up and become concretized in relation to multiple and conflicting sites of struggle, workers, the unemployed, even the designer resisters and, perhaps most importantly, with more or less disenfranchised ethnic groups. We need a richer political cartography than the opposition between the city and the country. Tempting as it is, sabotage combined with secession from civilization smells of the moralism we detected above, an ultimately anti-political purism.

That said, I understand the *desire* for secession: it is the desire to escape a seemingly doomed civilization that is headed for the abyss. The proper theological name for such secessionism is Marcionism, which turns on the separation of law from life, the order of creation from that of redemption, the Old and New Testaments. In the face of a globalizing, atomizing, bio-political and legal regime of violence and domination which threatens to drain dry the reservoir of life, secession offers the possibility of withdrawal, the establishment of a space where another form of life and collective intelligence are possible. Secession offers the possibility of an antinomian separation of law from life, a retreat from the old order through experiments with free human sociability: in other words, *communism*, understood as the "sharing of a sensibility *and* elaboration of sharing. The uncovering of what is common *and* the building of a force."[14]

It is also the case that something has changed and is changing in the nature of tactics of political resistance. With the fading away of

14 See "A Point of Clarification," a statement from January 2009 that appears at the beginning of the American edition of *The Coming Insurrection*, p. 5–19, see esp. p. 16.

the so-called anti-globalization movement, groups like the Invisible Committee offer a consistency of thought and action that possesses great diagnostic power and tactical awareness. They provide a new and compelling vocabulary of insurrectionary politics that has both described and unleashed a series of political actions in numerous locations, some closer to home, some further away. The latter is performed by what the Invisible Committee call – in an interesting choice of word – "resonance."[15] A resonating body in one location – like glasses on a table – begins to make another body shake, and suddenly the whole floor is covered with glass. Politics is perhaps no longer, as it was in the so-called anti-globalization movement, a struggle for and with visibility. Resistance is about the cultivation of invisibility, opacity, anonymity, and resonance.

*

I have my doubts about the politics of abstraction that haunts groups like the Invisible Committee. But if we reject such political experiments, then what follows from this? Are we to conclude that the utopian impulse in political thinking is simply the residue of a dangerous political theology that we are much better off without? Is the upshot of the critique of utopianism that we should be resigned in the face of the world's violent inequality and update a belief in original sin with a reassuringly miserabilistic Darwinism? Should we reconcile ourselves to the options of political realism, authoritarianism or liberalism, John Gray, Carl Schmitt or Barack Obama? Should we simply renounce the utopian impulse in our personal and political thinking?

If so, then the consequence is clear: we are stuck with the way things are, or possibly with something even worse than the way things are. To abandon the utopian impulse in thinking and acting is to imprison ourselves within the world as it is and to give up once and for all the prospect that another world is possible, however small, fleeting and compromised such a world might be. In the political circumstances that presently surround us in the West, to abandon the utopian impulse in political thinking is to resign ourselves to liberal democracy. Liberal democracy is the rule of the rule, the reign of law that renders impotent anything that would break with law: the miraculous, the moment of the event, the break with the situation in the name of the common. It is a political deism governed by the hidden and divine hand of the market. Other political forms of life are possible.

---

15 Ibid, p. 12.

*

Allow me a final word on the future. I'm against it. I think we have to resist the future, I mean resist the *idea* of the future, which is the ultimate ideological trump card of capitalist narratives of progress. I think we have to resist the future and the ideology of the future. But in the name of what? In the name of sheer potentiality of the radical past and the way that past can shape the creativity and imagination of the present. The future of radical, creative thought is its past, and radicalism has always driven a car whose driver is constantly looking in the rear view mirror. Some objects may appear bigger, some smaller.

Capitalism is an evil that presents itself as inevitability, as a destiny to whom the future by necessity belongs. Capitalism – at the level of ideology – has become a form of passive nihilist, quasi-Buddhist self-help amnesia, a new jargon of authenticity and well-being. All we have to oppose it is an understanding of history, a clear-sightedness about the structural injustices present and a willingness to take action, a need to confront commitment-free bovine contentment with the urgency of anguished commitment, the anguish of a demand as that which prepares the possibility of action. Such action should not just dream of a non-relation of law and life, and a secession from an allegedly doomed civilization, but requires that the relation between be decisively rethought. The world is shit, I agree; the problem is that it's our excrement.

Jon McKenzie

Abu Ghraib and the Society of the Spectacle of the Scaffold[1]

Two Anachronisms of the Performance Stratum

The scandal known as "Abu Ghraib" instantiates two political anachronisms that may very well come to define what I call the performance stratum, the global formation of power/knowledge which is currently displacing the disciplinary stratum analyzed by Foucault.[2] One anachronism, *the reemergence of sovereign power*, involves the expediency of discursive performatives, whether spoken or written. The second anachronism, *the reemergence of the spectacle of the scaffold*, involves the efficacy of spectacle, theatricality, and, more generally, embodied performance. I will very briefly outline the first anachronism with reference to an infamous series of "torture memos," and then turn to the main object of this essay, an analysis of the theater of torture enacted at Abu Ghraib prison. This theater can be understood, precisely, as a contemporary spectacle of the scaffold.

The first, more discursive, anachronism involves the reappearance of sovereign power, by which I mean the power of sovereign utterances to decide life or death - in a word - to execute. In contrast to discipline's universal, invisible, and continuous operation, Foucault described sovereign power as organized around a single sovereign body and as exercised through highly individualized, visible, and intermittent techniques. Its anachronistic return today, however, reroutes such sovereignty away from kings and their ministers and instead plugs it directly into the executive management of high performance organizations. In contrast to the plodding deliberations of rationalized bureaucracies, new "petty sovereigns" emerge fully authorized and directed to make decisions based on their expediency - their speed, their fitness to situation, their practicality, even their "actionability." Thus, in a series of brief memoranda written between January 25 and February 7, 2002, top Bush administration officials summarily declared that Taliban and al-Qaeda combatants were not covered by the Geneva Convention and,

---

1 This essay previously appeared in Patrick Anderson and Jisha Menon, eds., *Violence Performed: Local Roots and Global Routes of Conflict* (Hampshire: Palgrave Macmillan, 2009).

2 See Jon McKenzie, *Perform or Else: From Discipline to Performance* (London: Routledge, 2001), especially Part II.

in the following August, offered an unprecedented legal definition of torture, one so narrow that, short of death or loss of bodily organ, almost any level of pain and suffering could be justifiably inflicted in the name of the "Global War on Terror."[3] Such official memoranda articulated a (quasi)legal framework for the policies and procedures used in the detention, interrogation, and torture of prisoners at U.S. facilities in Bagram, Afghanistan; Guantánamo, Cuba; and eventually Abu Ghraib, Iraq (to name only the most well-known sites).

These "torture memos," however, must themselves be placed within a wider political framework, which legal scholars and administration officials call the "unitary executive," a controversial constitutional theory that vastly broadens executive power and reduces the ability of other governmental branches to provide checks and balances. "Unitary executive" means just that: executive power is unified, not divisible or limitable by anything outside of it. Beyond official memoranda, other means of exercising unitary executive power include public and secret executive orders, classified studies and findings, interpretative signing statements attached to legislation, and even seemingly mundane agency regulations. The power asserted by the theory of unitary executive can be understood in terms of Giorgio Agamben's "state of exception," in which sovereign decisions suspend the rule of law, even and especially to the point where the exception effectively becomes the rule. Butler explicitly theorizes the sovereign power of the Bush administration in terms of discursive performatives: "The future becomes a lawless future, not anarchical, but given over to the discretionary decisions of a set of designated sovereigns [...] who are beholden to nothing and to no one except the performative power of their own decisions."[4] Further, she describes this sovereign power as anachronistic and, significantly, as extending far down into bureaucracies, giving rise to low-level sovereigns. "These are petty sovereigns, unknowing, to a degree, about what work they do, but performing their acts uni-

---

3 See in particular the memos of Alberto Gonzales to President Bush ("Decision Re: Application of the Geneva Conventions on Prisoners of War to the Conflict with Al Qaeda and the Taliban," January 25, 2000), George W. Bush ("On the Humane Treatment of al-Qaeda and Taliban Detainees," February 7, 2002), and Jay S. Bybee to Alberto Gonzales ("Standards of Conduct for Interrogation under 18 U.S.C. §§ 2340–2340A," August 1, 2002). These and other memos can be found in Mark Danner's *Torture and Truth: America, Abu Ghraib, and the War on Terror* (New York: The New York Review of Books, 2004), a collection of essays, documents, and photographs.

4 Judith Butler, *Precarious Life: The Powers of Mourning and Violence* (London/New York: Verso, 2004), p. 65.

laterally and with enormous consequence."[5] I would argue that one must also consider petty, *non-state* decision-makers, such as the executives at Titan and CACI, two private military contractors currently being sued by former Abu Ghraib inmates. Thus I prefer to use the term "executive performativity" rather than "sovereign performativity." In some sense, executive performativity is an extension of what I have analyzed elsewhere as "high performance management," but one which suspends long-standing traditions of deliberative, highly rationalized bureaucratic decision-making and violates or suspends laws, contracts, and professional codes of practice, whether governmental or nongovernmental. Executive performativity represents a devolution of sovereign power at the same time as its resurrection in contemporary organizations.

My focus in this essay, again, is a second, closely-related anachronism, a more visceral enactment of power that Abu Ghraib incarnates but in no way exhausts. Alongside the gruesome scenes of Daniel Pearl's beheading and Saddam Hussein's hanging; alongside the globally broadcast bombings of Baghdad, Bali, Beirut, London, Manhattan, Tel Aviv, and many other cities; alongside the innumerable websites devoted to images of war carnage, executions, and other forms of political violence – the scenes from Abu Ghraib reanimate that extremely violent and graphic form of political theatricality which Foucault assigned to pre-disciplinary society and which he named "the spectacle of the scaffold."[6] Indeed, panopticism, as the visual regime of the enlightened human sciences, is precisely what displaced the visual regime of spectacle associated with sovereign power. The prison cell displaced the scaffold in the public square as the paradigmatic site where power and bodies meet. Today, however, scaffolds may be in cells, city streets, lonely landscapes, almost anywhere: it's the spectacle that has changed, shifting from highly localized spaces of temporal copresence to globally mediated spaces and times – or rather, all localized spaces of temporal copresence become potential nodes of transmission and reception in a worldwide electronic network of cameras, screens, databases, processors, and editing boards. In short, just as sovereign power has devolved and trickled down to mid- and even low-level officials, the spectacle of the scaffold has become networked and screenal: satellites, televisions, security cameras, facial and gestural recognition software, cell phones, Blackberrys, iPods, YouTube, Google Maps, The Memory Hole – all become means for capturing or

5 Ibid., p. 65.
6 See Michel Foucault, *Discipline and Punish*, trans. Alan Sheridan (New York: Vintage, 1979), especially Chapter 2.

being captivated by spectacles. Combining Foucault and Debord, two unlikely allies, we might say that on the performance stratum this second anachronism portends a *global society of the spectacle of the scaffold* – or global *societies* of the spectacle of the scaffold, as one can foresee such spectacles being deployed not only by fundamentalists, neoliberals, and neoconservatives, but even by those opposed to these social groupings.

One might object that torture and violence – and images of torture and violence – have long existed. In fact, the Abu Ghraib images have themselves been described in terms of late-19th and early 20th-century American lynching photos, Francisco de Goya's "The Disasters of War" prints (1810–20), and even ancient Greek sculpture.[7] Yet while one can find many historical precedents and analogues to Abu Ghraib (e. g., the racism, amateurism, and indexicality of lynching photos; the context of war and social upheaval surrounding Goya's prints; and the posed, almost sculptural arrangement of figures), what distinguishes the contemporary spectacle of the scaffold is its vast sociotechnical infrastructure. The technical infrastructure of television and the internet is both global and often real-time, on the one hand, and yet also local and even intimate, on the other. The images of the Hooded Man haunt the halls of Abu Ghraib but also the homes of people around the world. The same cell phones and laptops that carry words and pictures of loved ones also transmit anguished cries for help and images of bombing and carnage. And not just one or two images, or even ten or twenty, but hundreds upon hundreds and even thousands upon thousands of images. In the end, this global technical infrastructure decidedly does *not* mark a clean, absolute break from any and all historical precedents and analogues; more profoundly, via multimedia databases and hypertext markup language (html), these historical precedents and analogues are themselves being incorporated into the society of the spectacle of the scaffold. Indeed, this incorporation contributes to its anachronicity.

Abu Ghraib and the Total Theater of Torture

In addition to the general, if not universal, infrastructure of television and internet that supports it, the acts and images of Abu Ghraib are also underwritten by a much more specific sociotechnical infrastructure. Beyond the Bush administration's neoconservative cohort that

---

7 For an overview of such analyses, see Stephen F. Eisenman, *The Abu Ghraib Effect* (London: Reaktion Books, 2007).

produced the torture memos discussed above, another, longer-standing social paradigm was at work, a paradigm both coldly theoretical and ruthlessly "applied." I refer here to the paradigm of psychological torture developed by the CIA during the Cold War and used by the U.S. and/or its proxies in Vietnam, the Philippines, Argentina, and other countries. Here we have torture techniques developed and deployed internationally *in the name of democracy* – protecting American democracy, establishing and/or supporting democracy elsewhere, and "securing" democracy worldwide.

Significantly, in his recent book on the CIA's program of psychological torture, historian Alfred McCoy presents its overall implementation as *a type of theater*:

> the psychological component of torture becomes a kind of total theater, a constructed unreality of lies and inversion, in a plot that ends [...] with the victim's self-betrayal and destruction. To make their artifice of false charges, fabricated news, and mock executions convincing, interrogators often become inspired thespians. The torture chamber itself thus has the theatricality of a set with special lighting, sound effects, props, and backdrop, all designed with a perverse stagecraft to evoke an aura of fear.[8]

McCoy uses theatricality not as a metaphor, but as a robust analytical model. He is not the first to employ such a model to analyze torture and violence. Diana Taylor argues that the performance of torture in Argentina inscribed a nationalist narrative on the bodies of those expelled from the nation. More recently, sociologist Mark Juergensmeyer has analyzed religious terrorism in terms of "theater of terror" and "performance violence." At work in these analyses is a *certain* theatricality, and I too will use this concept to theorize phenomena far from theater proper. Significantly, the military itself calls its area of operations a "theater," a usage that dates from the 17th century.[9] Today, with the Global War on Terror, all the world's a bloody stage. Within this global theater, there is the Iraqi theater, and within it, the theatrical performativity of Abu Ghraib. Indeed, the military's own Criminal Investigation Division repeatedly uses the term "staged event" to refer

---

8 Alfred W. McCoy, *A Question of Torture: CIA Interrogation, from the Cold War to the War on Terror* (New York: Metropolitan Books/Henry Holt and Co., 2006), p. 10, emphasis mine. McCoy describes the development of the CIA paradigm of psychological torture in Chapter 2, "Mind Control."

9 Branislav Jakovljevic, "Theatre of War in the Former Yugoslavia: Event, Script, Actors," *TDR: The Drama Review* 43: 3 (1999): pp. 5–13.

to incidents at Abu Ghraib where soldiers posed or arranged inmates for viewing and/or photographing.

It is thus no accident that commentators have described the infamous Abu Ghraib photographs as "theatrical:" the poses of Lynndie England; the pyramid of naked inmates; the hooded figure holding electrical wires – these iconic images present tableaus of power and degradation. The performances seem scripted, directed, and enacted for an audience – and indeed they were. By whom and for whom? One only need to look at the casting: specific bodies – Arab, Muslim, and mostly but not entirely, male – were abused by Americans, both male and female, mostly white Euro-American but also African-, Latino-, and Arab-American, who acted under the orders of American commanders and officials. And we must also ask: by what means and to what ends were these bodies tortured? I propose to use theatricality as a way to analyze the techniques of America's torture machine.

Commentators have proposed many interpretative frames for understanding the events and images of Abu Ghraib: trophy photos shot by frat boys, tourist shots snapped by ugly Americans; porno pics taken by sex-crazed guards. More thoughtfully, Sontag framed them, in part, in terms of lynching photos, while Žižek argues that they document the initiation of Iraqis into the underside of American culture.[10] Art historian Stephen F. Eisenman argues the photos reveal a "pathos formula," often found in classical Western art, in which tortured individuals appear to sanction their own abuse.[11] While multiple frames are no doubt at work, I think the most important one is much more literal: it is the regimen of detention and interrogation instituted at Abu Ghraib at the recommendation of Major General Geoffrey Miller. This is precisely the regimen that McCoy calls "total theater."

General Miller, then the commander at Guantánamo, inspected Abu Ghraib in September, 2003. Following a summer marked by a sharp spike in insurgent attacks, the military sought better intelligence to counter the insurgency. Miller arrived at Abu Ghraib saying that "he was going to "Gitmoize" the detention operation."[12] After his inspection, the general filed a detailed report containing specific recommendations. These included the assignment of a Behavioral Science Con-

---

10 Susan Sontag, "Regarding the Torture of Others," *New York Times Magazine* (23 May 2004); Slavoj Žižek, "Between Two Deaths," *London Review of Books 26:11* (3 June 2004).

11 Eisenman, *The Abu Ghraib Effect*, p. 16.

12 Brigadier General Janis L. Karpinski, cited in "As Insurgency Grew, So Did Prison Abuse," *The Washington Post* (10 May 2004).

sultation Team, made up of psychologists and psychiatrists, and the incorporation of information technologies, particularly databases.

It is in the assignment of a Behavioral Science Consultation Team – or BSCT (pronounced "biscuit") – that we can best approach the theatrical performativity of Abu Ghraib, for it set the stage both in terms of scenes and images and *also the temporal unfolding of events.* While the scenes and images have received much popular and academic attention, their temporal and processual dimension has been largely overlooked. Beneath the spectacle of Abu Ghraib, there was plot, dramatic unfolding, and even character development – or rather, the decomposition of character and identity.

Miller developed and enhanced BSCT interrogation at Guantánamo, drawing on decades of CIA and military research into psychological methods of interrogation. McCoy argues that this research produced a radically new paradigm of torture, one that perversely complements the postwar emergence of human rights institutions. It is a "no touch" torture, a torture that leaves few visible marks on the body, precisely because it targets the mind – or rather, because it targets the mind through bodily sensation and stress, rather than primarily attacking the body through contact, twisting, or puncture. Erroneously called "torture light," its effects can be far more damaging and long-lasting than physical torture. There is a strong bias against recognizing psychological torture as torture, not only by folks such as Rush Limbaugh, who jokes about Muslims vacationing at "Club Gitmo," but even by past Congressional investigations into American torture programs. Even the United States' ratification of the Convention against Torture sidestepped the techniques I am about to describe. Thus the importance of understanding Abu Ghraib as psychological torture, and I believe theatricality provides a crucial lens for analyzing how this paradigm actually works, both spatially and temporally.

Until recently, the CIA's torture paradigm has consisted of two main methods: sensory disorientation, achieved by sensory deprivation and overload; and self-inflicted pain, such as stress positions and psychological manipulation. McCoy reads one of the iconic Abu Ghraib images precisely through this frame: "That notorious photo of a hooded Iraqi on a box, arms extended and wires to his hands, exposes this covert method. The hood is for sensory deprivation, and the arms are extended for self-inflicted pain."[13] The CIA torture paradigm targets the very sense of self and identity. Sensory disorientation techniques, including long periods of silence and darkness or, alternatively, loud

---

13 McCoy, *A Question of Torture*, p. 8.

music and strobe lights, aim to produce fear, a loss of spatial and temporal awareness, and emotional crisis and breakdown. Self-inflicted pain techniques include long periods of standing or squatting; shackling of arms and legs in painful positions, and informing prisoners that they could end the interrogation – simply by telling the truth. The goal here is to make prisoners blame themselves for their suffering.

For McCoy, one reason psychological torture is *total* theater is that it targets all of the senses: hoods, blackened goggles, and strobe lights target vision; earmuffs and loud music target hearing; gloves and mittens target touch; dietary changes target taste; and surgical masks target smell. We can see sensory disorientation at work in an image from Guantánamo released in 2002. It shows a group of orange-clad detainees kneeling in a fenced pen; they wear blackened goggles, earmuffs, wool gloves, and blue surgical masks. And we also see self-inflicted pain: these detainees are not praying, they are in kneeling stress positions. Ankles crossed, backs bent, wearing knitted caps in the Caribbean heat, they may have been forced to kneel for hours at a time.

General Miller's theater of torture actually "perfected" the CIA's psychological paradigm by adding two additional methods: "cultural shock" and the exploitation of individual vulnerabilities.[14] First, "cultural shock," which targets cultural values and sensitivities. McCoy gives this example:

Guantánamo's command began to probe Muslim cultural and sexual sensitivities, using women interrogators to humiliate Arab males. [...] According to a sergeant who served under General Miller, female interrogators regularly removed their [own] shirts and one [smeared] red ink on a detainee's face saying she was menstruating leaving him to "cry like a baby."[15]

Other cultural shock techniques include the shaving of hair and beards and the use of dogs to frighten and humiliate. Such techniques were imported and used at Abu Ghraib, as seen in the widely-published image of Lynndie England holding a leashed inmate nicknamed "Gus," taken in October 2003. In the uncropped version of this photo, another MP, Megan Ambuhl, looks on. Compare the scene to this Guantánamo interrogation log from December, 2002, almost a year earlier: "Began teaching the detainee lessons such as stay, come, and bark to elevate his social status up to that of a dog."[16] The Guantánamo detainee,

---

14 Alfred W. McCoy, interview by Amy Goodman, *Democracy Now* (http://www.democracynow.org/article.pl?sid=06/02/17/1522228, publ. 17 February 2006, cit. 10 November 2006).

15 McCoy, *A Question of Torture*, pp. 129–130.

16 Ibid., pp. 127–128.

Mohammed al-Kahtani, was also put on a leash and forced to be naked in front of female soldiers.

At Abu Ghraib, the military used cultural shock systematically. Here are extracts from a pamphlet given to Marines in fall 2003 to make them aware of Iraqi cultural sensitivities:[17]

> Do not shame or humiliate a man in public. Shaming a man will cause him and his family to be anti-Coalition
> The most important qualifier for all shame is for a third party to witness the act. If you must do something likely to cause shame, remove the person from view of others.
> Shame is given by placing hoods over a detainee's head. Avoid this practice.
> Placing a detainee on the ground or putting a foot on him implies you are God. This is one of the worst things we can do.
> Arabs consider the following things unclean:
> Feet or soles of feet.
> Using the bathroom around others. Unlike Marines, who are used to open-air toilets, Arab men will not shower/use the bathroom together.
> Bodily fluids (because of this they love tissue paper).[18]

As Mark Danner argues, interrogators and guards *inverted* such cultural sensitivity training at Abu Ghraib and reverse-engineered it to maximize shame rather than minimize it.

The other technique developed at Guantánamo was the exploitation of individuals' unique mental and physical vulnerabilities. Such exploitation allows interrogators to target an individual's ego in a highly effective manner, all the better to then erode and break it apart, so that the detainee transfers trust to his captors. As medical ethicist and MD Steven Miles contends, BSCT psychiatrists and psychologists identify vulnerable traits, as do physicians, medics, and nurses.[19] Such information is then conveyed to interrogators and filters down to guards – or may even filter up from guards, who spend long periods observing and handling inmates.

We can see such targeting of vulnerabilities in the nicknames given to Abu Ghraib inmates – nicknames such as "The Claw," given to Ali

---

17 Danner, *Torture and Truth*, p. 19.

18 "Semper Sensitive: The Marines' Guide to Arab Culture," USMC Division Schools. Reprinted in *Harper's Magazine*. vol. 308, issue 1849 (June 2004), p. 25–6. (http://www.harpers.org/SemperSensitive.html, cit. 12 November 2006).

19 See Steven H. Miles, *Oath Betrayed: Torture, Medical Complicity, and the War on Terror* (New York: Random House, 2006).

Shalal Qaissi, on account of his deformed left hand. "Shitboy" was the name given to an inmate referred to in records as "M-----." The military states he was "mentally deranged" and often smeared himself with feces. Military personnel also gave the name "Gilligan" to Abdou Hussain Saad Faleh, the inmate in the "The Hooded Man" photograph, presumably naming him after the bumbling TV character. *But how were individual vulnerabilities actually exploited?* "The Claw," "Shitboy," and "Gilligan" were no doubt names improvised on the spot by "creative" interrogators or guards and then exploited in subsequent abuses. McCoy writes:

> Thespians all, the torturers assume the role of omnipotent inquisitor, using the theatricality of the torture chamber to heighten the victim's pain and disorientation. Within this script, there is ample room for improvisation. Each interrogator seems to extemporalize around a guiding image that becomes imbedded in the victims' recollection of the event.[20]

The nicknames, I believe, functioned as guiding images for the performance of psychological torture. We can see how one such guiding image was employed by analyzing a series of images. As graphic as they are, individual photos only give a static impression of the theater of torture. To understand its process *in action*, we must look at a *sequence* of materials.

Violence Performed: "Shitboy"

Analyzing a series of digital images of M-----, the prisoner nicknamed "Shitboy," we can better understand the theater of torture's processual dimension. MPs recorded these images over a one-month period, from November 4 – December 2, 2003. Again, the military stresses that M----- was "mentally deranged," but given that the CIA torture paradigm sought to *produce* mental breakdown, M----- may well have been "deranged" *by* his treatment. At a minimum, we can see how guards exploited his vulnerabilities by enacting and elaborating the guiding image of "Shitboy" in their performance of torture.

The images of M----- are particularly graphic, as they both *represent violence* and *embody the violence of representation itself*. However, given that the events have been misrecognized as "hazing" antics or the deeds of a few bad apples – and that psychological torture para-

20 McCoy, *A Question of Torture*, pp. 83–84.

digm has been largely ignored, I think we have a responsibility to analyze both the theater of torture and the machine in which it operates. The images analyzed here can be found on Salon.com's "Abu Ghraib File" (www.salon.com/news/abu_ghraib), an archive that also includes annotations from the Army's Criminal Investigation Division (CID) and accompanying essays. I should also note here that there may well be other, undocumented scenes of M-----'s torture that occurred before, during, or after those described here.

The first known images of M----- were taken at 1:42 and 1:43 am on November 4, 2003. Two photos show him hanging naked and upside-down from his cell bunk in what appears to be a stress position. His calves stretch across the top bunk; his thighs, torso and head suspend down, supported on the floor by his hands, which rest on what appears to be a folded black cloth. His hands are placed together in a prayer gesture. Photos of other prisoners reveal they were often handcuffed to bunks in stress positions; handcuffs, however, cannot be seen in these images of M-----. According to CID notation of these images: "All investigation indicates he did this of his own free will, this was not a staged event." Already, we must ask what it means to attribute free will to someone who is a) subjected to a regime of psychological torture, and b) alleged to be "mentally deranged"? Yet if we do concede that M----- suspended himself from his bunk, these images also depict a staged event, staged not by MPs or interrogators but by M----- himself. As later images reveal, he is quite aware of the camera's presence and may well have been performing for it.

Because this first scene takes place in M-----'s cell, few other inmates could see him.

One week later, however, a much more public performance unfolded in the cellblock's central corridor, where it was documented by several images, two of which received wide publicity. In these two photos, taken late in the evening of November 12, one again sees M----- naked, but now walking with arms fully extended at the side and head bent back, an obvious stress position. But most disturbing about these images is that M-----'s entire body is covered with feces—head, arms, legs, and torso, front and back. In one photo, we see M----- from behind, walking toward Sergeant Ivan Frederick, who stands clutching a night stick. A second photo, taken moments later, shows M----- from the front, walking in the same manner. Significantly, both photos capture the scene's public nature, for we see the arms and heads of other inmates watching from their cells. M----- is being paraded before his fellow Iraqis and before the camera. How long this incident lasted is unclear, though two other images were taken ten minutes earlier from the cellblock's second floor walkway. These show M----- already covered with feces, but rather than walking, he kneels before Graner with hands atop his head. To the side stands civilian translator Adel Nakhla of Titan Corporation, no doubt translating Frederick's commands.

Here we see evidence of psychological torture that combines self-inflicted pain (stress position), cultural shaming (public display of nudity and excrement), and the exploitation of individual vulnerability (the targeting of a preexisting psychological disorder). M----- has been forced to kneel before the baton-wielding Graner and then paraded (and no doubt forced to stand for a long period) in full view of fellow Iraqis—all the while completely covered in feces. Indeed, these images may very well depict the initial formation of the "Shitboy" image, around which the MPs and interrogators would construct subsequent abuses. It should be noted that MPs later stated that M----- repeatedly smeared himself with feces, acts taken as symptoms of his mental disorder.

Nine photographs taken the next night demonstrate how long such sessions could last. At 10:04 pm on November 13, Sergeant Ivan Frederick photographed M----- standing with sandbags tied on his arms, placed there either for sensory deprivation or perhaps to prevent him from abusing himself. M----- stands in the corridor at one end of the cellblock, his black prison jumpsuit open and pulled down, exposing his upper torso. *Three and a half hours later,* at 1:39 am on November 14, M----- is photographed again, still standing, but now his arms extend forward with a sandbag on his right arm only. Two minutes later, Specialist Charles Graner photographs M----- with another camera from above on the second floor walkway. M----- is now turned around with arms extended on either side, head tilted back. Two more photos taken moments later by Graner show Frederick and a second MP, Sergeant Javal Davis, who smiles up at the camera. Significantly, these three photos reveal numerous stains on the floor beneath M-----'s bare feet, suggesting that not only has he been standing and turning for some time, but also that he has urinated on himself. (Graner later told Joseph Darby, the MP who would turn the infamous photos over to his superiors, that in regard to his abuses, "'The Christian in me knows it's wrong, but the corrections officer in me can't help but love to make a grown man piss himself.'"[21]) Additional photos taken with Frederick's camera depict further abuses. One shows M----- posed with both arms extended and curled on either side in a position reminiscent of a swan's neck. Another image, a headshot of M----- in profile, reveals something not legible in the other photos: his head has been shaved,

21 "Records Paint Dark Portrait Of Guard," *The Washington Post* (http://www.washingtonpost.com/wp-dyn/articles/A16832-2004Jun4.html, publ. 4 June 2004, cit. 12 November 2006).

except for a band of hair running from one ear to another, creating a sort of transverse Mohawk haircut. Finally, two photos taken at 1:52 and 1:53 am show M----- again wearing two sandbags, only now his arms have been bound tightly together with rope and a padlocked chain. In the final image, Graner stands behind M-----, holding him by the shoulders and grinning directly into the camera, apparently showing off his work.

Again, the temporal dimension of the Abu Ghraib theater of torture is crucial to understanding how the CIA regime of interrogation operates. As the scene just described indicates, detainees may be forced to hold stress positions for hours on end, a fact not captured by the more notorious single images. Intense physical and psychological pain arises not from blows delivered by another, but from sheer exhaustion and prolonged periods of immobility. The goal is to make the detainee blame himself for his suffering. A common outcome is incontinence, leading to self-disgust and, in cases where urination or defecation occurs in a space open to viewing by others, public shame. Both the personal and cultural sense of identity erodes in a highly calculated but gradual process.

We next see how this process unfolded – and also witness the elaboration of the guiding "Shitboy" image – on November 19, two full weeks after the first known images were taken. Two close-up images taken at 2:10 am show M----- lying naked on his right side on a pink foam bed pad, his upper body covered by a dark, stripped blanket. His ankles are bound with white, plastic ties, and in one image, it appears that his wrists are shackled behind him with metal handcuffs. Both images show M----- holding a yellow object; the CID notation reads, "Detainee inserts banana into his rectum on his own." A third image taken at 2:11 am reveals that these images were taken from the second tier walkway. The Sony camera has been zoomed out, and we see that M----- lies in the central corridor. It appears that his ankle restraints are chained to the bars of a cell door, and a pair of white underwear lies on the floor nearby.

We have here an inversion of the "Shitboy" image: instead of feces coming out of his rectum, M----- has been allowed to insert an object into it – or forced to do so: the trustworthiness of the CID notation is open to question, as it is likely based on testimony given by the very MPs who cuffed and placed M----- in the corridor, provided him with a banana, and then photographed him. The presence of the bedding is significant also. It has probably been dragged out of M-----'s cell along with him, and foam bedding will be used into the next scene of abuse. Thus, we may be witnessing the beginning of its incorporation into the "Shitboy" image.

This next torture scene begins ten days later, on the evening of November 28, and it embodies and then elaborates the "Shitboy" image in an extraordinary way. The first photograph, taken at 8:06 pm, shows M----- from the groin up, standing naked in the shower area of the hard site. M----- stands before a brick wall, the shower plumbing visible to his right. His body is marked with brown splotches. The CID notation reads: "The detainee is covered in what appears to be human feces." Feces has been smeared on each breast, the belly, the neck, and in the hair. Though M-----'s face has been digitally obscured, it appears that his chin, ears, and the left side of his face are also defiled, thus suggesting that excrement covers his entire face. The next two images, also time-coded at 8:06 pm, again show M----- standing, but now from the ankles up. Feces cover his genitals and inner thighs. M----- wears white surgical gloves whose fingers are covered with excrement. One photo depicts him with both arms at his side; in the other, it appears (again, his face has been digitally obscured) that he has put his right hand in his mouth, the grotesque irony being that M----- is using a hygienic glove to eat feces.

As with the images taken on November 12, these photos taken two weeks later depict the signature image of the "Shitboy" motif: M-----'s body smeared with excrement. One can only speculate how often this tableau was staged on nights not captured by digital cameras, either in secluded spaces such as his cell or the shower, or in open spaces such as cellblock corridors. This night, after again establishing the "Shitboy" motif, the guards will extemporize their performance in an open corridor, using objects previously deployed as props on earlier nights. The next sequence of photos, taken a little more than an hour after the shower images, begin with an image showing a cleaned-up M----- standing in an all-too-familiar pose, with arms fully extended at his side. Now, however, he wears a strange tunic-like costume: on closer inspection, one can see that it is a yellow foam bed mattress that has been folded over his shoulders to cover his body, front and back from the knees up. A slit has been cut in the bed pad's center, through which M-----'s head sticks out. Around his waist, a chain is being fastened tightly by Graner. Graner wears black gloves, an armored vest over his green T-shirt and camo fatigues. From his belt hang various "dangles": tools, cables, etc. The next image, taken at 9:13 pm, shows Graner posing beside M-----, leaning on his shoulders with both hands and smiling directly into the camera, as if showing off his improvised work.

Graner's work had only just begun. The next photo, taken at 9:16 pm, shows Graner kneeling on one knee, his right hand on the back of M-----, who now lies stomach-down on a litter, a cloth stretcher whose two support poles have small feet which keep the litter a few inches above the floor. The image has all the trappings of a trophy photo: Graner smiles broadly into the camera next to his "game." M-----, still wearing the foam tunic, lifts his head toward the camera; his face has been digitally blurred, but the head angle suggests that he too looks directly into the camera. We have here an image of abject humiliation and almost total subjection, a point I will turn to in a moment. Before doing so, however, I will note that the background of this photo reveals two remarkable things.

First, in the deep background on the left, there stands a second detainee; hooded with head bent toward the cellblock wall, he wears a smudged white gown and his hands appear to be tied behind his back. M----- thus may not have been the only person tortured this night. But even more significant, also on the left of this image but in the mid-range background, there stands a person holding up a second litter. Unlike Graner, Frederick, and the civilian translator Nadal seen in previous photos, this individual wears civilian clothing: black pants, green shoulder-bag, and bright white sneakers. *Such nonmilitary clothing strongly suggests that this second person was either a CIA interrogator or a privately contracted one.* In short, far from being "prep work" for subsequent interrogation, this entire scene may well have been part of an actual interrogation, if not of M-----, then of the hooded detainee or another person not visible in these photographs. Indeed, though there were special interrogation rooms at Abu Ghraib, Tara McKelvey reports that interrogations could also take place in "a cell, a shower stall, stairwell, or a supply room."[22] Other photos taken at Abu Ghraib have been described as showing "OGA" (i.e., "other government agency," a euphemism for CIA) personnel interrogating detainees in the open corridors of cellblock 1A.

Whatever the identity of this second person, he or she played an active role in this unfolding theater of torture, for in the next photograph the second litter has been placed on top of M----- to form what the guards called a "litter sandwich." Sandwiched face down between two litters, wearing foam bedding, chain belt, and arm restraints, M-----'s subjection has literally reached the bottom. The *coup de grâce* comes in the scene's final image, another trophy photo which depicts a second guard, Ivan Frederick, sitting atop M-----, who now raises his head to the camera. The subjection is now complete, the dominance of guard over prisoner, American over Iraqi, white-skinned over dark-skinned, military order over insurgent force, Good over Evil – all are both

22 See Tara McKelvey, *Monstering: Inside America's Policy of Secret Interrogation and Torture in the Terror War* (New York: Basic Books, 2007), p. 14.

allegorized and literalized. To coin a term, all become "litteralized" in the litter sandwich.

Such word play is not inappropriate here, for it may help reveal additional elements and moments in the improvisational development of M-----'s torture via the guiding image of "Shitboy." To begin with, *litter* read as stretcher can be associated with bed and bedding, in particular, with the foam pad seen here and in the earlier scene with the banana. As noted above, it is as if the bedding has become incorporated into the "Shitboy" theme, and one can imagine the guards joking, "Shitboy has made his bed and now must lie in it." (Recall, too, that the first images of M----- show him hanging from his cell bunk.) But *litter* can also refer to trash, especially pieces of trash left lying on the ground of public places, and here M----- has been trashed and left on the floor of the prison's public corridor. Significantly, *litter* is also associated with feces, for the term can refer to absorbent material, such as the dry granules found in cat litter. Here, the litter absorbs "Shitboy" into what might be called a "shit sandwich." Further, *litter* can refer to the surface layer of a forest floor, made up of decomposing matter such as twigs, leaves, and animals. Such rotting material can obviously be related to excrement. But more tellingly, the precise term *litter sandwich* is used in biology, where it refers to a framed, wire apparatus used to study the decomposition of organic matter in soil strata.

Taken together, the photographs taken from all the scenes analyzed here strongly suggest that M-----'s identity becomes decomposed into the image of "Shitboy." Again, such decomposition or breakdown of subjectivity is precisely the goal of psychological torture, a process that the month-long series of images just described documents with the methodical cruelty of an all-too-serious and all-too-prolonged sick joke, one in which sadistic humor is put to "intelligent" ends, those of military and national security intelligence. As one of the military whistleblowers, Sergeant Sam Provance, later recalled about the guards at Abu Ghraib, "They'd talk about their experience when the detainees were being humiliated and abused. It was always a joke story. It was like, 'Ha, ha. It was hilarious. You had to be there.'"[23]

One final document, a set of video clips taken the night of December 1, offers bone-chilling evidence of the effectiveness of psychological torture. M----- himself performs the final act of this particular theater of torture, though we would be more accurate saying that M----- "is performed" by this theater, for the agency of his actions now includes the Army, CIA, and Titan Corporation – or the torture machine itself. The

23 Provance, quoted by McKelvey, *Monstering*, p. 17.

performance was recorded on Graner's video camera, presumably by Graner. The Salon archive contains ten separate 15-second video clips and one 8-second clip of M-----, for a total of 2 minutes, 38 seconds. However, CID notation states that video was taken between 9:29 and 9:45 pm, so the events recorded unfolded for half an hour; moreover, additional still images of the same event are time-coded as occurring early on the morning of December 2 at 12:33 and 2:00 am, indicating that the torture lasted *at least four and a half hours*. This material, along with two other sets of video clips of other detainees – one of the infamous pyramid and group masturbation scenes – remains largely unknown in the U.S., where to my knowledge they have never been publicly broadcast (portions of them were broadcast in Australia). The clips on Salon.com are low resolution QuickTime movies and, significantly, their audio has been dropped out. No doubt full video and audio versions exist but have not been leaked to the public.

I will describe the video clips in the order posted on Salon.com, noting also that the file names suggest that other clips may exist. The first five clips of M----- were shot from the upper tier, peering down into the corridor below. In the first two clips, we see M----- from his left standing in profile, bent over at the waist with his head against a solid cell door. He wears a blanket of some sort. At first glance, it appears M----- may be praying, as his body rocks slightly, but on closer inspection we see that his wrists are handcuffed to the door before him. The next three clips reveal the horror of M-----'s performance: standing upright from his bent position, he leans back, still rocking his body slightly forward and backward. He then turns his head in the camera's direction and appears to look directly into the lens. Turning his head back, M----- extends his arms out and shifts his body weight back, bowing his body slightly at the waist. Seeming to take aim, he suddenly pulls hard on the handcuffs and slams the top of his head into the solid metal door. The blanket slips down, exposing his bare shoulders as his knees buckle. In the next clip, M----- appears dazed and shaken, his body shuddering as his head bends up and down. In the fifth clip, M----- prepares for another impact, standing and rocking, turning his head toward the camera, leaning back and again slamming his head into the door.

Again, CID notation indicates that the "self induced" actions captured on video lasted half an hour. The final six clips again record M-----'s ritualistic banging of his head into the metal cell door, only now the cameraperson has moved down to the cellblock floor. In the first of these clips, we see M----- standing full length in profile, but now in a mid-range shot taken from his right side. He wears sandals, and we can see that his blanket bears a large blue floral pattern. From this angle and distance, we more fully sense the force of his head hitting the door, twice within a 15-second span: the rhythm of his impacts has increased and once again he turns his head briefly toward the camera. The next, 8-second clip starts from the same angle, but M----- now squats on his feet, balled up and teetering no doubt after another head-slamming. The camera then moves quickly toward and behind M-----, the lens pointing toward the concrete floor, the bars of several other cell doors, and the cameraperson's walking feet. The next two clips, each 15 seconds long, show M----- closer up from his left side, waist to head in three-quarter view. In one clip, we see M----- standing before the door, whose green surface we now see is marked with two bright bloody spots, one where his head hits the door, the other where he rests his head while bent over at the waist. The second of these two clips shows M----- again slamming into the door. In the tenth and final video clip, the camera towers over M-----, who squats below. Solarized lens flares give the image a dark red hue, then a light green one, as M----- squats and rocks, tilts his head back, and then stands up again. He again looks into the camera and we see that the right side of his forehead is bloody and raw. M----- grimaces, and he appears to be crying and/or crying out.

Taken together, all of these materials demonstrate that Abu Ghraib's theatrical performativity was not limited to poses and images, settings and props. The total theater of torture also operates via a temporal, processual dimension that has been largely ignored by commentators; however, this dimension is crucial to understanding the underlying regime of psychological torture and interrogation at work in Abu Ghraib and elsewhere. M----- was subjected to over a month of painful and humiliating abuse in sessions sometimes lasting several hours each. The photographs and videos clearly demonstrate that military personnel (and possibly CIA personnel and/or private military contractors) employed this regime's four main components on the detainee: sensory deprivation, self-inflicted pain, cultural shock, and the targeting of individual vulnerabilities. With respect to the latter, I have tried to show that "Shitboy," beyond its function as a nickname for M-----, also served as a *topos* upon which his captor improvised and deve oped a highly individualized yet highly public performance designed to decompose his subjectivity. Bodily organs and gestures, as well as specific objects, entered into the processual development of the "Shitboy" topos, effectively driving a wedge between M-----'s corporeal and psychosocial sense of self. Even if he was mentally unstable before his capture, guards and interrogators spent weeks exploiting his vulnerabilities, both in isolation and, more often, in public. In the end, the question of whether his pain was self-inflicted or not is irresolvable and even irrelevant: his performance was both scripted and improvised by guards and interrogators within a codified theater of torture designed to produce self-inflicted pain as a means of breaking down his identity.

Coda: Media Shock and Counterperformativity

The CID report on Abu Ghraib also indicates that M----- was not a "high value" prisoner, meaning that he was not thought to possess valuable information, in which case guards likely used his serial abuse in order to intimidate other prisoners, in both live and recorded performances. Now given the widespread use of media, not only at Abu Ghraib, but reportedly also at Bagram and Guantánamo, I believe that media forms a fifth element of the CIA's paradigm of psychological torture, one we might call "media shock." Spectacular abuses perpetrated in isolated cells or rooms targeted the psyche of the prisoner in question. But inmates also report being repeatedly photographed and then told that humiliating images would be shown to family and friends if they did not cooperate. Recall here the Marine Corps brochure's comments about shaming Iraqis in front of others. And, indeed, the majority of known photographed abuses occurred in the central corridor before the eyes of other inmates, who were themselves shamed and intimidated by being forced to watch – and to watch American men and women take photographs and videos of the abuses. In addition, guards reportedly used such photos as screen savers and openly displayed them on prison walls where inmates could see them, effectively telling them that "this can happen to you." In short, the force of theatrical performativity at Abu Ghraib, including media shock, first of all struck the inmates, as both objects and viewers of torture. The public scandal then communicated that force around the world.

The spectacle of the scaffold thus returns both in the cells and corridors of Abu Ghraib and other sites, and through television, computer, and other media networks, by which it reaches a global audience. But in between the local and global audiences, the performative force of the spectacle was radically transformed.

This transformative process began on January 13, 2004, when Graner handed Specialist Joseph M. Darby two CDs containing hundreds of images. Disturbed by what he saw on the CD, Darby turned over the images to CID, and they soon became central to "Article 15–6 Investigation of the 800th Military Police Brigade," a.k.a. the "Taguba Report," which was initiated in late January. By April, a selection of images had been leaked both to CBS and to reporter Seymour Hersh and then subsequently made public by *60 Minutes II* and *The New Yorker*, unleashing the images' performative force around the world. But a strange, yet hopeful, thing happened in this globalization, something that began with whistle-blower Darby's reaction: the performative force of the spectacle inverted and turned on itself. Reframed and publicized by CBS and Hersh, the poles of Good and Evil reversed, as it were, and the persons shamed in the images became England, Frederick, and Graner, and beyond, the U.S. military and, further still, the United States itself. This profound reversal was captured in a political cartoon that appeared soon after the scandal broke. Composed by Tim Menee of *The Pittsburg Post-Gazette*, the cartoon depicts Uncle Sam standing atop a cardboard box with wires attached to his fingers and wearing a black hood and robe; next to him are scrawled the words "UTTER HUMILIATION." Other cartoons – published in the U.S. and abroad – expressed a similar sentiment, using Uncle Sam or other figures associated with the U.S., such as the Statue of Liberty or Lady Justice.

Such reversibility of performative force can be understood in terms of what Butler has called "queering," "resignification," and, following Brecht, "refunctioning." Similarly, Donald MacKenzie, a noted sociologist of science and technology, has recently found that certain economic models, after initial performative success in making reality conform to them, may eventually "alter economic processes so that they conform less well to the theory or model" and may even lead to economic crisis. MacKenzie calls this possibility "counterperformativity,"[24] and while he focuses on economic models, one can extend this concept to potentially *any* model or theory. Indeed, McCoy's study of the CIA model of psychological torture argues that its use by the Philippine military on suspected Communist insurgents in the 1970s and 1980s helped create a group of egomaniacal officers who later tried to overthrow the very government (that of Ferdinand Marcos) on whose behalf they had originally tortured people.[25] In the Iraqi theater of war, the counterperformativity of CIA torture techniques includes the creation of more rather than less insurgency, the production of useless rather than useful intelligence, and the generation of psychic violence not only on

---

24 See Donald MacKenzie, *An Engine, not a Camera: How Financial Models Shape Markets* (Cambridge, Massachusetts: The MIT Press, 2006), p. 19. MacKenzie's primary case study is the 1998 hedge fund crisis associated with Long Term Capital Management (LTCM), a firm that had deployed an economic model known as "Black-Scholes," first to make and then to lose billions of dollars. MacKenzie develops a sophisticated model of performativity, of which "counterperformativity" is one component.

25 See McCoy, *A Question of Torture*, chapter 2.

torture victims but also on the torturers themselves. In this light, the images of torture at Abu Ghraib may have even helped, counterperformatively, to produce in the U.S. public what Eisenman calls "the Abu Ghraib effect," that is, "a kind of moral blindness [...] that allows them to ignore, or even to justify, however partially or provisionally, the facts of degradation and brutality manifest in the pictures."[26] In other words: in the name of morality, (some) Americans blinded themselves to morality.

There is a lesson here about violence performed, violence analyzed, violence cited and incited. One could protest that the very analysis attempted above – a detailed performance analysis of the images of M-----'s torture – could itself contribute to the systematic violence it seeks to critique, could perpetuate the media shock rather than counter it, could contribute to the society of the spectacle of the scaffold rather than warn against it. Similarly, one could protest that political and/or artistic protests against Abu Ghraib, Guantánamo, and Bagram (for instance, protest marchers dressed in black hoods and orange jumpsuits, the performances of interrogation by Coco Fusco or Fassih Keiso, certain graffiti and installation work by Banksy, the film *The Road to Guantanamo* by Michael Winterbottom and Mat Whitecross – all of which can be read as counterperformatives of the CIA torture paradigm), could themselves incite further torture. Such risks are unavoidable, given that the iterability of any and all performances and performatives insures both their possible misfiring *and* their possible success, their very performativity and counterperformativity. No amount of interpretative framing or historical contextualization can ward off such citationality, as framing and contextualization themselves entail citation networks. One could, alternatively, simply withdraw and refuse to cite the violence, whether in words or in images – but that is precisely the move made and encouraged by the Bush administration, which has fought the release of images, as well as further inquiries that would investigate the chain of command and potentially connect torture images to torture memos, theatrical performativity to executive performativity. In an age of global performativities, of performative powers operating on both local and global scales, what is needed is more connecting, citing, and critiquing of violence performed, not less, and countering the spectacle of the scaffold and the theater of torture may well depend on counterperformative spectacle and theater. The risks of producing them are great, but the risks of not doing so are greater still.

---

26 Eisenman, *The Abu Ghraib Effect*, p. 9.

Anneka Esch-van Kan

"Torture Chicks"
Resistance and the Political in Coco Fusco's *A Room of One's Own* and *A Field Guide for Female Interrogators*[1]

Dear Virginia, [...]
Your atelier becomes my torture chamber.[2]

Are we ethically obliged to look at the media relics of war, crimes, and torture? Or are we turning into voyeurs who continue the violence when we consume images? The pictures of torture, including humiliation, mental stress, and sexual assaults, inflicted on inmates by their guards and interrogators in US prison camps in Guantánamo and Abu Ghraib, have given, again, particular relevance to these questions. The horrifying pictures that reveal the paradoxes at the heart of American democracy[3] were partly printed in newspapers and circulate widely on the internet. Many felt obliged to respond to those images – to those that gained public awareness as well as to the openly acknowledged existence of many others that are still hidden from public view.[4] If it were legitimate to speak of an ethical imperative that urges us to actively consider these images, how could we fulfill this obligation in a responsible way? While it is certainly important to acknowledge and regard "the pain of others,"[5] Susan Sontag warns against the implications of sympathetic stances: These lead to an identification with the

1 Many thanks go to Erin Treat for carefully proofreading this essay.

2 Coco Fusco, *A Field Guide for Female Interrogators* (New York: Seven Stories Press, 2008), p. 8.

3 In her *New York Times* article "Regarding the Torture of Others," Susan Sontag stresses that the practice and (public) response to torture is far more than a momentous "scandal," but that it points at a paradox at the heart of American democracy by shedding light on the willingness to use violence to spread democratic values and by revealing two tendencies in contemporary American culture: the celebration of a "culture of shamelessness" and the "reigning admiration for unapologetic brutality." Susan Sontag, "Regarding the Torture of Others," *New York Times* (23 May 2004), (http://www.nytimes.com/2004/05/23/magazine/regarding-the-torture-of-others.html?pagewanted=all&src=pm, publ. 23 May 2004, cit. 30 August 2012).

4 Donald Rumsfeld, for example, openly admitted that "[t]here are a lot more photographs and videos that exist," and that "[i]f these are released to the public, obviously, it's going to make matters worse." Donald Rumsfeld, quoted in Robert Plummer, "US powerless to halt Iraq net images," *BBC News Online* (http://news.bbc.co.uk/2/hi/americas/3695897.stm, publ. 8 May 2004, cit. 30 August 2012).

5 Susan Sontag, *Regarding the Pain of Others* (New York: Farrar, Straus and Giroux: 2003).

victims and too easily let us off the hook and allow us to ignore our own complicity "to what caused the suffering."[6] "Our sympathy" – Sontag emphasizes – "proclaims our innocence as well as our impotence."[7] This is why Sontag decidedly opposes the views of Virginia Woolf, who in her 1938 book-length essay "Three Guineas" responded to a series of war photographs by using them as a plea against war in general. She criticizes Woolf's identification of the depicted sufferers as "anonymous, generic victims"[8] and insists on the necessity of supplementing images with captions that explain their (political) contexts and reflect upon their historically specific implications and consequences.[9] Sontag argues that photographs can ultimately only "supply [...] an initial spark"[10] for a serious engagement with wrongs, (political) violence, and injustices, but that "they are not much help if the task is to understand."[11]

Cuban-American performance artist/scholar Coco Fusco draws both on Sontag and Woolf's ethico-political and emancipatory writing in a series of works (2005–2008) dedicated to the use of torture in general, the specifics of the most recent American practices in prison camps outside the U.S., and the role of women as perpetrators in particular. In *A Field Guide for Female Interrogators*, Fusco openly articulates that she felt ethically obliged to respond to the pictures of torture inflicted on others by American military personnel and – as a woman and feminist – even more so when she learned that female soldiers played a prominent part in this.[12] Instead of taking the easy path of identifying with the victims – risking a fall into the trap of the so-called *ethical turn* and losing sight of politics[13] – Fusco only takes her ethical shock and anger as an "initial spark" and closely investigates the circumstances and structures that make torture likely to happen. It becomes unmistakably obvious that Fusco – without exception – opposes torture; but neither the legitimacy of torture, nor the bashing of the so-called "Bush-administration," nor the search for persons responsible in the military are the subject of the series of artistic projects. Instead, Fusco decided "to pose as a student"[14] and "learn their [the perpetrators']

6 Ibid., pp. 102–103.
7 Ibid., p. 102.
8 Sontag, *Regarding the Pain of Others*, p. 9.
9 Ibid., pp. 9–10.
10 Ibid., p. 103.
11 Ibid., p. 89.
12 Fusco, *A Field Guide*, p. 9.
13 Judith Butler, p. 127.
14 Fusco, *A Field Guide*, p. 65.

language"[15] in order to arrive at an understanding of the logics and (institutional as well as cultural) premises that make such horrifying actions possible[16]: What kind of education do interrogators go through? What kind of reasoning are they trained to follow? Which practices are explicitly authorized and which practices might be silently sanctioned (e.g. by the dropping of charges)? How do interrogators and guards become capable of torture and other atrocities? What role does language and the debate surrounding the range of meanings of "torture" play? How do the specifics of this discourse as well as the media representation of the recent "torture scandal" shape public opinion? And is it possible that the modest public outcry might hint at a paradox of American democracy that cannot be belittled as manipulation and opinion making?

In order to develop an informed perspective on these questions, Fusco – together with an all-female group of scholars and artists – signed up for a course by retired U.S. Army interrogators on interrogation techniques and resistance tactics for prisoners of war. The camp, designed for civilians, adapted elements of military SERE trainings, which teach soldiers tactics for survival, evasion, resistance, and escape. Initially introducing herself as "a university professor who was conducting research on military interrogation as political theater"[17] – a half-honest disguise[18] –, she soon realized that the instructors were surprisingly open to debate and suspiciously unafraid of becoming subject of critical scrutiny. They signaled their readiness to take part in public discussions and allowed Fusco's team to film their experiences in the training camp. This material, together with her extensive research including a number of interviews with scholars and military personnel, later became part of the documentary movie *Operation Atopos* (2006), which follows the women's "extended trip into the fantasy world of

15 Ibid., p. 29.

16 Susan Sontag emphasizes that "the issue is not whether the torture was done by individuals (i.e., 'not by everybody') – but whether it was systematic. Authorized. Condoned." And she continues: "[t]he issue is not whether a majority or a minority of Americans performs such acts but whether the nature of the policies prosecuted by this administration and the hierarchies deployed to carry them out makes such acts likely." Sontag, "Regarding the Torture of Others".

17 Fusco, *A Field Guide*, p. 68.

18 In *A Field Guide*, Fusco stresses that her original "disguise" was at least partly accurate, as she actually conceives of military interrogation as a practice that shows many similarities to theater and performance. Explaining to what extent her disguise was not "untrue," she writes: "I do see interrogation as a form of intercultural theater imposed upon an unwilling audience of one" (ibid.).

military interrogation."[19] The material and experience also played into and significantly shaped Fusco's other productions and texts on the same topic. In 2005, Fusco presented *Bare Life Study #1* in Sao Paulo, Brazil: "a group street performance using routine methods of humiliation in military prisons as choreography."[20] Fusco – in uniform – urged a group of students in orange jumpsuits to clean the ground in front of the U.S. consulate with toothbrushes. Between 2006 and 2008, she developed her lecture-performance *A Room of One's Own: Women and Power in the New America* (2006–2008), which was presented as a work-in-progress at The Kitchen (2005) and premiered at Performance Space 122 (P.S. 122) in 2006, both in New York City. Enacting the part of a pro-military, pro-"torture," yet still feminist female interrogator, Fusco introduces a manual on sexual tactics to be used by female interrogators in particular.

Her 2008 book *A Field Guide for Female Interrogators* (2008) includes this manual, in which Fusco and graphic artist Dan Turner put together sexual tactics that reportedly were used by American interrogators. The largest part of the book, however, consists of an extensive letter to Virginia Woolf. In that letter, Fusco critically engages many of the topics that played into her other artistic projects on a theoretical level, but keeps a safe distance from academic writing or an author's note by the many-faceted combination of materials and the decision to directly address a historic person. Fusco repeatedly ties her arguments back to – or contrasts them with – Woolf's views, and thereby positions her reflections within feminist discourses. She emphasizes how much the world and our conception of it has changed, and how this makes it untenable to hold on to Woolf's highly moralizing perspective – even though she strongly honors her writing and contribution to the feminist cause. Fusco admits that she is "resigned to the persistence of war,"[21] and champions the necessity of developing new approaches to resistance that would allow us to confront the complexities of our time and go beyond easy classifications and binaries such as good and evil, or female and male. In this, she agrees with a great number of contemporary artists and scholars, who have been trying to develop forms of resistance (in art) that move beyond taking (political) sides or advocating specific positions. Qualifying this widespread – and often militant – resistance against the announcement of (political) opinions,

---

19 Ibid., p. 27.

20 Fusco, "Performing the Institutionalization of 'Bare Life,'" (http://hemispheric-institute.org/journal/3.1/eng/artist_presentation/cocofusco/index.html, cit. 30 August 2012).

21 Ibid., p. 9.

Fusco openly declares that she "won't accept torture as a legitimate component"[22] of war. Yet, even though this conviction of hers certainly makes itself felt as an undercurrent in her performances and parts of the *Field Guide*, Fusco's work still resists a reduction to mere messages. This is mainly achieved by the complexity of her series, which multiplies perspectives, transgresses genre boundaries, and most importantly, confronts different discourses.

In the performances, the movie, and the book, the general investigation into the conditions that make the use of torture likely, the urgent question as to whether the actions were politically calculated or otherwise sanctioned, and the exploration into the (shaping of) public opinion are strongly interconnected with thoughtful reflections on the role of women in the military. This nexus, then, is the real centerpiece of Fusco's recent works. Countering her own surprise and shock about the active role of female soldiers and interrogators in practices of torture,[23] Fusco makes common stereotypes both of femininity and the military explicit, pits them against each other, and reveals how these in many ways naïve and improper but very powerful images are consciously exploited. Fusco puts the recent instances of and debates on torture into immediate context with the ongoing struggle for equal rights and treatment for women, critically considers the use of sexual tactics, and suggests that the frequent depiction of women as perpetrators contributed to the relatively modest public outcry in response to the scandal.[24] The critical impulse, however, is bidirectional: Fusco not only points at the exploitation of female sexual violence and stereotypes of femininity in practices and representations of torture, but also targets the desperate attempts of feminist scholars to either ignore or read the role of women in the military (and even in the "torture scandals") in a way that still allows conceiving of women as victims, not perpetrators.[25] This is reflected in Fusco's decision to give her lecture performance the well-thought-out title *A Room of One's Own*, which bears the potential to shock and provoke audiences – and feminist

22 Ibid.

23 Ibid., p. 25; Coco Fusco, "Performing the Institutionalization of 'Bare Life.'"

24 Fusco, *A Field Guide*, pp. 38–40.

25 "It seems to me that the phenomenon of instrumentalized female sexual violence raises many disturbing questions, not only for those who are concerned about the use of torture by the U.S. military, but also for feminists who are accustomed to conceiving of women as victims of sexual violence, not as agents." Coco Fusco, "Authors Note to 'A Room of One's Own,'" *TDR – The Drama Review* 53:1 (Spring 2008): pp. 139–140.

audiences in particular[26] – by explicitly referring to Virginia Woolf's essay of the same title from 1929[27] – that is, to one of the main references and most-often cited texts of the feminist movement in the 1970s. The female interrogator who – in form of the lecture performance – offers a "briefing"[28] on sexual tactics makes the bitterness of the comparison even more explicit, when she welcomes the audience with the following address:

> Ladies and gentlemen, it was the great British writer Virginia Woolf who argued that every woman had to have a room of her own in order to manifest her strengths. At the onset of the new millennium, American women finally have what they need to demonstrate their prowess. The War on Terror offers an unprecedented opportunity to the women of this great country.
> Our nation is putting its trust in our talents, and is providing the support we need to show the world that American women are the *linchpin* in the worldwide struggle for democracy. That struggle for democracy is being waged by women plying their trade in rooms just as Woolf imagined. These are simple rooms furnished with nothing more than a desk and a couple of chairs. And in these sanctorum of liberty, American women are using their minds and their charms to save American lives. I am proud to be one of those women. We are leading our nation's effort to rid the civilized world of terrorism. We are carving a place for ourselves in history.[29]

Fusco, who performs the part of the interrogator herself, is dressed in a camouflage uniform and a visor cap that hides her hair and gives her a stern appearance. She speaks from a lectern positioned center stage with a huge American flag as a backdrop – a typical setting for official speeches that emphasizes the declared patriotism of the orator. To her left is a projection surface that depicts the American Eagle, a standard symbol for the United States that in the context of the War on Terror has repeatedly been turned into a visual equivalent of a war cry. Starting from the quoted address, the screen is used for the PowerPoint presentation that accompanies the "briefing." On the opposite side of the stage, there is another screen that monitors a sparsely equipped prison cell – indicated by a rectangular shape of light. Before a prisoner in orange jumpsuit is brought in, the projection surface shows a map

---

26 "The comparison was intended to shock anyone who clings to outdated ideas about women's relationship to power." Fusco, *A Field Guide*, p. 8.

27 Virginia Woolf, *A Room of One's Own* (London: Hogarth Press, 1929).

28 Fusco, "Author's Note," p. 140.

29 Coco Fusco, "A Room of One's Own," *TDR: The Drama Review* 52:1 (Spring 2008): p. 136–159, pp. 142–143.

of Guantánamo Bay and thereby suggests that the cell represents this specific secret U.S. prison camp. The simulated CCTV footage[30] naturally comes with a continuously running time display that in contrast to photographs – and in line with McKenzie's argument in this book – stresses the importance of sequences, time, and duration in the use of torture.[31] It is also marked with a subtitle: "Gitmo [Guantánamo] Live." Additionally, there is a small table and chair down stage right, which holds telephone and communication devices as well as technical equipment for the creation and playing of visual and auditory material and effects. A video camera is installed center stage and records the entire performance. This underlines the status of the "briefing" as a well-calculated performance and (political) staging. The entrance to the show already includes the calling of cues and commands that unmistakably make clear that Fusco's lecture performance not only adopts military perspectives and arguments, but also simulates the military's performances for its personnel and the public; *A Room of One's Own* then is a "performance of a performance."[32]

Fusco does not try to *represent* the use and justification of torture by the U.S. Army, but *repeats* and *extends* its performance. *Simulation* is of utmost importance in Fusco's entire series: *A Room of One's Own* is a "counter-performance"[33] that simulates a military briefing and – with PowerPoint and CCTV footage – also makes use of media that are commonly part of military presentations. Furthermore, the entire

---

30 Fusco speaks of a "simulated CCTV video." Fusco, "Author's Note," p. 140.

31 Fusco's artistic approach to the topic shows many parallels to McKenzie's deliberations. She emphasizes the necessity of considering the photographs and the execution of torture by American interrogators in a complex way that critically investigates how these phenomena are bound to contemporary American culture and politics. She reflects on the media and techniques of presentation that are involved in practices of torture and/or that are used in its representation and media transmission. And she also conceives of interrogation as a form of theater or performance. The re-enactment of prisoner abuse on stage – recorded by the simulated CCTV technology – affirms McKenzie's claim that sequence and duration are important aspects of torture. Fusco does not smear blood into the inmate's face, nor does she force him to stand naked in front of the audience; her methods are in fact "harmless" compared to the "sexual tactics" described in the briefing. Yet long durations, dehumanizing ways of address, and the constant surveillance already made me – as an audience member – feel alarmingly uncomfortable.

32 Uros Cvoro, "Torture Chicks: feminist artist responses to Abu Ghraib photographs," (http://www.inter-disciplinary.net/wp-content/uploads/2011/04/cvorofpaper.pdf, publ. April 2011, cit. 30 August 2012).

33 José Esteban Muñoz, "Performing the State of Exception. Coco Fusco's *Operation Atopos* and *A Room of One's Own*," *TDR: The Drama Review* 52:1 (Spring 2008): pp. 137–139, p.137.

series is based on Fusco's experiences as a participant in a training camp that simulates the immersive simulations that are used in military training. The doubling or multiplication of simulation reveals the "intangible and symbolic dimensions"[34] of war and exposes the fact that "[w]ars don't just happen on the ground," but that they "take place in our minds."[35] Fusco's move to inscribe the highly contested female "sexual tactics" into the symbolic universe of the U.S. Army is very close to the faking of websites and appropriation of identities by activists such as the Yes-Men, who in a similar vein turned the language of – for instance – the World Trade Organization against itself. Fusco makes tactical use of simulation to shed light on the military mindset and to reveal the preposterousness of the position of women in the U.S. Army.

A Room of One's Own and Fusco's entire series on torture is particularly interesting in the context of this book, because it strongly relies on and relates to recent debates about the resistant potential of art – as it shows in the well-reflected use of simulation; because it entangles aspects of thinking, resisting, and reading the political; and because it engages the question of method on several levels. First, it describes and demonstrates various methods of torture – in the narrow sense of the word – and insists that "sexual tactics" definitely need to be counted in. Second, the documentary movie and the book make Fusco's methodical proceeding and her tactics of approaching the topic explicit. Third, the techniques of artistic (re)presentation and tactics of resistance – and here I am consciously avoiding the term "method"[36] – are clearly related to recent theories of resistance and the political. Fourth, the series challenges standard methods of analysis, as it transgresses genre boundaries, mixes media, breaks with conceptions of self-contained art works, and balks at any attempt to read the performances, the movie, and/or the book on a semantic level only. The series combines philosophical thought (most prominently in *A Field Guide*), investigative research (particularly evident in her participation in the training camp and her extensive research and interviews on methods of interrogation), activist intervention (specifically her appearance as an inter-

34 Fusco, *A Field Guide*, p. 10.

35 Ibid.

36 The term "method" suggests that there is a clearly defined way to an equally defined goal. This cannot be claimed for tactical practices that gain impact by their potential for quickly adapting to changing circumstances, and it also does not quite meet artistic practices and techniques that are freely employed – as many scholars and artists nowadays would probably claim – in a tactical fashion.

rogator in front of an art school[37] and the street performance *Bare Life #1* as a form of public demonstration), and political theater (mainly in *A Room of One's Own* – a stage performance for a paying audience that presents a lecture given by a fictional persona, a hyperpatriotic female military interrogator who describes effective methods to protect the American homeland and its people). Even though foci can obviously be determined, forms of thinking, resisting, and reading the political mark not only the series as a whole but also each individual project, and I argue that this close entanglement of perspectives and points of attack is crucial for the resistant potential of Fusco's work and an important element for contemporary political art in general.

Starting from the widespread assumptions that the *grand narratives* of former times have died out, that art has lost its political function and is unlikely to effect change, and that partisanship and advocacy of opinions eventually play into mainstream culture and politics, how could it still be possible to critically engage with the contemporary world? How could it be possible to challenge the way our living together is organized and the way political decisions are formed and executed? What possibilities might be left to destabilize the given *distribution of the sensible* – as Jacques Rancière coins it – that determines what can be said, heard, or seen?[38] How could the theatricality of everyday and public life be brought to light and critically challenged? Which tactics could be of use in developing forms of thought and expression that escape the confines of a given *distribution of the sensible* and thereby make *politics* occur as an event that interrupts *police* – both in the Rancièrian sense?[39]

In the last two or three decades, questions such as these have preoccupied many scholars and artists. Yet, they gained particular relevance in the so-called "War on Terror" that has made the paradoxes at the heart of Western democracies clearly visible and generated the urgent need to develop powerful forms of resistance and critique. This pressing situation has further spurred on the so-called *ethical turn*, which opposes the wariness towards taking clear positions and the theoreti-

37 In January 2007, Fusco was invited to speak at the symposium "The Feminist Future" at the Museum of Modern Art in New York City. She addressed the audience in character of a representative of the U.S. Army and "congratulated [her] peers in the art world for their strategic containment of feminism and their effective use of women" (Fusco, *A Field Guide*, p. 93). Her talk is published in *A Field Guide*: Coco Fusco, "Our Feminist Future," *A Field Guide*, pp. 93–105.

38 Jacques Rancière, *The Politics of Aesthetics*, trans. Gabriel Rockhill (London/New York: Continuum, 2004), pp. 12–19.

39 Jacques Rancière, *Disagreement. Politics and Philosophy*, trans. Julie Rose (Minneapolis: University of Minnesota Press, 1998).

cally supported ambivalence of (postmodern) critical practices that often focus on the destabilization of binary logics and the disclosure of general structures and premises that limit our perception and thought. Yet many – such as Judith Butler and Simon Critchley in this book, as well as Rancière in his essay "The Ethical Turn of Aesthetics and Politics"[40] – have argued that this is, in fact, a misleading consequence of the discontent with deconstructivist thought, the highly philosophical theories of radical democracy, and poststructuralist-inspired conceptions of resistance and the political in the arts. Especially in the context of the American political rhetoric of the past decade, it becomes very problematic indeed to turn political arguments into ethical ones; by applying binaries between good and evil and claiming to fight for humanity, equality, and freedom, critically-intended projects fall in line with mainstream discourses and finally contribute to the alarming vanishing of politics.[41] Hence, the question arises whether there could be another way to envisage resistant practices that hold up to the standards of theoretically informed perspectives and still allow for active engagement in concrete situations that might include ethical stances. Fusco's series on torture searches for such a form of resistance – in art and beyond – and I would like to argue that it meets this challenge.

Fusco's decision to "learn the language" of the military and try to understand the training and logics of interrogators instead of bemoaning the victims and shouting out for justice is clearly connected with the theoretically supported conviction that there is no "outside" and that resistance can only ever happen from within.[42] According to Michel de Certeau, *tactics* – as opposed to *strategies* – wind themselves through a given order or system to find ways to destabilize it from within.[43] Fusco proceeds tactically when she uses the language and rules of the military and feminist discourse to destabilize both. The confrontation of these discourses forms a Lyotardian *différend* in that two incompatible systems of rules confront each other, justify massively conflicting perspectives, and cannot in any way be reconciled.[44] This is why it is factually impossible to reduce Fusco's projects to a set of messages.

---

40 Jacques Rancière, "The Ethical Turn of Aesthetics and Politics," trans. Jean-Philippe Deranty, *Critical Horizons* 7.1 (2006): pp. 1–20.

41 Compare Judith Butler in this volume, as well as Rancière "The Ethical Turn".

42 Compare the writings of Michel Foucault, Gilles Deleuze, Michael Hardt and Antonio Negri among many others.

43 Michel De Certeau, *The Practice of Everyday Life*, trans. Steven Rendall (Berkeley: University of California Press, 1984), esp. pp. 51–55.

44 See Jean-François Lyotard, *Differend. Phrases in Dispute*, ed. Wlad Godzich, trans. Georges van den Abbeele (Minneapolis: University of Minnesota Press, 1988).

In *A Room of One's Own*, Fusco uses the tactic of *overidentification*[45] and pushes military rhetoric to extremes. She sticks to the channels of communication and ways of representation used by the military and uses them to present "sexual difference as completely subsumed under the symbolic law of the military"[46]; what is usually communicated and taught in a negative way – that is, tactics that are not supposed to be used and information that is (officially) provided to secure the fair treatment of prisoners – is turned into a manual of approved methods of interrogation and is affirmed as part of military training. Fusco performs without any irony. Despite a certain level of absurdity, the persuasive power of military reasoning is hardly diminished; the female lecturer proclaims that the allocation of responsible positions to women in the military should be celebrated as a (final) success of the struggle for women's equality and sticks to the unpopular argument of many politicians and military representatives in rejecting a definition of "sexual tactics" as torture.[47] She argues that "[m]odern-day interrogation is not torture," and explains that "[i]nflicting physical pain is utterly ineffective on hardened terrorists who have no regard for life."[48] The central question here is obviously not the ethical defensibleness of "sexual tactics" or torture, but the effectiveness of methods to obtain information: "Pain is useless when you are after the truth."[49] Rather than "inflicting pain," interrogators are advised to apply "stress."[50] This leads the lecturer to the definition of "[m]odern interrogation" as "the calculated deployment of mental and physical pressure by experts."[51]

Probably military briefings would not open with a reference to Virginia Woolf and – at least at this point – they would certainly not present "sexual tactics" as part of basic training, but despite these alienations, the lecture-performance seems to strictly follow military logics and reasoning. The goal is to get information from suspects or

---

45 Cvoro, "Torture Chicks".

46 Ibid.

47 "There was also the avoidance of the word 'torture.' The prisoners had possibly been the objects of 'abuse,' eventually of 'humiliation' - that was the most to be admitted. 'My impression is that what has been charged thus far is abuse, which I believe technically is different from torture,' Secretary of Defense Donald Rumsfeld said at a press conference. 'And therefore I'm not going to address the 'torture' word.'" Sontag, "Regarding the Torture of Others".

48 Fusco, "A Room of One's Own," p. 144.

49 Ibid.

50 Ibid.

51 Ibid.

confidants, and any method to get there is judged by its effectiveness.[52] When female interrogators resort to stereotypes and misogynistic prejudices, it is undoubtedly approved by the interrogators and their superiors if it shows results. In *A Field Guide*, Fusco points out that "[w]hen she asked a few young women who had served how they felt about being asked to use their sexuality as part of their patriotic duty, they seemed to have difficulty understanding the question."[53] This lack of understanding makes the incompatibility of military and feminist discourses blatantly obvious. Responses of feminist audience members, who felt wounded and apparently accused Fusco of having severely harmed the feminist cause by celebrating the work of female interrogators as one of its successes,[54] are equally telling of the fundamental disagreement. And so is Fusco's finding that with rare exceptions (such as Angela Davis), feminists close their eyes towards violence performed by women, and her declarative statement that "[w]e don't really have a language for comprehending female sexual aggression as rape [or as torture], which diminishes our ability to perceive it as such."[55]

On the one hand, the lack of a language for female violence, feminist audiences' feeling of having been wounded, and the lack of understanding between Fusco and military personnel hints at the impossibility of a negotiation between the discourses. On the other hand, however, the missing vocabulary for violence inflicted on others by women and stereotypical depictions of women are tactically played out in interrogations and public representations in the context of the "torture scandals." Fusco suggests that the fact that many of the published photographs depict women in the act of degrading prisoners might follow a rationale.[56] The laughter of audiences at the graphics in *A Room of One's Own*, which were later published in *A Field Guide*, is proof of the effectiveness of the crossing of discourses and of the incapacity of accepting the seriousness of female sexual aggression as torture. This is also reflected in the spreading of notions such as "torture lite"[57] or "torture chicks,"[58] which undermine the seriousness of "sexual tactics" as violence and torture. And it also becomes obvi-

---

52 "They [the instructors of the training camp standing in for the military] have no trouble with the use of force as long as they can justify it as necessary. In their world, everything, including hurting people, can be rationalized." Fusco, *A Field Guide*, p. 77.

53 Ibid., p. 49.

54 Ibid., pp. 80–81.

55 Ibid., p. 54.

56 Ibid., p. 26.

57 Ibid., p. 38.

58 Ibid., p. 20.

ous in the media representation of female military police depicted on several of the photographs, such as the extensive public discussion of Lynndie England's private life and social background that picture her "as a victim."[59] In *A Field Guide*, Fusco makes the potential consequences of these shifts from one discourse to the other explicit when she asks: "Can poor, uneducated women who themselves are victims of their boyfriends in addition to being tools of an authoritarian power structure like the military be blamed for violating human rights as part of their job? If torture involves women doing things to men of a sexual nature, which has been the case in numerous interrogations in Guantánamo, Iraq and Afghanistan, can it even be called torture?"[60] The shift to feminist discourse obscures the violence precisely because military and feminist discourses are mutually exclusive when it comes to the relation of women and violence, or women and power. The *différend* between military and feminist discourses[61] creates a situation in which a mutual understanding becomes impossible and in which there is no ground for communication; feminists lack the language to describe female violence, and serving women are devoid of a vocabulary that would allow understanding the problematic use of misogynist prejudices and stereotypes in the military.

The juxtaposition of different discourses that form a *différend*, the tactical use of simulation, the decision to destabilize a given *distribution of the sensible* from within, and the general focus on the conditions that limit what can be perceived, expressed, or thought firmly ground *A Room of One's Own* and Fusco's other projects on torture in recent philosophical debates on resistance and the political. However, one might argue that Fusco merely applies philosophical insights to critically engage with the "torture scandals," but that her series does not contribute much to the discussion of the resistant potential of art in our time. Quite to the contrary, I am convinced that Fusco's series has the potential to provide stimulating impulses to recent debates: The

---

59 Fusco, "Author's Note," p. 139.

60 Fusco, *A Field Guide*, pp. 39–40.

61 In this article, I am entirely leaving out intercultural aspects that play into *A Room of One's Own* and further complicate the role of women (in the military) and the use of "sexual tactics." The lecture includes a passage on "the Arab mind" that is based on material and handbooks reportedly used by the military. In the reenactment of prisoner abuse on stage – that runs parallel to the lecture – it turns out that the inmate is Pakistani and does not understand Arabic. Responding in Urdu and broken English, he tries to communicate that he wants to speak to a male officer. It is certainly promising to further explore the role of American and Arab stereotypes and prejudices as well as the relation of ethnic discourse to the *différend* between military and feminist discourses.

complex interconnection of the individual projects – which emerge out of each other, provide material for one another, or offer readings of earlier parts of the series – allows Fusco to multiply perspectives, confront incompatible discourses, and blur the boundaries of art, life, and scholarship.

She breaks away from the awkward tendency to pronounce certain forms of political art dead only to advocate another. Instead of putting all of one's eggs in one basket, Fusco combines diverse forms of expression without valuing one more than the other, without using the potential of one to argue for the inefficacy and misguidedness of another: Documentary, tactical simulation, activist demonstration, and scholarship coexist, break through each other, confront each other, and comment on one another. Fusco's series on the "torture scandals" and the role of female interrogators in the U.S. Army blurs the boundaries between thinking, resisting, and reading the political by combining art, scholarship, and activism in an investigative approach, a form of scenic research. She combines various approaches to political art and levers out distinctions between "political theater" – that is, theater that explicitly addresses politics – and "the political in theater" – that is, theater that shifts focus from content to form and explores the conditions of possibility, and the limits of perception and thought. She not only addresses a hot-button issue of our time, but also complements her intriguing analysis of the unsettling consequences of the *différend* between military and feminist discourses with a decidedly ethical and critical stance. In *A Field Guide*, she openly opposes torture, explores the rationale behind its use, exposes factors that make the use of torture likely, clearly identifies female "sexual tactics" as torture, and at the same time criticizes the feminist belief in the ultimate victimhood of women and the ignorance of many feminists towards female violence. Even though other projects do not explicitly verbalize these claims – *A Room of One's Own*, for example, strictly sticks to military rhetorics – , convictions clearly accompany her performances, the book, and the movie.

Yet despite this decidedly ethical attitude and clear positioning, Fusco's series escapes the traps of the *ethical turn* and stays at a safe distance from agit-prop theater. The rejection of torture plays into each single project, but Fusco neither loses herself in accusations nor in arguments over the legitimacy of the use of torture. Rather, she explores the range of its meanings and the particular role of the language used to describe it. Furthermore, she zooms in on the role of female interrogators in practices of torture and explores the relation between women and power both from a military and a feminist perspective. The clash between those discourses leaves audiences with a sense of unease; it destabilizes both perspectives and provokes disturbing questions that are finally left open. How does the fact that female interrogators have prominently participated in and enacted torture potentially change (feminist) perspectives on the interrelations between gender and violence? What consequences could we draw from the impossibility of reconciling feminist and military discourses? How could we arrive at a language that allows understanding feminine violence as well as the exploitation of misogynist feminine stereotypes in the military? And, perhaps most importantly, what cultural and political changes would be necessary to make torture less likely to happen?

Andreas Hetzel

Prendre la parole
Voices of Resistance in Contemporary Theory

I want to consider whether there can be a speech beyond the "one" language we know, and whether such speech may connect to a certain notion of politics. I want to start from a rhetorical point of view, because classical rhetoric does not know anything like our modern concept of language in the sense of a system of rules or competences; the classical authors only had a concept of speech, which is always already concretely situated, addressed and efficient.[1] Following traditional rhetorics, I assume that we speak more than one language whenever we speak, and that this is true in a twofold sense. Neither do we simply actualize a system of meanings, rules, and competences, nor do we restrict ourselves to the limits of one single language or even one discourse. A counter-hegemonic speech as suggested in acts of translation, of *seizing the word* (*prendre la parole*), and of catachrestic resignification, can only repeatedly redraw the limits of languages and discourses, introducing language less as its own precondition than as its result.

The perspective of a counter-hegemonic or resistant speech connects to a number of political questions: How may those who have no share nor space in our time articulate themselves? Which events of enunciation correspond to their precarious forms of life? What concepts can describe such events most adequately? In order to answer these questions, I recur to three recent theoretical propositions: First, to Jacques Derrida's and Judith Butler's concept of a *translation* that precedes any single language logically and genealogically, and that relegates the very notion of single languages to the realm of theoretical fiction; secondly, to Jacques Rancière's notion of *seizing the word*, i.e. of facing Louis Althusser's theorem of appellation (which assigns the subject to its place within the symbolic order) by an insistence on the possibility of inventing a paradoxical language, of being heard even while disregarding rules of established languages and discourses; thirdly, to Butler's *catachrestic resignification*, which critically appropriates or recodes a given ascription of identity.

1 Andreas Hetzel, *Die Wirksamkeit der Rede. Zur Aktualität klassischer Rhetorik für die moderne Sprachphilosophie* (Bielefeld: Transcript, 2011).

1. Translation

"What is proper to a culture is to not be identical to itself."[2] Its eccentric identity as claimed by Derrida hails from a doubly negatory relationship. The proper, familiar and shared horizons of meaning represented by any culture are in a certain way nothing other than the other of its other. That other at once stabilizes and destabilizes each culture. From this perspective, every translation can also claim a certain priority before its original. For only translatability into the foreign language constitutes the ever precarious identity of a native tongue. For Derrida, we never speak only one language, much less a native tongue. Language, and especially "my" language, hails from the other in several ways; it never truly belongs to me, it was there before me, its effects are incalculable to me. Even my native language would be foreign in this sense, and any communication within a native language shows traces of translation. Derrida points out that a language "consists only of transference," and that all we have here is "a thinking through of transference, in all the senses that this word acquires in more than one language, and first of all that of the transference between languages."[3] He even goes so far as to "risk a single definition of deconstruction" which centers on translation: "*plus d'une langue* – both more than a language and no more *a* language."[4]

Following Derrida, Homi K. Bhabha conceives of culture as a whole as something "translational,"[5] as a shifted and shifting, translated and translating practice that can only be grasped within the shifts, transfers and supplementations of cultures, a plural for which each singular culture is understood as that self-identical horizon of meaning. A rhetorics of cultural translations would have to examine the metaphors, metonymies and catachreses dressing this translation for each case. As opposed to an objectivist study of culture reifying each single culture, such a rhetorics of the cultural would focus on the in-between and on the interjections, on articulation that takes place at the margins and at the limits.

---

2 Jacques Derrida, *The Other Heading. Reflections on Today's Europe*, trans. Pascale-Anne Brault and Michael B. Naas (Bloomington/Indianapolis: Indiana University Press, 1992), p. 9.

3 Jacques Derrida, *Memoires. For Paul de Man.*, trans. Cecile Lindsay, Jonathan Culler, and Eduardo Cadava (New York: Columbia University Press, 1986), pp. 14–15.

4 Ibid., p. 15.

5 Homi Bhabha, *The Location of Culture* (London: Routledge, 1994), p. 247.

Following again Derrida's and Bhabha's de-position of the identitary concept of culture, and accepting the priority of translation before the translated, Judith Butler redresses the relationship between universalism and particularism in cultural theory and seeks an explication of universality *as* translation. It is only by starting with practices of translation and hybridization that particular cultural identities can be addressed retrospectively. Butler explains culture in this sense to be no "bounded entity,"[6] but "a relation of exchange and a task of translation"[7]: Translation that always takes place in the impossible space between cultures would then be culture in the most proper sense. It is connected to a universalizing effect that can never be arrested nor projected onto any fixed structure. With this argument, Butler joins the tradition of Walter Benjamin's counter-factual "language as such" (*Sprache überhaupt*[8]), a postulated universal language towards which individual languages are transcended in the (always impossible) moment of translation, but which can never be hypostatized *as a universal language* or replaced by the practices of translation.

Butler transforms universality into a "labor of transaction and translation which belongs to no single site, but is the movement between languages, and has its final destination in this movement itself."[9] This marks a post-foundationalist turn in universalist thought. Here, universality no longer results from suspending particularities in a universal horizon of reconciliation, but rather it shines through any particular perspective as its specific claim to a universal audience transcending that same perspective.

As a practice and process, translation precedes that which is translated: "Translation is no reproduction; there is nothing given beforehand that could then be translated"[10]; it transcends limits and first begets the very territories between which it oscillates by traversing their limits. Like metaphor, it transfers something from one territory to the other, transforming source and target language in this process. "Translation and translated text" are "host and guest to each other as

6 Judith Butler, "Restaging the Universal: Hegemony and the Limits of Formalism," Judith Butler, Ernesto Laclau, and Slavoj Žižek, *Contingency, Hegemony, Universality. Contemporary Dialogues on the Left* (London/New York: Verso, 2000), pp. 11–43, p. 20.

7 Ibid., pp. 24–25.

8 Walter Benjamin, "Über Sprache überhaupt und über die Sprache des Menschen," *Gesammelte Schriften*, Bd. II.1 (Frankfurt/M.: Suhrkamp, 1980), pp. 140–157, p. 145.

9 Judith Butler, "Competing Universalities," Butler, Laclau, and Žižek, *Contingency, Hegemony, Universality*, pp. 136–181, p. 179.

10 Felix Christen, *Eine andere Sprache. Friedrich Hölderlins große Pindar-Übertragung* (Basel: Engeler, 2007), p. 15.

strangers. Their place is another language yet to be conceived."[11] That other language plays into any speech that never belongs completely to any one language.

2. Seizing the Word

Rancière develops his concept of *seizing the word* on two different grounds: Once as part of his projected history of the proletariat, and then also in the course of his attempt to redefine political philosophy. For Rancière, a politics that lives up to its name cannot be enclosed in the limits of any institution, societal system or discursive field, but coincides with a struggle concerning those very limits. It is only "a dispute about the existence of politics through which politics occurs."[12] Authentic political practice does not fulfill established rules, but permanently seeks out their positing and replacement. From this perspective, the political concerns a fundamentally disruptive struggle in which literally everything is at stake: the object of the struggle as well as the criteria by which the dispute might be settled, and likewise the identity of the struggling parties. Politics is not exhausted in parliamentary dispute, but begins only when those parts of the population that lack institutional representation, such as the proletariat or the *sans-papiers*, demand the "institution of a part of those who have no part."[13]

"Speaking out [*Prendre la parole*]"[14] is, in Rancière's thought, to invent a language for the shareless, claiming an audience but without submitting to the rules of an established discourse. Any genuinely political event is in this sense "tied to an excess of speech in the specific form of a displacement of the *statement*: an appropriation 'outside the truth' of the speech of the other (of the formulas of sovereignty, of the ancient text, of the sacred word) that makes it signify differently."[15] The politically subversive speech act retroactively creates its own author-subject. While Althusser emphasizes the objective side of subjectivation and describes the subject as an effect of certain dispositives

11 Ibid.

12 Jacques Rancière, *Disagreement: Politics and Philosophy*, trans. Julie Rose (Minneapolis/London: University of Minnesota Press, 1999), p. 14.

13 Ibid., p. 11.

14 Ibid., p. 37.

15 Jacques Rancière, *The Names of History*, trans. Hassan Melehy (Minneapolis/London: University of Minnesota Press, 1994), p. 30; In the same book he describes the political event as the "entrance of the people from anonymity into the universe of speakers" (Ibid., p. 44).

and ideological appellations, Rancière points out the resistant quality of the subjective practices that face the power of dispositives. For him, a subject emerges at the very moment when it leaves its assigned place and audibly articulates an inaudible demand, something that is impossible within the hegemonic regime of representation. Its interjections do not only interrupt certain discursive routines, but announce a new ballgame for all discursive processes. To successfully seize the word is to transform the generative situation, and to revise what Stuart Hall called the global "regimes of representation."[16]

With his concept of *seizing the word*, Rancière can refer to a rhetorical tradition. In the first book of his *Politics*, Aristotle introduces man as a *zoon politikon* and shortly thereafter as a *zoon logon echon*.[17] Politics and logos, power and language, are close siblings in this foundational document of occidental political thought. This already expresses a basic insight of modern theories of power: As every power requires symbolical articulation, any lingual utterance coincides with effects of power. Both take place in a space of power that provides the very meaning, audibility and possibility of the utterance. But at the same time, lingual utterances offer their own effects on the spaces of power in turn, shifting their borders and redefining the realm of the sayable.

Aristotle describes the *polis* as the epitome of the political and as a kind of hybrid between power and language. It marks a space of *logoi*, of public speeches brought forth by the free and the equal in order to settle the matters of the community. The free and the equal mutually empower themselves to institute the *polis*, a task that tends towards infinity. As a space of the political, the *polis* has clear boundaries; it is defined by multiple outsides, not only in the shape of other *poleis*, but also in the shape of an inner outside, of the *oikon* as an unpolitical space of dominance over women, children, and slaves. Rancière shows how Aristotle's *Politics* can be read as a foundational document of the political as well as of post-politics.[18] It denies some groups among the populace the competence for politics. To define the border between the political and the non-political is an eminently political gesture, as Carl Schmitt has shown. In Aristotle's text, politics is thus born twice: as a radical democracy, in which all may decide all (or speak about all), and as a definition of those persons that cannot speak, and those

16 Stuart Hall, ed., *Representation. Cultural representations and signifying practices* (London: Sage, 2010).
17 Aristoteles, *Politik. Griechisch und Deutsch*, ed. Franz Susemihl (Leipzig: Wilhelm Engelmann, 1879), 1253a.
18 Rancière, *Disagreement*, pp. 1–20.

topics that cannot be spoken about. A definition that is itself political in a larger sense, but that Aristotle does not declare as such.

Scholars have tended to interpret the postpolitical aspect of Aristotle's *Politics* as an atavism, a concession to either his teacher Plato or to an aristocratic zeitgeist. But Aristotle is by no means a representative of aristocracy. As a metic, he himself falls under the verdict of lacking the very political ability which he formulates. The metics are not far removed from slaves and barbarians, as they are all *aneu logou*, without language. From this point of view we should ask ourselves from what place it is that Aristotle himself speaks. Perhaps that peculiar place should be characterized as the proper place of a philosophy that understands itself as a form of discourse beyond politics, but that certainly does intervene in a concrete political manner, as Aristotle himself proves. The metics' intervention first of all consists in anchoring the difference between the spaces of the political and the pre-political in the orders of being: "Who is by his nature (*physin*) not his own, but another's, and yet is human, is by his nature a slave."[19] The slave is reduced to a prosthesis of his master, "an animated but separate part of his body."[20] Slaves have a soul, but no reason; the latter they require from their masters who convey it by means of language: "The slaves must be cautioned and reasonably taught even more than children."[21] While children, slaves, women, and enemies are permanently spoken about in the first book of the *Politics*, they never speak themselves.

But as Rancière as well as Agamben[22] have pointed out, Aristotle does not only exclude some groups from the political space, but also divides the very concept of the *demos*, the people, itself. In some passages of the text, *everyone* counts as *demos*; in others, it is only the poor. Aristotle describes democracy, the dominance of the *demos*, as a *parekbasis* or "degeneration"[23] of polity, because democracy does not serve "the best of the community," but only "the advantage of the poor."[24] As is the case in Plato, democracy is here used synonymously for a dominance of the mob. The rich are few, the poor are many. Polity, as opposed to democracy, respects the minority rights of the rich; it

---

19 Aristoteles, *Politik*, 1254a.

20 Ibid., 1255b.

21 Ibid., 1260b.

22 Giorgio Agamben, *Means without end. Notes on Politics*, trans. Vincenzo Binetti and Cesare Casarino (Minneapolis/London: University of Minnesota Press, 2008), pp. 29–36.

23 Aristoteles, *Politik*, 1279b.

24 Ibid.

could be characterized as a democracy that spares the inequalities of property, that accepts, naturalizes and de-politicizes the economical difference. But for Aristotle, it remains "accidental that the one [the rich] are few and the others [the many] are poor."[25] In this remark, there is some revolutionary potential. The division of the polis into rich and poor does not seem to be founded in nature in the same way as the differences between men and women or between free men and slaves. It is not necessary that few are rich and many are poor. A differently distributed community remains conceivable: for instance, one in which everyone is rich. The status of the *demos* would then have to change; the distinctions of "all" and "mob," of democracy and polity, would fall away. But this possibility is denied by Aristotle as a kind of threat, a *parekbasis* from the proper path.

That path of strict social classification is justified through a cosmological argument: "The opposition of dominance and servitude appears wherever something consists of several parts and constitutes a unity."[26] Aristotle's model, not unlike Plato's, is the dichotomy of body and soul, which does perhaps always serve to justify hierarchies. It is similar to the opposition of male and female: "the woman's decorum is silence," as Aristotle quotes "the poet."[27] As in Plato, the cosmological argument in Aristotle serves to de-politicize the relationship between the included and the foreigner, between men and women, between the owners and the owned. In this foundational text of political thought, metaphysics and cosmology entertain a metapolitics concerning the delimitation of the political, which is always connected with a denial of the political. In this sense, we can only arrive at the political once we decouple politics and metaphysics, once we de-spatialize it and stop thinking of it as an exclusive sphere. This is precisely what is at stake in ancient rhetorics, which Rancière recurs to in his concept of *seizing the word*.

First of all, Aristotle strictly distinguishes politics from economics, as the latter is the most unpolitical discipline of all; the *oikon* counts as a sphere of the mere reproduction of life, of necessity and dominance. Every free and equal citizen is head to an *oikon*. His freedom and equivalence appear as an effect of his private dominance, of the women's, children's, and slaves' lack of freedom and equivalence. Although Aristotle does concede that "every family is a part of the state,"[28] it is so only in the sense of what Rancière has called the

---

25 Ibid., 1280a.
26 Ibid., 1254a.
27 Ibid., 1260a.
28 Ibid., 1260b.

"part of those who have no part [*la part des sans-part*]."[29] Politics and economics correspond to two utterly different types of space: Politics denote the public and open space of the *agora* and of participation, economics denote the excluded and invisible space within the four walls of a home.

In the first book of his *Politics*, Aristotle distinguishes two forms of economics: Economics proper, a kind of economy of subsistence forever assigned to the living center of hearth and home, and chrematistics, a kind of catachrestic abuse of economics, which leaves its place and conquers space and time, replaces commodities with money, and produces worth from commodities. Aristotle radically rejects this second form, describing it in terms of an alienation. But I want to ask if we might not begin with Aristotle and yet conceive of a not only chrematistic and catachrestic, but also abusive politics, a politics that ignores the peaceful limits of the *polis*, as well as all the borders that Aristotle and the classical *polis* have created for the political?

There are hints to such a politics, and thus to a speech of the speechless, both in ancient rhetorical tradition and in Rancière. Rhetorics has always been suspected of incorporating an apology, as well as a technique, for a speech of dominance. It has defended itself by showing that the rhetor not only raises his voice in service to power, but even more so in service to the powerless. A good speaker will speak for the good cause, for instance by pleading a wrongly accused man's innocence. The craft does not sell out to anyone and for any use: "And the speaker will not defend everyone," as Quintilian maintains, "he will not open the safe haven of eloquence to pirates, and he will mostly make his support depend upon the case."[30] Cicero likewise emphasizes that the orator must assist the weak and shareless most of all. The speaker has to prefer the defense to the prosecution, "more so when saving someone threatened and oppressed by a powerful man's influence."[31] Though rhetorics might not yet be acquainted with the possibility that those lacking a place in society seize the word, it does at least allow for a complementary strategy of lending them a voice.

It is Rancière who begins to conceive of that other possibility, which might correspond to the catachrestic politics described above. In Rancière's thought, *seizing the word* is about inventing a language for the shareless who claim an audience without submitting to the rules

---

29 Rancière, *Disagreement*, p.9.

30 Marcus Fabius Quintilianus, *Institutionis oratoriae*, ed. Helmut Rahn (Darmstadt: WBG, 1995), XII 7, 4.

31 Marcus Tullius Cicero, *De officiis/Vom pflichtgemäßen Handeln*, ed. Heinz Gunermann (Stuttgart: Reclam, 1976), II 51.

of an established discourse. "The ailment of politics is first the ailment of words."[32] What threatens the self-sufficiency of the political sphere are the "poorly used words or unwarranted phrases [...], superfluous words, words that designate nothing other than the very targets against which they place weapons in the killers' hands."[33] These words are unheard in a twofold sense; inaudible and yet claiming an audience. They create a lingual "nonplace,"[34] they dislocate the interdependent orders of the sayable and the political. For Rancière, this has mostly been the case for the declarative speech acts of democratic revolutions, from ancient times unto the presence.

Rancière locates one such non-space where the "deceptive event of excessive speech"[35] becomes audible in the 16th chapter of Tacitus' *Annales*. This author closely binds rhetorics to a radicalized concept of democracy. In his *Dialogue on the Orator*, Tacitus explains that rhetorics become possible if and only if "*omnia omnes poterant*,"[36] if everyone can do everything. In the 16th chapter of the *Annales*, Tacitus reports a revolution by Roman legions in Pannonia. He dates this revolution to the interregnum following the death of Augustus. The insurrection is led by a "certain Percennius," a simple soldier, but one who understands oratory as well as theatre, as Tacitus points out. It is only against the backdrop of the interregnum that Percennius can raise his demands: For a loosening of military regulations, for participation, for just treatment and pay, and for a settlement for soldiers' retirement. It is the interruption that "erected the nonplace in the place, gave speech to the one who had no place to speak,"[37] as Rancière describes it. As a simple soldier, Percennius belonged to the share– and speechless, to those who could not be subject of any politics by definition: "Percennius had no place to speak. Nevertheless, Tacitus makes him speak."[38] Tacitus calls on the impossible voice of Percennius in his text, but only to immediately bid it silence once more, to reject it as inappropriate, to describe his demands as ill-founded and to restitute legitimate power. His historiographical discourse is on the side of the victors, as is almost every historiography. Tacitus attempts to draw potency away from any future reference to Percennius by proscribing

---

32 Rancière, *The Names of History*, p. 19.
33 Ibid.; translation modified, AH.
34 Ibid., p. 18.
35 Ibid., p. 24.
36 Tacitus, *Dialogus de oratoribus/Dialog über den Redner*, ed. Dietrich Klose (Stuttgart: Reclam, 1981), 40, 3.
37 Rancière, *The Names of History*, p. 25.
38 Ibid., pp. 25–26.

the language that Percennius will have spoken. And yet for Rancière, this is another, impossible voice claiming valence and audience despite this historiography of dominance. It is towards this voice that Rancière adopts a perspective of Benjamin's "saving critique." He reconstructs the unfulfilled demands of the simple Roman soldiers and orients them towards the current demands of the shareless. Percennius' voice can once more be taken from the victors' discourse, here: the historiographers' discourse, in the way of a revolution or an event: "the entrance of the people from anonymity into the universe of speakers,"[39] the opening "of a class that is no longer a class but the 'dissolution of all classes.'"[40]

3. Catachrestic Resignification

More recently, Judith Butler has also developed an interest in similar moments where the word is seized. She describes an interesting example: "In the spring of 2006, street demonstrations on the part of illegal residents broke out in various California cities, but very dramatically in the Los Angeles area. The US national anthem was sung in Spanish as was the Mexican anthem."[41] George Bush reacted by claiming the American hymn was only to be sung in English. To sing it in Spanish amounts to a catachrestic or parekbatic political act in Butler's interpretation. The singing is heard in the non-place, on the streets: "The street is exposed as a place where those who are not free to amass, freely do so."[42] Butler wants to "suggest that this is precisely the kind of performative contradiction that leads not to impasse, but to forms of insurgency."[43]

The fruitful performative contradiction to which Butler alludes is found in any antihegemonial declarative speech act: "'Declaring' becomes an important rhetorical movement, since it is the very freedom of expression for which it calls or, rather, it is the very call of freedom. Freedom cannot pre-exist this call […], but can only exist in its exercise."[44] In the same way that revolution is bound to an event for Rancière, Butler points out that

---

39 Ibid., p. 44.

40 Ibid., p. 92.

41 Judith Butler and Gayatri Chakravorty Spivak, *Who Sings the Nation-State? Language, Politics, Belonging* (London/New York/Calcutta: Seagull, 2007), p. 58.

42 Ibid., p. 63.

43 Ibid.

44 Ibid., p. 48.

> no radical politics of change is possible without a performative contradiction [...]: It is not as if everything is done by means of language, as if one could say, 'I am free, and so now my performative utterance will set me free.' No. But to raise this demand for freedom is to begin to exercise it, and to demand its legitimization afterwards; its means declaring the gap between exercise and realization closed and bringing both into the public discourse in a way that makes the gap visible and leads to its mobilization.[45]

Butler refers here to theories concerning the politics of language, which she previously developed by tracing catachresis. In previous texts, she began with the "catachrestic resignification"[46] within hate speech. Ascriptions of simultaneous subjectivation and exclusion, such as being gay, can be appropriated by the subjects of the appellation and turned against their grain: It is as if the appellation suddenly goes nowhere. An example might be found in Hall's discussion of being black:

> We said: "You have spent five, six, seven hundred years developing a symbolic system in which 'black' became a negative factor. Now I don't want to have any other term. I want this negative term, that most of all. I want a part of that thing. I want to remove it from its previous articulations and their religious, ethnographic, literary and visual discourses. I want to tear it out of that previous articulation and articulate it anew."[47]

Translation, *seizing the word*, and catachrestic resignification, can each count as rhetorical figures par excellence; they do not simply belong to a language, but rather they shift lingual limits in their process of figuration. The three figures constitute the theoretical reflex of a lingual pragmatics or politics denying any interpretation by theories of action like those found in post-Wittgensteinian speech act theory. Those theories imprison utterances between the poles of a speaking subject, monolingual rules, and a pre-lingual world, robbing them of their transfiguring force.[48] Translation, *seizing the word*, and catachrestic resignification, each denote a certain negativity or freedom within speech: an irreducibility of utterances to transcendental conditions of

45 Ibid., p. 66.
46 Judith Butler, *Bodies that matter. On the discursive limits of "sex"* (London/New York: Routledge, 1993), pp. 223–240.
47 Stuart Hall, "Old and New Identities, Old and New Ethnicities," *Culture, Globalization, and the World System*, ed. Anthony D. King (London: Macmillan, 1991), p. 41–68, p. 54.
48 Hetzel, *Die Wirksamkeit der Rede*, pp. 54–70.

possibility. There is something about the exercise of these utterance events that cannot be traced back to transcendental conditions. The interjections by "subjects" of translation, of the seized word, and of catachrestic resignification, redefine the field of the sayable through their utterances; along with the positing of this field, the interjectors invent and position themselves. The subject neither controls the effect of its speech, as it does in classical speech act theory, nor is it controlled *by* language, as would be the case in Heidegger's late philosophy or certain theories of discourse. Political interjections open a zone of indeterminacy between languages and cultures; they confront the seclusion of cultures with a possibility of freedom that seeks to claim an audience, at all times, and in all places, in ever new shapes.

(Translated by Stephan Packard)

III. Reading

Anneka Esch-van Kan and Philipp Schulte

Introduction

To discuss resistance is not necessarily to resist. Indeed, there is a yet present and virulent concern that the very act of interpretation might symbolically reintegrate previously edgy, often extra-lingual tactics, profoundly subverting an original and basic desire to deny the symbolic and its hegemonies. But what role does that leave for scholarly research and reflection upon resistances? How is it possible to approach evasiveness and enter an – inescapably lingual – orbit? What function could the exemplary singularity, the particular performance, installation, or production, take in an abstract argument on practices of resistance? The concluding section of this volume on *Thinking – Resisting – Reading the Political* assembles contributions that deal immediately with concrete, most often artistically intended objects conspicuous for their participation in the political. They demonstrate a number of diverse manners in which one might deal with aesthetic practice in theory.

Dealing, that is, by accompanying, flanking the objects of these analyses, in a sometimes peaceful, sometimes controversial co-existence, ever aiming for a productive interaction of theory and artistic practice. In many cases, this means abandoning the fixation of meaning by lingual and hermeneutic interpretation and translation, and recognizing both treatments of the world as autonomous and mutually emancipated. In this way, both modes can be realized freely and art can be taken seriously as an experience of ever specific situations most of all (separated from the obligations of construing mediations and messages). How can such a co-existence of theory and practice be conceived? How can the mutual neighbourhood, even friendship – in Marcus Steinweg's terms[1] – between two fields that constantly tax and reflect each other, be expressed without giving way to any claims of hierarchy or unidirectional determination?

"[*N*]*e jamais s'excuser, ne jamais s'expliquer*"[2] – "*never apologize, never explain*": Roland Barthes begins his thoughts on the "pleasure of the text" with this description of a reader's attitude in the moment of pleasure: in that moment, in which the reader's body becomes rel-

---

1 Compare Marcus Steinweg, *Kunst und Philosophie /Art and Philosophy* (Cologne: Walther König, 2012).

2 Roland Barthes, *Le plaisir du* texte (Paris: Editions du Seuil, 1973), p. 9, translation S.P.

evant, which does not have "the same ideas as I."[3] Wolfgang Iser's *Akt des Lesens*, the action of reading, also begins with the unfolding of effects that a text can only commence as it is read.[4] "Gaps" (*Leerstellen*) in artistic and philosophic texts engage the readers' imagination as their occupant. They rupture expectations of annexability, reading becomes an event – and vice versa, the act of writing becomes performative, its perlocutionary consequences necessarily transgressing authors' intentions. Such *reading*, then, is no hermeneutic interpretation of a given semantic conglomerate, but a translation of some of its particular aspects into the language of another field, that of theoretical reflection, conscious of inevitable omissions, additions, rearrangements, and re-contextualizations. To read resistance is then not to envelop and embed symbolically the resistant element in that as which it is read, but to translate it – wherever possible – into a new form, e.g. that of a scholarly treatise, in which it can continue to take effect; not least in order to give new impulses for resistant artistic practice, as yet another answer and transformation.

And yet the question remains: Under which conditions can a text, a piece of art be read as political, or as resistant? And how can its resistant quality be maintained in the course of its symbolic transformation during the act of reading – if at all? What manners of conception and reception are required, enabled, or even demanded by resistant performances, installations, films, and texts? While some of the contributions in this final section reflect on such questions in a general way, others demonstrate some examples of a possible reflective treatment of resistances in art.

"How do we listen, see and read while claiming a critical stance?"[5] Armen Avanessian starts with this question and reads "political theories (not) reading." He is concerned with the tensions between political and aesthetic theory, emphasizing the dependence of certain philosophical concepts of politics and the political upon contemplations of the arts. Avanessian shows that a dominance of literary forms as philosophical points of reference has recently shifted in favour of visual arts, and pinpoints differences in the respective location of the political: The aesthetic orientation contributes to the shape of abstract theory. In describing this mutually informative "aesthetico-political episteme," Avanessian argues that narrative models circle a more recent "realism of reference" and extend its influence into theories of the political. The

---

3 Ibid., p. 94.

4 Wolfgang Iser, *Der Akt des Lesens. Theorie ästhetischer Wirkung*, 4th edition (Munich: Fink, 1994).

5 P. 221.

interrogative stance of this text demonstrates an inevitable unsettledness proper to the interrelating opposition of aesthetics and politics, negating any stability of interpretation sometimes claimed by analyses that meander in turn between the arts and the construction of theory.

And yet once literary theory or even history has materialised, its commentary can hardly help but invite a reading that considers it as a fixation of its commented originals' topics and meanings. Wim Peeters examines the politics of a commentary which, at least in the 20th century, knows this effect all too well, and produces a number of rebellious tactics and movements that resist, sometimes overcome and sometimes reshape the process of such fixations. Broch's 1945 novel *The Death of Virgil* serves as a three-fold example of commentary, commented text, and methodically balanced object of a reflective analysis that discovers the bounds and binding mechanisms of commentary while experiencing it. In this, Peeters' argument hails back to Balke's treatment of reiteration and re-interpretation in the first section of this book. It is no coincidence that both focus on the iteration, commentary, and destabilisation of the text of the *Quijote* in Borges' *Menard*. Ultimately, it is the aesthetically co-produced sovereignty of the authoritatively stated intent, the oath that stands as the image, if perhaps not the real possibility, of denying the constant and indefinite "chattering" of comments and commentators, settling also the unsettled stance of a democratic sphere of continuous re-interpretation that they sustain.

In "Realism Today," Juliane Rebentisch continues the discussion of changing and redistributed forms of realism in current arts. In reference to theories reaching back to the early 20th century, she shares Avanessian's diagnosis of a present return of realisms, though not in a renewed claim towards a political dimension of representation, as in a direct visibilisation of minorities or grievances. Starting from the dissolution of boundaries between the arts, a stated experiential quality of art, and a societal change towards a performative turn, Rebentisch reconsiders concepts of realism: While maintaining a fidelity towards the object and its necessarily consequential involvement in ethical, political, and aesthetic discourses, she emphasizes that contemporary (and especially resistant) art does not refer to realities as much as it critically questions a society that consists in reality's representations. This leads to another plea for a post-mimetic realism, in which Avanessian's treatise, Rebentisch's argument, and Nikolaus Müller-Schöll's and Philipp Schulte's observations on post-dramatic theatre converge.

Müller-Schöll connects to Derrida's shortest attempt at defining deconstruction – "more than one language, no more language" – and demonstrates several examples from experimental theatre that allow us to watch the disappearance of previous constructions of clearly defined roles and their concomitant ascriptions of identities. Müller-Schöll understands this "as the expression of a kind of collective unconscious, a reference to the roles' common roots in prior structures, and ultimately in a community that is constantly exposed to its own alteration."[6] These post-mimetic procedures are contrasted to the traditions of the 18th and 19th centuries still dominating many established theatres today. Far from merely constructing correlations between deconstruction and certain performances, Müller-Schöll demonstrates the former's involvement in the very theories and methods of artistic productions. His foregrounded interplay of theory and practice thus mirrors the self-relation of the analysed examples of scenic research.

Philipp Schulte continues this interest in experimental forms of theatre that evade the concept of oeuvre and consider themselves as practices of investigation. His description of "critique and style in contemporary performance arts" in the mode of "alternative genealogies" presents the lecture-performance *Product of Other Circumstances* by the French choreographer and dancer Xavier Le Roy as well as the production *Into the Skirt* by Japanese performance artist Mamoru Iriguchi. In both cases, their scenic research questions the relationship between theory and practice, as well as that between scientific research and artistic creation. It is in direct reference to core concepts of the political that these performances develop their own resistant potential. Both artists, in spite of their considerable differences, develop pieces within the tension of integration and de-integration in the symbolic orders of a style of dance, an economic system of marketing, or of heteronormative practices. Combining Le Roy's works with a reading of Foucault and Butler, Schulte emphasizes the usefulness of a concept of style in conceiving of these phenomena of a (not merely) artistic de-submission; meanwhile, the analysis of Iriguchi's performances denotes a proximity to the philosophical textual form of critical genealogy.

While these experimental forms have little traction in popular media, Stephan Packard continues a similar line of questioning into a critical reading of serial genre television, focusing on *Dexter*'s apotheosis of serial killings. In a return to Jacques Rancière's concepts, Packard is led by the observation that recent TV productions maintain a plurality of genres mirroring the distinct and defined multitude of arts in the representative regime, but appeal to a "dark and gritty" ethical aporia

---

6 P. 265.

where they claim a transgression towards an aesthetics of suspended reference as a most pessimistic realism. The serial killings committed by the main character, traumatized but not to be analysed in terms of his trauma, can be compared to the aesthetics as well as the philosophical quandaries of Paul Kammerer's *Law of the Series*, a metaphysical exaltation of seriality as a principle for cultural studies as well as scientific research. In both cases, Packard argues, an "operative monism" is brought to bear, distinct from straightforward monistic approaches by its ultimate dualist world view, and yet ever prone to introducing monistic interludes that short-circuit reference as well as abstraction and ironically deny realism even while they argue its binding powers to negate any ethics that would accompany the world as it is with any idea of what should be. The argument culminates in a re-examination of the relationship between theory, method, and reading, claiming that naïve forms of direct application can be criticized for just such an operative monism, and might be corrected or replaced by a consciously reticent use of the concept of "consequences" from reading theory for reading arts instead. In this vein, Packard also resists, as it were, our ideas of a purely co-existent, rather than critically interpretative and productively hermeneutic, relationship between analytic methods and their arts.

Between arts and politics, the topics of this section are summarized and once again measured against the previous themes in this volume in Gabriel Rockhill's "Critical Reflections on the Ontological Illusion." Criticizing seemingly hermeneutical assumptions, he outs the *talisman complex*, "according to which the politics of art amounts to a political force inherent in works of art that is supposedly capable of producing political consequences through a nebulous, preternatural alchemy."[7] He reveals the myth of a naturally pre-determined distinction between the episteme of art and that of politics, criticizing the conviction of so many critics that the analysis of any politics of arts will inscribe an immediately political potential, or any direct political competence, into the artistic objects themselves. Once again emphasizing the irrationality of such direct applications, Rockhill presents an argument for considering pieces of art as "social objects in the sense of being polyvalent phenomena with a multiplicity of dimensions, nodal points in a complex of social relations that are irreducible to a single or definitive relationship."[8] He sketches and supports a radical and inescapably resistant historicism as a methodological alternative, going far beyond the established descriptions of circumstances of societal

---

7 P. 311.
8 P. 314.

structures, productive procedures, and contemporary habits of reception. Rather than paying lip service to such circumstances, the pieces of art themselves are to be considered as purely and thoroughly social phenomena, necessitating an equally radical sociologism that can be immediately read as resistance, instead of precariously maintaining an assumed resistant impulse from the aesthetic talisman with which the reading began.

(Translated by Stephan Packard)

Armen Avanessian

Reading Political Theories (not) Reading
Towards a Contemporary Realism of Reference

1. Aesthetic Dimensions of a Political Imperative

In this essay I want to investigate a self-reflexive dimension of resistant thinking in the humanities, or disciplines that are related to art and literature. How do we listen, see, and read while claiming a critical stance? Or is it not just an illusion of being political when we often simply apply Marxist notions, Rancièrian concepts, or Badiouian gestures to the literary or aesthetic objects we write about? Are we usually just (ab)using certain political vocabularies without any political relevance, or even worse: are we only pretending to have political relevance at the expense of any true political dimension of our (intellectual) practice? I will surely not be able to answer such broad questions, and perhaps it is not even possible to answer them in such a general way. Still it is necessary and possible to do a close analysis of the two respective fields: political theory and the aesthetic, or in my own case, political theory and literary theory.

Instead of giving final answers or solutions as to how political and aesthetic theory should relate to each other, I will approach my questions from two different angles. The second part of my analysis will consist in an example – different (contemporary) concepts of "realism" in art and literature. In order to point out some diachronic as well as synchronic nuances, the first part of my investigation will be dedicated to some – admittedly very general – thoughts about what I would like to call both our past and contemporary *aesthetico-political episteme*. This latter task will mainly be done by means of questions and observations, such that some hypotheses will necessarily not be covered within the framework of a short essay.

To begin with, I will try to differentiate the demand for "resistant thinking" both systematically and historically. Obviously, historical differences indicate that there is no political imperative outside ever-changing aesthetic parameters (which often remain unnoticed). This became especially poignant to me when reflecting upon the invitation to the conference that was the source for this volume. I immediately realized the following discrepancy: I am working in the early twenty-first century, mainly on contemporary literature, while the political theories that shape the current (by no means trans-historical) imperative are in many cases *informed* by – and by that I understand: have their aesthetic background in – traditional and modernist literature, including the now classical avant-gardes. Already here we have different, slightly contradictory layers in the *political* dimension of the imperative to resistant thinking within the field of literary theory.

But to make things even trickier, the literary material I work with, and that I am supposed to work on in a critical way, is hardly known to most of my colleagues from other fields. Nevertheless, the aesthetico-political imperative to "resistance in thinking" is necessarily directed at my work as well. And while this is rightly so, I am still confronted with a certain mismatch both historical and disciplinary: an asymmetry that is both synchronous and diachronous.

And as it obviously cannot be an option to abandon the political imperative in one's work, I will for now try the following: to understand a bit better the art-theoretical or art-specific implications of a recent emphatic valorization of political ideas and concepts such as the *truthfulness of the political event*, taken in the sense of a *radical interruption*. What I am especially interested in is not so much whether one supports the political views implied by these ideas. My working hypothesis in the following – and always in light of the analysis of different concepts of "realism" and "reality" in the second part of my paper – is that it is always necessary to be aware of these epistemological structurings and their tacit valorizations, which are (at least partly) shaped by underlying aesthetic implications and preferences (just think, for one example, of the affinities between the categories of the "event" and the field of the performative, an affinity that cannot be stated so simply for literature.)

The main question in this context is: which model do we use to think about the political, or more precisely, which understanding of aesthetic experience do we use for the role of the viewer, reader, or recipient of an artwork. My underlying hypothesis is that there is not just a political dimension to the arts and to aesthetics, but a basic aesthetic dimension to political theories as well. Let me stress that my assumption is neither that the political, and therefore also resistance, can simply be traced back to aesthetic preferences, nor do I want to repeat a negative judgment that the "dominant political concept of the left today is an aesthetic one."[1] Rather I "simply" want to investigate different artistic

---

1 "The implicit dominant political concept of the left today is an aesthetic one. This is the context in which contemporary models of engaged artists and artistic practices must be examined. Models of political art today tend to meld with an aesthetic understanding of the political." Michael Hirsch, "Subversion und Widerstand: 10 Thesen über Kunst und Politik," *Inaesthetik* 1 (June 2009): pp. 7–23, here p. 9, translation A.A.

or aesthetic role models for shaping "the political," or our thinking of the political. From this point of view it might be possible to see how the political – understood in its fundamental incommensurability to representations, discourses or institutions – is thought differently from perspectives informed by, for example, a deconstructive reading of literature on the one hand, or a theory of performative visual art on the other. Naturally, understanding the political as interruption has an impact upon the range and possibility of each theory of politics.[2]

2. Different role models and role media

If one thinks of historical examples for different socio-cultural role models, and/or the historical variability of aesthetico-political role media (*Leitmedien*), each one with its particular concept of immersion and participation, various examples come to mind. Consider the role taken on by paintings in the late eighteenth century, during the French Revolution (as demonstrated impressively by T. J. Clark in his book *Farewell to an Idea*[3]), or consider music as an aesthetico-political role medium some 70 years later in Germany, and the way Nietzsche reflected upon this in his *Birth of Tragedy*. Obviously, Nietzsche's thinking of the political, his idea of a political polis, of a unification of the people, was heavily influenced by the idea of musical tragedy, a specific politics of merging the people in the way language and music are merged into one by the *Gesamtkunstwerk* opera. From Schopenhauer to Wagner to Nietzsche and beyond, nineteenth-century German culture was dominated by the hegemony of music, and this musical ideal resulted in corresponding political ideas.

Now I do not claim that there is a linear story to be written about a hidden political parergon, a history of different competing arts being the sole model for ideas about how political revolutions or political change has been thought in the past. What I do claim, though, is that we might be able to learn something not just about the reality we theorize, but about the implicitness of some of our expectations regarding this theorizing, especially concerning the application of terms that seem to have taken over as dominant metaphors from older ones. It seems to me that political *metaphors we lived by* (to paraphrase

2 Also the dominant artistic medium is surely not *the* political message, but it is most definitely important not just for how the political is thought, but for how reality is conceived.

3 Timothy James Clark, *Farewell to an Idea: Episodes from a History of Modernism* (New Haven/London: Yale University Press, 2001).

Lakoff/Johnson[4]) in the eighties and nineties were, for example, those of "transgression" or "subversion." It seems to me that during the last few years, it is rather concepts such as "rupture" or "break" which urge us to think the political in quite a different way. But what if this is a trap laid out by a hegemony of a recently fashionable vocabulary biased towards an application to the visual arts?

3. Political Applications and a Criticism of a Regime of Language-Politics

As an exemplary thinker for a past paradigm of academic political theory, some still call it "postmodern," I want to briefly mention Derrida. I will only focus on two elements here: the *second* is a politics of language that, *first*, results from the role of both fictionality and also narrativity in Derrida's thinking. In particular, narrativity concerns the quasi-"ontological" status of the origin of law as fictional, based on later narrativizations of an event that never occurred as such, and which only comes into existence retroactively. Derrida's insight into the effect of fictionality is strongly based on the experience of reading not just philosophical but also literary texts.

Derrida's "method" is most of all a method of reading, a reading and re-reading that he also applied to non-literary objects such as political questions. Deconstruction therefore has various affinities to an aesthetic device. It is what can be called deconstruction's aesthetico-political richness that made it such a popular strategy of discursive and non-discursive strategies of resistance throughout the last decades of the twentieth century. Of course deconstruction was not alone but connected very well to a certain understanding of Bakhtin (especially his concept of the "hybrid") and others, for example in Judith Butler's theory.

A good example of such a language-oriented paradigm in political theory itself is Gibson-Graham's *Postcapitalist Politics* and their attempt to find another "language politics"[5] as opposed to capitalocentrism's

---

4 George Lakoff and Mark Johnson, *Metaphors we Live By* (Chicago: University of Chicago Press, 2008).

5 J. K. Gibson-Graham, *A Postcapitalist Politics* (Minneapolis: University of Minnesota Press, 2006), pp. 54–59. Their underlying methodological framework is not necessarily structuralist – but still, the basic assumption is that only through such a different language can the "variety of noncapitalist economic activities" fuse "into a unity," something that must remain beyond every Marxist discourse, which can only see pre-capitalist or primitive capitalism everywhere it looks.

dominant economic discourse. Gibson-Graham's methodology, and also their political practice, is fully based on their trust in a "constitutive power of discourse" for the political or social critique, and a belief in "political effectivity of theory and research" qua "insight into the ultimate undecidability" that "poststructuralist thinking offers."[6] Another famous example of such a political theory heavily influenced by deconstruction (with its heyday in the last two decades of the twentieth century) is the post-Marxist theory put forward by Ernesto Laclau and Chantal Mouffe.[7]

It has somehow become very fashionable – a kind of radical chic – to criticize the weakness and emptiness of such attempts. All kinds of symbolic (minority) politics, together with their underlying deconstructive assumptions, have recently been the object of heavy criticism. Given the fact that capitalism is easily able to accommodate and exploit all the demands of identity politics, a more radical constructivism has been called for, more radical than the one offered by a discursive understanding of society and the political. Most articulate in this respect is probably Alain Badiou's accusation of practically everyone, from the representatives of Anglo-Saxon empiricism to Foucault, as an "antiphilosophical" invariant in critical philosophy: a historicist suffocation of the event owing to a nominalist use of explanatory language: "within the constructivist vision of being, and this is the crucial point, *there is no place for an event to take place.*"[8]

When I quote Badiou here, it is less because his argument is particularly nuanced, but rather because of its clarity. The passage quoted shows the characteristic traits that have recently, although only decades after having been published, become fashionable, and that are forming a typical (all too often only rhetorical) pattern. The pattern consists of: a refusal of language (and the whole of structuralism); a negligence of the (merely) symbolic; as well as a fascination with the event and powerful activism.[9]

---

6 Ibid., p. 54.

7 Ernesto Laclau and Chantal Mouffe, *Hegemony and Socialist Strategy* (London: Verso, 1985).

8 Alain Badiou, *Being and Event*, trans. Oliver Feltham (London/New York: Continuum, 2006), p. 289.

9 Now it is not my concern to discuss the obvious merits of Badiou's philosophy in contrast to the possibly pacifying effects of his theories on the "empty set," once applied to politics (by his disciples); what I am solely interested in are the aesthetico-political framing conditions behind this desire to shift away from any language-related "symbolic politics."

I am also interested in the general tendency of such shifts, which is not at all refuted by the fact, for instance, that Badiou himself is active as a literary author. I also can-

4. Hegemonic Exclusion or Integration

As indicated above, my hypothesis is that instead of a dominant connection of reading and of language to the symbolic politics that went along with these, and which were still in place a few years ago, we are today experiencing a shift towards a dominance of the visual and performative. By this I mean that "criticism" and "resistance" – whether in thinking or in political action – tend to be conceived, though not always with any degree of awareness, according to a simplified aesthetic model of the visual arts. I am by no means trying to describe a necessary opposition or fight between literature and visual art as to which is a better role model or role medium for political intervention. Instead I use the two in order to make visible an (aesthetico-political) shift, which also occurs within artistic fields and their related disciplines themselves.[10]

Obviously, these very preliminary aesthetico-political observations should be corroborated with some sociological, cultural, and most of all economic data. Unfortunately, I cannot investigate the institutional, financial, and geopolitical background in order to analyze a possible art-theoretical hegemony in contemporary culture. Instead, I argue that any such hegemony is simplifying and misleading, and that by no means should we attempt to go back to the good old days of a literature-dominated culture. I want to make a case for a *post-medium condition* (Rosalind Krauss)[11] not just in art theory but in political thinking as well. The most recent tendencies of narration, as well as understandings of fictionality, in the visual arts today are thus not only aesthetically relevant, but also have an impact on how we can and must think about the critical quality of the arts and literature. In this context, Peter Osborne has recently pointed out that "the generic post-medium concept of art reincorporates 'literature,' returning it to its philosophical origins in early German Romanticism. Post-conceptual art articulates a post-aesthetic poetics."[12]

---

not go into the special role that Mallarmé plays for the (not only aesthetic) thinking on the event in French post-war philosophy.

10 For example, I learned during the Gießen conference that in dance studies as well, such a shift away from identity politics towards more "direct" and "general" political questions might have occurred.

11 Rosalind Krauss, *A Voyage on the North Sea: Art in the Age of the Post-Medium Condition* (London: Thames & Hudson, 2000).

12 Peter Osborne, "The Fiction of the Contemporary. Speculative Collectivity and Transnationality in The Atlas Group," *Aesthetics and Contemporary Art*, ed. Armen Avanessian and Luke Skrebowski (Berlin: Sternberg Press, 2011), pp. 101–123, here p. 118.

In order to show that this dissolution of the hegemony of art forms and media also has an impact on (how to think) their political capacities, I will distinguish three different forms of realism. Eventually, it will become clear that many current aesthetic attempts to grasp the social and cultural reality we live in do share some traits that I want to sum up under the label of a *realism of reference*. Such a desire to produce effects which refer to reality as changeable – rather than as copying or imitating reality – are obvious in various contemporary trends like the *hegemony of the reenactment* (Simon Critchley)[13] in the visual arts, the performative in theatre (in pieces that are less and less text-based), and new forms of narrativity in contemporary fiction.

5. Different Realisms

In the following I intend to show how such historically different hegemonies also imply and produce different understandings of "reality," different understandings of what our reality is and of what should be changed politically. It will become clear that these historical differences cannot be separated from each of their aesthetic backgrounds. In order to understand how we tend to think of or conceive "reality" today, I then investigate how a contemporary notion of realism might be different to other realisms; different, first, to a historical realism of the nineteenth century, which could be called a *realism of the narrated*. Such a *realism of the narrated* is full of trust in the ability to depict a reality, to understand it, and as a consequence also to help change this reality. This traditional realism has of course been repeatedly contested by various avant-gardes since the beginning of the twentieth century (in stark contrast to so-called *socialist realism*, which more or less maintained the aesthetic premises set a century before).

Thus what I see as a second, *modernist realism of the signifier*, or a *realism of abstraction*, no longer believes in the power of direct or narrative mimesis, but inverts both principles. Even so, by employing an anti-realist propaganda, this (sometimes even formalist) realism is not necessarily less realistic. It is just that its modernism assumes an underlying "real" that has quite different traits or features. A notion like "traumatic realism," as announced by the art historian Hal Foster, implies a "real" that is hardly ever accessible, and eventually

13 Critchley's phrase at the *Thinking – Resisting – Reading the Political / Dance, Politics & Co-Immunity* Conference in Gießen 2010; see also his contribution to this volume.

can only crystallize via the most rigid procedures of abstraction.[14] The poetological slogans in this context are the revolutionary ones of antinarrational novels, antifictional factography, or, to borrow the expression Barthes uses in his famous text about the *effet du réel* in Balzac: an *intransitive* use of language as opposed to a *communicative* one.[15]

I have the impression that today we are not only obviously witnessing a new interest in realism and in grasping our political reality. I also think that this revival of realism and the new interest in its capacity for resistance – and I strongly believe that these two belong together – must be distinguished from earlier revivals of critical realism: such as, for example, the photo-realism we have known for decades, or the necessary realistic practices of various marginalized groups (think for example about many artistic reactions to AIDS), or minorities attacking an aesthetic mainstream often expressed by a high-brow conceptualism or formalism.

6. A new Interest in Realism Today: Realism of Reference

I believe that today we are confronted more and more with quite a different realistic claim. One of the most telling examples of this is the new interest in such terms as "fact" or "facticity," or the "thing" in various contexts and disciplines that have in the past been rather methodologically opposed to investigating any such ontological "realness" of things. But I am less interested in discursive symptoms than in distilling a new way of understanding realism and reality, which cannot be seen as a variation of older notions. For this idea, which I call a *realism of reference*, I recognize at least three theoretical contexts, in which I see the appearance of such a new desire for reference that cannot be derived from older or known conceptions of realism (either mimetic or formalist). New attempts to understand what reference means can be seen in such heterogeneous "disciplines" as ontology (for example, the object-oriented philosophical tendencies in "speculative realism"), in cognitive science (e.g. the neurobiological realism of Lakoff/Johnson), or in science studies.

Now what the contemporary tendencies mentioned here share – and in this respect they are part of a shift away from the semiotic dominance discussed before – is a common direction in attacking postmodernism,

---

14 Hal Foster, *The Return of the Real: The Avante-Garde at the End of the Century* (Cambridge, Mass./London: MIT Press, 2001).

15 See Jacques Rancière's analysis of this in *The Politics of Literature*, trans. Julie Rose (Cambridge, UK: Polity Press, 2011).

without falling back into a neo-classicism or retro-avant-gardism. This can be shown by the new meaning and importance of apparently aesthetic concepts like "narrativization." I will only cite one example of this, Bruno Latour's *constructivism*, according to which there is "no single [anthropological, A.A.] attribute, that isn't at the same time social and narrative as well."[16] Of special significance for this renewed interest in the narrative and specifically the literary dimension of every relation is Latour's understanding of what he calls "internal reference." "Reference" for him does not mean "an outer referent [...] but the quality of a chain of transformations."[17] Internal reference is a concept that has its origin in semiotics and indicates "those elements, which produce the same difference between the various levels of meaning within a text, that they also produce between text and outer world."[18] Therefore the internal referent concerns the assemblages, shifts, and also differential breaking points between elements. Such referential points – they are also the starting points of potential resistance! – also transcend the well-known dialectic of form and content, of inside and outside etc. Because they are on the one hand elements *within* narrations, they create effects of reference within the narration, and on the other hand they enable and regulate their external reference.

7. Conclusion

Although I can only provide a rough sketch here, it should be clear that such epistemological reflections might also provide the requirements for an aesthetico-political model that could liberate itself from the hegemonic doctrine of modernist art firmly established within political discourses. This doctrine operates with dated oppositions (for example between the performative vs. the narrative), internal political contradictions (avant-garde-revolutionary nostalgia in contemporary art in view of completely altered socio-economic circumstances) or at least inner-aesthetic tensions (like the *hegemony of the reenactment* in contemporary art).

Actually the aim of many contemporary trends within this new aesthetico-political regime whether in so-called popular culture, literature, or art as seen at the various biennales, is to produce (new) effects of reference between the artistic inside and the social outside;

---

16 Bruno Latour, *Pandora's Hope: Essays on the Reality of Science Studies* (Cambridge, Mass.: Harvard University Press, 2008), p. 14.

17 Ibid.

18 Ibid., pp. 379–380.

effects of reference, which should not be confused with attempts to depict or illustrate reality in a mimetic way. When one thinks about the narrative structures not just in literature but also in visual media – one good example are the efforts to develop new narrative strategies in popular culture, especially in TV series over the last decade – one immediately has to ask oneself: what could such things, actants, facts, or documents be, that do not just stand for the specific plot, but for new attempts to make visible, or better, to make accessible what by definition is hard to trace: streams of data, streams of money, streams of people, etc.? And how can they become agents of narrative transformations in novels or films?

One of the main difficulties in thinking about these (not necessarily literature-bound) new tendencies of narration and fictionality expressing such an inner referentiality, is to think about the possibility of a new realism of referentiality outside the terms already established by literary theories, but also by the visual arts and film studies. The difficulty is, for example, to produce and understand reference not in terms of mimesis or within the framework of visual indexicality; to understand internal referentiality not as formal mimesis; to understand the involvement of a reader or viewer as an active part in any narration (but not as passive immersion); to understand the relation between internal and external elements (but not as a mode of participation); to understand narrative procedures in relation to (and not independent of) the mediality in which they are produced.

If I finish with some thoughts about such a narratological implementation of reenactment in fiction per se, this is definitely not simply in order to turn the hierarchies around (back to the dominance of literature or music), but to indicate the necessity of a post-medium condition also in modes of thinking about politics. These modes of political theorizing do always have an aesthetic dimension, as Jacques Rancière has famously shown. Because obviously, the more artistic, poetic, visual, narrative, etc. devices we have, the better: sometimes in order to produce visibility, sometimes to produce invisibility, sometimes to break up wrong connections, sometimes to produce stable connections and new meanings. In the exact same way, we need both to fight for apparently minor progress on cultural and social fronts, and the most detailed analysis possible of capitalism's functioning while avoiding economic reductionism. In order to achieve this, we need to overcome the narrowing down that goes along with the various paradigms of our critical "thinking resistance," and extend the post-media condition from its position in aesthetics to its manifestations and implications in politics.

Wim Peeters

Contesting "the Democratic Chattering of the Letter" Politics of Commentary in 20th Century Literature

In the prologue to his collection of stories *The Garden of Forking Paths* (1941), the famous Argentinian writer Jorge Luis Borges states that it is completely outmoded to write a voluminous opus:

> The composition of vast books is a laborious and impoverishing extravagance. To go on for five hundred pages developing an idea whose perfect oral exposition is possible in a few minutes! A better course of procedure is to pretend that these books already exist, and then to offer a résumé, a commentary. [...] More reasonable, more inept, more indolent, I have preferred to write notes upon imaginary books.[1]

This statement is a rebellious act, aiming at the very heart of the Western text system. The politics of writing and reading are at stake here. What would happen if everybody started writing comments, or even worse, comments on non-existing texts? Michel Foucault calls the role of commentary to mind:

> [...] commentary's only role [...] is to say at last what was silently articulated 'beyond', in the text. By a paradox which it always displaces but never escapes, the commentary must say for the first time what had, nonetheless, already been said, and must tirelessly repeat what had, however, never been said.[2]

How can one still base our society on authoritative texts, when all we have left is to comment, without a possibility to compare the commentary with that upon which it is commenting? The commentary would lose the paradoxical status it holds in our society. The differentiation (*décalage*[3]) between canonical texts and their commentaries is,

1 Jorge Luis Borges, *Ficciones* (New York: Grove Press, 1962), pp. 15–16.
2 Michel Foucault, "The Order of Discourse," trans. Ian McLeod, *Untying the Text: a Poststructuralist Reader*, ed. R. Young (Boston, Mass./London/Henley: Routledge and Kegan Paul, 1981), pp. 48–78, pp. 57–58.
3 Michel Foucault, *L'ordre du discours. Leçon inaugurale au Collège de France prononcée le 2 décembre 1970* (Paris: Gallimard, 1971), p. 25.

as we all know, one of the main strategies to limit the proliferation of discourse.[4] As Foucault sees things,

> commentary is designed to keep the authoritative, not to say authoritarian, texts (e.g., religious and legal texts, but also literary classics), alive, to explain them, but also to institute and defend the rightness of the exegetes' own interpretations. Commentary allows us to infinitely produce new texts that pretend to speak about the same text, the text commented on, and reveal its meaning while adapting the discourse to a changed world (the eternal problem of theological and juridical exegesis).[5]

The first function of authoritative texts is to provide relief: They curtail the power to have the last say, the power to educate or just the power to comment. To prevent general confusion, societies must protect the "imperative form" of their central texts against unregulated commentary and chatter, as the philosopher and sociologist Arnold Gehlen puts it (drawing here on the legal historian Rudolf von Ihering).[6] The artificial boundary between text and commentary allows us to stipulate a certain content. This brings relief and enables us to react appropriately and resolutely to the flow of ("zu- und abfließende"[7]) new information. When Foucault sums up the authoritarian text that may come into question to be commented on, he mentions literary texts as well as legal and religious texts, but he attributes to literature a "curious status."[8] Why is that? Is literary communication too wasteful and time-consuming, as Borges suggests? Or is it that the literature is itself commentary nowadays, comment-fiction? Foucault aims at Borges' fictitious review of the work of *Menard*, a writer who comments on *Don Quijote* by repeating it word for word. This kind of literature resists its fate, not having the power to say: No further comment. As Foucault puts it:

> Plenty of major texts become blurred and disappear, and sometimes commentaries move into the primary position. But though its points of applica-

---

4 Compare: Foucault, "The Order of Discourse," pp. 56–57.

5 Jørgen Dines Johansen, *Literary discourse: a semiotic-pragmatic approach to Literature* (Toronto: University of Toronto Press, 2002), p. 77.

6 Arnold Gehlen, *Urmensch und Spätkultur. Philosophische Ergebnisse und Aussagen*, ed. Karl-Siegbert Rehberg, (6th enhanced edition Frankfurt/M.: Vittorio Klostermann, 2004), p. 45.

7 Ibid., p. 44.

8 "[...] les textes religieux ou juridiques, ce sont aussi ces textes curieux, quand on envisage leur statut, et qu'on appelle 'littéraires'; dans une certaine mesure les textes scientifiques." Foucault, *L'ordre du discours*, p. 24.

tion may change, the function remains; and the principle of differentiation is continuously put back in play.[9]

Why is literature able to attract comments at all? How is it connected to the force of law? Where does the idea, that literature has the power to function as a constitutional or foundational text, originate from?

The nexus of sovereignty and fiction determines the office of the poet, the *officium poetae*. The latter was incarnated prototypically by artists still close to "scholastic naiveté". Ernst H. Kantorowicz has disclosed this type of governance, in which the poet has been assigned a prescribed position.[10] In the 14th century, the sovereign and the poet are on the same level. Both deliver glory and are thus laureates. Petrarca is the prototype for this kind of poet. Why did this structure exist? The secular, or respectively the ecclesiastic sovereign and the poet had the ability – just like god – to create something from nothing. Thus they have an officium in common. The sovereign could release laws that had been inscribed into his heart by god. The poet is authorised to cover with his imagination that void, in the name of which the sovereign legislates, according to the poetic principles he embodies, or – to say it in Petrarca's words – "to interweave [the void] into a cloud of fiction."[11] He invents the fictitious words for the "omnipotence that administers the nothing."[12] He is the only authorised speaker regarding sovereign fiction. He delivers the images for the miracle of the *translatio imperii* (transfer of rule). He is the "sovereign of sovereigns," and the French legal historian Pierre Legendre emphasizes that it is for that reason that the *officium poetae* was the term for the supreme office in the state. The poet is the speaker of the *capital reference* and is indispensable for instituting the subjects based on a fiction that can only be verbalised poetically. He provides the poetic commentary on the law, the thrilling words that can enthuse the subjects with the legal order.[13]

---

9 Foucault, "The Order of Discourse," p. 57.

10 Ernst H. Kantorowicz, "The Sovereignty of the Artist. A Note on Legal Maxims and Renaissance Theories of Art," *Selected Studies* (Locust Valley, New York: J. J. Augustin Publisher, 1965), pp. 352–365, pp. 362–363.

11 This definition of the *officium poetae* originates from the *Privilegium* which was handed over to Petrarca on the occasion of his crowning ceremony in 1341 at the Capitol in Rome and is said to have been at least inspired by the poet himself. Compare: Kantorowicz, "The Sovereignty of the Artist," p. 362.

12 "[L]a tout-puissance maniant le Rien." Pierre Legendre, *Paroles poétiques échappées du texte. Leçons sur la communication industrielle* (Paris: Édition du Seuil, 1982), p. 213. Translation mine.

13 Ibid., p. 212.

Just as much as legal commentaries were being examined, and those without imperial allowance were suppressed, the poet was subjected to an examination. In the end, however, no legislator has been able to prevent the hypertrophy of poetical commentaries. Since the middle of the 17th century, many German universities have begun to crown poets too and to provide them with doctoral caps, which is why, "as sneering voices have put it, in Germany there were more *poetae laureati* than there were real poets in the whole rest of the world."[14] Once the bureaucracy takes on its own dynamics and gets detached from sovereign or human values, the double leadership structure "poeta – principe" suffers a loss of authority, and the unintended other poetry of this system of power is set free: it exhibits itself as fictitious. This happened in the course of the 19th century. Modern writers prefer to contrive their office autonomously, or they refuse any office that would imply that they turn into a poet of the nation or the people. [15] Confusing mountains of books are the consequence. The poet's suitability for his office is no longer examined in advance by a central authority. Now everyone can excommunicate and be excommunicated. In modernity, the "democratic chattering of the letter"[16] – as Jacques Rancière puts it – is spreading its untameable power.

Famous are the words of the French poet Paul Valéry, who was one of the first to diagnose this devaluation of literature. Ironically, he might have been the last to enjoy the status of *poet laureate*. In the preface to his text, "An Evening with Monsieur Teste," from 1895, he emphasises his disgust over the vagueness and impurity of literature. His "Monsieur Teste" attests[17] to the impossibility to express clear ideas with the trillions of words that have already been sent into the world.[18] Even more radically, in an aphorism dating from 1959, he rejects the fiction behind the *poet laureate*. Valéry frowns upon the image that "represents" poets "receiving the best of their work from some imagi-

---

14 Translation mine. Compare: Ulrich Raulff, "Der Traum vom ästhetischen Staat und die Diktatur der Dichter," *Vom Künstlerstaat. Ästhetische und politische Utopien*, ed. Ulrich Raulff (Munich/Vienna: Carl Hanser Verlag, 2006), pp. 7–17, p. 13. In Italy every Ph.D. is called *Laureato*.

15 E.g., Voltaire was to be crowned *poeta laureatus* by the people. He felt flattered, however refused the office. Compare: William Marx, "Le couronnement de Voltaire ou Pétrarque perverti," *Histoire, économie & société* 20/2 (2001): pp. 199–210, pp. 200–203.

16 Jacques Rancière, "The Politics of Literature," *SubStance* 33/1 (2004): p. 20.

17 In Roman law, *testis* means *attestor*.

18 Paul Valéry, "Monsieur Teste," *Collected Works*, vol. 6, ed. and trans. Jackson Mathews (Princeton, New Jersey: Princeton University Press, 1989), p. 4.

nary creature."[19] For him, literature is not even worth being criticised anymore. Creative embarrassment becomes a topic. The silence or the "unworking" (Maurice Blanchot) of the poet becomes an alternative. A poet is needed that takes a dogmatic stand, without impurifying it with words. Literature has to regain power to repeat an elementary institutional practice: the radical circumcising of public speech in the name of the truth.[20]

Concerning poets such as Valéry or Hugo von Hofmannsthal, Blanchot remarks in his essay *Where does Literature go?* (1953) that in times in which literature seems to lose its "honour,"[21] becoming non literature, the writer's preoccupation seems to be the ceaseless search for the true nature of literature. In the 20th century, literature reinvents itself based on its own impossibility. Blanchot phrases the aesthetics for this kind of literature. It does no longer "expect to be made possible by a transformation of the world; rather, in a transformed world literature will be able to realize its own essence by ceasing to be possible."[22]

For Blanchot, this new condition of literature overlapped with what happened during the May 1968 Revolution. Following Blanchot one might say that the May 68 Revolution might have been the one that came closest to the condition of modern literature.[23] Fifteen years after the events in Paris, Blanchot wrote in *The Unavowable Community* that this revolution was "without project."[24] Compared with the more traditional revolution, this one, as Paul Zahir interprets Blanchot, "did not revolve around the siege and occupation of the symbolic center."[25] Blanchot's view on 68 may be a bit idealistic, but one

---

19 Paul Valéry, *Cahiers / Notebooks 2*, ed. Brian Stimpson, Paul Gifford, and Robert Pickering, trans. Stephen Romer (Frankfurt/M./ Berlin/ Bern/ Bruxelles/ New York/ Oxford/ Vienna: Lang, 2000), p. 198. "C'est une image insupportable aux poètes, ou qui leur devrait être insupportable, que celle qui les représente recevant de créatures imaginaires le meilleur de leurs ouvrages." Paul Valéry, "Autres Rhumbs" (1926), *Œuvres*, Tome II, ed. and annot. Jean Hytier, (Paris: Gallimard, 1960), p. 681.

20 Compare: Pierre Legendre, *L'Empire de la vérité. Introduction aux espaces dogmatiques industriels. Leçons II* (Paris: Fayard, 1983), pp. 115–116.

21 Maurice Blanchot, "Où va la littérature?," *Le livre à venir* (Paris: Gallimard, 1959), pp. 271–272.

22 Denis Hollier, *Absent Without Leave. French Literature under the Threat of War*, trans. Catherine Porter (Cambridge, Mass: Harvard University Press, 1997), p. 8.

23 Compare: Maurice Blanchot, *La communauté inavouable* (Paris: Gallimard, 1983), pp. 52–53.

24 "Sans projet" (ibid.).

25 Zakir Paul, "Introduction: 'Affirming the 'Rupture'," Maurice Blanchot, *Political Writings 1953–1993*, trans. Zakir Paul (New York: Fordham University Press, 2010), p. li.

thing is indisputable: Much more blood could have been shed, but that didn't happen. The movement limited itself to permanent "explosive communication."[26] To Blanchot, this was a revolution of the word. The radical negation of the established social order did not find its way out of words any more. "Saying it was more important than what was said. Poetry was an everyday affair."[27] Nevertheless, this revolution could not be neutralised by somebody calling it a fictitious revolution, since it only happened in speech. This opinion would never have thelast say.

The revolution actualised itself the moment freedom of speech was granted to everyone. In consequence all communication was being levelled. All originality was being communalised. Every slogan, every sentence belonged to the public, became literally a common place. Thus all radical negation was disempowered, as it could endlessly be executed in language. The failure of the revolution of the world remained part of the revolution of the word. The priority of the saying over the said is [a] reminder for Blanchot that "politics is embodied in speech, in the power to endlessly say no, in refusal without end, the only power 'irreducible to any power' [...]."[28]

May 68 was a completely novel *communist* community, "which no ideology was able to recuperate or claim as its own."[29] This community had to remain unspoken. The finiteness of May 68 consisted in the fact that its discourse was without end. The question whether the revolutionary event had taken place or not could never be answered, since all answers were acceptable. So every answer would pass on the question. Already in 1968, Roland Barthes wrote his answer in *Writing the Event*. For him, the spoken word was "the event itself."[30] The revolutionary event and the witness' comment became indistinguishable. The transistor radio functioned as an "auditory prosthesis."[31] It produced breathless comments on the events from reporters, demonstrators or bystanders, informing everybody in real time about the impact of their actions. But not only that: "by the compressing of time, by the

---

26 "[C]ommunication explosive." Blanchot, *La communauté inavouable*, p. 52.

27 Maurice Blanchot, *The Unavowable Community*, trans. Pierre Joris, (Barrytown, New York: Station Hill Press, 1988), p. 26; "Le dire primait le dit. La poésie était quotidienne." Blanchot, *La communauté inavouable*, p. 53.

28 Cited in: Paul, "Introduction: Affirming the 'Rupture,'" p. li.

29 Blanchot, *The Unavowable Community*, p. 26; "que nulle idéologie n'était à même de récupérer ou de revendiquer." Blanchot, *La communauté inavouable*, p. 53.

30 Roland Barthes, "Writing the Event," *The Rustle of Language*, trans. Richard Howard (New York 1986), p. 149–154, pp. 149–150.

31 Ibid., p. 150.

immediate resonance of the act, it inflected, modified the event; in short, wrote it."[32] Barthes is in a euphoric mood: He divines a "fusion of the sign and its hearing, reversibility of writing and reading which is sought elsewhere, by that revolution in writing which modernitiy is attempting to achieve."

Since the boundaries between writing, commentary, and political event have become indistinguishable, literature adopts the ubiquity of the comment to look for the truth in discourse. Borges, Franz Kafka, and Robert Walser already experimented with fiction as comment or comment as fiction, since the classification of these kinds of text had become reversible. Just to drop a few other names: In the second half of the 20th century, Hermann Broch, Edmond Jabès, Giorgio Manganelli, and Nathalie Sarraute offered commentary as strictly literary work. In the view of the German writer and film maker Alexander Kluge, commentary mutated into "the basic form of text."[33] Of course this classification is fictional itself. Kluge turns around the "worn-out myth"[34] of the canonical text and its ancillary commentary. But his new hierarchy debunks itself as a mere construction, which pretends to an overview of the vast production of text. Comment-fiction functions as a transgression of the sovereignty of classic literature. Let me focus on one example.

Shortly after World War II, Broch's novel *The Death of Virgil*, published in 1945, reenacts the last 18 hours in the life of the Roman poet. Broch, having called himself a poet on several public occasions, is seeking out common grounds with the author of the *Aeneid*. In part four of the book, *Earth – the Expectation*, the author recalls the legend according to which the poet ordered the destruction of his unfinished *Aeneid* in the moment of his death. The novel is – in Broch's own words – a "lyrical commentary"[35] in which he questions the poet's

---

32 Ibid.; "La parole [...] était l'événement même."; "[...] par la compression du temps, le retentissement immédiat de l'acte, elle [la radio] infléchissait, modifiait l'événement, en un mot l'écrivait: fusion du signe et de son écoute, réversibilité de l'écriture et de la lecture qui est demandée ailleurs, par cette revolution de l'écriture que la modernité essaye d'accomplir." Roland Barthes, "L'Écriture de l'événement," *Communications* 12 (1968): pp. 108–112, pp. 108–109.

33 Quote as found in: Georg Stanitzek, "Autorität im Hypertext: 'Der Kommentar ist die Grundform der Texte' (Alexander Kluge)," *Internationales Archiv für Sozialgeschichte der deutschen Literatur* 23/2 (1998): pp. 1–46, p. 1.

34 Roland Barthes, *Criticism and Truth*, trans. and ed. Katrine Pilcher Keuneman (London/New York: Continuum, 2007), p. 24.

35 Hermann Broch: *"Erzählung vom Tode" (Der Tod des Vergil) [I] und [II], Kommentierte Werkausgabe*, vol. 4, ed. Paul Michael Lützeler (Frankfurt/M.: Suhrkamp Verlag, 1976), pp. 458, 462.

place in modernity. So in Broch's version, the prototype of the imperial poet,[36] Virgil, places himself next to modern writers such as Valéry, Arthur Rimbaud, or Hofmannsthal, who radically renounced fiction in their work. In the core scene of the book, Virgil comments on his decision to burn his *Aeneid*, thus disputing emperor Augustus' claim to his work. He resists being put in the exclusive position of "superb creator" next to the emperor, delivering the foundational authoritative words for power. Broch's achronistic Virgil abdicates as prototype for the *poeta laureatus*.

Octavian, the Roman emperor Augustus, tries to talk him out of his destructive plan. An intense discussion between Virgil and Octavian unfolds regarding the significance of the *Aeneid* and the emperor's claim on the poet's work. Virgil wants to destroy his work, as he believes his *Aeneid* would reveal only beauty without insight.[37] The emperor's insistence seduces the Roman poet to comment on his own work. When he explicitly calls his words a commentary, the emperor calls out: "A commentary by Virgil on his own work! Who would want to miss that!"[38]

In Broch's version, the problem of commentary derives from the same source as the foundational fiction for Rome. That is no coincidence. In fact, Broch's novel thrives on it. The Name Virgil stands for a referential structure that is Roman, and that still influences the way we differentiate between text and commentary today. The Roman Empire survived in the form of the order to interpret. You will remember: The first meaning of the Roman word *imperium* is *order*. The empire migrated from the map to the library.[39] Ever since the *Corpus iuris*, the Justinian body of civil law (529–34 A.D.), Rome has set the norm for commentary. The empire of authoritative text was founded in Rome and it ceaselessly attracts commentary. Every literary canon, every edition of classics, inescapably descends from the Roman Empire of text.[40]

---

36 Dante, alongside Petrarca the second prototype of poet laureate, did not randomly opt for Virgil as companion for hell and *Purgatorio*.

37 Hermann Broch, *The Death of Virgil. A Novel*, trans. Jean Starr Untermeyer (New York: Vintage Books, 1995), p. 123.

38 Ibid, p. 330; "Ein Kommentar des Vergil zu seinem eigenen Werk! Wer möchte solches versäumen!" Hermann Broch, *Der Tod des Vergil*, p. 310.

39 Compare: Manfred Schneider, *Der Barbar. Endzeitstimmung und Kulturrecycling* (Munich/Vienna: Carl Hanser Verlag, 1997), p. 42.

40 Compare: Cornelia Vismann, "Unentrinnbares Rom," *Referenz Rom. Materialien*, ed. Michael Kempe and Cornelia Vismann (Frankfurt/M.: Max-Planck-Institut für europäische Rechtsgeschichte, 2002), p. 19 (http://www.rg.mpg.de/de/forschung/vismann-referenz-rom, cit. January 2012).

Broch transposes the division between legitimate commentary and text back to the fictional birth of the reference: Rome as primal scene. This Virgil not only practises criticism himself. He also is aware of the affection of his writing by chatter and commentary, and thus qualifies as a modern writer. Like Borges' *Menard*, Broch's novel is an allegory elaborating on the relocation of writing in modern society: The "democratic chattering of the letter"[41] (Rancière) subverts the distinction between the poetic and the critical function of writing.

In the light of the catastrophe of World War II and the abusive reference to Rome, Virgil's refusal to give away his *Aeneid* as the foundational myth of the resurrection of Rome as a *second Troy* becomes meaningful. The emperor competes with Virgil as commentator when it comes to appropriating the epic for purposes of political affirmation. Octavian as a figure anachronistically represents the ideological era and its instrumental relation towards art and truth. For him, terms such as law, freedom, and security can take on completely conflicting and arbitrary meanings. Augustus is "clever enough to wrap himself in the glittering and seductive mantle of freedom, trickily disposing its folds so as to conceal how it is patched and pieced together with scraps of meaningless and outworn form."[42] Augustus' regime wages a "commentary war"[43] against other opinions. It principally does not question the postulated superiority of power over the text. For Augustus, the *Aeneid* only serves as pre-text, not as ground for further action.

Virgil, on the contrary, argues on the basis of the Roman-Christian conception of text. He doubts that the words of his *Aeneid* immanently are sovereign enough to allow access to a truth that always steps back behind the text. Virgil's denial of his work lies founded in his love for the *holy text* underlying all words and commentaries. Broch's Virgil has to loose ground against Augustus. He perceives his own words as well as those of the emperor as idle talk.[44] The antagonism between the *realpolitiker* and the idealistic poet is reconciled when Virgil, in his last hours, forgets his institutional body and discovers the amicable mortal fellow man in Octavian. In the name of friendship, Virgil bestows his *Aeneid* on Octavian unconditionally and asks for the grace for his slaves

41 Rancière, "The Politics of Literature," p. 20.

42 Broch, *The Death of Virgil*, p. 365; "[Augustus] versteht [es] sich in dem schillernd verführerischen Gewand der Freiheit aufzuspielen und solcherart mit gauklerisch geschicktem Faltenwurf zu vertuschen, wie arg es aus überlebten und nichtssagenden Formelfetzen zusammengestückt und zusammengeflickt ist." Broch, *Der Tod des Vergil*, p. 343.

43 "[U]ne guerre par le commentaire." Legendre, *L'Empire de la Vérité*, p. 42.

44 Broch, *The Death of Virgil*, p. 385.

to be released after his death. As a sign of acknowledgement, Augustus lays "a small laurel branch plucked from the wreaths [...] that he had held between his fingers on the bed-cover."[45] For the reader, this token of fame and honor signals the reintegration of the *Aeneid* into the imperium of texts. But is it legitimate?

With his comment-fiction, Broch demonstrated what poets, psychoanalysts, and language philosophers in the 20th century have pointed out repeatedly: that no text can gain authority by itself. Liberalisation of speech constantly invites us, through permanent discussion and countless comments, to come to an "institutional consensus" on the in- or exclusion from the imperium of texts. As an unwanted side-effect of this, the power of language to trivialize the distinction between text and commentary becomes visible. The call for a sovereign fiction able to channel and contain this force grows louder. This king within the text is no longer the originator of the law, nor is he the *poet laureate*. In speech, and even more so in writing, there lives a tyrant "that incessantly needs to be converted back into a legitimate monarch."[46] Broch's Virgil contests the tyrannous political claim for decidedness in the use of language; then again, he keeps searching for a mode of language to overcome endless comment.

In the moment of death, the poet Virgil describes "a bush with golden leaves"[47]: eventually and symbolically, *cognoscere* and *amare* are brought together, two attributes the *poet laureate* traditionally possesses.[48] In the end, and this is remarkable, Virgil perceives

> the pure word which it was, exalted above all understanding and significance whatsoever, consummating and initiating, mighty and commanding, fear-inspiring and protecting, gracious and thundering, the word of discrimination, the word of the pledge, the pure word.[49]

---

45 Ibid., pp. 396, 398; "[e]inen kleinen, aus den Kränzen gezupften Lorbeerzweig," den "er zwischen den Fingern gehalten hatte, auf die Bettdecke hin." Broch, *Der Tod des Vergil*, pp. 373, 375.

46 Translation mine. Compare: Manfred Schneider, "Der König im Text. Autorität in Recht und Literatur," *Zeitschrift für Ideengeschichte* III/1 (2009): pp. 48–63, p. 63.

47 Broch, *The Death of Virgil*, p. 426; "Ein Strauch mit goldenen Blättern." Broch, *Der Tod des Vergil*, p. 402.

48 Jürgen Heizmann: *Antike und Moderne in Hermann Brochs "Der Tod des Vergil." Über Dichtung und Wissenschaft, Utopie und Ideologie* (Tübingen: Gunter Narr Verlag, 1997), p. 129.

49 Broch, *The Death of Virgil*, p. 481. "[Vergil vernimmt] das reine Wort, das es war, erhaben über alle Verständigung und Bedeutung, endgültig und beginnend, gewaltig und befehlend, furchteinflößend und beschützend, hold und donnernd,

Broch's oath [*Eid*] is the speech act *pur sang*. It is *pure* in the sense of Walter Benjamin. "In the essay on language, pure language is that which is not an instrument for the purpose of communication, but communicates itself immediately [...]."[50] Like Broch, Giorgio Agamben rediscovers the language of the oath in his 2008 essay *The Sacrament of Language*.[51]

Many scholars have tried to explain the oath's force by placing it in the realm of magic or religion. Because it implies divine sanction in case of perjury, this archaic instrument of power functions as a guarantor of truth. In the course of the development of civilization, so the argument, due to a separation of law and religion, the oath has lost its force and has become more or less irrelevant. But how then to explain the enigmatic appeal that this speech act has preserved to our times?[52] Agamben argues the other way around. According to the Italian philosopher, "the magico-religious sphere does not logically pre-exist the oath, but it is the oath, as an originary performative experience of the word, that can explain religion (and law, which is closely connected with it)."[53] The oath is the foundational speech act that as a *sacrament of language* solemnly re-establishes the unique bond between man and language. It reproduces the "first promise" of man to "put himself at stake in language" by means of "distinguish[ing] and [...] articulat[ing] together life and language, actions and words" in an ethical and political way.[54]

Agamben's comment on the oath sheds a new light on Kafka's famous fragment number 45 from December 2, 1917:

> The choice was put to them whether they would like to be kings or kings' couriers. Like children they all wanted to be couriers. So now there are a great many couriers, they post through the world, and, as there are no kings left, shout to each other their meaningless and obsolete messages. They

---

das Wort der Unterscheidung, das Wort des Eides, das reine Wort." Broch, *Der Tod des Vergil*, pp. 453–454.

50 Giorgio Agamben: *State of Exception*, trans. Kevin Attell (Chicago/London: The University of Chicago Press, 2005), p. 62.

51 This title is a reference to Paolo Prodi's book on the history of the oath: *Il sacramento del potere. Il giuramento politico nella storia costituzionale dell'Occidente* (Bologna: Il Mulino, 1992).

52 *Fatale Sprachen. Eid und Fluch in Literatur- und Rechtsgeschichte*, ed. Peter Friedrich and Manfred Schneider (Munich: Wilhelm Fink, 2009), p. 11.

53 Giorgio Agamben: *The Sacrament of Language. An Archeology of the Oath (Homo Sacer II, 3)*, trans. Adam Kotsko (Cambridge, UK: Polity Press, 2011), p. 65.

54 Ibid., p. 69.

> would gladly put an end to their wretched lives, but they dare not because of their oath of service [Diensteid].[55]

There is no legitimate sovereign or poet laureate left that can institute or at least explain the bond holding the society of couriers together. The mute remembrance of the high esteem of the oath suffices to keep the couriers endlessly passing on their meaningless messages. Why is this oath still in power, causing so much fear? In Kafka's fragment only the oath has the power to cover up its own emptiness, its own turn to bureaucracy. It even seems to gain power, once it no longer refers to a higher principle that transcends it. Among couriers there is no possibility to reflect upon the speech act separate from service. Since their form of communication only consists in passing on messages, they cannot differentiate between authoritative text and comment. They have no means to comment upon the origin of the power of the oath. They will never discover that the oath is highly unsusceptible to commentary and chatter. For Agamben, this is communication in its purest form. Agamben bets us that the oath will outlast the grasp of our scientific-industrial society.

> [...] because what human beings have to communicate to each other is above all a pure communicability (that is, language), politics then arises as the communicative emptiness in which the human face emerges as such. It is precisely this empty space that politicians and the media establishment are trying to be sure to control, by keeping it separate in a sphere that guarantees its unseizability and by preventing communicativity itself from coming to light.[56]

In the "age of the eclipse of the oath,"[57] as Agamben describes our times, the oath still has the power to question the bond between man and language. We are still under the spell of Broch's Virgil or Kafka's fragment. Literature functions as a political commentary on the oath, in the sense that it exhibits "*a mediality: it is the act of making a means visible as such*" [emphasis in original].[58] Agamben regards "being-into-language itself as pure mediality, being-into-a-mean as a irreducible

---

55 Franz Kafka, *The Great Wall of China and Other Pieces*, trans. Willa and Edwin Muir (London: M. Secker, 1933), p. 265.
56 Giogio Agamben, *Means without End. Notes on Politics*, trans. Vincenzo Binetti and Cesare Casarino (Minneapolis: University of Minnesota Press, 2000), p. 95.
57 Agamben, *The Sacrament of Language*, p. 71.
58 Agamben, *Means without End*, pp. 115–116.

condition of human beings."[59] It is its immunity against endless commentary or empty words that makes the oath still irresistible as a political act in its purest form.

59 Ibid., p. 115.

Juliane Rebentisch

Realism Today
Art, Politics, and the Critique of Representation[1]

Primarily instigated by the 6th Berlin Biennale in 2010, the German discussion over the possibilities of an aesthetic realism has come to new life; arguments have been exchanged in academia as well as in the broader public sphere. Participants in these debates are recognizably attracted by the concept of realism, but they also evince a certain hesitation to claim the label for their own practice or to actually use this highly fraught term to describe contemporary art in general. Instead, their arguments quickly veer toward very fundamental issues; it is the ethics and politics of today's art most generally that are at stake.[2] Yet it strikes me as no coincidence that the general problem of the relationship between art and reality and the related issue of whether and how to accept the heritage of the realisms of the twentieth century become prominent at a time when contemporary art receives greater attention from institutions and critics. For the normative sense of *contemporary art* is that it should make its historic present present to us. It is supposed to be an art of its time – with regard both to the state of artistic consciousness (in technical as well as critical terms) and to its relationship to the social and cultural reality in which it originates. These two criteria decide whether an art is worthy of its present, whether it can do justice to it. That also means that there may be current artistic productions that fail to meet this double requirement, because they are anachronistic, regressive, or obsolete in one or both of the dimensions I have mentioned.

The debate on realism has always closely tied the notion of artistic progressiveness to the question of how artistic production relates to its social and cultural outside. To isolate considerations of formal creation from art's reference to that outside is to bid farewell to the project of realism. For unlike such formalism, realism is by definition impure. It

---

1 Originally published in German as "Realismus heute. Kunst, Politik und die Kritik der Repräsentation," *WestEnd. Neue Zeitschrift für Sozialforschung* 2 (2010): pp. 15–29.

2 Witness the debates over realism in the pocket guide to the 6th Berlin Biennale for Contemporary Art, which bore the title *what is waiting out there*; compare Kathrin Rhomberg, ed., *was draußen wartet / what is waiting out there: 6. Berlin Biennale für zeitgenössische Kunst / 6th Berlin Biennale for Contemporary Art* (Cologne: DuMont, 2010).

is always already open to an ethical, political, and epistemic demand: realism – as a stance, a project, a production – requires fidelity; fidelity, that is, to a reality that needs to be done justice in ethical, political, and epistemic terms. Realism attests to reality; it does not engender it. This implies that those who commit themselves to the realist project, and hence to fidelity to reality, must be the contemporaries of this reality. On the other hand, the realist project amounts to more than a positivist or automatic registration of something already given. Realism thus opposes formalism, but it does not necessarily oppose abstraction.

The relation of art to its social outside cannot be dissociated from questions of representation. For realistic art renders an *image* of reality. This means that the relationship between realism and reality is dialectical: the image of reality does not exist before realistic representation; but what is represented is still considered to be a given, however latent, or else the representation would not be realistic. The project of realism brings forth, makes visible – realizes – what is given as reality. Now realism was understood as a decidedly critical project in the great aesthetic debates of modernity, as distinguished from naturalism by the fact that the reality that appears in this general definition is social reality. But the critical perspective contains more than that. For the realistic image itself is supposed to have a potentially interventionist quality. It does not merely aim at representing the social world, but at once also at changing it. This lends the realist's fidelity to reality a double character: it is committed to what is given, yet for the sake not of this given but of the possibility of its practical transformation.

What we have to consider now, however, is how we are to understand this nexus more specifically today. For those who currently return to the problem of realism do so in light of changes which art and its theory have undergone over the past forty or fifty years – profound changes, no doubt, that are not least associated with a crisis in the philosophy of history and its constructions that defined the modern debate on realism. The key terms we may use to outline the most crucial of these developments are the *dissolution of boundaries* and *experience*. The former concept – the German has a single noun for it, *Entgrenzung* – has in recent years become a widely established title for a development in art that, as it pursues modern art's impulses toward open work-forms with a new radicalism, fundamentally calls into question not only the system of the arts but also the closure of the individual work. Yet in doing so it subverts the presupposition on which any aesthetic of truth, including that espoused by the philosophy of history, rests, as such an aesthetic must rely on the idea that the work is an objective given. The concept of experience, on the other hand, has become a key term in an aesthetic theory that has evolved not least in response to the tendencies toward boundary-dissolution in the arts; to this theory, the truth-content of the works of art can no longer be understood within the conceptual framework of a philosophical system nor, hence, of a historico-philosophical construction.

And yet a certain urgency still pertains to the question of contemporary realism –particularly in the realm of the visual arts, where developments toward the dissolution of the boundaries of art and between the arts have been most radical[3] – indicating that the question of art's relation to social reality is fundamental; it concerns even our contemporary understanding of art at its very core. For it entails questions about the ethics, the politics, and the epistemology of art – and these are hardly mere ancillaries to the conception of art itself. Rather, they concern art's right to exist at all: the question, *Wherefore art?* This question, however, has become a problem only under the conditions of modernity. For it is art's attainment of autonomy, its liberation from service to church and state, that gives rise to the discomforting thought that art might have cut the ground from under its own feet by emancipating itself from these functions, that its freedom might be no more than a veil over its servitude to a new master: the market. The discourse of realism has insistently highlighted the question, *Wherefore art?* – and that explains the central role this discourse has played in debates over aesthetic modernity. Today's return to the problem of realism in art and art theory, too, is about these fundamental issues and not merely about an *-ism* to be filed among all the other *-isms* in a history of styles. The quickest glance at the great debates over realism

3 Of all the arts, the visual arts have most distinctly developed into meta-arts. After Duchamp's radical inclusion of non-artistic elements in art, they are no longer solely or even primarily oriented by the questions, *What is painting?* or, *What is sculpture?* Instead, these questions are now subordinate to the more fundamental question, *What is art?* But once the concept of art as a whole is at stake, it can no longer make sense to conduct the engagement solely on the previously demarcated territory of a theory of the genres. That is why institutions devoted to the visual arts have made an unquestioned policy of being open to inter-media experiments whose roots lie in other arts; think of artists in the wake of John Cage – from Yoko Ono to Tony Conrad – as well as representatives of experimental film – from Harun Farocki to Michael Snow: today they all find their audiences primarily in visual arts institutions. The theater, too, to the extent that it has become postdramatic, laps over into installative and performative practices that might just as well be categorized as visual art. In a parallel development, the (academic) critical discourse of art that has accompanied these shifts has long ceased to be the privilege of art historians, and has become open to interdisciplinary exchange. These developments explain why today's engagements over the concept of art as such will with striking frequency, though of course not exclusively, take place in the institutional framework of the visual arts.

of the 20th century may clarify what is systematically at stake; it will at once serve as a backdrop highlighting the situation in which the problem of realism is taken up again today.

I.

As is widely known, Georg Lukács believed that art primarily served political insight. In showing the reader details of his own social reality, the realist novel is supposed to present to him that reality in its entirety – its laws, the tendencies of its development, and the role of man within, in short: its objective truth.[4] The possibility to recognize that truth at all is of course predicated on socialism. What makes this definition of art problematic in the first place is the idealist premise of a philosophy that not only claims insight into the totality of reality, but even into the logic of its historical unfolding.[5] For our context, however, it is just as problematic that this model reduces the function of art to illustrating vividly what has already been understood. Yet the primacy of extra-aesthetic social analysis defined not only Lukács' theory of realism, but also that of his opponents. For example, the so-called expressionism debate of the 1930s – among its participants, all in exile, Ernst Bloch was Lukács' leading opponent – already revolved around the question whether expressionist depictions of the rifts that mar the world and the subjects alike express the true nature of late capitalism, or are mere symptoms of false consciousness, obstructing actual insight into that nature. Whether the one or the other side was right, however – whether the realism of totality or, on the contrary, the realism of diremption, the novel of the 19th century or that of 20th-century expressionism, was to be distinguished as realist or rejected as antirealist – is a question whose answer is found not in close contemplation of the art, but rather on the territory of the philosophy of history.[6]

---

4 Compare, e.g., Georg Lukács, *Wider den mißverstandenen Realismus* (Hamburg: Claassen, 1958), p. 105.

5 See the criticism of this point in Lukács in Albrecht Wellmer, "Kommunikation und Emanzipation: Überlegungen zur ‚sprachanalytischen Wende' der kritischen Theorie," *Theorien des Historischen Materialismus*, ed. Urs Jaeggi and Axel Honneth (Frankfurt/M.: Suhrkamp, 1977), pp. 465–600, pp. 477–478, and Jürgen Habermas, *The Theory of Communicative Action*, trans. Thomas McCarthy (vol. 1: *Reason and the Rationalization of Society*, Cambridge, UK: Polity Press, 1984; vol. 2: *Lifeworld and System: A Critique of Functionalist Reason*, Cambridge, UK: Polity Press, 1987), vol. 1, p. 364.

6 For a critique of the debate over expressionism from the perspective of aesthetics, see also Rüdiger Bubner, *Ästhetische Erfahrung* (Frankfurt/M.: Suhrkamp, 1989),

When Theodor W. Adorno began to quarrel with Lukács' notion of realism in the late 1950s, he, too, returned to an extra-aesthetic philosophy of history. Although the pessimism of his critique of reason was diametrically opposed to Lukács' socialist optimism, it drew no less vehement opposition. Indeed, the objections Jürgen Habermas raised against the totalizing traits of the critique of reason first framed by Adorno and Max Horkheimer in the *Dialectic of Enlightenment*[7] could not but damage the plausibility of the dialectical construction Adorno had used in his aesthetic theory to recover the aspirations of critical realism in his own fashion. What is most immediately remarkable about Adorno's response to the challenge of realism, however, is that it goes hand in hand with a defense of aesthetic difference. For unlike Lukács, Adorno does not conceive of the relationship between art and science as one of kinship. Art, he writes, "will never say, as knowledge usually does: 'this is so' [...] Instead, it says, 'this is how it is.'"[8] Objectivity in art, in other words, is not created by pulling into art an external and already given meaning as though that meaning could remain in art what it was. For though art may receive its materials from reality, it does not conserve them unaltered; they are transmuted into an image. The quality of semblance that distinguishes art from reality cannot be subtracted from it. To reduce it to a purely external feature, as though art "were merely reproducing the world," just "without claiming to be immediately real itself,"[9] is to misapprehend the essence of art. Aesthetic objectivity, Adorno argues, thus arises quite differently: only in and through the intrinsic organization of the work of art – in its coherency.

At the same time, however, Adorno charged this notion of aesthetic difference itself with the contents of a philosophy of history. On the one hand, he considered the coherency of aesthetic structural creations to be in and of itself an expression of a reconciled coalescence of rationality and mimesis, which he contrasted with a historical reality determined throughout by instrumental reason as its negative image. But as this theory of reconciliation defined art as fundamentally separate from an unreconciled reality, it could fulfill its realist commitment to making an unreconciled state of affairs appear only by enacting a paradox: it had to turn against the aspect of untruth about the truth of the

---

pp. 24–26.

7 Habermas, *The Theory of Communicative Action*, vol. 1, pp. 366–399.

8 Theodor W. Adorno, "Extorted Reconciliation: On Georg Lukács' *Realism in Our Time*," Theodor W. Adorno, *Notes to Literature*, trans. Shierry Weber Nicholsen, vol. 2 (New York: Columbia University Press, 1991), pp. 216–240, p. 232.

9 Ibid., p. 224.

aesthetic semblance of reconciliation itself, by coherently shaping the negation of aesthetic coherency.[10] Formalism and realism thus coincided in Adorno. For it is the principle of the creative formation of coherency itself – not the concrete material rendered coherent in each instance – that is here made to bear the historico-philosophical burden. Yet this move ultimately identifies the concrete content of the individual works with an idea of art in general that has its place in a philosophy of history.[11] Even Adorno's virtuosity in interweaving his idea of art, motivated by his philosophy of history, with the analysis and assessment of concrete works, could not quite conceal the unmediated identification of this idea with the concrete content of the works. To the contrary: the dogmatic features and probably also the esotericism in Adorno's criticism rendered this problem most conspicuous.

II.

Today, we find ourselves far removed from these approaches to the problem. By allowing elements of reality to permeate the boundary separating it from that reality, contemporary art subverts a premise on which socialist realism's central notion – that art should represent the world by way of a model – is based. For this notion depends not least on our ability to distinguish the model from what it represents, i.e. empirical reality. Contemporary art, on the other hand, in its tendency to dissolve boundaries, destabilizes the distinction between art and non-art, between artistic representation and empirical reality. Yet by doing so, it evidently contravenes Adorno's formalist meta-realism as

---

10 Accordingly, the *this-is-how-it-is* of art contains an ambivalence that dialectically enacts within itself the realist project's double aspiration to be faithful to reality – in the insight into the bad existing state of affairs, and in the perspective toward reconciliation. The *this-is-how-it-is* of aesthetic coherency, then, must remain related within the work itself to the *this-is-how-it-is* of an unreconciled real world. Yet even this second meaning of art's *this-is-how-it-is* does not coincide with the assertive statement that *this is so*. Art does not predicate unreconciled reality; it expresses it. Its aim cannot be the coherent representation of an unreconciled world – as though art were nothing more than yet another cognitive medium. Rather, the aspiration to render an unreconciled world apparent requires acknowledgement of the chasm that severs art from reality; it can refer only to the plane of aesthetic semblance itself. For the ambivalence of Adorno's *this-is-how-it-is* more generally, compare Alexander García Düttmann, *So ist es: Ein philosophischer Kommentar zu Adornos "Minima Moralia"* (Frankfurt/M.: Suhrkamp, 2004).

11 For a more detailed critique of this point in Adorno, compare Albrecht Wellmer, *Zur Dialektik von Moderne und Postmoderne: Vernunftkritik nach Adorno* (Frankfurt/M.: Suhrkamp, 1985), pp. 31–32.

well. For even the idea of a reconciliation to be experienced in art – however dialectically refracted it may be – is tied to the presupposition of a "second reality"[12] of the work separate from all other reality. It is not by chance that Adorno conceives the adequacy of the work as the objective coherency of its structure.

However, contemporary art does not simply suspend the difference between art and non-art, between artistic representation and empirical reality. Rather, it understands that difference in a fundamentally different way: the difference between art and non-art can no longer be objectivated as a border between a self-contained work of art and its outside, but manifests itself in the specific reflective structure of the experience that distinguishes our relation to art from all other theoretical and practical manners of living in the world. The aesthetic quality of the object is not tied to certain properties of the object that are defined in advance, but must instead be understood as the product of a process of experience initiated in the engagement with the object. That is to say, the aesthetic object becomes apparent as an aesthetic object only in its interaction with an experiencing subject; the latter is likewise transformed as it relates to the object, becoming an aesthetic subject. Subject and object of aesthetic experience, in other words, are aesthetic only through and in their *becoming* aesthetic. If, under the conditions of the dissolution of boundaries, the aesthetic can no longer be understood as the objective other of the non-aesthetic, that does not imply a renunciation of aesthetic thinking but rather a shift within that thinking.[13] Far from facing the non-aesthetic as its external other, the aesthetic consists solely in its reflective transformation.

This might best be explained by examining some spectacular cases of art integrating elements of an extra-artistic reality. In 2000, Santiago Sierra exhibited illegal immigrants in cardboard boxes at the KW Institute for Contemporary Art, Berlin; on other occasions, representatives of the international precariat allowed him to tattoo a line onto their backs, or dye their hair for money.[14] But such *reality bites* do not make art disappear into life – the agents in turn become dramatic actors and thus elements of an exhibition or performance. Just as these works obviously cannot be totally abstracted from the bodily and social

12 Bubner, *Ästhetische Erfahrung*, p. 33.

13 For a more extensive discussion of this point, compare Juliane Rebentisch, *Ästhetik der Installation* (Frankfurt/ M.: Suhrkamp, 2003).

14 The works bore the simple titles *Workers who cannot be paid, remunerated to remain inside cardboard boxes* (KW Institute for Contemporary Art, Berlin, 2000); *250 cm line tattooed on 6 paid people* (Espacio Aglutinador, Havana, 1999); *133 people paid to have their hair dyed blonde* (Arsenale, Venice, 2001).

reality of their performers, the beholder also cannot be prevented from viewing them not primarily as a moral and/or political reference to the precarious living conditions of the extras, but as ultimately staged – and hence, in the broadest sense of the term, fictional – works of art. This very fact provoked a certain moral discomfort in Sierra's audience. He was accused of exploiting his performers for the effects of a media spectacle whose putatively enlightening effects actually came down to the standards of the schadenfreude pornography mass-produced for today's commercial television stations, where the reality and liveness of the miserable is turned into a showcase fetish.[15] We might ask, of course, whether an art that so obviously brands itself as cynical is in fact really cynical. The artist indeed believes that he is merely holding a mirror up to the cynicism of society – which would in turn render him decidedly uncynical. By itself, that is hardly enough to acquit Sierra's art of the charge that it operates in a manner continuous with a spectacular logic which is part of the problem of exploitation rather than part of its solution. But that charge ignores a crucial factor that makes Sierra's works function in more complex ways than the artist himself seems to have conceived: it is precisely by deranging the boundaries between fiction and reality, between art and non-art that Sierra's work – in contradistinction to reality shows on television – problematizes the position of spectating or beholding. The spectator or beholder here becomes a part of what is going on; he shares some responsibility for the situation. Still, the moral act of freeing the illegals from their undignified position beneath the cardboard would imply no less of a categorical mistake than that of the yokel Stanley Cavell mentions who storms the stage in order to save Desdemona from the black man.[16] Yet it is obviously no more instructive to merely insist that what we are looking at is just art. The very point of these works, if they have one at all, is the situative discomfort that calls the accepted safety of the audience's position into question, and does so to the very degree to which the boundaries between the aesthetic and the non-aesthetic, between art and non-art, between reality and fiction are at stake in a

---

15 On what appears, at least at first glance, to be a close proximity between "a sensationalist new realism in the visual arts" and "new formats in the mass media," Diedrich Diederichsen, "Realitätsbezüge in der bildenden Kunst: Subjektkritik, Repräsentationskritik und Statistenkunst," *Realismus in den Künsten der Gegenwart*, ed. Dirck Linck, Michael Lüthy, Brigitte Obermayr, and Martin Vöhler (Berlin: Diaphanes, 2010), pp. 13–28, pp. 14–15.

16 Compare Stanley Cavell, "The Avoidance of Love. A Reading of King Lear," *Must We Mean What We Say? A Book of Essays* (Cambridge: Cambridge University Press, 1976), p. 329.

doubtlessly serious aesthetic play.[17] Yet this play does not elicit any specific political stance. It does no more than reflectively address the position of the spectator, including the moral problem of voyeurism it may entail in extra-aesthetic contexts.

Even the most drastic adoption of elements of reality into art, however, is anything but a simple expression of its greater proximity to reality. In art – and today's boundary-dissolving productions illustrate this with particular clarity – reality is always a highly ambivalent parameter. The elements taken from extra-aesthetic contexts and adopted into art do not, that much is clear, signify reality; but neither *are* they simply reality, as Peter Bürger claimed in his *Theory of the Avant Garde* [18] Instead, they linger in a peculiar in-between: removed from their original contexts and brought into one of representation, they become dissimilar to themselves without ever clearly adopting the status of a sign for something else. How – and that always also means: as what – they appear to us in any particular instance is accordingly not an objective fact, but inseparable from ourselves and the imaginative dimensions of our experience.

Aesthetic semblance, however, can then no longer be understood as a semblance of reconciliation in the objectively given coherency of the thoroughly composed work of art; rather, it manifests itself as the correlate of aesthetic experience on the side of the object.[19] Because the processes of aesthetic experience never terminate in some objective meaning, the viewer is at once confronted with himself: in the mode of aesthetic semblance, he encounters his own projection of meaning along with the cultural and social influences that shape it. For a theory of experience, it is precisely here that the aesthetic harbors a unique ethical-political potential, created in and by the very suspension of immediate understanding in favor of a reflective engagement with its cultural and social horizons. Whether such an experience leads to an

---

17 It is not by coincidence that the concept of the situation taken in this sense becomes relevant also in the contemporary postdramatic theater; compare Hans-Thies Lehmann, *Postdramatic Theatre*, trans. Karen Jürs-Munby (New York: Routledge, 2006), pp. 122–25.

18 Peter Bürger, *Theory of the Avant-Garde*, trans. Michael Shaw (Minneapolis: University of Minnesota Press, 1984), p. 78.

19 As Bubner (*Ästhetische Erfahrung*, p. 43) explains this phenomenon, "there is no image in which that, and nothing but that, is to be seen which the beholder sees in it; no poem in which that can definitely be read which we read in it; and no piece of music where listening closely is enough to hear what offers itself in the aesthetic experience [...]. The aesthetic experience sees something that cannot be ascertained, and that is there, for that very reason, ever and again."

actual change of mind that might pass into political action, however, is a matter art itself does not decide.

III.

To the extent that we may nonetheless maintain a cautious reference to an ethical-political potential of aesthetic experience, the latter must be defined on the basis of an intrinsic logic of the aesthetic, of aesthetic difference. Yet from the perspective of a theory of experience, this aesthetic difference no longer coincides with that between reconciled semblance and real unreconciliation. Today's advanced art, in fact, firmly defies any attempt to commit it to a utopian position separated from reality by an unbridgeable chasm. It is a turn not against utopia altogether, but toward a different understanding of the utopian. Art no longer offers itself as the placeholder for utopia, because it is faithful to the fact that utopia's original place is not in art but in politics.

We may well recognize a certain parallelism between this shift and developments in critical theory: when Adorno portrayed art as the residue of the utopian other, he did so not least based on his problematic diagnosis that the sphere of conceptual thought was thoroughly corrupted, as it were, by instrumental reason. Habermas' critique of this diagnosis fundamentally changes the constellation of reality, art and utopia. As he argues convincingly, conceptual thought comprehends not only the objectivation of reality in the context of instrumental action, but also the intersubjectivity of communication, the mimetically open relationship between subjects.[20] Therefore, "the utopian perspective migrates into the sphere of discursive reason itself."[21]

The title of the utopia associated with this perspective is a "communication free of domination." But if this utopia is to be understood as practical and political, the idea that we can experience no more than an anticipative semblance of it, and worse, experience even that much only within art, would amount to a betrayal of its practical-political core. It is precisely in the name of political utopia that the utopian pathos must be subtracted from art.[22] Under these circumstances, to persist in stylizing art as the semblant fulfillment of a good, true, and right life is no more than an ideological degradation of art to a mere

---

20 Habermas, *The Theory of Communicative Action*, vol. 1, pp. 389–390.

21 Wellmer, *Zur Dialektik von Moderne und Postmoderne*, p. 21.

22 For the critique of the aesthetic utopia, see also Martin Seel, *Die Kunst der Entzweiung: Zum Begriff der ästhetischen Rationalität* (Frankfurt/M.: Suhrkamp, 1985), pp. 325–333.

affirmative beautiful semblance that compensates for a bad reality and thus contributes to its continuance.

But we also cannot dispose of the problem of a compensatory functionalization of art by negating all aesthetic difference – and that means: the aspect of semblance in all art – and turning art directly into an instrument of the practical-political realization of utopia. That is the problem of today's relational aesthetics in particular.[23] To declare art a privileged medium of social integration is to perform a paradoxical sublation of art and life that cements the very difference between reconciled artistic practice and unreconciled reality. The difference, however, is then no longer aesthetic but social: a communicative practice celebrates itself in the protected space which the institutions of art afford, and relates to its other, to unreconciled conditions, merely from the distance of such privilege.

If there is an idea in Adorno that critical contemporary art can connect to at all, it is that the utopia of reconciliation can appear in authentic, uncorrupted art only in an act of negation: in and through its reference to an unreconciled reality. But as the concept of utopia has shifted, so has that of unreconciled reality. Reality can be called unreconciled no longer because it is entirely controlled by instrumental reason, but because the communicative relationships between its subjects are factually distorted. These distortions, however, arise not only from processes of economization and bureaucratization that "colonize" a communicatively integrated life-world from the outside, as Habermas suggested in his *Theory of Communicative Action*;[24] rather, they also result from unequal social distributions of power inherent to the process of communicative action itself.[25] As the early Habermas himself had pointed out in *Knowledge and Human Interests*,[26] this explains why there are struggles that must first confront the social conditions of

---

23 I am referring only to the program of relational aesthetics – compare especially Nicolas Bourriaud, *Relational Aesthetics* (Paris: Presses du réel, 2002) – and not necessarily also to the art associated with it. For what the latter accomplishes is, upon closer inspection, usually fairly distinct from social integration: it consists in turning *participation* into an object of aesthetic reflection, precisely stripping it of its immediate practical meaning. See also Juliane Rebentisch, "Participation and Reflection: Angela Bulloch's *The Disenchanted Forest x 1001*," Angela Bulloch, *Angela Bulloch: Prime Numbers*, exh. cat. (Cologne: Walther König, 2006), pp. 87–107.

24 Habermas, *The Theory of Communicative Action*, vol. 2, p. 522.

25 For a critique of this point in Habermas, compare Axel Honneth, *Kritik der Macht: Reflexionsstufen einer kritischen Gesellschaftstheorie* (Frankfurt/M.: Suhrkamp, 1989), especially pp. 296–306.

26 Jürgen Habermas, *Knowledge and Human Interests*, trans. Jeremy J. Shapiro (Cambridge, UK: Polity Press, 1987), pp. 53–63.

reasonable communication so that communicative action may be set free and rendered communicative in the first place. Yet as Jacques Rancière in particular has emphasized in recent years, such struggles are always also contentions over the communicative parameters and social patterns of perception, the vocabularies and images in which a society articulates its self-conception.[27]

Struggles for recognition have shown that the question of representation is not merely an issue of symbolism. Representation creates and maintains social perception as a part of the *materiality* of social reality: it constitutes a differentiation within the field of the sensible that assigns some to the center, others to the margins, affording more rights and greater political weight to some than to others. The problem that women, blacks, or gays face, as the American art critic and theorist Craig Owens wrote in the 1980s, is not a lack of representation. Rather, the hegemonic representations of these groups are such that the visibility they grant them reinforces their very political invisibility.[28]

But while social movements work to oppose hegemonic representations with representations of their own in order to enable the marginalized to represent, and speak for, themselves – in short: to make them appear as political subjects –, the critique of representation in the arts articulates itself in a fundamentally different way. For the sea change in aesthetic thought has consequences even where art turns to the problem of representing the world and thus seems at first glance to operate within the paradigm of the old realism: art today refrains from seeking the true image. It is no longer engaged in disrupting the opaque surfaces of the world in order to reveal its hidden meanings, its laws or its truth; instead, it engages with a world already disclosed by representation. The reality to which contemporary art refers in these contexts, and of which it makes us conscious, is the reality of representation. And yet the act of bringing that representation to present itself is initiated by artistic operations that deliberately subvert the referential inference from representation to what is represented. This also means that the critique of representation cannot, or at least not primarily, be conceived as a contribution to the political visibility of marginalized groups.

---

27 Jacques Rancière, *Disagreement: Politics and Philosophy*, trans. Julie Rose (Minneapolis: University of Minnesota Press, 1999), pp. 43–60.

28 Craig Owens, "'The Indignity of Speaking for Others:' An Imaginary Interview," *Beyond Recognition: Representation, Power, and Culture*, ed. Craig Owens, Jane Weinstock, and Barbara Kruger (Berkeley: University of California Press, 1992), pp. 259–262, p. 262.

IV.

It is here that art today differs explicitly from those realist projects that take the critique of representation to be mostly concerned with criticizing the exclusion of the poor and oppressed from the worldview of the powerful. Think of the historic example of Jacob Riis, whose photo reportage *How the Other Half Lives* confronted the upper and middle classes of late 19th-century America with the conditions in the slums of New York.[29] As late as the 1970s, the same impulse motivated Jacob Holdt's documentation of African-American ghettos.[30] These realisms, their enlightening potential notwithstanding, always already had a double flipside: on the one hand, they exploited their subjects; on the other hand, the images thus produced lent themselves to voyeuristic consumption. The problems of a realism so conceived became evident once more in the wake of the AIDS crisis. Douglas Crimp, for example, harshly criticized Nicholas Nixon's *People with AIDS*[31] for a return to a conception of realism that is perhaps well-intentioned, but factually reactionary in its exploitation and fetishization of its subjects.[32]

But the debates over an activist use of photography during the AIDS crisis have also forcefully drawn our attention to another problem, one that demonstrates that art does not simply withdraw from the task of political representation on a whim, but that this abstinence has to be understood as an insight into the intrinsic and fundamentally different logic of the aesthetic. For these debates revealed that it was impossible to decide, without further context, which picture would best accomplish the task of representing the crisis. Depending on the context, it might make sense to show the mortal suffering of those stricken by the disease in detail – or on the contrary, to refrain from dragging it all into the light.[33] It was context that decided whether and in what form it was politically sensible, or morally adequate, to show images of suffering. It is no coincidence that a combination with text was often sought in

29 Jacob Riis, *How the Other Half Lives* [1890] (New York: W. W. Norton & Company, 2009).

30 Jacob Holdt, *American Pictures: A Personal Journey through the American Underclass* (Copenhagen: American Pictures Foundation, 1985).

31 Nicholas Nixon and Bebe Nixon, *People with AIDS* (Boston: David R. Godine, 1991).

32 Compare Douglas Crimp, "Portraits of People with AIDS" [1992], *Melancholia and Moralism: Essays on AIDS and Queer Politics* (Cambridge, Mass.: The MIT Press, 2002), pp. 83–107.

33 Dirck Linck, "'Mourning and Militancy:' Künstlerische Reaktionen auf die Aids-Krise," *Realismus in den Künsten der Gegenwart*, ed. Michael Lüthy, Brigitte Obermayr, and Martin Vöhler, pp. 29–50, p. 44.

order to extend the images toward their political context,[34] corroborating Walter Benjamin's insight that "all photographic construction must remain arrested in the approximate" without "inscription."[35] Taken by itself, it seems, photography almost inevitably succumbs to the ideological – Roland Barthes would have said: "mythical"[36] – tendency to sanitize what it represents by suppressing the complexity of the political contexts with which it is tied up. For the picture without any commentary, as Susan Sontag has also emphasized on several occasions, can do no more than register misery; it shows that misery exists – but explains nothing.[37] It can thus at best appeal to a politically empty and quickly transient compassion, a sympathy for humankind in general that lacks the necessary focus to translate into a self-sustaining motivation of political practice. It is easy to get used to the fleeting effect of such pictures – and to the mere factuality of the misery they document. This is why those artistic productions remain unpersuasive whose sole claim to the political rests in the fact that they depict some miserable circumstances. Their only immediate political effect is the exploitation of their subjects by the artist under whose name the images are shown. To avoid such politically and morally counterproductive effects, the image requires further explanation – in the form of a political commentary, for instance, that relates my own world to that of the image and points out my implicit place in the image. What I am driving at is quite a familiar nexus: the more defined its context, the better the meaning of an image can be controlled. Control over its context, in other words, though it can never be total, is what any documentary must attempt if it aspires to enlighten. This also means that the documentary image is not created in the instance when it is shot, but in retrospect, in the work of its contextualization. The controlling regard for the context, then, is a crucial component not of any photograph, as Benjamin had suspected toward the end of his *Little History of Photography*, but certainly of any documentary use of pictures.[38]

---

34 Ibid., p. 46.

35 Walter Benjamin, "Little History of Photography," *Selected Writings*, vol. 2: *1927–1934*, ed. Michael W. Jennings, Howard Eiland and Gary Smith, trans. Edmund Jephcott and Kingsley Shorter, (Cambridge, Mass.: The Belknap Press of Harvard University Press, 1999), p. 527.

36 Roland Barthes, *Mythologies*, trans. Annette Lavers (New York: Hill and Wang, 1972), pp. 144–145.

37 Susan Sontag, *Regarding the Pain of Others* (New York: Farrar, Straus and Giroux, 2003), p. 42 and pp. 116–117.

38 See also Juliane Rebentisch, "Das dokumentarische und das ästhetische Bild," *Chile International. Kunst – Existenz – Multitude*, ed. Andreas Fanizadeh and Eva-Christina Meier (Berlin: ID-Verlag, 2005), pp. 45–58.

V.

Now the debate over the political use of pictures only raises the question of a politics of art with renewed urgency. Art, I would argue, functions as the structural *irony* of the documentary register; for in an inversion of the logic of enlightening documentation, it functions by isolating its elements from the contexts in which they are embedded in the life-world. This allows for the form of depiction to assume a potential independence from the depicted content, gaining a weight of its own and coming to the fore in its own material reality. This does not result in a formalism, however, but rather in a tension between the depiction and the depicted that disintegrates all evident meaning and calls the referential inference from the representation to the represented into question.

From the perspective of the documentary, oriented as it is towards an offering of insight, this would certainly seem to be a highly problematic dynamic. We might even say that it confirms an age-old – in fact, Platonic – resentment against art: that it requires a specialization in questions of representation but is nonplussed when it comes to the truth of what it represents. But what Plato could only regard as a weakness turns out, at this juncture, to be the specific strength of art. For it employs this dynamic to serve a critique of representation that, unlike the enlightening critique of representation in documentary works, proceeds in a strictly negative fashion.

As an example, consider *The Bowery in Two Inadequate Descriptive Systems*, a fairly well-known work by the American artist Martha Rosler from 1974–1975. It consists of a series of sheets, each of which combines a black-and-white photograph with a text plate showing a few words arranged in the style of concrete poetry. The conventional photographs of derelict shops on New York's Bowery show nothing spectacular; they simply quote some very familiar sights from the neighborhood. The words assembled in the text plates, on the other hand, are taken from no less familiar descriptions of what was then a so-called deprived area, focusing on the desolate state of its perpetually intoxicated residents. This is obviously a form of montage, not just of images and text, but of fragments of reality into art. But these fragments collected from reality are already representations of reality. Her claim to accuracy, as Rosler later commented on her work, was made "in relation to representations of representations, not representations of truth."[39] If we were to call Rosler's piece a documentary of

39 Martha Rosler, "In, Around, and Afterthoughts (on Documentary Photography)" [1981], *The Contest of Meaning: Critical Histories of Photography*, ed. Richard Bolton

the realities of the Bowery, we would therefore have to call it at best a documentary of the second order. But even that description strikes me as ultimately misleading. For the critical potential of this work unfolds decidedly not in the enlightening logic of the documentary, but rather in that of the aesthetic. The work explains nothing; text and image precisely fail to converge in one meaning. Instead, we, the beholders, are required to establish the connection between image and text in an experimental act. We can only quote the contexts in which it might make sense to assign these words to these images, but there is no objective basis for this act within the work itself. In aesthetic experience, we gain no more than a refracted sense of the meaning of that present which the art presents, so that the way any particular representation appears – and that means: what it makes appear – at once refers us back to ourselves and to the cultural and social worldviews at work in our acts of understanding. Such art precisely disrupts an approach aimed at enlightening us about a state of affairs in the world, in favor of a reflective confrontation not only with the political implications of culturally and socially fabricated worldviews, but also with the cultural and social prejudices with which we ourselves face the world and its images.

The question may be raised whether the strict opposition between documentary procedures on the one hand and their ironic representation in art on the other hand is in fact plausible. Yet I believe that any art that deserves its name refers to the logic of representation in a negativist-ironic fashion, even in cases in which we may at first be tempted to assign it to the documentary genre. One good example would be Allan Sekula's idiosyncratic photographic essay *Fish Story*[40]; another, Sharon Lockhart's formally rigorous film *Lunch Break* (2008). Both take up a positively classical genre of critical documentary photography: labor. But they do so in a way that reflectively blocks any attempt to read the images they generate as pure and simple representations by always also exhibiting the strategies of representation themselves.

Yet art that suspends our direct access to the world and documentary work bent on enlightenment are not rivals for the same project – the point obviously cannot be to pit one against the other. In order to take seriously the intrinsic logic of art, however, we have to accept it as complementary to the logic of the documentary. In it, art remains faithful to the double aspiration of the old realism: fidelity to the given for the sake of its practical transformation. For it is in and through its negativity that this art enables a distancing reflection on the implications

---

(Cambridge, Mass.: MIT Press, 1992), p. 303–342, p. 325.

40 Allan Sekula, *Fish Story* (Düsseldorf: Richter, 2002).

of our existing worldviews – and our investment in them –, and opens them up for the possibility of change.

Again, such a genuinely aesthetic experience does not relate to the utopia of a communication free of domination in the manner of its semblant fulfillment. Rather, the aesthetic suspension of the logic of culturally and socially operative representation remains fully conscious that, in political terms, its word cannot be final. Politically, the logic of representation simply cannot be suspended. There can be no justice and no freedom without determined political subjectivity, and that is to say, without its political and juridical representation. The new social movements have always demanded a *different* representation, transforming the political invisibility of the marginalized into a political visibility. Far from suspending the logic of representation, the partial political successes they have achieved have reinstalled this logic by framing a new political subjectivity: workers, women, homosexuals, blacks. But any political representation contains an aspect of flat-out assertion that is concealed to the extent that it veils its own rhetorical nature. For as a rhetorical act, any representation always also indirectly points toward the indeterminacy of what it first renders determinate – and hence toward a potentiality that may always also call it into question again. So if art refrains from any positive representation of social reality, it does so not least in order to expose social realities as representations, and thus expose also their rhetorical nature, suspending the naturalizing inference from the representation to those it represents. Art gains (meta-)political meaning not least by revealing the positing acts, along with their rhetorics, at the foundations of our political worldviews. In doing so, it points toward the potentially endless struggle over the conditions under which a communication free of domination would be possible.

(Translated by Gerrit Jackson and Stephan Packard)

Nikolaus Müller-Schöll

Plus d'un rôle
Playing Together in Contemporary Dance, Theatre, and Performance

On and Off Roles

Some erosions proceed so slowly that we only notice them once the complete ruin at their very end, like some sudden catastrophe, reveals that an architecture, an era, and sometimes even a whole world have disappeared. This is true of the *role*, as we will see when we look back to the stages of the 20th century from our vantage point as defined by early 21st century experiments in theatre, dance, and performance. More closely even than most of the other central notions of bourgeois theatre and classical drama theory, the *role* is conceptually tied to modern views of the subject: that self-empowered, present sovereign that was coined in the 18th century. A master of its own house, this subject could set its affairs in order by the use of its own reason, if only it would for once aspire to such use.[1] The acme of subject philosophy – that time of great designs of subjective systems and models of onto-theological communities fully owning their own substance – coincides with the emergence of modern role concepts in a thoroughly bourgeois literary theatre: Its actors are to offer up body, voice and face to a fictitious figure that becomes the character that they are to play, and play as "naturally,"[2] as they can. This 18th century talk of the natural demands ever more refined methods, which theoreticians readily invent while critics guard them – and while the actor is instituted as his own first critic in the course of his specific self-duplication.[3] Even such an immanent view of the foundational writings of drama theory in the 18th century suffices to show the phantasmatic quality of their regulated purity. However, in the light of the most recent debates on

1 See Immanuel Kant, "Beantwortung der Frage: Was ist Aufklärung?," *Werke*, vol. 9 (Darmstadt: Wissenschaftliche Buchgesellschaft, 1975), pp. 53–61; p. 53.

2 On "nature" in the 18th century, see Paul de Man, *Allegories of Reading. Figural Language in Rousseau, Nietzsche, Rilke and Proust* (New Haven/London: Yale University Press, 1979); Jacques Derrida, *Grammatologie* (Frankfurt/M.: Suhrkamp, 1988); Günther Heeg, *Das Phantasma der natürlichen Gestalt. Körper, Sprache und Bild im Theater des 18. Jahrhunderts* (Frankfurt/M./Basel: Stroemfeld, 2000).

3 See Johannes Lehmann, *Der Blick durch die Wand. Zur Geschichte des Theaterzuschauers und des Visuellen bei Diderot und Lessing* (Freiburg: Rombach, 2000).

issues of community, these writings appear as parts of an immunization strategy ultimately aimed at protecting the community – in a state, but also in a microcosm such as the theatre – from its outside, at sealing it off against touch, against contamination, and against that *munus* to which *communitas* traditionally referred, those bonds to the other that at once constitute a law and a gift.[4] The actor is reduced to his role in play, supposedly merged into it, and can be regarded as an equivalent of that naked or mere life, which, separated from its specific form, stands in the middle of the calculations of modern politics.[5]

The dominant theatre of the 19th and 20th century transforms the *work done on a role*, still a fragile concept in the 18th century, into a program that has defied all tendencies to the contrary and survives even today in the inert institutions of German straight theatre, and in the instructive training that guards its doors. So is it a timeless *conditio sine qua non* of theatre? Of course not, as any look at other cultures or even occidental theatre's own history will show. The role in today's sense was recognized only in modern times, and from early on in the 20th century, it has gradually begun to crumble.[6]

I would like to recall just some of the steps in the slow demise of a self-identical role in play:

– Bertolt Brecht's work can be read as a reaction to at least five great challenges haunting the self-conscious, present subject since the mid-19th century: namely war, commodity economy, pleasure principle, logo-centrism's destruction, and the insights coming from physicists such as Albert Einstein and Werner Heisenberg. Brecht's epic theatre answered these challenges by exposing the role's difference from the actor playing it. His model of the *learning play* (Lehrstück) had a ten-

4 See Roberto Esposito, *Communitas* (Zurich/Berlin: Diaphanes, 2004); Roberto Esposito, *Immunitas* (Zurich/Berlin: Diaphanes, 2004); Cornelia Zumbusch, *Die Immunität der Klassik. Reinheit, Schutz und Unempfindlichkeit bei Schiller und Goethe* (Frankfurt/M.: Suhrkamp, 2011).

5 On the disruptions that should contextualize research into the development of modern acting in the second half of the 18th century, see Giorgio Agamben, "Lebens-Form," *Gemeinschaften. Positionen zu einer Philosophie des Politischen*, ed. Joseph Vogl (Frankfurt/M.: Suhrkamp, 1994), pp. 251–257; as well as all of the volumes on changing modern politics that Agamben collected under the project of the "homo sacer"; Michel Foucault, *Sexualität und Wahrheit*, vol. 1. (Frankfurt/M.: Suhrkamp, 1988); Michel Foucault, *Il faut défendre la société* (Paris: Gallimard, Seuil, 1997); and beyond those, we might also recall the parallel between the emergence of bourgeois theatre and the institutions of the clinic and the prison as described by Foucault.

6 On the history of the role, see Ulrike Haß, "Rolle," *Metzler Lexikon Theatertheorie*, ed. Erika Fischer-Lichte, Doris Kolesch, and Matthias Warstat (Stuttgart/Weimar: Metzler, 2005), pp. 278–283.

dency to turn the role – especially in *Maßnahme* – into a merely preliminary, and only a posteriori fixable, construct of an ever different play.[7]

– Gertrude Stein's, Samuel Beckett's, Heiner Müller's, Elfriede Jelinek's and Sarah Kane's plays, or rather: texts, each in their own way, don't allow for roles except as quotations, repetitions, fragmentations, and as the result of a lingual and text-spatial mise-en-scène that exposes its literariness, its own lingual construction.

– The various rediscoveries of the *commedia dell'arte* and of the *harlequin principle*[8] have produced plays with unchanging masks, which can be separated from their actors and may stand in for, without ever being consumed by, transient roles in the course of play. Specifically, this is the case in the stage practice of avant-garde theatre from Edward Gordon Craig, through Wsewolod E. Meyerhold, Jacques Copeau, Max Reinhardt and Brecht, to Jean-Louis Barrault, Dario Fo, Ariane Mnouchkine, Benno Besson, Eugenio Barba, Giorgio Strehler, Roberto Ciulli, and to Forced Entertainment.[9]

– But most important is the rediscovery of the chorus, much spoken of in the last two decades. It might be traced as a consideration of men of their crowds, of Proletarian non-heroes, and of the choral origins of Greek theatre, from Brecht through Heiner Müller to Einar Schleef. Schleef's staging practice and theory gave light to the chorus as an object of repression that began with the reforms of acting practice in the standing theatres of the 18th century.[10]

As I intend to show in the following examples situated between current choreography, performance, object, and straight theatre, the disappearance of the *role* in today's stage experiments can be understood as the expression of a kind of collective unconscious, a reference to the roles' common roots in prior structures, and ultimately in a community that is constantly exposed to its own alteration.

---

7 See Nikolaus Müller-Schöll, *Das Theater des ‚konstruktiven Defaitismus'. Lektüren zur Theorie eines Theaters der A-Identität bei Walter Benjamin, Bertolt Brecht und Heiner Müller* (Frankfurt/Basel: Stroemfeld, 2002); Nikolaus Müller-Schöll, "Die Maßnahme auf dem Boden einer unreinen Vernunft," *Maßnehmen*, ed. Inge Gellert, Gerd Koch, and Florian Vaßen (Berlin: Theater der Zeit, 1999), pp. 251–267.

8 See Rudolf Münz, *Theatralität und Theater. Zur Historiographie von Theatralitätsgefügen* (Berlin: Schwarzkopf & Schwarzkopf, 1998), pp. 60–65; Ulrike Haß, *Das Drama des Sehens. Auge, Blick und Bühnenform* (Munich: Fink, 2005), p. 160–171.

9 See Nikolaus Müller-Schöll, "Der 'Chor der Komödie'. Zur Wiederkehr des Harlekin im Theater der Gegenwart," *Performing Politics*, ed. Nikolaus Müller-Schöll, André Schallenberg, and Mayte Zimmermann (Berlin: Theater der Zeit, 2012).

10 See Einar Schleef, *Droge Faust Parsifal* (Frankfurt/M.: Suhrkamp, 1997).

Playing the Role Text instead of Roleplay (Chétouane)

Director and choreographer Laurent Chétouane began to dissolve the mapping of players to roles in his staging of Müller's *Bildbeschreibung*. He has since continuously refined this process.[11] His most recent straight theatre is characterized by a transfer of methods from contemporary dance theatre to his playful treatment of text. This was first to be observed in his Weimar staging of *Faust II*,[12] which emerged from the previously performed dance piece #2: "Antonin Artaud liest den 2. Akt von Goethes *Faust 2*" ["Antonin Artaud reads the second act of Goethe's *Faust 2*"]. Like the subsequent work on *Faust I*, on which I will focus here, it can be understood as an accolade to changeability, a night of metamorphoses.[13] It is framed by a question which determines all of Chétouane's recent work: that of the possibility of playing *together* as a group. Its preliminary culminations are *dance piece #4*, titled *Leben wollen (zusammen)* [*Wanting to live (together)*],[14] *Horizon(s)*[15] and the consequent stagings of *Dantons Tod*,[16] and of *Das Erdbeben in Chili*.[17]

Chétouane's *Faust I* can be understood as an improvisation on motifs and topics from Goethe's *Faust*, as developed from the dance pieces. It was Chétouane's second work in Cologne, after a previous show devoted to Brecht's *Fatzer* and Friedrich Hölderlin's *Empedokles*. When these are viewed alongside *Faust II*, the roots that reach back to *Fatzer* are evident in the presentation.[18] Heiner Müller once

---

11 See Nikolaus Müller-Schöll "Raisonner sur scène," *Resonanz. Potentiale einer akustischen Figur*, ed. Karsten Lichau, Viktoria Tkaczyk, and Rebecca Wolf (Munich: Fink, 2009), pp. 291–306.

12 Johann Wolfgang Goethe, *Faust II*, Nationaltheater Weimar [National Theater Weimar, Germany], directed by Laurent Chétouane, Opening: 20 March 2008.

13 Johann Wolfgang Goethe, *Faust I*, Schauspiel Köln [Municipal Theater Cologne, Germany], directed by Laurent Chétouane, Opening: 17 October 2008.

14 Tanzstück #4: *leben wollen (zusammen)*, Sophiensäle Berlin [Germany], choreography by Laurent Chétouane. Debut: 13 September 2009. See Roland Barthes, *Wie zusammen leben* (Frankfurt/M.: Suhrkamp, 2007).

15 *Horizon(s)*, PACT Zollverein Essen [Germany], choreographed by Laurent Chétouane. Debut: 20 May 2011.

16 Georg Büchner, *Dantons Tod*, Schauspiel Köln [Municipal Theater Cologne, Germany], directed by Laurent Chétouane, Opening: 16 January 2010.

17 Heinrich von Kleist, *Das Erdbeben in Chili*, Schauspiel Köln [Municipal Theater Cologne, Germany], directed by Laurent Chétouane. Debut: 27 January 2012.

18 Friedrich Hölderlin/Bertolt Brecht, *Empedokles Fatzer*, Schauspiel Köln [Municipal Theater Cologne, Germany], directed by Laurent Chétouane, Opening: 22 February 2008.

called *Fatzer* Brecht's *Faust*[19]; along the same lines, one might say that Chétouane took *Faust I* to be Goethe's *Fatzer*. Although the material might have been shaped into a play and canonized in that form, it still retains the quality of a great fragment that bursts through all form, indeed one of the great historical fragments in German literature. The actors were to take as the central thesis Mephisto's self-definition in response to Faust, in which he claims to be "a part of the part that once was all…".[20] All players of that night, six actors and two dancers, play with the text of their roles, imagining what those roles are about. In this sense, there is no reading of the whole, no preceding idea or great narrative that could connect everything on stage and anchor it in some reference. But neither are there any incorporated roles or characters. In their place, an unknown textual object appears, inspiring the imagination of the agents who play and move to it, who perform it in a permanent together and against each other, representing and enacting it without making it their own. The manner in which the text is spoken emphasizes the continuance of language rather than its imposed structure, and several speakers play together for one character, or rather: figure, the text re-emerges in variants conveying its potential polyphony precisely because there is no dialogue, drama, nor conflict to draw away our attention. It appears as a kind of minimalist lingual music, a many-shaped material offering itself up for play *en gros* and *en detail*, and in different ways: Sometimes in the manner of a piece of dance theatre accompanied by straight spoken sequences, where the text is spoken standing up, lying down, in and through an assortment of different positions. Sometimes again in the manner of an improvisation for scenic practice reminiscent of jazz sessions. Sometimes, in the manner of ensemble movements: All will move in a circle and speak the text in turn. Or else, all will occupy themselves with the objects and materials found in different parts of the stage as they take up the text from one another. Auerbach's Cellar is turned against itself: One agent, the "party pooper," is playing classical music at the piano, while the "cool party" next to him attempts to draw him in. The Walpurgisnight breaks into the piece almost as a *mise-en-abyme*: A curtain opens, and a film is projected on the far wall, introducing the events as some kind of surreal dream collage. All of this seems like an attempt to find out, together, just what this is all about in the first place: what, for instance,

---

19 See Heiner Müller, "Fatzer ± Keuner," *Material* (Leipzig: Reclam, 1990), pp. 30–36; p. 35.
20 Johann Wolfgang Goethe, *Faust*, ed. Albrecht Schöne (Frankfurt/M.: Deutscher Klassiker Verlag, 2005), p. 65.

this "Faust" may be, this man, this piece of theatre, this myth. A night spent in search, a kind of scenic research.

The movements include dancing and pacing elements; the latter at first appear as mere activities on stage, not primarily representative, albeit not completely devoid of representation; perhaps no more than the emergence of a representation that will never be perfected but always remains in a state of being-made. It is as if we were witnessing a rehearsal, an impression not least supported by the actors' everyday clothes: socks for the actors, bare feet for the dancers.

Similar to the dancers in Chétouane's dance pieces, the players in all parts of this event never define themselves merely through an imaginary situation from the play's plot, but always also through the situation of the event, that is to say through the fact that they and the audience share a space , the "Halle Kalk." In this outer performance area of Cologne's theatre, figures rather than characters emerge, figures which one might consider to be nothing but the operative unity[21] of their acting, of their collective play with the text of roles. No fourth wall closes off the space. When the actors look at us, they recognize us, see us, perceive us and themselves in a two-edged relation of gazing and gazed-upon. As such, they do not necessarily play for us, but neither is there any moment in which they play as if we weren't there.

The Role that was Never Heard of Again
Nature Theatre of Oklahoma

Chétouane's dissolution of bourgeois roles goes back to the very specific context of his own work. But at the same time, he also shares a greater connection with scenic research happening in many other places, all of which gradually approaches a similar dissolution of the role. *Life and times – Episode One* is a music dance performance of almost four hours.[22] First developed by Pavol Liska and Kelly Copper at the Wiener Burgtheater, it is now enacted by an ensemble of six

---

21 As Gabriele Brandstetter explains, the choregraph Willam Forsythe conceives of the characters in his choreographies as "operative units" (see Gabriele Brandstetter, "Figura: Körper und Szene. Zur Theorie der Darstellung im 18. Jahrhundert," *Theater im Kulturwandel des 18. Jahrhunderts. Inszenierung und Wahrnehmung von Körper – Musik – Sprache*, ed. Erika Fischer-Lichte and Jörg Schönert (Göttingen: Wallstein, 1999), pp. 23–38; p. 23).

22 My description focuses on the "New York Version" of *Life and Times – Episode One*, which I saw at the Summerfestival Hamburg at Kampnagel on 12 August 2010.

performers and three musicians under the name of the *Nature Theatre of Oklahoma*. Three women and three men sing through the story of an American childhood and youth, told in the first person. The narrative consists of thoroughly trivial reminiscences, the everyday peculiarities of neighbours, school incidents, and small catastrophes: The love interest that has a crush on yet another pupil, the shocking view of Dad on the toilet, and so on. A scansion is achieved by a repeated "uhm" that interrupts the singing and refers to the source of the text: a 16-hour telephone interview that the directors conducted with a 34-year-old woman. If we listen only to the content of the text, we hear an American woman engaged in small talk about the times that were. But in opposition to this movement, these everyday memories are represented far out of their usual proportion: There is the great length of the evening, as well as the great weight afforded to the lovingly told anecdotes, which are slowed down by their transfer to music. The musical style is poached from Country, Weird Folk and movie scores. As has been rightly remarked, this institutes the "recitative as a dramatic form"[23] that renders trivial small-town stories as an oratory of everyday life. The very simple setting includes an illuminated backdrop, and the actors enter through hatches in the floor: an allusion to the world of variety shows and musicals, albeit only in the manner of a citation or rough sketch. We might call this scenic pop-art: Not unlike Roy Lichtenstein's overproportional comic panels or Andy Warhol's soup tin motif, a common living environment, deprived by industrialisation of any originality or uniqueness, is exhibited by methods that can be traced back to the renaissance: Proscenium stage and panel painting. The difference between the quoted form and its new object, between the spiritual storytelling of oratories that promise salvation to humanity on the one hand, and the everyday life in the middle of nowhere on the other, points to a radical disillusionment. Nothing but an empty shell, a comical remnant, is left of the subject that once inherited God's place in the midst of secularization along with all the claims and hopes of the modern age.

This difference between quoted form and trivial content alludes to the program promised by the name of the "Nature Theatre of Oklahoma." It refers to Franz Kafka's novel *Der Verschollene* (*The Man Who Was Never Heard of Again*, previously titled: *America*). In it, the "great theatre of Oklahoma" famously advertises for staff with these words: "Everyone is welcome! If you want to become an artist, sign up! We are the theatre that can use anyone, everyone in their own

23 In the words of the program from Kampnagel.

place."[24] Walter Benjamin commented: "By what criteria applications are decided is an enigma never to be solved. Talent as an actor, which might be your first thought, does not seem to play any role at all."[25] The casting for the performance – in the Nature Theatre's rather than the Burgtheater's version – recalls these sentences: The performers may be viewed as intruders on stage, chosen throughout by the one principle that they should exceed all measure (of mediocrity). They neither fit the flawless world of variety shows suggested by the set design, nor do they demonstrate the almost seamless merging of text, role and actor towards a character or figure that usually dominates casting choices in actors' theatre: A bit too fat, a bit too small, a bit too skinny, a bit too sweaty, their bodily appearance continuously detracts from the narrative, reshaping it and adding to it. The cast's movements do not recall dance art or dance theatre, but rather the moves of cheerleaders and of show dancing, even of rhythmic gymnastics. Referring the descriptions in the text back to the persons on stage produces many comical effects. We are not encountering actors from a new young generation, but performers conspiring to stage such a youth together. The disproportional representation of an ultimately anonymous character's story is reflected in the distributed work of its representation, occupying no less than six singers. While each of the six sings some text contributing to that character's figure, none of them merges with the "I" of these statements, or if they do, it happens only for some short moments. This is why one of the many bits of food for thought offered by the performance concerns an utterly new relationship between text, actor, role, and figure. The person that played the bourgeois stage of the 18th century was connected to the text through the role, in order to create the figure as a character. The Nature Theatre's play shifts these connections in several ways: Performers sing the character's text, entering and exiting its figure with their song, shaping it by singing and by a rudimentary embodiment, figuring, but never quite figuring *out*, the character by playing it together. What their play does not include, however, is any type of role.

---

24 Franz Kafka, *Der Verschollene* (Frankfurt/M.: Fischer 1994), p. 295.

25 Walter Benjamin, "Franz Kafka," *Gesammelte Schriften*, vol. II, 2. (Frankfurt/M.: Suhrkamp, 1980), pp. 409–438; pp. 422–423.

Roles in Negotiation
Ivana Müller: Working Titles

A third example, Ivana Müller's conceptual theatre work, might yield the richest insights for the question of role; for it demonstrates the allegorical character of all roleplay obscured within the traditions of the 19th century. In her much discussed and celebrated work *While we were holding it together,*[26] five performers rigid in five different poses spend an hour imagining what brought them there: Are they taking part in a family excursion, are they animals in a zoo, showpieces in a museum, or soldiers in some army? They keep reintroducing themselves in different ways, each with sentences beginning with "I imagine…," and in presenting their roles, they also showcase that very act of their presentation. We might consider this performance a roleplay in a permanent *statu nascendi*, an imagination at a threshold to the possible narratives that remain untold. Similar to baroque allegorical representations, the event sees the performers stand for all kinds of things, and thus ultimately also for nothing. But at the same time, they only collect the set of possible roles for which they stand by virtue of this one constellation of poses, which is held but for a certain time. This fact refers us to their mere *Dasein (Being there)* in a community and, more precisely, to Dasein's inalienable connection to a *standing for*. *While we were holding it together* ultimately showcases no more than mere bearers of presentation and role, the being that precedes any instance of roleplay. Although the classical view is that this vehicle should be made invisible, it will not be vanquished by any amount of work done on the role, because it is no role and yet is the very thing that makes roles possible. It constitutes their involvement in a scenic constellation, in short: their *representability*.[27] It is in the more or less involuntary faltering of a hand or the blink of an eye, in those moments in which the outlines of the exhibited tableau vivant begin to shiver, that we glance that bearer.

---

26 For detailed information on the contributors and dates, see www.ivanamuller.com, pub. unknown, cit. 17 August 2011).

27 Such *Darstellbarkeit* goes back to Benjamin's family of "-barkeit" concepts, such as *Mitteilbarkeit*, "communicability" (see Walter Benjamin, "Über Sprache überhaupt und über die Sprache des Menschen," *Gesammelte Schriften*, vol. II, 1 (Frankfurt/M.: Suhrkamp, 1980), pp. 140–157; pp. 145–146; Müller-Schöll, *Das Theater des 'konstruktiven Defaitismus,'* pp. 89–100 and pp. 152–156; Samuel Weber, *Benjamin's -abilities* (Cambridge: Harvard University Press, 2008).

In her next work, *Working Titles*,[28] Müller has four players with seven puppets present a silent series of tableaus in eight chapters. They are baroque emblems given meaning and a kind of life by titles, projected onto the backdrop. The puppet show is characterized by two peculiarities: For one, it is not only the inanimate puppets, but also their players that stay silent through most of the piece, likewise receiving their meaning from the projected titles. Furthermore, the simply fashioned puppets, reminiscent of shop windows, all lack heads. From the very start, this emphasizes that nothing that happens in the performance can be separated from a process of imagination that involves players and audience alike, while at the very centre an uncloseable gap remains: the absence of face. This becomes most prominent when we are told that one of the puppets is black. But we also notice the same effect when some scenes are connected to several interpretative possibilities, and when other stories are rewritten. The motti of the scenes are, as announced in the title of the performance, "working titles:" titles which are subject to change, and titles which are themselves at work. In connection with the players and puppets standing in front of them, they construct new figurations. In doing so, they demonstrate the principle of playing roles: That the role one plays in a certain context is the effect of a text which has literally been written onto one's body. However, the evening tells us that one's body never becomes mere blackboard or matrix. It alters the inscribed story in ways never quite to be predicted, it distracts from that story and reformulates it by transferring the letters, the significant, "dumb" (Lacan)[29] material of language, onto the stage as bodies. Everyone appearing in these performances has no choice but to continue in a constant negotiation of the role that they will eventually have played. What this work demonstrates about roleplay in general is how roles depend upon assignments, which may be discretionary, but never quite arbitrary, given their attachment to different specific ensembles.

---

28 My text goes back to the staging at the Live Art Festival at Kampnagel, Hamburg, 19 May 2010.

29 See Jacques Lacan, *Encore. Das Seminar Buch XX* (Weinheim/Berlin: Quadriga, 1986), pp. 19–30.

Plus d'un rôle
More Than One Role and No More Roles

Remember that the classical concept of the *role* in theatre can be considered (as I hinted at in the beginning) to be an equivalent of a *naked* or *mere life*, which is reduced to a perfect object of control at the centre of the modern political[30]; and remember that its successive determination, isolation, and construction may also be considered as a form of immunization against the disturbances threatening the shape of the role through the body, as well as through the perception of the theatre situation, of the auditorium, of the divided time and the language connecting the roles. The historical stations of the role's erosion can then also be read as stations of theatre's resistance against the ideology of the political as such: against the notion that there could be an in any way pre-stabilized order of the political and of politics, and that such an order could be founded on anything but an ultimately always aporetic, antinomical, and contradictory core.

In other words, the destruction of the role can be seen as a symptom of a paradigm shift that is played through in contemporary scenic practices, in which players can claim that they no longer play roles, but *are there* as performers to perform certain rules of play. And it is also played through in the many rediscoveries of the chorus, and in the transfer of practices from dance theatre, choreography, and object theatre to the ways of play that make straight theatre. In theatre, the paradigm shift connected to these symptoms is itself a reaction to changes no less radical than those that first initiated modernity and its theatre of roles in the 18th century. Then as today, the central question is how to think the *together*, the community or society[31]; and as in the 18th century, theatre is once more both a mirror and a part of the society that surrounds it.[32] As a part of its society, it undergoes the same disbanding of traditional community structures: The ensemble as a kind of theatrical conspiracy against its city, country, and universe appears as an obsolete organizational community, much like marriages, fami-

30 See Giorgio Agamben, "Lebens-Form," pp. 251–257. His formula of "bare life" goes back to Walter Benjamin's early work and specifically refers to his theories on the philosophy of history (for a critical review, see Burkhardt Lindner, "Der 11.9.2001 oder Kapitalismus als Religion," *Ereignis*, ed. Nikolaus Müller-Schöll (Bielefeld: Transcript, 2003), pp. 196–224; pp. 204–209.

31 On the question of community, see most of all Jean-Luc Nancy, *Die undarstellbare Gemeinschaft* (Stuttgart: Edition Patricia Schwarz, 1988).

32 See Jean-Luc Nancy, "Theatereignis," *Ereignis*, ed. Nikolaus Müller-Schöll (Bielefeld: Transcript, 2003), pp. 323–330.

lies, companies, unions, churches, and nations: an anachronism facing contrary economic conditions that have long begun to transform the actors, directors, and technicians of a production into small "Ich-AGs," Ego Corporations Ltd. which are only punctually allied corporations constituted by one person each. As a mirror to its society, theatre no longer suggests through its play that today's conditions allow for any unfragmented unity on whatever level, least of all the unity of a – and of only one – role. In its resistance against an ideology of role, this kind of play may help us better understand the economical and political, ultimately societal processes that are no longer intelligible to the categories of a philosophy of consciousness. If there is any commonality to the different variations of eroding roles, it might be what choreographers and directors such as Chétouane, Müller, Liska, and Kelly have understood: That we are all formed by the fact that – to allude to Derrida's famous verdict about language – we play *plus d'un rôle*: more than one role and no more roles.[33] In this condition lies the point from which every community were to begin – and in which the commonality of any community will irreconcilably end.

(*Translated by Stephan Packard*)

33 See Jacques Derrida, *Memoires* (Vienna: Passagen, 1988), p. 31.

Philipp Schulte

Alternative Genealogies – Critique and Style in Contemporary Performance Art: Xavier Le Roy and Mamoru Iriguchi

"What Is Critique?"

"What is critique?" – Michel Foucault dedicated a lecture to this question in 1978.[1] Twenty-two years later, Judith Butler did the same, and presented a detailed analysis and interpretation of Foucault's text.[2] "What is critique?" – to both theorists, this is the short form of a question that I would like to put this way: How can we develop a "reflected intractability [*l'indocilité réfléchie*]"[3] in order to desubjugate ourselves and to escape reigning discourses – at least potentially or temporarily? Butler draws our attention to a fascinating aspect of Foucault's lecture: She points out that it is highly performative. Foucault tries to do what he explains, he rehearses the act of desubjugation. When asked where the *decision-making not to be governed* comes from, he answers very artfully: "I was not referring to something that would be a fundamental anarchism, that would be like an originary freedom, absolutely and wholeheartedly resistant to any governmentalization. I did not say it, but this does not mean that I absolutely exclude it."[4]

On the one hand, Foucault's model does not utilize an originary freedom as its ontological driving force. On the other hand, it does not *not* do so. Judith Butler argues that we can only properly understand this and other parts of the lecture if we keep in mind *how* Foucault stages what he says. Butler believes that Foucault's words are "*artfully* rendered" stagings rather than assertions:

> The staging of the term is not its assertion, but we might say that the assertion is staged, rendered artfully, subjected to an ontological suspension, precisely so it might be spoken. And that it is this speech act, the one which for a time

---

1 Compare Michel Foucault, "What is Critique?," trans. Lysa Hochroth and Catherine Porter, *The Political*, ed. David Ingram (Oxford: Blackwell, 2002), pp. 191–211.

2 Compare Judith Butler, "What is Critique? An Essay on Foucault's Virtue," *The Political*, ed. David Ingram (Oxford: Blackwell, 2002), pp. 212–228.

3 Compare ibid., p. 220 and Foucault, "What is Critique," p. 194. For Foucault and Butler this intractability implicitly derives from a state of self-reflection. The starting point of their (and my) investigation is the origin of the power to self-reflect.

4 Foucault, "What is Critique?," p. 208.

relieves the phrase, "originary freedom," from the epistemic politics within which it lives which also performs a certain desubjugation of the subject within the politics of truth.[5]

Butler calls Foucault "oddly brave"[6] because he gestures towards the *originary freedom* knowing that it is impossible to ground his claim. His artful, tongue-in-cheek utterance shows that he just accepts this epistemological groundlessness. "Critique begins with the presumption of governmentalization and then with its failure to totalize the subject it seeks to know and to subjugate."[7]

According to Butler, Foucault's lecture is all about artful stagings and experimental tryouts of alternative practices within the framework that the reigning discourses provide. This staging activity is considered creative because it can transcend and even partially defy the normativity of those discourses. Butler points out that for Foucault, "there can be no ethics, and no politics, without recourse to this singular sense of poiesis."[8] The subject appears once again as both created and creating, simultaneously and without any implied temporal priority. Foucault calls the singular *poiesis,* which emerges from the tension between forming and being formed, self-stylization. This is a well-coined term – especially from a theatre studies perspective, as I hope to show –, because the notions of style and stylization can help us grasp the exemplary subjectivating processes of subjugation and desubjugation *performed on stage* with the methods of performance analysis. In this context, I suggest distinguishing performative acts on stage as acts that either *fit* or *do not fit* certain given conventional frames. "Style" is then a preliminary proposal for a term that denotes this distinction, to be complemented by the idea of a *critical genealogy* as found in the philosophy of Nietzsche, Foucault and Butler.

The term "style" fits with the discussed model of subjectivation quite well, given its trajectory. Since the middle of the 18th century it has paradoxically denoted two conflicting aesthetic concepts. On the one hand, style is considered to be one of various perceivable, isolatable, normative elements that characterize a work of art. Here, style is committed to a principle of continuity, which is linked to and adheres to an artistic tradition. Style is understood as conformation to an already

---

5 Butler, "What is Critique?," p. 224.

6 Ibid.

7 Ibid.

8 Ibid.

existing system of values, a submission to a given norm. Artistically, style primarily denotes workmanship, the style of production.[9]

According to Aleida Assmann, it was a revolution of style in 18th century England that introduced the second concept of style at least to the field of literature. The increasing alphabetization had given rise to new profane genres, which gradually superseded all kinds of religious literature and sparked literary criticism. Foucault argues similarly when he attributes the emergence of critique and the question of *how not to be governed thus* to the fact that the plurality of written interpretations weakened the pope's exclusive oral power over the Christian creed. The second dimension of the notion of style, dominant today, enters the stage: style as individual deviation. It is a hybrid of the old concept of imitation and the more recent concept of creation.[10] However, deviation is only possible within the norm, and desubjugation only at the cost of subjugation. Thus, style is the creative version of critique, looking out for individual alternatives to be governed thus.

Art, especially performative art, always oscillates between traditional stylistics and individual style. Contemporary theatre research therefore needs to pay attention to both: to the defining stylistics, theatrical formats, and genres of different epochs on the one hand, and to singular theatre phenomena on the other. Only in this way can the interdependence of gradually emerging stylistics and suddenly erupting individual styles be understood. The notion of stylistics alludes to a canon of rules to be observed, whereas style means to know the rules and to play with them. One of the artists who explore the artistic and subjective potential of style is the dancer and choreographer Xavier Le Roy; another is the London-based performance artist Mamoru Iriguchi, who works with certain performative elements in his performances orientated towards certain aspects of critical genealogies.

---

9 Compare Hans-Martin Gauger, *Über Sprache und Stil* (Munich: C. H. Beck, 1995).

10 Compare Aleida Assmann, "'Opting in' und 'opting out'. Konformität und Individualität in den poetologischen Debatten der englischen Aufklärung," *Stil. Geschichten und Funktionen eines kulturwissenschaftlichen Diskurselement*es, ed. Hans-Ulrich Gumbrecht and K. Ludwig Pfeiffer (Frankfurt/M.: Suhrkamp 1986), pp. 127–143.

Rehearsing the Revolt: Desubjugation as Stylization in Xavier Le Roy's *Product of Other Circumstances*

A black rehearsal stage. It is empty except for a projection screen upstage, a laptop on a small stool in the left downstage area, and, centerstage, the performer, a man in his late forties wearing a T-shirt and loose-fitting trousers. The man is Xavier Le Roy. He watches his audience taking their seats. From time to time he nods to someone. As soon as everybody is seated, he begins: "Let's start." He takes off his glasses and his shoes, then goes upstage and starts to dance. At first, Le Roy moves very slowly, his hands at a strange angle and his fingers cramped, as if he was trying to repel something. He mainly moves on the floor, spreading his arms wide, as if he was holding something invisible. Sometimes he appears to be mimicking an animal. His facial expression is striking, too: His eyes are closed most of the time, his mouth is distorted, then he opens it to make guttural, rattling, sucking sounds. The dance sequence is reminiscent of Butoh. After five minutes Le Roy stops abruptly, takes a sip of water and addresses the audience once again: "This dance is a part of a story I would like to tell you this evening. The story will be about two hours long." This is the beginning of the lecture performance Product of Other Circumstances *from 2009.*

The development process of *Product of Other Circumstances* started with choreographer Boris Charmatz reminding his friend Le Roy of his own boisterous statement that he could learn how to dance Butoh in two hours, and asking him to do so during the festival "Re-Butoh". In *Product of Other Circumstances* Le Roy humorously and charmingly presents the intermediate result of his work. He tells the audience how he approached Butoh with the help of his own experiences and memories – as well as with Google, Wikipedia, YouTube, and additional textbooks. He explains how he did research in his free time and he even presents two short choreographies – a reenactment and a sequence of his own, inspired by the results of his research. By allowing us to observe a two-hour learning process (even though the actual research took more time) he indirectly keeps his promise to become a Butoh dancer in two hours. In *Product of Other Circumstances*, we observe the antagonism of subjugation and desubjugation on at least three levels: in relation to its "prequel" *Product of Circumstances*, and the "style" of the genre of lecture performance; in relation to the "styles" of Butoh; and finally in relation to the conditions of art institutions.

Product of Circumstances and *Product of Other Circumstances*

On a first level, *Product of Other Circumstances* deals with its own "prequel," the widely noticed and academically much discussed performance *Product of Circumstances* from 1999. It is through this performance that the *lecture performance* became a very popular genre, especially among choreographers and dancers.[11] What is more, *Product of Circumstances* initiated a certain style that by now has become mainstream in the contemporary performance context. The lecture performance as such plays with the rules and norms of mainstream academic presentations. The narration of *Product of Circumstances,* too, deals with conforming to norms and not conforming to norms, when Le Roy, who has a Ph.D. in molecular biology, describes his desire to dance and his physical inability to fulfil the requirements of certain dance styles, when he talks about his academic career and his scepticism towards the scientific community. Le Roy goes even further. The title *Product of Other Circumstances* already reveals that there is a strong connection to the first lecture performance that made him famous ten years before.

Le Roy thus undermines the expectations raised by a genre that he helped establishing. Instead of talking about how *he* has become what he is today, he talks about how his current *performance* has become the way it is. With *Product of Other Circumstances* Le Roy shows that style, in the sense of desubjugation, can withstand only temporarily, namely in rehearsal-like situations; and by citing *Product of Circumstances* he somewhat proves that style, once fully developed, tends to turn into stylistics – a fixed set of styles. To experience style as a momentary, imaginary, artful freedom is only possible in a rehearsal, understood as a situation of free play where everything *can*, but nothing *has to* be fixed.

To Know How To Dance Butoh and To Rehearse Butoh

Product of Other Circumstances approaches the subject of following the rules and not following the rules on a second level when Le Roy mentions his claim to be able to learn Butoh in two hours, the starting point of the work. The claim resembles those of the self-improvement industry: "Learn Chinese in two months," "Lose ten pounds in two

---

11 The term "lecture performance" refers to a genre in performance art that uses means of academic presentations, in particular those of the classic academic lecture.

weeks," "Understand Hegel in two days." The fact that the "style" of Butoh is more than vague makes it clear just how presumptuous and unrealistic it is to try to *learn* it in two hours. Kazuo Ono coined the term Butoh more as a label for a certain attitude towards dance rather than as the name of a specific dance form. Hence, the internet provides only contradictory definitions of Butoh: "There is no set of style, and it may be purely conceptual, without any movement, with or without ordinance."[12] However, it is possible to *rehearse* this liminal dance practice. This is what Le Roy artfully shows on stage, maybe as artfully as Ono's term presents itself. Le Roys individual approach to Butoh's vague stylistics is the topic of *Product of Other Circumstances*.

At the beginning of the performance Le Roy clarifies what he did *not* do to learn Butoh. He did not travel to Japan, and he refused to participate in Butoh workshops because of a lack of time and a small production budget. In his performance, he looks into Butoh unsystematically and from a very personal point of view. He focuses on his memories and on the things that strike him in the Internet's information potpourri: "You'll never know with the Internet..." For instance, as he googles *Butoh in two hours*, an entry about himself appears which advertises the Re-Butoh festival. The anecdote reflects what the whole performance is about: We are unable to isolate the circumstances that shape us from ourselves. We are products of other circumstances but we also leave traces in the discourse that become circumstances for others and, again, for ourselves.

There is a discrepancy between the claim to be able to *learn Butoh in two hours* and the difficulty to identify a certain Butoh style. And there is a discrepancy between the claim to be able to *learn Butoh in two hours* and the actual factors of production such as time, money and the physical possibilities the choreographer has to work with. These discrepancies constitute the framework in which Le Roy is able to follow or violate rules: first, the rules of marketing in the performing arts, and second, the vague "rules" of Butoh stylistics that were developed by Ono, and adapted and distorted by other dancers. Le Roy recollects these stylistics in order to develop his own Butoh style, not to learn Butoh.

Three dance sequences structure the performance. They illustrate the processes at work when we try to appropriate something alien by

12 All unreferenced quotations in this section are Xavier Le Roy's and were drawn from the video recording of *Product of Other Circumstances* performed at the rehearsal stage of the Institute for Applied Theatre Studies on November 13, 2010 during the international double symposium "Dance, Politics and Co-Immunity" and "Thinking – Resisting – Reading the Political" at Justus-Liebig-University, Gießen.

the means of our own potential and desire. The above described early sequence prepares the audience for the two hours that follow. Some members of the audience may already sense that what they see is an approach to Butoh. However, the dance precedes any verbal contextualization. The opposite is the case with the second dance, which is performed one hour later. By then, the audience already knows what Le Roy's performance is about, and this second dance is contextualized. The contextualization has a specific function. It is supposed to make the audience reflect on what they see and not just identify and evaluate it. In retrospect, Le Roy explains the first dance and its technique, that he imagined concrete pictures, a man, an animal, a tree, which inspired him to associatively create his movements. In his second dance, however, Le Roy re-enacts a Butoh choreography that he saw years before, relying only on his memory and on a video documentation. Here Le Roy does not experiment with specific stylistics but strictly plays by someone else's rules, which is not what he actually planned to do: "You have to find your own Butoh and this was not really my Butoh, it was their Butoh... So I dropped the idea." At the end of his performance, Le Roy finally presents the provisional outcome of his research that he has been explaining to the audience for almost two hours. These detailed explanations are important because they let the audience realize the context in which Le Roy choreographed himself. We now know that we are supposed to see Le Roy's experimental setting and recognize Le Roy as a person who physically deals with the somehow given and at the same time vague stylistics of Butoh – sometimes conforming to them and sometimes transforming them creatively.

The Person and the Institution

On a third level Le Roy demonstrates the processes of opting in and opting out of the contexts of institutionalized contemporary dance and its theatre and festival system. This has always been an important aspect of Le Roy's work. What does it mean to describe a performance on stage during the performance itself? Instead of just presenting the outcome of his rehearsals, Le Roy incorporates the rehearsal process in his performance. As a choreographer he refuses to comply with the art market's demand for a coherent and entertaining product. Thus, Le Roy undermines the administrative conventions of the performance art market. He even talks about this process in *Product of Other Circumstances:*

End of August I got this receipt from the production office. And that was somehow interesting: the proposal was 1,300 Euro. My first reaction was: "Wow. Two hours work and maybe ten or twenty minutes dance – that's very well paid." But of course at this time already I failed because I worked much more than two hours.

And at the end of the performance he becomes even more explicit:

The French administration sends me a letter every year telling me how much I earn by the hour, or what I should earn. And last year it was 29 Euros an hour. So I did this very fast calculation: 1,300 Euros, 12% for the administration and production, and the rest… counting the taxes and all this: I should have worked 26 hours. But of course I worked more. And then I thought, what does that mean? It was interesting for me to realize that I have done this, in a way, more in my free time than in my time where I am supposed to work. So the conclusion of this would be that this work is more like amateur work, a work that is done as a hobby piece. […] What the whole story produces is also a space for me to be detached from certain pressures or expectations. I was not at all in that situation where I had to look for a co-production to find the money and to pay the people, or to find the time to get the people together, the premiere and all that. This proposal somehow freed me from those conditions.

Le Roy enjoys working under such *other* circumstances – free from pressure and expectations. The "freedom" of the rehearsal allows him to escape the necessity of meeting the requirements of the professional art system at least temporarily, and it is a prerequisite of artistic creativity. And even though the final performance is subject to the pragmatic constraints of a festival or theatre, this freedom of the rehearsal remains as an artful staging and a subtle reference to the necessity of such a freedom, which the artist has to negotiate with the commissioning and sponsoring institutions again and again.

In *Product of Other Circumstances,* Le Roy lets the audience witness an enabling de-ontologisation of that "freedom," of Butoh as a dance form, and also of Le Roy's potential to act subversively. The performance meticulously explains its own process of creation and verbally contextualizes its artistic means and matters, thus disclosing that all the artistic decisions are not fixed but could be dismissed at any time. Le Roy learns *something similar to* Butoh; he experiences *something similar to* creative freedom given the requirements of the professional art market; and he is able to refer to this freedom in demonstrating *something similar to* a subversive attitude towards this system. The freedom Le Roy experiences while rehearsing *Product of Other Circum-*

stances is closely related to the originary freedom to which Foucault refers by "not referring" to it. This kind of freedom is always relational, a *freedom from something*, and Le Roy's performance shows once again that it only exists in relation to circumstances. Le Roy is able to temporarily deviate from the norms of Butoh or the performance art market by pointing out these norms. His freedom emerges under restricting circumstances. His account of these restricting circumstances is simultaneously the account of his artful handling of these circumstances – "this dance is part of a story…". Le Roy cannot plausibly explain the origin of this subversive self-stylization. Neither could Foucault, who instead developed a Nietzschean genealogical construction. Philosopher Martin Saar describes Nietzsche's genealogical style as a "critically motivated art of drastic depiction."[13] Nietzsche's stylization in *On the Genealogy of Moral*[14] is, of course, different from Foucault's stylization in "What is Critique?," just as Foucault's stylization is different from Le Roy's in *Product of Other Circumstances*. All three positions stylize themselves and their (speech) acts by different means. However, there is one important similarity: they all narratively and performatively construct an unprovable "originary freedom" which is not an alternative to apparent certainties but a "critical questioning of the contemporary self-conception."[15]

Only subjects who refuse to think of themselves as completely subjugated can rehearse the act of de-subjugation. They accept that the "originary freedom" cannot be proved and engage in an artful self-stylization. This is the claim that Le Roy's performance suggests: philosophy and art allow types of utterances that create spaces that enable the development of style that opts in and opts out; spaces where subjects may look for "something similar" to the originary freedom and temporarily dismiss whatever it is that determines them.

---

13 Compare Martin Saar, *Genealogie als Kritik. Geschichte und Theorie des Subjekts nach Nietzsche und Foucault* (Frankfurt/M.: Campus, 2007), p. 139. Translation A. S.

14 Compare Friedrich Nietzsche, *Zur Genealogie der Moral. Eine Streitschrift* (Stuttgart: Reclam, 1988).

15 Saar, *Genealogie als Kritik*. p. 141. Translation A.S.

Opting out: Mamoru Iriguchi's Experiments with Critical Genealogy[16]

London-based Japanese performance artist Mamoru Iriguchi works in such a space of de-subjugation. His project *Into the Skirt* allows me to expand my argument. The telling of alternative stories can be understood as an artistic strategy to reflect and opt out. Iriguchi's performance begins like this:

Mamoru Iriguchi[17] *stands in the middle of a small black box stage and faces the audience. He wears wide pyjamas (strangely shaped at the hips) with a lot of pink fighter jets on them. "It's me, seven years old," he says. "I wish I'd be wearing something prettier than this. Fighter planes were not my cup of tea."*[18] *He talks about his neighbourhood friend Rita, whom he envied for her pink flowered pyjamas. However, since seven-year-old Mamoru considered himself a "pretty scientifically-minded person" who looked at the world through logic, this was no big deal to him. To prove his* junior ego's *analytical skills, Iriguchi brought a huge scrapbook containing all kinds of alleged observations. He picks up the book from the floor and opens it. Iriguchi uses the actual book's blank pages as a screen for a video projection in order to display the pictures in Mamoru's scrapbook.*

"Chapter One is on science. I was particularly interested in biology." We see the silhouette of a hen and a rooster right behind her. This is a depiction of "Melting," a procedure during which a male "hands over" a small amount of sperm to the female. However, young Mamoru failed to quite understand how that worked. After a lot of research he came to the "logical conclusion" that the hen must have an orifice on the nape of her neck.

Mamoru turns a page: "Chapter Two is on fairy tales." Sleeping Beauty used to be his favourite tale. He especially liked the idea of being kissed awake by "Prince Charming." The projection shows the princess in the

---

16 Parts of this paragraph are a translation based on an earlier article: Philipp Schulte, "Von der Wichtigkeit, nicht ernst zu sein. Die alternativen Genealogien in den Performances Mamuro Iriguchis," *Subjekt: Theater. Beiträge zur analytischen Theatralität. Festschrift für Helga Finter zum 65. Geburtstag*, ed. Gerald Siegmund and Petra Bolte-Picker (Frankfurt/M.: Peter Lang, 2011), pp. 259–271.

17 In the following I will refer to the *performance artist* Mamoru Iriguchi as "Iriguchi" and to his *performed* young alter ego as "Mamoru."

18 All unreferenced quotations in this section are Mamoru Iriguchi's and were drawn from the video recording of *Into the Skirt* performed during the Plateaux Festival at Künstlerhaus Mousonturm in Frankfurt/Main on May 1, 2010.

same position as the hen with prince Charming behind her. The book's appendix contains a picture of Judy Garland, whom Mamoru admires.

It is obvious how closely the three chapters of his book about biology, fairy tales and Judy Garland are connected when Mamoru, who has changed out of his pyjamas into a hoop skirt, ostentatiously struggles to lay four cardboard eggs while singing *Somewhere Over the Rainbow*. *Into the Skirt* deals with the tension between Mamoru's infantile "scientific" interest in the inevitably heterosexual act of procreation, and his imaginary identification with the fairy tale princess and Judy Garland.[19] Mamoru's idiosyncratic story about the biological creation is set in contrast to what Iriguchi, the performer, has made of himself. All the funny, oneiric, and metaphoric pictures, actions, and stories which Iriguchi presents in *Into the Skirt* oscillate between normed expectations and subjective self-stylization. Iriguchi's silly fictions turn out to be a tongue-in-cheek critique of what is considered normal in the process of individuation.

At the beginning of the second part of the performance, Mamoru shows his book once again. Seven years have passed since his first entries. He compiled the additional material at the age of fourteen. Mamoru still wears his pink pyjamas and he still adheres to the same structure: the two chapters and an appendix. However, even though his drawings remain naïve, he has learned many of the disillusioning biological facts about reproduction. He now knows about the penis and the vagina and the injection of sperm (although his infographics are still a little bit inaccurate). Mamoru knows more about fairy tales, too: "Sometimes original stories are much more grotesque." Instead of romantically kissing her awake, the prince ordinarily rapes her. "He just has sex. That's right! After the sex she is still sleeping, and Prince Charming runs away. How irresponsible is that?!" Mamoru still keeps Judy Garland's photograph in the appendix, but it is almost covered by new, conventional hetero-pornographic pictures. These pictures are chaotically arranged and run counter to the diagrammatic order of the previous chapters.

---

19 Concerning Judy Garland's role as a gay icon compare: Charles Kaiser, *The Gay Metropolis 1940 – 1996* (New York: Houghton Mifflin, 1997); John Loughery, *The Other Side of Silence: Men's Lives and Gay Identities. A Twentieth Century History* (New York: Henry Holt and Company, 1998); Neil Miller, *Out of the Past: Gay and Lesbian History from 1869 to the Present* (London: Vintage UK, 1995); The National Museum & Archive of Lesbian and Gay History, ed., *The Gay Almanac* (New York: Berkeley Books, 1996).

There seems to be a structural similarity between Iriguchi's artistic strategy, his obviously fictitious stories of the origin of the self, and the academic form of the *critical genealogy*. The latter is extensively used by philosophers such as Nietzsche, Foucault, and, to a lesser extent, Judith Butler. Artist as well as philosophers critically ask "where" certain phenomena come from in order to show that seemingly natural circumstances and assumptions are historical products, and that alternatives are possible. Iriguchi's fictitious tales of reproduction hint in this direction. Saar believes that the familiar metaphor of birth is a common sign of the critical genealogies' typical "obsession with the true and the false origins, ancestry, roots, and their power."[20] Nietzsche's *The Birth of Tragedy from the Spirit of Music* is a well known example for the attempt to criticize a *status quo* by imagining its origin. Saar asserts that "[...] since Nietzsche, the notion of genealogy has promised to merge the critique of the present with the knowledge of the past by attributing a critical significance to historicity and the specific origin of its subject matters."[21]

This "knowledge of the past," however, is nothing that one can "reveal" or "discover" with the traditional methods of historical analysis. In a strict sense, it is no *knowledge* at all but the assumption of an often fictitious event that the author needs to make his point. Saar makes this clear: "True, possible, and fictitious stories can all function as an objection against current values and practices,"[22] and flippancies and ways of getting off track in particular render this kind of resistance possible. Genealogical texts employ certain rhetorical techniques in their narration and their argument which make them oscillate between academic and aesthetic writing. Saar describes the most important features of this style, such as interest in stories of origin, direct addresses to the reader, a tendency to dramatize and hyperbolize the fictionalization of common knowledge and the aspect of the seemingly possible. Many of these structural features occur in Iriguchi's work as well. Even though Iriguchi's obsession with procreation and birth is singular, the following aspects of his work are typical for many recent performance art projects.[23]

---

20 Saar, *Genealogie als Kritik*, p. 23. Translation A. S.

21 Ibid., p. 9. Translation A. S.

22 Ibid.

23 Besides Xavier Le Roy's works there are for example lecture performances by Lebanese media artist Walid Raad and some works by Belgian choreographer/director

On top of Iriguchi's interest in birth, the performance *Into the Skirt* shares at least two more characteristic traits with critical-genealogical texts. The first one is the direct address to the audience, which is actually quite common in contemporary performance art. Nietzsche used the direct address as well as hyperboles and polemics to provide his readers with an entertaining read and hence to reach a broader audience than an academic essay would. By being addressed directly, the reader, as the agent of the concept of self in question, is supposed to develop self-doubts and to contemplate alternative concepts of self. Iriguchi does exactly the same when he directly addresses his audience. The "self" that is to be examined turns out to be at once the subject matter as well as the addressee of the critique. The reader and the audience are supposed to recognise themselves in this defamiliarized form because it is for their own sake that the story of subjectification is told.[24] Iriguchi tells a (possible, fictitious) story about *his own* development (what he thought at age seven and age fourteen). The spectators, however, who are directly addressed, are implicitly invited to think about *their own* history, the steps of *their own* development that made them what they are.

A second characteristic of critical genealogies is the already mentioned tendency to dramatise and hyperbolize. Saar even calls Nietzsche's technique "the art of exaggeration,"[25] and it is due to this *hyperbolic pretense* that Nietzsche's highly constructed and extremely simplified depictions of the origin have "a 'reality effect', seemingly describing or even explaining a real event or process."[26] However, this is not only a rhetoric trick to gain attention, but an illustration of how discursive powers create subjectivity. Philosopher David Owen even calls this technique "a form of affective performance which seeks to communicate particular affective dispositions to the reader" and not to argue in favour of a certain position.[27]

In *Into the Skirt*, Iriguchi uses pictures and symbols in a similarly simplifying, almost overly explicit way:

The audience is given to understand that Mamoru masturbates. The fruit of this act is a white foam pony called Snowwhite (which has

---

Michael Laub, to name just three. Compare also Philipp Schulte, *Identität als Experiment. Ich-Performanzen auf der Gegenwartsbühne* (Frankfurt/M.: Peter Lang, 2011).

24 Compare Saar, *Genealogie als Kritik*, p. 140.

25 Ibid.

26 Ibid., pp. 140–141.

27 David Owen, *Nietzsche, Politics and Modernity: A Critique of Liberal Reason* (London: Sage, 1995), p. 47.

been hidden under Mamoru's pyjamas). On this pony Mamoru rides through a projected sky and fights a wicked witch with a cardboard-penis sword. The fighter planes from his pyjamas support Mamoru in the fight. The witch's motherly curses, such as "It's 7 am!" or "You wetted the bed again!," are projected as well and accompanied by the sounds of Mamoru's alarm clock. Mamoru shatters the curses with his unsubtle sword.[28]

This is how Iriguchi stages the contradictions between an as yet undirected libido and the organising norms of everyday life. His hoop skirt, the eggs, and his imitation of Judy Garland are colourful and humorous illustrations of the battle against heteronormativity.

The already mentioned scrapbook scenes contrast Mamoru's private imaginary world and the symbolic normative order. If we compare the seven-year-old's book to the fourteen-year-old's, we see how drastically the experiences of the older Mamoru have overwritten the almost romantic world view of the younger Mamoru. The facts of procreation, the violent truth behind the fairy tale, and heterosexual pornography discredit Mamoru's idea of a procreational bite and his soft spot for Prince Charming and the young Judy Garland as naive and unnecessary. Iriguchi fictionalizes this general conflict through a funny story about a particular subjective development, and at the same time, he hints at the possible but discursively rejected alternatives, as on the stage it is *not* unthinkable for a man to identify with Judy Garland instead of a male porn star. According to Saar, Nietzsche's genealogical fictions point out that "social forms always demand some kind of adaptation, and that taxing the costs of this adaptation is the first step towards a re-evaluation of these forms."[29] Iriguchi breaks down the costs of growing up by showing us the incompatibility of some childhood desires with the norms of the grown up society.

Saar mentions yet another characteristic aspect of genealogy: being seemingly possible. Genealogies are always polemic counter-truths, "undocumented, hypothetic accounts that are supposed to change the self by telling a scandalising history of the self."[30] Foucault, too, believes that it is possible "to make fictions work within truth, to induce truth-effects within a fictional discourse, and in some way make the discourse of truth arouse, 'fabricate' something which does

---

28 There is an obvious affinity between Iriguchi's work and Freudian psychoanalytic theory, which itself shows characteristics of *critical genealogy*, such as questioning the mechanisms of subjectification and pointing out possible alternatives of living.
29 Saar, *Genealogie als Kritik*, p. 64. Translation A. S.
30 Ibid., p. 65. Translation A. S.

not as yet exist, thus 'fiction' [*fictionne*] something."[31] Even though Mamoru Iriguchi's scrapbook and his stories about his *junior ego's* preoccupation with Judy Garland might not be authentic, they never seem to be impossible fictions. Iriguchi's performance "fictions" in a Foucauldian sense. The mere existence of Mamoru's ideas, which obviously deviate from the dominant discourse, questions this very discourse at least for a moment.

However, while the philosophical genealogies mentioned above focus on certain cultural developments and concepts and try to point out alternatives to the dominant perspectives on these phenomena, Iriguchi only tells his own story. He seems to have no interest in revolution or ethical re-evaluations. But Iriguchi's approach is not naïve. His performance challenges heteronormative standards of masculinity by drafting a homosexual genealogy and enforcing it on stage. Clearly he stands in the tradition of those performance artists who since the 1960s have used the stage to try out deviant forms of existence in front of an audience. Not being subject to economic and political interests completely, the field of performance art allows a testing of identities that would be scandalised elsewhere. Thus Iriguchi's own private genealogy renders visible the power system that surrounds and shapes him and all of us.

To Irritate What Is Taken for Granted

Both genealogical texts and Iriguchi's artistic work aim to criticize the way we are formed by a discursive system or a symbolic order. This is also true for an earlier lecture performance by Mamoru Iriguchi, *Pregnant?!*. Once again, Iriguchi combines a humorous fictionalisation

31 Michel Foucault, "Interview with Lucette Finas," trans. Paul Foss and Meaghan Morris, *Michel Foucault: Power, Truth, Strategy*, ed. Meaghan Morris and Paul Patton (Sydney: Feral, 1979), pp. 298–309, p. 74. See also Foucaults formulation in his lecture "Von der Souveränität zur Disziplin": "Die Reaktivierung lokaler, 'unmündiger' (wie Deleuze vielleicht sagen würde) Wissensarten gegen die wissenschaftliche Hierarchisierung der Erkenntnisse und ihrer eigentlichen Machteffekte ist das Projekt dieser ungeordneten und zerrissenen Genealogien. Kurz gesagt: Man könnte vielleicht sagen, dass die Archäologie die für die Analyse lokaler Diskursivitäten geeignete Methode und die Genealogie die Taktik wäre, die ausgehend von den so beschriebenen lokalen Diskursivitäten die sich davon ablösenden 'ent-unterworfenen' Wissensarten funktionieren lässt." (Michel Foucault, "Von der Souveränität zur Disziplin," lecture from January 7, 1976, *Kritik des Regierens. Schriften zur Politik*, selected and with an afterword by Ulrich Bröckling (Berlin: Suhrkamp 2010), pp. 9–39, p. 17.

with a genealogical critique when he uses a very detailed PowerPoint presentation to illustrate his (possible) development in his mother's womb. At the same time he overlays this narrative with a fictional story of his own pregnancy and his giving birth to seven small rabbits. Iriguchi confronts his male body with aspects of motherhood (partly through projections onto his body) and tells a story of origin that differs from the conventional form. He raises doubts about the present form of power by examining which of his personal desires cannot be brought in line with the symbolic order with which he has to comply. Foucault says that "there is no first or final point of resistance to political power other than in the relationship one has to oneself."[32] Iriguchi experiments with precisely this relationship of the self to itself as a relationship between accepting what you are and rejecting the necessity to be that way. By such means he questions the allegedly predetermined development of "the subject" in a very similar way to Le Roy's performing acts of subjugation and desubjugation on stage.

One of the prominent characteristics of Iriguchi's genealogical technique is, as stated, the permanent direct address to the audience. In his case it also needs to be viewed as an appeal. The relationship of the performance artist on stage to himself – similar again to Le Roy's not in its form but in its structure – makes the audience wonder about their own relationship to themselves, and at least temporarily allows them to think: *not like this*.

(Translated by Anna Schewelew)

32 Michel Foucault, *The Hermeneutics of the Subject: Lectures at the Collège de France 1981–1982* (New York: Palgrave Macmillan, 2005), pp. 251–252.

Stephan Packard

Why Are Story Arcs Dark and Gritty? On the Metaphysics of Seriality in *Dexter* and Kammerer

During the last two decades, popular serial storytelling, especially in US TV productions, has shown two interweaving tendencies, each receiving broad and, in its own way, thorough critical attention. On the one hand, plotting has moved away from standalone episodes presenting similar contents for each installment, and towards a greater emphasis on *story arcs*, plots that continue through many or even all episodes of a series, rendering each installment functionally dissimilar, unique, and indispensable viewing. On the other hand, there has been a second and critically celebrated move towards plots and characters that showcase problematic morals, address ethical quandaries, and depict a world in which morally righteous behaviour is unsuccessful, impossible, and indeed mostly unrecognizable.

In the joint discourse of studio PR, mainstream journalist criticism, and the increasingly solidified documentation and discussion of viewer experiences on internet fora, certain shows or specific runs of such a show's episodes will be praised by pointing out in the genre vocabulary that they "continue the mythology," i.e. emphasize the story arc, and that they are "dark and gritty," i.e. present unsolved moral dilemmas. In order to understand these phenomena more clearly, I want to ask why these two changes seem to be so closely related, and what further identification happens in the course of their convergence: Why is it story arcs specifically that are dark and gritty? And why is this combination so often understood as adding value, as double criteria for quality?

For both these changes are typically described within the shows and their paratexts with appeals to an added aesthetic value. This usually points to the perceived virtues both of complex storytelling and of mature ethical debate. It is also accompanied by an employment of artistic choices elevating the differentiation and complexity of imagery, montage, and dialogue, often introducing devices from shorter genres established in video formats, such as music clips, advertising, and contemporary short film. So in their technique, their criticism, and their quotations, TV serials have entered a phase of aesthetic emphasis, and the two central changes of serial continuity and moral aporia are indeed increasingly referred to as an establishment of *art* out of what has previously been called *genre* television.

1. Genre TV and Representation

If the emphatic aesthetics of long modernity have moved the established singularity of art beyond those instructive definitions of distinctive arts' plurality which structured the canons and paragones of classical tradition, the popularity of significantly named "genre productions" has retained, reframed, and revived a system of separate rule-based games. Each game is not devoted to a *mimesis* of reality's assumed integrity, but each is liberated from such adherence by the regulations of its very own *mimeses*, with their own "expression codifiée d'une pensée ou d'un sentiment."[1] To shift from one popular genre to another is to switch codes, to wander from one mood of representation to another, while the object of representation has long diffused. It is in the diffusion that the divisioned aesthetics of popular genres sometimes renew an appeal to that supposedly modern beyond while dwelling on this side of its frontier. Theirs is a subliminal appeal that confuses the exalted aesthetics of suspended representation with the ethical potential of shared imagery, and identifies both by placing them in the neglected space of the represented real. In the persistent representative regime of arts as genres offered by current popular TV, the break with representation that redefines aesthetics since the 18th century adopts a specific shape, even as it re-enters the precedent reign of learnable and teachable artistic operations.

Popular TV serials, especially but by no means only since the advent of internet fandom, famously exist in a space of constant paratextual commentary[2]: Interpretations that fix and re-settle connections between

---

1 Jacques Rancière, "Le Destin des Images," *Le Destin des Images* (Paris: La Fabrique Éditions, 2003), pp. 7–39, p. 21.

2 This is now perhaps one of the best researched, most densely described, and most often repeated discoveries of the presently obvious in media studies. Among many others, see Steven Johnson, *Everything Bad is Good for You* (New York: Riverhead, 2005); Henry Jenkins, *Fans, Bloggers, and Gamers: Exploring Participatory Culture* (New York: UP, 2006); Karen Hellekson and Kristina Busse, *Fan Fiction and Fan Communities in the Age of the Internet* (Jefferson, NC: McFarland, 2006). For the development of seriality in other media since the eighteenth century, see Robert Darnton, "Readers Respond to Rousseau: The Fabrication of Romantic Sensibility," *The Great Cat Massacre And Other Episodes in French Cultural History* (New York: Basic, 2009): pp. 215–256; Linda K. Hughes and Michael Lund, "Linear Stories and Circular Visions. The Decline of the Victorian Serial," *Chaos and Order. Complex Dynamics in Literature and Science*, ed. N. Katherine Hayles (Chicago: University of Chicago Press, 1991): pp. 167–194; Linda K. Hughes, *The Victorian Serial* (Charlottesville: University Press of Virginia, 1991); Jennifer Hayward, *Consuming Pleasures. Active Audiences and Serial Fictions from Dickens to Soap Opera* (Lexington: University Press of Kentucky, 1997). Roger Hagedorn has presented a compelling

episodes and cross-references between elements, but rarely identify an ulterior meaning or referent. Theirs is a strikingly Alexandrian practice, which culminates in a care for the text that consequently disregards its reference in favour of its structure, though not in the mode of formalism, but as artistic appreciation. The aim of such interpretation is rarely to render transparent the thought or sentiment expressed, but to deal in the lucidity of the code governing the expressions. Perhaps the most striking illustration is the now accepted fusion of the concepts of *trope* and *topoi*. The famously enormous and growing popular wiki database on *TV Tropes*[3] collects the units of genre codes: the "Spin Attack" that migrates a video game move into action scenes' choreography on TV, the "Defeat by Modesty" as a recurring gambit in gender relations, the "Unfazed Everyman" exemplified by Douglas Adams' Arthur Dent longing for his usual cup of tea in an alien spaceship: they each have entries. Each entry is an exercise in criticism with all the trappings of classical rather than modern aesthetic appreciation: Is the form useful for the genre? When is it used well, and which techniques make it effective? The site defines the eponymous tropes as "devices and conventions that a writer can reasonably rely on as being present in the audience members' minds and expectations."[4] This is clearly accurate, but it is not at all what classical rhetorics would have considered tropes: figurative expressions that introduce doubled references, proper and improper, by means of metaphor, metonymy, symbolisms, and so forth. Rather, it is much closer to a definition of topoi, or motifs. But the topoi of popular genre television are understood and celebrated as tropes, improper expressions that position thoughts and sentiments by the very act of encoding them, distinct from any proper reality.

TV Tropes' entry on "Police Brutality" briefly mentions that though this motif deals with "Truth in Television to some extent, this is often exaggerated in fiction," and having thus separated the artistic operation from its representational object, goes on to describe only the topos: "Some types of policemen [...] are thugs who take a cruel pleasure in beating and tormenting people they don't like, for no reason at all. And often this is a category that contains pretty much everyone." There is an obvious critical potential and some room for resistance here (a note goes on to mention that illegal immigration "even in Britain does not carry the death penalty, whatever the Daily Mail thinks"). However,

---

argument for the emergence of serial structures from the economics of media innovations: "Technology and Economic Exploitation: The Serial as a Form of Narrative Presentation," *Wide Angle* 10.4 (1988): pp. 4–12.

3 *TV Tropes* (tvtropes.org, est. 2004, cit. August 2012).

4 Ibid., "Home Page."

the explicit criticism is directed towards an ironically expressed narratological and dramaturgic displeasure over the accepted topos' avoidance of deeper characterisation – as antagonists act "for no reason at all," by means of the code for representing police.[5]

The entries on "Justified Tropes" and "Truth in Television" deal more directly with the Aristotelian principle of verisimilitude: As Aristotle ascribes to tragedy the deeper truth of depicting general likeliness instead of historical fact, he considers its relation to confirmed reality:

> [...] the possible is also believable; while we will not necessarily believe in the possibility of what never happened, in the case of actual events it is clear that they are possible; it would not have happened, if it were impossible.[6]

TV Tropes' discourse almost perfectly repeats but reverts this central instruction for representational drama:

> Once in a while, a TV show does something that actually happens in Real Life. Don't worry, it never lasts, and they soon slip back into their old habits. [...] Technically, these tropes do not need to be Justified Tropes, since they are truth.[7]

Real Life is a quotable point of reference rather than the real referent of art; habits outweigh, or rather, they incorporate such Real Life in their lists of accepted operations, and deal more comfortably with the techniques of justification for their motifs than the technicality of truth. This is an explicit principle of this method of TV criticism ruling out disagreement from the stage of wiki entries, and consigning it to the orchestra of fora, following the habitual necessities of the wiki media culture:

> Note that a work portraying real life is still a work – such examples are about how the work portrays real life, not about real life itself. [...] Real Life does not have an author in the same way as a film or other work does, and we see real life from the inside rather than from the outside. Thus, tropes that are objective in works are often highly subjective in Real Life. And since trope pages are not discussion forums, a debate about who is right and

5 Ibid., "Police Brutality."

6 Aristotle, *Ars Poetica*, ed. R. Kassel (Oxford: Clarendon Press, 1966): 1451b, translation S.P.

7 *TV Tropes*, "Truth in Television."

who is wrong is a distracting (and maybe even destructive) case of natter or Edit War.[8]

The article on "Darker and Edgier," *TV Tropes*' version of the "dark and gritty" theme, concludes with the same refrain: "No Real Life Examples, Please! If you want to debate about how dark the world is/was, Take It to the Forums."[9] Finally, the system is hermetically sealed in the entry on the "Real World Episode," which concerns, of course, not any real world, but narratives that meander between separate staged realities embedded in each other by metadiegesis.

In detailing the "representative regime of the arts," Jacques Rancière pointed out Diderot's criticism of Creux' portrayal of Septimus Severus, the first Roman emperor of African descent, as too dark-skinned: Regulation by representation, not as adherence to similarity with the real world, but to the rules that order the practices and operations of the art according to the habitual categories of representation.[10] Genre TV's fiction seems at first to repeat that distinction, as with the black Presidents that denoted near-future SF scenarios before 2008, which *TV Tropes* considers ended rather than validated by Barack Obama.[11] But instead of ordering the perception of reality by its categories, the representational scheme in the genre TV discourse is built on an ironic detachment of real life from the Real Life, which usually protects both from questioning. It has, in this sense, adapted the removal of the represented object that marks the aesthetic regime of art, but not as a turn from representation. But in the course of its own turn, it re-establishes, as we will see, *ex fortiori* the aesthetics of exaltation, by accepting the rare reference to the real in the mode of the sublime, the symbolization of an Other and of emphatic truth in the shape of a symbolic suspension of its codes. In a popular version of the movement that Rancière has criticized – and I will return to this at greater length – under the name of the "ethical turn," it also returns to the ethical regime of the image, but thus identifies it with the real as glanced in aesthetic exaltation and as identified with that which is, rather than what could or ought to be. Even beyond the irony of separating the trope of Police Brutality from the police brutality supported by the *Daily Mail*, this signals acceptance of its reality as governed and covered by the political habitus of a media portrayal that is morally rejected, but to which

8 Ibid., "No Real Life Examples, Please!"

9 Ibid., "Darker and Edgier."

10 See Jacques Rancière, "La peinture dans le texte," *Le destin des images*, pp. 79–102, pp. 85–6.

11 *TV Tropes*, "President Minority" in "Our Presidents Are Different."

the irony critically resigns. A critique of such practice must then focus on that kind of ideology in which the exposure of Žižek's "totalitarian laughter"[12] does not suffice, for accepting the removal of reality effected by such irony still places the real in the ethically suspended space of sudden aesthetic revelation, of a perceptually foreign event that is granted the power of disrupting the habitual irony, and grants the subject an opportunity for an unironic loyalty, a fealty to that which was previously rejected as reality, resurfacing as Truth.

Instead, the following will continue to frame current changes in TV serial formats in terms that consciously reach towards, but do *not* fully identify with, concepts taken from Rancière's considerations of ethics, aesthetics, and politics. I will examine in greater detail how the celebration of ethical aporia touches upon the famed "ethical turn" in the precise form in which Rancière reveals and criticizes its abandonment of right in favour of fact, supplementing a realm of ultimate identification of ethics, politics, and art, in lieu of a perceivable distinction between what is and what should be. In this view, the dismissal of the field of possibilities dependent on the paradigmatic sameness of stand-alone episodes, and the embrace of the continuing series of things that senselessly happen each after the other, prepare a space for the ethical problems resulting from dismissing ethics' evaluating difference. And I will continue to analyse what follows from the assumption that the space prepared for talk of the newly claimed aesthetic quality opposes the technical expertise of genre requirements much as an "aesthetic regime" of singular art opposes the catalogue of arts provided by a "representative regime" proscribing the techniques of each form.

For both aspects, I will refer to the series about the serial murderer "Dexter," which epitomizes the "darker and grittier" style as well as the appropriation of a rhetorics of the sublime in order to point towards the evasive real. I will then seek out parallels between this convergence of seriality from series and serial, and the lawfulness of the series as a modern metaphysical concept exemplified several decades earlier, in Paul Kammerer's *Gesetz der Serie*, and continuing in some aspects of the popular discourse on science today. For this, I propose a concept of *operative monism* to describe the recurrent aesthetic and paradoxical restriction of representation within a representative regime.

And yet by turning to such universalisations, the unease of metaphysics also returns to the process of reading. For such an appropriation of Rancière's concepts is clearly problematic, and its implied problems eventually repeat main topics of the ideology of serial violence in

---

12 Slavoj Žižek, *The Sublime Object of Ideology* (London: Verso, 1989), p. 23.

Dexter, and the operative monism in Kammerer. So the argument leads to a reflection on the extent to which legitimate consequences can be drawn from the suggested ways of thinking politics for our reading of further media phenomena and their resistant valence; and specifically, what might sensibly happen to those concepts when they encounter the popular productions of mainstream media industry.

2. The Trauma Lost in the Serial

The TV show *Dexter* began in 2006 and is still running. It focuses on the title character, a compulsive serial killer who poses as a forensic blood splatter analyst for the Miami Police Department and tries, but often fails, to channel his urge to murder into a selective killing of other murderers who escape formal justice. Immediately, the seeming justification for the character is exposed as a feint: This is not the story of a murderer to benefit mankind, but always already an ironic turn on the possibility of telling that story. The series originally began as a TV adaptation of Jeff Lindsay's 2004 novel *Darkly Dreaming Dexter*, but although Lindsay has also gone on to turn the novel into a series, the TV production went in quite a different direction after its first season.[13]

In producers Daniel Cerone's, Clyde Philipps', and Melissa Rosenberg's screen version, originally developed by *Sopranos* co-producer James Manos Jr., the format that at first mirrored one novel per season, and thus at least partially closed one story with each season finale, eventually introduced forebodings and finally true cliffhangers in their season endings, opening the whole of the series up for the increasingly uninterrupted and unending stream of dominant story arcs. Along with this structural change, they introduced an increasing interest in secondary characters, including a cast of Dexter's love life, sister, and colleagues in story-lines that feed partially off the detective genre, but are in other parts more at home in soap opera. Even from the very start, their stories would not conclude with the end of a season. And what is perhaps most important, the TV producers did not follow the novels' eventual revelation of Dexter's compulsion to murder as a possession by a supernatural and millennia-old evil entity, an offspring of the Biblical Moloch. So while the novels reify Dexter's evil in the shape of a transcendent power and different person opposing Dexter's better

---

13 Jeff Lindsay, *Darkly Dreaming Dexter* (New York: Doubleday, 2004); *Darkly Devoted Dexter* (2005); *Dexter in the Dark* (2007); *Dexter by Design* (2009); *Dexter is Delicious* (2010); *Double Dexter* (2011). Daniel Cerone et al. (prod.), *Dexter* (John Goldwyn Productions/Showtime Networks, 2006–2012 and ongoing).

qualities, the TV series does not allow for such a clean if ludicrous separation of good and evil, nor for the inclusion of such a metaphysical Other. Instead, Dexter's killings remain the result of a traumatic slaughter experienced as a young child, and resurface in an automatism deeply connected with each and every facet of Dexter's person – who also functions as a main narrator through voice-overs.

But the beyond quickly resurfaces through the emphasized aesthetics of violence and storytelling, which coincide in *Dexter*. For this concept of trauma, continuously alluded to but never connected with concepts of therapy, re-appropriation, or even symptomatic recoding, is no longer a tool of psychoanalytic enlightenment, creating *ego* where *id* was, but a stoppage to all analysis. When Dexter does submit to psychotherapy, its success – staged as the most consciously farcical parody of sudden healing revelations so common in genre television, and so foreign to actual analysis and therapy – is measured by the speed with which the cured Dexter runs from the middle of his session to his girlfriend and then his next victim, finally freed of a doubled impotence that retarded the storyline.[14] This view of trauma stubbornly insists on the *id*'s perpetuity, and in fact, exclusive reality: Even when clouded, any revelation leads back to the traumatic core, and then remains there indefinitely, a testament rather than a resignification of the real.

It is especially in contrast to Dexter's forensic work that his own automatic killing is put into perspective: The methods, actions, and even pathologies of other killers are open to scientific analysis and sometimes even to deliberate change. But Dexter's murders go on as unstoppable as they are unpredictable. His kind of "killer is an artist,"[15] a genius with no further explicit knowledge of his craft, who embodies the disjunction of unconceivable beauty and realized artistic concepts that marks the aesthetic regime of singular art.[16] Dexter's dark ethics and artistry are hard-wired into that part of the material universe that is not even accessible to scientific investigation, but is always to be accepted as a pure matter of fact, and to be dealt with only by an aesthetics of the factual. In a purely operative sense of both words, this aesthetics of fact favours a certain kind of "monism" against all "dualism;" as we will see, monism and dualism here connect not to the most common sense of the philosophical dichotomy, but to a tradition of 20th century notions of the series likewise devoted to aesthetic factuality.

---

14 "Shrink Wrap," *Dexter* 1.08 (Nov 19, 2006).

15 "Dexter," *Dexter* 1.01 (Oct 1, 2006), 27:20.

16 See Jacques Rancière, *Ist Kunst widerständig?*, trans. Frank Ruda and Jan Völker (Berlin: Merve, 2008), esp. pp. 16–17.

So like many parallel shows, the series grows darker as its storytelling grows more continuous. That increase in continuity entails both the developing societal framework surrounding Dexter, and the reduction of scansion in Dexter's personal story, as the season conclusions gradually replace endings with moments of sublime violence: Instead of finding and killing another serial killer, as in the first season finale, the fourth season has Dexter discovering his murdered wife and blood-soaked infant, and the sixth season allows his sister to watch, shocked and awed, the ritualized murder of that year's main antagonist.[17] Perhaps the most emphatic disruption of the order of representation occurs in the seemingly perfect ending to season three, Dexter's wedding, which has a diegetically utterly inexplicable drop of blood appear on his bride's white laced dress, a foreboding authorial comment that underlines the continuing darkness of further promised seasons in opposition both to the concept of narrative conclusion and to representative storytelling.[18]

While eschewing pulpish genre stereotypes such as the fantastical evil spirit from the ancient past, this favours a purported realism that is no less an aesthetic creation for its avoidance of obvious fictional markers. For the removal of Dexter's murdering force from insight does not oppose mysticism to science, but rather opposes mystical along with scientific explanations to the mere quality of inexplicable, objectified fact. And crucially, it is closely connected to the formal and filmic choices underscoring the simultaneous move towards an emphatically stated art. This, then, is the specific character of the TV series' ethical turn and the shape of the maturity so often ascribed to it: To narrate evil as a transcendent metaphysical concept is a genre stereotype; instead, narrating it as something hardwired into the matter of the universe is supposed to reflect that greater insight which at once aspires to beauty. For it is the beauty of the presented object that repeatedly halts investigation into Dexter's urges in a turn upon rhetorical models of the sublime.

It is here that the three strands of the series' intensified aesthetic reach come together: The dismissive quotation of genre standards as topoi that are blind and uninterpreted tropes, the operatively monist identification of evil with matter, and the subsequent identification of both with sublime beauty. The show's introduction sequence has become famous by now and showcases this filmic approach that also applies to many other details of motif, framing, and sequence through-

---

17 Respectively: "Born Free," *Dexter* 1.12 (Dec 17, 2006); "The Getaway," *Dexter* 4.12 (Dec 13, 2009); and "This is the Way the World Ends," *Dexter* 6.12 (Dec 18, 2011).
18 "Do You Take Dexter Morgan?," *Dexter* 3.12 (Dec 14, 2008).

out every episode. Set to a mollified county fair and barrel organ tune, the intro consists almost exclusively of expanded bull lens close-ups of objects and gestures: A mosquito sucking on Dexter's arm, then flattened by his other hand, but with each view of a human limb separated from the whole of the body, which remains off-screen; a likewise separated cut to his facial hair, and then to the razor moving along his throat almost as if about to slit it; the t-shirt pulled over his head almost as if suffocating a victim; the shoe-laces pulled tight almost as if in a strangling movement. The human body reduced to its limbs as partial objects gains a starkly material presence that is identified with two other aspects: the threat of sharp, pointed, hard-edged inanimate objects, and the suggestion of a murderous inclination implied, but never admitted to, by the everyday actions of a man washing, clothing himself, and preparing breakfast. The underscored recurring views of blood – sucked by the mosquito, one drop drawn by the razor, and imitated by ketchup on the plate and blood orange juice in the squeezer – plays with splatter movie conventions, but also references the general idea of *suture* within any montage, and stitches the veiled presence of murder to the aesthetic of the depicted objects' hyper-presence.

Each image is isolated; each image is metaphorical, but resolves not to a proper reference, but to a topos that the genre considers as regulated code, as trope. And yet by the extreme exaltation of each motif, the imagery renders the trope as if it were its own ideal reference, a truth shining through in these moments of beauty. It is here, in the metaphors of the breakfast routine, that violence is aestheticized to a much greater degree than in the many depictions of actual violence and murder that run through most episodes. Its version of the sublime calls forth persistent and unending interpretations, while at the same time halting all further semiotic engagement with a double barrier: For as Dexter's murders are beyond explanation, so do the pictures require no further understanding, as they are presented as already beautiful.

This is the reverse of the show's claim to a higher aesthetics, and it is also the main reason why I am treating so extensively the gulf between the popular production and its formal and material reach towards emphatic art. In many other cases, analysis might best proceed by ignoring traditional distinctions of high and low art, or of art and popular entertainment, when considering the devices and methods of a given text. But in *Dexter* and many similarly positioned shows, this departure from mass entertainment is a conscious and explicit part of the work's own poetology. It constantly points out that it is a popular TV show full of popular genre conventions, and yet goes beyond that. By doing so, it establishes a border between the genre elements it boldly goes on using and the moments of ostentatiously reaching beyond to a different aesthetic. That border runs through the structure of the series as well as each episode; it even divides scenes. Across those divides runs a tension at once employed to tie together and to separate Dexter's violence and the universe's general evil on the one hand, and on the other hand its aesthetic representation that veils this evil and draws its beauty from it.

For the fabric that represents and occults violence continues from the aspects of a young man's morning routines to a whole tapestry of bourgeois identity; it is ideological in a precise sense: It can share one monistically conceived reality with the very violence that it denies because it is always already its deliberate falsification, dependent upon the falsified content of the representation even as that content depends on its misrepresentation. In this way, it denies operative dualism by the very act of covering violence with a second identity, and presenting that cover-up openly and as if by unavoidable necessity. It is not any body's and object's hyperbolic presence that entails Dexter's violence, but the objects and inscribed bodies of a specifically structured and situated life: Middle class, a bachelor's apartment in a complex near the beach, later on replaced by a suburban home with a wife and her kids from a previous marriage.

The series invests many genre elements in this play of hide-and-seek, recurring both to the establishment of lawful order in optimistic detective stories, as Dexter or his police team capture criminals, and to the social standards of soap opera motifs in the team's dalliances and love affairs and divorces and petty enmities. Their genre functions are always ready to be interrupted by an aestheticized staging of their duplicity, recalling Dexter's murdering compulsion. At the same time, they also serve as an important structuring element that turns large parts of the plot into an application of farce, as Dexter's constant lies to hide his murders entail further lies and further lies, eventually entangling with the many smaller lies told by everyone around him. This goes on until he finds himself, for instance, enrolled in a 12 steps program, because it was easier to pretend that the drugs and syringe that were found in his car and that he uses to immobilize his victims were part of an addiction. Often, this is played for an effect of tragic irony, as Dexter and other characters unknowingly express Dexter's truth in puns and slips of the tongue. The dark comedy created by these constellations is no mere by-product – it takes up much more space, time, and effort than that. Rather, it concerns the series' main conceit in a profound way, because it negotiates and reinforces the separation of violence from its dependent representation in that which hides it. Alcoholism and drug abuse treated in self-help groups fit the pretense suburban existence better than compulsive murder; but it also quickly becomes a stand-in for Dexter's actual struggle with his urge to kill, as he attempts to apply the 12 steps to his own betterment – and inevitably realizes that his violent secret is beyond all therapy. In this as in so many other configurations of the farce, the basic message is clear – and it is expressed with suffocating directness in a voice-over monologue opening one such episode:

> We all have something to hide, some dark place inside us we don't want the world to see; so we pretend everything's okay, wrapping ourselves in rainbows. And maybe that's all for the best; because some of these places are darker than others.[19]

This message lies at the heart of *Dexter*: Yes, your identity as an upstanding citizen is a sham. But everyone has some dark deviance inside himself, albeit none as interesting as that of our main character. The ongoing pretense is always ultimately strong enough to cover your darkness; it is reliable not because it is accurate, but because it doesn't have to be. *Ex fortiori*, it is that hidden darkness that gives the construct of our society strength, and its aspects a dark and gritty beauty. The message is somewhat immunized by its explicit falsehood, its submission under an unapologetic false consciousness and the dispensation hailing from its rhetorical irony. The quoted voice-over accompanies images of a flowing fabric in rainbow colours, again heavily aestheticized, and ultimately revealed to be a part of a kindergarten game in which parents cover and uncover their kids in a colourful tent. Again, materiality is celebrated as sublime and textual coherence suggestive of unavoidable ethical failure.

The expanding fabric of societal relations in the increasingly developed supporting cast, coupled as it is with the increasing reliance on ongoing story-arcs, takes its cue not only from this farce, but also underscores yet again the all-encompassing, operatively monist representation in which everything is connected to everything by virtue of being misrepresented in a shared pretense that draws aesthetic pleasure from its suggestive secret. It adds a dimension of appellation supporting Dexter's self-positioning in his superficial role, his named identity being provided by its falsehood:

> The babysitter doesn't trust me because of the lies. Lumen doesn't trust me because of the truth. There must be a name for that. Oh, right: Dexter Morgan.[20]

---

19 "First Blood," *Dexter 5.05* (Oct 24, 2010): 3:20–23.
20 "Beauty and the Beast," *Dexter 5.04* (Oct 24, 2010): 22:50.

In the genre, this kind of farce that completely defines a secondary identity finds its prototype in the relationship between Superman and Clark Kent, which is often parodistically referenced in *Dexter*. It is worth remembering here that the Clark Kent identity was only invented after the Superman character, and that the further development of Kent's relatives, friends and colleagues was driven not only by immanent needs of storytelling, but by a specific pragmatic requirement: The Superman character was deemed too iconic by US courts to enjoy full copyright protection on its own. As this copyright sought by publishers had to apply not to a specific single text, but to a property extending over the disjointed installments of an ongoing series, that property needed a solidifying element, eventually recognized in the stitched-on realization of the character as a middle-class reporter, following the landmark decision by county judge August Hand in 1940.[21] The further development of Dexter's supporting cast similarly helps to distinguish its intellectual property from its adapted basis in Lindsay's novels. The addition of a strong supporting cast to the duplicitous main character is thus a genre convention doubly immersed in the need to tie that character to the ownership of middle-class ideology: It achieves this by offering societal, appellative recognition of citizen identity, as well as by turning the whole of the character into property both within the diegesis and without.

3. Seriality, Operative Monism, and Method

If this all-encompassing fabric of *Dexter*'s reality is indeed a kind of *operative monism*, denying the differences of interpretation and representation in favour of an ultimately un-othered real, its specific metaphysics deserve more detailed analysis. For the genre series, it first implies the move from paradigmatically repeated shapes of interchangeable episodes to an unending stream of linear installments, but also to the dismissal of ideal ethical standards beyond the unavoidable reality of the thoroughly bloody facts: Story-arcs that appear to tend, by their very structure, to that "dark and gritty" reality they extoll. The accompanying aesthetic focus on material hyper-presence, and the combination of all three aspects in a universal conscious misrepresentation, denies any more truthful outside.

---

21 For a detailed analysis, see Stephan Packard, "Copyright und Superhelden. Über die Prägung populärer Mythologie durch textuelle Kontrolle," *Justitiabilität und Rechtmäßigkeit. Verrechtlichungsprozesse von Literatur und Film in der Moderne*, ed. Claude D. Conter (Amsterdam: Rodopi, 2010): pp. 109–126.

This use of the term "monism" requires some clarification. It may not at first seem to fit very well many of the more influential definitions given to the term in dominant philosophical discourse. It does, however, fit very closely to one somewhat strange instantiation of the concept in the midst of 20th century's fascination with seriality, exemplified by Paul Kammerer's *Gesetz der Serie* from 1919.[22] Kammerer is famous today mostly for two things: As a biologist, he fabricated evidence for an inheritance of acquired characteristics, along the lines of what we now usually refer to as Lamarckism. And he authored this amazingly idiosyncratic and yet influential book, *The Law of the Series*, which also has a troubling relationship with empirical proof, as Kammerer keeps on insisting himself. As he develops a general theory of the series that is supposed to explain phenomena at all levels of the world, from basic physics to the most complex cultural achievements, he points out that he is both unhappy with his oeuvre's tendency to move beyond empiricism, and yet unable to deny the driving force of his speculation. He hopes desperately that later researchers will claw back his theory into the field of experimental evidence, but realizes in many places that its very structure is hardly commensurable to this kind of testing, that it focuses on an interpretation rather than a depiction, even as it denies the validity of such representation. The problem is that his notion of the series is supposed to explain certain phenomena of bundled and clustered events and permanent similarities and patterns by reference only to the series itself – but cannot help but introduce transcendent notions to describe those similarities and hold on to those patterns. I want to examine this as a close analogy to the way that the uninterrupted and uninterpreted series of Dexter's killings and the serial of *Dexter*'s episodes is interpreted only by an explicitly false and farcical veil of suburban identities, the middle-class ruse turning into the only perceivable pattern of any constancy.

The specific monism in Kammerer is perhaps best described as an attempt to recapture an Aristotelian realism of form that places the existence of the recurring shapes observed in his series only in the existence of the shaped elements themselves, but with a much greater concern for insisting on the purely monist foundation of such a view, as only it can promise objective truth to Kammerer's fiercely scientistic stance. Two comparisons – one with psychoanalysis, the other with

---

22 Paul Kammerer, *Das Gesetz der Serie* (Stuttgart: Deutsche Verlags-Anstalt, 1919). I am here indebted to Aage Hansen-Löve's work on the history of formalism and structuralism. In a talk at Munich in 2010, he hinted at the similarities and differences between Kammerer's concept of the series and the paradigmatically-bound concept of the linear syntagm in structuralist semiology.

theories of biological evolution – may serve to elucidate his position, and underscore the analogy to the serial principles in *Dexter*.

In many ways, Kammerer's fascination sounds and feels like Sigmund Freud's interest in the strange things that people say and do. His book begins with three chapters' worth of a catalogue of individual case studies,[23] each told very much in the style of a novella, arranged around the surprising and unheard novelty of the central event: After meeting no acquaintances throughout the course of weeks, a person runs into several on the same day. After being placed in the 18th row in a concert, Kammerer finds himself in the 18th row of another concert hall on the very next night. Shortly after noticing the surname *Tyrolt* on a portrait, he notices the same name on a newspaper column. A man recites a nonsensical rhyme to a friend; the very next day, his sister-in-law, who was not present, recites the same rhyme to the same friend. Freud often fastens on to the same kind of patterns: As commonalities between elements of a dream as well as a series of associations interpreting a dream, but also as features of Freudian slips, of witty remarks, and ultimately of cases in which he suspects that actual telepathy is taking place. Jung intensified the same method in his notion of synchronicity.

But what sets Kammerer completely apart from Freud and Jung is his insistence that there must be no common cause, no third power outside of the series that can explain these recurrences. Instead, he refers to concepts of an inertia, of a sameness developing in, not beyond, the elements of the series. This exclusion happens by explicit definition; it can therefore never be tested by experiment. In this, it goes beyond its own driving interest in a pure reliance on testable facts happening after facts. It hails from method, and not from the object to which that method is applied. It is diametrically opposed to the psychoanalyst's introduction of an unconscious – mostly individual in Freud, partially common in Jung – that stands beyond the series of its symptoms and indications, and that offers a key to evaluate and change its automatism. This is the same difference that occurs in the twisted use of trauma in the *Dexter* tale: Knowing that his murderous urge continues the slaughter of his childhood neither explains it nor offers any kind of help, but instead serves to permanently close the series of murders in on itself.

---

23 For a view of this assembly of coincidences leading to an abandonment of coincidence in the monist structure of the series, see Henning Ritter, "Der Zufallsjäger. Paul Kammerer und das Gesetz der Serie," *Kunst der Serie*, ed. Christine Blättler (Munich: Wilhelm Fink, 2010), pp. 43–55.

Kammerer's work on series is connected to his work as a biologist mainly by a reinterpretation of genealogical inheritance. Histories of biology usually connect his work to Lamarckism; and indeed Kammerer insists that the force of the series suffices to perpetuate an acquired change in an organism in that creature's offspring, and that no third instance is necessary that might conserve the organism's identical shape in some other form, and cause parent and child to develop the same characteristics. In its dismissal of a separate realm of form, this approach subscribes to a monism even more rigid than Darwin's. But unlike pure Lamarckism, Kammerer again positions himself in a precarious spot half-way towards a begrudging dualism by referring to Richard Wolfgang Semon, who developed the concept of the "mneme," an encryption of shapes in nervous cells, to account for the persistence of acquired forms. By placing this recording device firmly within the material existence of the body shaped by the recorded form, Semon still upheld a kind of monism; but in Kammerer's application of the method, it receives a more dualist taste, as the encountered relatives, the repeated rhymes of brothers and sisters in law, and many others of the examples he discusses do not readily offer a material carrier for the mneme. The construction of a representation of the interpretative pattern in the material object gives way to strongly rhetorical accolades of that object's ability to reach into the shaping forces of itself and its surroundings, to become a scripture, or "engram" in Semon's words, that is completely identical to its own realization-as-interpretation in the unalterable development of a serial event. There is a deeply aesthetic quality to this ascription first evident in the Greek name of the Muse Mneme, and running throughout Kammerer's devoted portrayal of Semon's ideas. It closely mirrors *Dexter*'s aesthetic fascination with the objects of middle-class everyday life that hint at the underlying patterns of bloody murder in a way that ultimately betrays its own monist conception.

It is worth detailing the difference between such operative monism, with its disjointed alternation between continuous representation and its aesthetic fracture, and the concepts of continuum in monist semiotics as a purely representative method. Charles Sanders Peirce' monism is no less rigid – all phenomena refer back to but one essence of being, explained in one strict assembly of triadic relations between Firsts, Seconds, and Thirds[24] –, but never submits to the paradoxical version of a determinism of materiality as understood to eradicate ethical choice. Instead, in an opposition he subsumes under the headings of

24 See Charles Sanders Peirce, "A Guess at the Riddle," *Writings*, ed. Nathan Houser et al., vol. 6 (Bloomington: Indiana UP, 2000), pp. 165–210.

a monist "idealism" versus a monist "materialism,"[25] Peirce advocates tychism, outlining the endless possibilities of new semiotic relations in new encounters of elements,[26] a generalization of Darwin that moves evolutionary biology in a quite different metaphysical direction.[27] Such a monism that goes beyond mere operations of fracture interfering in an adapted dualist model of cognition and matter introduces a much different view of the promise of the future: While for Kammerer, the monist interpretation of Darwin allows us to become "work-masters of the future" precisely by governing through the inevitabilities of racial genetics,[28] it does so precisely by empowering us through the necessity of continued inherited serial characteristics:

> Und der Mensch sieht also auch die Mittel und Wege, seiner Feinde Herr zu werden: die Medizin, die individuelle und die Rassenhygiene, die Heilung des privaten wie des öffentlichen Lebens, die geistige und politische Aufklärung der Massen und aller Mittel Mutterboden, die Naturwissenschaft, hier in erster Reihe die Biologie.[29]
> [And man thus also recognizes the means to master his enemies: medicine, individual and racial hygiene, the cure for private and public life, the spiritual and political enlightenment of the masses, and the mother soil of all such means, here foremost biology.]

Thus issues of ethics and politics become inseparable from science, both appearing as knowledge of the immutably continuing series, eliminating all variety of what might, could, or should be. In Rancière's criticism of the more recent "ethical turn," this identification is described clearly, and connected to the recent reversal of the allegiance of such philosophy to a catastrophe, which while wandering between past and present, reiterates the aesthetically removed space of truth glimpsing an inevitable real:

---

25 On the possibility of a monist idealism in Peirce, see also Thomas A. Goudge, *The Thought of C. S. Peirce* (New York: Dover, 1969), esp. pp. 274–280. Helmut Pape, *Der dramatische Reichtum der konkreten Welt* (Weilerswist: Velbrück, 2002), esp. pp. 346–365.

26 Charles Sanders Peirce, "Design and Chance," *Writings*, vol. 4 (Bloomington: Indiana UP, 1989), pp. 544–554.

27 Compare Nathan Houser's interpretation in "Introduction,", Ibid., pp. xix-lxx, p. lxx.

28 Paul Kammerer, *Sind wir Sklaven der Vergangenheit oder Werkmeister der Zukunft? Anpassung, Vererbung, Rassenhygiene in dualistischer und monistischer Betrachtungsweise* (Vienna: Anzengruber, 1913).

29 Ibid., p. 33.

> C'est [...] une réversion du cours du temps: le temps tourné vers la fin à réaliser – progrès, émancipation ou autre – est remplacé par le temps tourné vers la catastrophe qui est en arrière de nous. [...] Cette disparation tendancielle des différences de la politique et du droit dans l'indistinction éthique définit aussi un certain présent de l'art et de la réflexion esthétique.[30]

Ex negativo, this reading of the identifications that are the eliminating operations of operative monism opens up a space to reconsider alternatives that include alternatives. It has been argued that the genome, in today's understanding of inheritance, fulfills some of the aspects of the form in Aristotelian realism for the same reasons as did Semon's mneme, and that view has been confronted with the same kind of objections. In a similar way, the purely *operative* monism that characterizes a method even at the cost of creating a false representation in lieu of a truly dualist container of form is still a fascination and problem in current debate. In empirical psychology, it has been called the problem of *neuro-realism*.[31] Their observation in examining news reports in mainstream media about functional MRI scans of neurological mechanisms convinced them that there was a problematic misinterpretation of scan results in the public discourse, and feeding back into medical research itself. That interpretation considered a pattern of human behaviour – successful or pathological or neutral – more "real" if it corresponded to an observable organic process. So for instance, one article claimed, "Now scientists say the feeling is not only real, but they can show what happens in the brain to cause it." Another said: "Patients have long reported that acupuncture helps relieve their pain, but scientists don't know why. Could it be an illusion? Now brain imaging technology has indicated that the perception of pain relief is accurate." The problem here is that the supposed monism – only what happens in this one material world really happens – is coupled with a self-denying dualism that first accepts the fact of pain relief being reported by patients, then considers the same relief more justified if it is doubled in a different act of perception.

---

30 "This reverses the course of time: that time which was directed towards an end as its realization – progress, emancipation, or something else – has been replaced by a time directed towards a catastrophe that lies behind us. [...] As the differences between politics and law tend to disappear in an ethical lack of distinction, this also defines a certain present of art and of aesthetic reflection." (Translation mine.) – Jacques Rancière, "Le tournant éthique de l'esthétique et de la politique," *Malaise dans l'esthétique* (Paris: Galilée, 2004), pp. 143–173., here esp. pp. 157–159.
31 First described in Eric Racine, Ofek Bar-Ilan, and Judy Illes, "fMRI in the public eye," *Nature Reviews Neuroscience* 6 (2005): pp. 159–164.

This problem of method, I think, points to a deeper engagement with seriality in contemporary discourses. It delineates precisely the imagination of Dexter's killing urge, which is introduced as an effective cause, and yet is at once denied any accessible existence by means of science, mysticism, therapy, or even interpretation. Instead, it is bound by the aesthetic insistence on the power of the uninterpreted object even as that object stands in for a representation that is justified because it is overtly false and incomplete. It is worth noting that Aristotle's own psychology frames the problem of potentially doubling the observed facts by observing them in the body as well as the soul again as a problem of methodology, and not of metaphysics. While he never doubts his hylomorphism, Aristotle describes characteristic unease towards this problem at the very beginning of *Peri psyches* for the very reason that he has to decide on a method to look at psychological events – either as purely belonging to the psyche, or as repeated in the body:

> Sometimes these phenomena are thought to pertain only to the soul, and sometimes, although hailing from the soul, they may belong to the whole nature of the animal. The greatest difficulty here is choosing how to grasp some knowledge of this. [...] It might be supposed that there is but one common method (*mia tis einai methodos*) [...] but if there are several methods [...], the difficulty becomes that much worse.[32]

So this returns to the problem of methodology. I have tried to give an account of the aesthetics and implied political dimension of *Dexter* as an example for the contemporary unity of continuous storytelling and a "dark and gritty" "ethical turn" in popular TV. That account is heavily influenced by observations found in Rancière's various writings. The quotation and dismissal of genre topoi in favour of an inaccessible aesthetic experience of greater art is conceived along the lines of Rancière's aesthetic regime, which keeps the representative techniques of the regime of the many arts handy as it redefines art as the one thing transcending all explicable technique. My look at the introduction sequence of *Dexter* could be very shortly rephrased as an observation of the *naked image* hinted at in the isolated shots of single objects, its turn into a montage of *ostentative images* in its aesthetic claim, and the combination of both in *metamorphical images* that exercise that kind of "silent speech" that characterizes the work of art in the aesthetic regime: On the one hand demanding their interpretation

---

32 Aristotle, *Peri psyches*, ed. Edwin Wallace (Cambridge: UP, 1882), 402a, trans. S.P.

as signs of the cruelty and violence they hide, they at the same time insist on arresting that interpretation, keeping it ever unsatisfactory, as their mere celebrated presence counters its semiotic meaning. The problem of operative monism in creating a third tier to conserve the general shapes informing the series of signs could be likewise restated as the problem of rediscovering an *archi-resemblance* between technical *resemblance* and *image*. And while I have carefully refrained from using all these terms because I am wary of grafting them onto such perhaps different objects and questions and even interests, the whole shape of my argument attests to consequences in method that come, not least, from reading Rancière.

The unease here comes from suspecting a Kammererian mistake. There is a danger that we may fasten onto ultimately superficial similarities, and recognize the nonsense rhyme repeated by brother and sister-in-law everywhere. Look, I ran into so many acquaintances today, and none yesterday! It must be a series of attractions! Look, there's an archi-resemblance! And a series of images opposing their resemblances! It must be the aesthetic regime at work. These doubts continue, pertaining to any case in which we try to do what some other analysis has already done, but for a different object.

So I would like to close with two suggestions, one concerning consequence and one concerning operative methods. The spectre of an "application" in the worst possible sense is striking. I would like to reinforce the idea that we might sometimes better speak of "consequences" when describing the methodological changes effected by such readings, rather than try and isolate terms and concepts and make them "applicable" to any observation, like a toolbox that can be carried around as far as we like. In this reading, I have tried *not* to "apply" Rancière to *Dexter*, but to allow a number of sensibilities developed in reading his work to come through in my reading of TV serials. More importantly, I have tried to show that it is often useful to identify the operative methods that are themselves involved in the things we're looking at, placing their claim to methodology alongside our own. The latter also may allow us to consider in which cases it is useful, after all, to carry a toolbox to a site where it did not originate, and discover, for instance, alternatives containing alternatives in a richness in *Dexter* that is not ultimately enclosed by its own method of conscious misreading.

Gabriel Rockhill

Critical Reflections on the Ontological Illusion
Rethinking the Relation between Art and Politics

Ontological Illusion

The common starting point for reflections on the relationship between art and politics is a series of three central questions: What is art? What is politics? What is the connection between art and politics? This *terminus a quo* is apparently so self-evident that there has been very little critical reflection on what this series of questions actually entails. While it is true that the responses have varied widely, they nonetheless tend to share the same methodological framework, which might be referred to as a descriptive ontology: they purport to provide an account of the being of art and politics as well as the nature of their relationship. The guiding assumption is that art and politics have identifiable natures that can be definitively described. Modifying the level of analysis or the terms of relation does not necessarily change the methodological orientation. In other words, if the initial question is *what is literature?*, *what is film?* or *what is democracy?* the same basic methodological framework is operative. This is equally true in the case of an individual work of art or a particular instance of "politics." At base, it is a matter of responding to the question *ti estin* – what is (an entity)? – with an ontological description of the nature of a particular object, activity or relationship.

This common sense starting point runs the risk of orienting the entire discussion of art and politics around competing definitions of their nature and rival accounts of their privileged meeting ground. Such a *terminus a quo* is based on what I propose to call the ontological illusion, that is to say the myth according to which art and politics have stable natures that can be identified once and for all. Moreover, the relation between them is often thought in causal terms: a particular work of art or type of artwork provokes or contributes to a specific political action (or not). Such a relationship makes sense within the framework of what I call the talisman complex, according to which the politics of art amounts to a political force inherent in works of art that is supposedly capable of producing political consequences through a nebulous, preternatural alchemy. The talisman complex tends to center the discussion of art and politics on the productive side of art by focusing primarily on the art object or artistic activity as such, occasionally linking these to the particular artistic intentions imbued within them. It thereby brackets, to a greater or lesser extent, the social distribution of works of art and their reception by a public. The political dimension of art is thus reduced to the supposed power of a particular talisman-like object or practice. It should be noted, moreover, that this complex also prevails in the various attempts to delegitimize political art or reveal the vacuity of particular politicized work, as if the fact that a specific work or group of works did not instigate revolutionary transformation was in itself an indictment of its politicity, if not of political art *in toto*.

Consider, for instance, the various and sundry claims made regarding the supposed failure of Pablo Picasso's *Guernica* (1937). In 1948, Jean-Paul Sartre raised the rhetorical and sardonic question: "does anyone think that it won over a single heart to the Spanish cause?"[1] If the answer is clearly "no" for him, it is in part because paintings do not express unambiguous meanings that could galvanize spectators. Instead, they present imaginary objects and feelings that cannot be clearly committed to a political cause. Theodor Adorno, in spite of his truculent and unrelenting criticisms of Sartre's conception of commitment, nonetheless shared his view of *Guernica* and sought to extend it to Bertolt Brecht: "Sartre's candid doubt about whether *Guernica* had 'won a single person to the Spanish cause' certainly holds true for Brecht's didactic drama as well."[2] These types of categorical judgments are largely founded on the assumption that the politics of art amounts to the potential for individual works to function as autonomous and sovereign sources of political transformation. In sharp counter-distinction to this approach, which is dependent upon the supposed autarchy of the isolated work of art, I maintain that it is essential to examine the complex and diverse ways in which aesthetic practices are intertwined with the social fabric. In the case of Picasso, for instance, it should be remembered that he provided direct financial support to the Spanish Republic and that he established a fund for Republican exiles, which benefitted from many charitable exhibitions:

> *Guernica* was given to the Spanish Republic by Picasso, and he also conferred the 150,000 francs he had received for expenses to the fund for Republican exiles. The fund also benefited from the proceeds of the many charitable exhibitions of *Guernica* and its related works, and from the sale of the limited folio edition of *Songe et mensonge de Franco*. It has not been

---

1 Jean-Paul Sartre, "*What Is Literature?" and Other Essays* (Cambridge, Massachusetts: Harvard University Press, 1988), p. 28.

2 Theodor Adorno, *Notes to Literature*, vol. 2, ed. Rolf Tiedemann, trans. Shierry Weber Nicholsen (New York: Columbia University Press, 1992), p. 84.

> confirmed that Picasso actually financed the purchase of warplanes as has been alleged. Instead, he donated milk for the children in Barcelona. He signed numerous declarations in support of the Republic and became involved with several refugee relief organizations. He participated in fund-raising efforts such as exhibitions and auctions to benefit Spanish refugees, and was particularly active in securing the liberation of Spanish intellectuals from French internment camps. Mercedes Guillén, the wife of the Spanish sculptor Balthazar Lobo, recalled how helpful Picasso was in obtaining green cards for Spanish exiles.[3]

These were not simply individual acts of Picasso the citizen that could somehow be separated from those of Picasso the artist. They were acts rendered possible, in part, by his social status as an artist and the relative popularity as well as the financial success of *Guernica* and other works. Picasso himself recognized the fundamental impossibility of separating the artist from his or her social and political being:

> What do you think an artist is? An imbecile who only has eyes if he is a painter, or ears if he's a musician, or a lyre at every level of his heart if he's a poet, or even, if he's a boxer, just his muscle? On the contrary, he is at the same time a political being, constantly alive to heart-rending, fiery or happy events to which he responds in every way.[4]

The peremptory judgments issued by Sartre and Adorno effectively illustrate the role of the interpreter within the framework of the ontological illusion and the talisman complex, which is to identify *the* politics of art, to determine *the* political effects of artistic endeavors. The guiding assumption is that art and politics are separate entities, and that each artistic object or practice has its own proper politics that can be objectively identified as such. The fundamental hermeneutic presupposition is hence that there is an *epistéme* of art and politics, a strictly determined knowledge regarding the political efficacy (or inefficacy) of particular works. Moreover, it is widely assumed that the role of the interpreter is simply to describe what exists in the "nature of things," so to speak. There is often, therefore, a short-circuit between subjectivity and objectivity insofar as the supposedly objective politi-

---

3 Gertje R. Utley, *Picasso: The Communist Years* (New Haven, Connecticut: Yale University Press, 2000), p. 25. It is also important to note that the Spanish government was "disappointed with Picasso's insufficiently partisan approach" and "considered removing the canvas from the pavilion, but were deterred only by their fear of adverse publicity" (ibid., p. 24).

4 Cited in Gertje R. Utley. *Picasso: The Communist Years*, p. 1.

cal effects of art are determined based on the subjective experience or point of view of the interpreter. In the worst cases, this leads to a complete uniformization of artistic reception via hermeneutic hegemony: a singular experience of a work of art or a specific judgment is hegemonically imposed as a general or even universal experience or judgment without considering the variability operative in the social reception of works of art.

The talisman complex often leads to the identification of a privileged meeting ground between art and politics or a prototypical form of political art. One can think, for instance, of Sartre's decision to focus on prose writing as the only art form capable of being "committed" because it uses words to produce meaning (instead of feelings or imaginary objects). He thereby restricts the entire discussion of artistic commitment – at least in "*What Is Literature?*" (1948) – to prose writing, whereas music, painting and poetry are held to be outside the field of commitment in the true sense of the term because they do not produce meaning.[5] One might also consider Georg Lukács' valorization of realism as the literary form capable of truly mirroring the deep forces of reality at work behind the fleeting appearances of the world. He thereby rejects what he referred to as the introversion of formalism and the extraversion of naturalism, neither of which are interested, according to him, in the social totality and the essential, subterranean mechanisms of historical development. Both thinkers end up producing relatively schematic formulas: *this* art is political and *that* art is not political; *this* art is politically progressive and *that* art is politically regressive. Outside of a few exceptions, which usually occur nonetheless within a rather rigid class determinism, there is little attempt to think works of art as social objects in the sense of being polyvalent phenomena with a multiplicity of dimensions, nodal points in a complex of social relations that are irreducible to a single or definitive relationship.[6]

The ontological illusion and the talisman complex are ultimately rooted in a social epoché: an individual thinker purports to determine

---

5 Sartre does assert in "*What Is Literature?*" that the very act of writing – whatever one's intention may be – necessarily implies a commitment, and he also mentions that the desire to discuss the poet's commitment can only make sense if it is understood as the commitment to *losing* and to the failure of the human project. Moreover, we should note that Sartre significantly reworked the stark opposition between poetry and prose as early as "Black Orpheus" (1948), where he discusses the functional and committed aspects of black poetry (see "*What Is Literature?*," pp. 289–330).

6 There are, as we will see, at least some partial exceptions in Sartre's work.

the very being of art and politics, as well as the nature of their relationship, by bracketing their sociality and thereby establishing a fixed, univocal determination of social phenomena. In other words, the social is bracketed by a transcendental determination of the nature of art and politics from a subjective point of view in the social field that purports to grasp the objective nature of phenomena. This ultimately leads to a fundamental impasse: if what we call politics necessarily has a social dimension, and the ontological illusion and talisman complex lead to a bracketing of the social, then they foreclose the possibility of actually thinking the political dimension of works of art, their social politicity. More so than an impasse, this might be best described as a cul-de-sac insofar as the various authoritative statements on the particular political nature of works of art are destined to endlessly turn in circles around one another. Since the ultimate arbiter seems to be the subjective point of view of the interpreter, claims cannot be mediated by an account of the social distribution and reception of works of art, or simply reinserted in a broader description of the ongoing social negotiations over the supposed nature of art and politics.

This social epoché reduces works of art to a singular, atomistic existence and usually situates them in a binary normative framework in which there are only two possibilities: either a work of art helps a particular political agenda or it hinders it. There are thus only two viable judgments, and the task of the critic often becomes one of drafting a long list of "good" and "bad" works. Such an approach excludes the complexity and variability of social phenomena such as works of art, which – instead of acting like fixed talismans with a single and unique power – can and do have variable effects at different levels that are irreducible to the simple opposition between positive and negative. For instance, it appears that R. W. Fassbinder – often presented as the quintessential German dissident – had at least some partial supporters on the right as well as among conventional members of the establishment. Indeed, he defended accepting money from conservatives in order to make complex politico-psychological films that do not allow for the easy identification of good and evil so common to moralizing political films. "If someone objects, as some of my friends do," Fassbinder declares, "that you shouldn't make films with the money of rightists, all I can say is that Visconti made almost all his films with money from rightists. And always justified it with similar arguments: that they gave him more leeway than the leftists."[7] Fassbinder is an excellent example not only of the ways in which works of art

7 Michael Töteberg and Leo Lensing, eds., *The Anarchy of the Imagination* (Baltimore/London: The Johns Hopkins University Press, 1992), p. 61.

qua social phenomena are irreducible to the binary normative framework of "good" and "bad," but also of the ways in which artists themselves have at times sought to undermine this very framework. To take but a single and brief example, it is worth recalling how Fassbinder attacked – from the left, so to speak – mainstream feminism and gay rights by making a film about lesbian relationships, *The Bitter Tears of Petra von Kant* (1972), in which caustic sadomasochistic battles contravene the acquiescent models of social-engineering multiculturalism (in which works of art are used to construct positive role models that break with the negative stereotypes of mass culture).

The compression and uniformization of the social dimension of works of art in what I am calling the social epoché is often closely linked to a reductive conception of history, if not an outright exclusion of historicity through a historical epoché. In extreme cases, art and politics are presented as transhistorical or ahistorical constants, as if they had existed as discrete phenomena since time immemorial. When history is taken into account, as in much of the Marxist and neo– or post-Marxist tradition, for instance, it is often reduced to what I call its vertical or chronological dimension. The horizontal dimension of the geographic distribution of events is thereby forgotten in favor of a more or less homogenous conception of periodic blocks of time, as if there were a *Zeitgeist* unifying all of the developments of a particular moment. Moreover, the complex strata of various social formations and practices tend to be occluded in favor of a more or less monolithic vision of society. By excluding both the horizontal dimension of geography and the stratigraphic dimension of social practice, historicity is thereby reduced to supposedly univocal blocks of time.

Rethinking Art and Politics

In order to reopen the question of art and politics in a new light and chart out novel territory for rethinking their relations, it is necessary to begin by breaking with the ontological illusion in all of its forms: there is no being of art and politics, and there is no essential and unique relationship between them. In direct opposition to the conceptualist assumption that there is a fixed notion – transhistorical or extrasocial – of art and politics, I maintain the position of radical historicism: art and politics have no stable natures but are differentially constituted socio-historical practices. Radical historicism should be clearly distinguished from reductive historicism, which consists in reducing all historical phenomena to a fixed set of determinants. If everything is in history (radical historicism), this does not mean that everything can be explained by a series of historical determinants as if history were only a form of destiny (reductive historicism). The adjective *radical* indexes the dynamic role of different forms of agency in history and the fact that historical developments are never absolutely determined. It also refers to the dissolution of the very objects of history: if history is *radical* it is precisely insofar as its objects are only provisory formations in the torrent of time. It is for this reason that I also distinguish radical historicism from selective historicism, which purports to separate the chaff of historical appearances from the true wheat of the stable entities behind historical change. Art and politics are not simply historical in the sense that they have undergone changes through time. They are radically historical insofar as there is no being or essence that unifies them across time. Borrowing a term that Daniel Dennett has used in a different context, we might say that radical historicism unleashes a "universal acid" that dissolves all categories and containers into the flow of time.[8] It is for this reason that the Foucauldian distinction between analysis and analytic – also developed in a different context – proves particularly useful. Whereas the historical analysis of art and politics tends to be founded on selective historicism and the assumption that these are natural objects with their respective histories, the historical analytic of aesthetic and political practices begins the other way around, by exploring the complex set of relations that are labeled "art" and "politics" at diverse points in time. This does not mean, of course, that there are not identifiable entities or phenomena in a particular socio-historical conjuncture. It simply means that these are not historical constants, but are rather the result of intricate socio-historical negotiations and their institutional sedimentation. This is one of the reasons why radical historicism goes hand in hand with radical sociologism: all human phenomena take place in society, but this does not mean that they are reducible to a particular state of the social.

In short, I propose to jettison the ontological illusion that undergirds much of the debate on art and politics in favor of a radical historicist analytic of practice, according to which "art" and "politics" are recognized as socio-historical concepts in struggle. Instead of searching for the privileged point of intersection or natural link between them, it is imperative to recognize that various relations are constructed and dismantled in the social sphere through a series of ongoing negotiations (and that the critic plays a crucial role in these struggles). It is for these reasons, among others, that it is important to categorically reject

8 See Daniel C. Dennett, *Darwin's Dangerous Idea: Evolution and the Meanings of Life* (New York: Simon & Schuster, 1995), pp. 61–84.

the talisman complex, which reduces the politics of art to the supposed inherent power of artistic objects and practices to provoke political consequences. Objects of art in their traditional sense do not have, in and of themselves, an innate political power.[9] They might be imbued with a particular political agenda or orientation, but this does not mean that they have a political force that can be identified once and for all as being part of their constitutive nature. Moreover, by reducing the politics of art to the so-called political power of artistic products (as well as to a largely monocausal relationship between art and politics), the talisman complex forecloses the truly social dimension of works of art and thereby acts as a bulwark against understanding the veritable social politicity of aesthetic practices. In other words, one of the fundamental problems of the talisman complex is that it purports to give an account of the politics of art by bracketing the social dimension of aesthetic practices and focusing solely on artistic products. In so doing, it tends to remove art from the social arena and thereby occlude its veritable political dimension insofar as politics – as it is understood in our conjuncture – is necessarily a social phenomenon.

The critique of the talisman complex therefore requires overcoming the social epoché that has plagued much of the debate on art and politics. Instead of according pride of place to aesthetic products and their supposed political power, the analytic of aesthetic practices I propose focuses on the truly social dimension of these practices by studying not only the works themselves but also the complexities of their production, their distribution in society and, finally, their reception by the public. In short, it is a matter of examining works of art as social phenomena instead of as isolated atoms with a supposedly innate politicity. It is, of course, still necessary to examine in detail the works themselves by studying their propositions and strategies, their implicit political implications, as well as their potentialities. But it is equally necessary to consider, as I've just mentioned, three different dimensions of their social existence as works of art.

At the level of production, it is important to examine the socio-historical conjuncture, the set of operative practices in this conjuncture,

9 I am not considering here, for the sake of concision, works of art that are themselves forms of political action, like Gianni Motti's U.N. intervention in the 53rd session of the Commission on Human Rights in Geneva (Motti occupied the seat of the absent Indonesian delegate and made a speech that helped instigate a walkout by representatives of the American Indians and other ethnic groups prior to the vote on the 48th resolution concerning ethnic minorities). However, it should be noted that even these aesthetico-political acts do not produce univocal social effects. In other words, they do not function like talismans with innate political powers.

the cultural field of possibility, the social and economic forces at work, the material conditions of production, the artist's training and acquired dispositions, and everything that goes into the act of producing particular works of art. To take a single example of the relevancy of this dimension to the politicity of aesthetic practices, we can note that it is rather one-sided to critically dismantle the particular political agenda manifest in various Hollywood films, for instance, if the product is not situated in relationship to a system of production in which the Pentagon has played a central role by bartering military expertise and extremely expensive military equipment against the right to censorship. "Millions of dollars can be shaved off a film's budget if the military agrees to lend its equipment and assistance," writes David L. Robb in his book *Operation Hollywood*, "and all a producer has to do to get that assistance is submit five copies of the script to the Pentagon for approval; make whatever script changes the Pentagon suggests; film the script exactly as approved by the Pentagon; and prescreen the finished product for Pentagon officials before it's shown to the public."[10] An additional example of the importance of the system of production might be taken from Frances Stonor Saunders' enlightening work on the central role played by the CIA – and particularly the Congress for Cultural Freedom – in the production and circulation of artwork during the international *Kulturkampf* of the Cold War era.[11]

Secondly, regarding distribution, it is necessary to foreground the real social circulation of works of art by studying their distribution and accessibility, their cultural framing, the institutions that present them, and so forth. For instance, it is clear that the modern museum, which began to emerge around the end of the 18th century, has played a key socio-political role by making art – in principle – more accessible to the masses, solidifying and codifying a cultural heritage and shared conception of the past, and also linking national artistic traditions to the cultural identity of emerging nation-states. An institution like the modern museum has also played a significant role in the articulation of various aesthetico-political rejections of "establishment art" and bourgeois institutions since at least the end of the 19th century. To take a more specific example of a slightly different nature concerning the political dimensions of aesthetic distribution, it is interesting to note that John Pilger's documentary, *The War on Democracy* (2007), which was in part an attack on the new political imaginary of the "War

---

10 David L. Robb, *Operation Hollywood: How the Pentagon Shapes and Censors the Movies* (Amherst, New York: Prometheus Books, 2004), p. 25.

11 See Frances Stonor Saunders, *The Cultural Cold War: The CIA and the World of Arts and Letters* (New York: The New York Press, 1999).

on Terror," was not distributed in the United States. Pilger writes that a major New York distributor said to him: "You will need to make structural and political changes. Maybe get a star like Sean Penn to host it – he likes liberal causes – and tame those anti-Bush sequences."[12] This flagrant example reveals the very close links between politics and the distribution of works of art.

Finally, concerning the role of reception, it is imperative to recognize that works of art do not play univocal roles in the social matrix, and their political dimension cannot be determined once and for all. They necessarily have a multidimensional social existence insofar as they are subject to different interpretations and points of view, but also to variable cultural contexts and modes of social framing. We might take our cue – up to a certain point – from a statement made by Sartre: "There is no art except for and by others [*Il n'y a d'art que pour et par autrui*]."[13] In order for a work of art to function as such, it needs to circulate in society and have its own proper social existence. In so doing, it takes on a life of its own by being interpreted in various ways, put in relationship to different works, placed in sundry contexts, and so forth.

This brings us to the role of the critic and interpreter. Rather than simply describing, from the sidelines, the politics supposedly inherent in works of art, the critic plays a crucial role in the politicity of works by entering into the socio-political battlefield over their reception. He or she does not simply draw out potentialities but rather formulates arguments and politicizes the work in various ways and according to a particular orientation. We should not assume, however, that the work is thereby sullied and debased, for the battles of interpretation are part of the social life of the work itself. This does not mean that there are not better or worse interpretations, but rather that this very distinction is negotiated through social institutions – in the broad sense – and the struggles around them. Another way of putting this is by extending one of Cornelius Castoriadis' claims regarding politics: just as "there is no science of politics," there is no *epistéme* of art, there are only ongoing social struggles over meaning and values (as well as the institutionalized results of previous struggles).[14] This is one of the reasons why it is essential to reject the hermeneutic hegemony which consists in

---

12 John Pilger, "Hollywood's New Censors" (http://www.antiwar.com/pilger/?articleid=14271, publ. 19 February 2009, cit. 13 June 2011).

13 Sartre, "*What Is Literature?*," p. 52.

14 Gabriel Rockhill, ed., *Postscript on Insignificance: Dialogues with Cornelius Castoriadis*, trans. Gabriel Rockhill and John V. Garner (London/New York: Continuum Books, 2011), p. 11.

trying to pass off a personal interpretation for a universal attribute of a particular work, or, in the language I have just evoked, making an informed interpretive opinion into a form of infallible scientific knowledge (which does not mean that interpretation is infinitely open, a point that I have argued in great detail elsewhere).[15] The position I maintain is twofold: on the one hand, it is necessary to recognize the plural nature of artistic reception and jettison the naïve and self-serving belief in artistic *epistéme*. On the other hand, such a recognition should by no means hinder us from intervening in the field of social negotiation in the name of a particular politicization of aesthetic practices. Instead of hermeneutic hegemony, I therefore argue in favor of pragmatic interventionism: the role of the interpreter is to intercede in a particular conjuncture not simply in order to describe a purportedly universal trait but rather to directly participate in the production of an artwork's politicity by formulating informed opinions on its political valence. This requires, as I've mentioned, that we recognize the multiple dimensions of works of art in their social existence, and that we break with the simple binary normativity that has plagued a significant portion of the debate on art and politics by reducing it to categorical judgments opposing "good" political art to "bad" political. The social inscription of works of art is much more complicated than this schematic framework would lead us to believe.

We might consider in this regard Georg Lukács' attempt to make Honoré de Balzac's own political positions and artistic intentions secondary to his unique brand of realism, which, for him, coalesced with Karl Marx's description of the history of capitalism. Even if Balzac did provide a detailed portrait of the wretched transformations of modern capitalism, it is difficult to deny that his work was widely read and appreciated by the bourgeoisie, and interpreted along more conservative lines. In other words, his works were intertwined with diverse publics and various political orientations, which reveals the extent to which they were not politically univocal, in spite of what Lukács might have wanted to believe. We could also consider one of Adorno's passing statements in a letter to Walter Benjamin in 1936: "The laughter of the audience at a cinema – I discussed this with Max [Horkheimer], and he has probably told you about it already – is anything but good and revolutionary; instead, it is full of the worst bourgeois sadism."[16]

15 See, for instance, *Logique de l'histoire: Pour une analytique des pratiques philosophiques* (Paris: Éditions Hermann, 2010).
16 Theodor Adorno, Walter Benjamin et al., *Aesthetics and Politics: The Key Texts of the Classic Debate within German Marxism*, ed. Ronald Taylor (London/New York: Verso, 2002), p. 123.

Here we have a case of the reduction of social reception to a univocal political meaning, as if everyone laughing in the cinema were simply manifesting the same fundamental trait. It is, of course, important to emphasize that this is only a passing statement made in a letter from 1936 and that Adorno did not maintain this methodological orientation throughout his entire corpus. For instance, he occasionally invoked the "split consciousness" of the cultural consumer capable of seeing through the products of the culture industry while nonetheless indulging in them.[17] Nevertheless, in this particular proclamation he does purport to have access to *the* effect of the cinema *per se* (via, we can presume, his personal experience of individual films), thereby collapsing the density of the social fabric into a singular and monolithic reception. The critic judges *for everyone* and *in the place of everyone else*. There is no attempt in this passing statement to take into account the multifaceted topography of the receivers of cultural production. Moreover, Adorno's operative normative categories clearly reveal the binary value system at work. There are apparently only two possibilities: either laughter at the cinema is good and revolutionary, or it is bad and reactionary. He excludes the possibility of variegated and differentiated forms of reception in favor of a global conclusion concerning the political meaning of laughter at the cinema in general. This is why the problem with his assessment is not its cultural conservatism but its method. Indeed, the opposite claim would have been equally faulty. In both cases, abstract conceptualizations purport to reduce social phenomena to a single concept and unique value, as if they had a singular meaning. The critic thereby pretends to have *epistéme* concerning the definitive nature of a multifaceted social event.

---

17 See, for example, Theodor W. Adorno, *The Culture Industry: Selected Essays on Mass Culture* (London/New York: Routledge Classics, 2001), p. 196: "What the culture industry presents people with in their free time, if my conclusions are not too hasty, is indeed consumed and accepted, but with a kind of reservation, in the same way that even the most naive theatre or filmgoers do not simply take what they behold there for real. Perhaps one can go even further and say that it is not quite believed in. It is obvious that the integration of consciousness and free time has not yet completely succeeded. The real interests of individuals are still strong enough to resist, within certain limits, total inclusion." Also see the section in J. M. Bernstein's "Introduction" entitled "Seeing Through and Obeying" (ibid., pp. 12–16).

Conclusion

In conclusion, I would like to return to the core of the matter and provide heuristic labels for the two general positions I have been describing. The first might be generically referred to as *the politics of art* insofar as it is founded on the ontological illusion that each of these entities has a fixed being and a privileged relation that we can definitely describe via the lens of *epistéme*. The politics of art concentrates on the supposedly unique power of talisman-like works of art to produce political effects and generally assumes that the role of the interpreter is to authoritatively make claims regarding the nature of art in general or the singular political meaning of particular works. Rather than isolating art from its social inscription, rarifying politics as a discrete element, and then searching for their supposedly privileged link, it is necessary to break with the politics of art in favor of examining and participating in the *social politicity of aesthetic practices*. This means undermining the ontological illusion and the talisman complex by a radically historicist analytic of practice, which reveals that there is no being of art and politics or privileged relation between them. Instead, these are taken to be socio-historic concepts in struggle. It is therefore absolutely necessary to abandon the social epoché that has acted as a bulwark against understanding the social politicity of works of art in order to analyze – in addition to the works themselves – three important social dimensions of aesthetic practices: production, distribution and reception. This does not condemn us, however, to simply describing these various dimensions from the sidelines, so to speak. On the contrary, it is imperative to maintain what I call the dual position, which consists in simultaneously recognizing the polyvalent status of artwork in its social inscription and pragmatically intervening in the sphere of collective negotiations with strong arguments concerning the political elements operative in various aesthetic practices. It is my hope that this displacement from the politics of art to the social politicity of aesthetic practices will open novel space for rethinking the complex relationship between what is called "art" and "politics."

Contributors

Armen Avanessian studied philosophy and political science in Vienna, as well as literary studies at Bielefeld. After finishing his PhD thesis in 2004, he spent several years as a freelance journalist and editor in Paris and London. Since 2007 he has been a researcher at the Peter Szondi Institute for Comparative Literature at Freie Universität Berlin, and at SFB 626 *Ästhetische Erfahrung im Zeichen der Entgrenzung der Künste*. He was a visiting fellow at Columbia University's German Department in 2011, and at Yale University's German Department in 2012. Publications include: *Phänomenologie ironischen Geistes. Ethik, Poetik und Politik der Moderne* (2010); *Präsens. Poetik eines Tempus* (with Hennig, 2012); *Vita aesthetica. Szenarien ästhetischer Lebendigkeit* (ed. with Menninghaus/Völker, 2009); *Form. Zwischen Ästhetik und künstlerischer Praxis* (ed. with Hofmann/Leeb/Stauffacher, 2009); *Aesthetics and Contemporary Art* (ed. with Skrebowski, 2011).

Friedrich Balke is Professor for the History and Theory of Artifical Worlds at the Media Faculty, Bauhaus-University Weimar and spokesperson of the DFG-Research Training Group *Media of History – History of Media*. His areas of teaching and research focus on the cultural history of political sovereignty, governmentality and modern biopolitics, interrelations of media and forms of knowledge, aesthetic theory, and French philosophy. His books include *Der Staat nach seinem Ende. Die Versuchung Carl Schmitts* (1996); *Gilles Deleuze* (1997); *Ästhetische Regime um 1800* (ed. with Maye/Scholz, 2008); *Figuren der Souveränität* (2009); and *Die Wiederkehr der Dinge* (edited with Muhle/von Schöning, 2011).

Judith Butler is Maxine Elliot Professor at the Department of Rhetoric and Comparative Literature, and Co-director of the Program of Critical Theory at the University of California, Berkeley. She received her Ph.D. in philosophy from Yale University. Her research interests include continental philosophy and critical theory, gender and sexuality, literary and cultural studies, race and ethnicity, as well as political and social thought. She has authored numerous landmark studies such as *Gender Trouble: Feminism and the Subversion of Identity* (1990); *Bodies That Matter: On the Discursive Limits of "Sex"* (1993); and *Undoing Gender* (2004). Recent publications include: *Precarious Life: Powers of Violence and Mourning* (2004); *Frames of War: When Is Life Grievable?* (2009); *Is Critique Secular?* (2009); *The Power of Religion in Public Life* (2011); and *Parting Ways. Jewishness and the Critique of Zionism* (2012).

Simon Critchley is the Hans Jonas Professor of Philosophy at the New School for Social Research and part-time Professor of Philosophy at Tilburg University. His books include *The Ethics of Deconstruction: Derrida and Levinas* (1992); *Very Little...Almost Nothing* (1997); *Continental Philosophy: A Very Short Introduction* (2001); *On Humour* (2002); *The Book of Dead Philosophers* (2009); and *The Faith of the Faithless* (2012). He has just finished writing a book on *Hamlet*, to be published in 2013. His work has been translated in many languages. Critchley is series moderator of "The Stone," a popular online philosophy column for the *New York Times*, and he contributes to it regularly, as well as writing for *The Guardian*.

Anneka Esch-van Kan studied Theatre Arts and American Studies at Frankfurt/M., Giessen, Stony Brook (USA), and Münster. She is a member of the Graduate Centre for the Study of Culture at the University of Giessen, where she has recently submitted her PhD thesis *Representation of Crisis – Crisis of Representation. The Politics of Aesthetics and 21st Century. Political Theatre in the United States*. Her research interests include the relations between politics and aesthetics, experimental theater in Europe and the US, contemporary (American) drama, poststructuralist philosophy, and points of contact between theories of culture and disability studies. Publications include: "The Documentary Turn in Contemporary Drama and the Return of the Political: David Hare's *Stuff Happens* and Richard Norton-Taylor's *Called to Account* (2007)" (*A History of British Drama*, ed. Baumbach/Neumann/Nünning, Trier: WVT, 2011); "Ein-Brüche / trotz allem. Zur 'Politik der Bilder' im amerikanischen Theater seit dem 11. September 2001" (*9/11 als kulturelle Zäsur*, ed. Seiler/Poppe/Schüller, Bielefeld: transcript, 2009); "Amazing Acrobatics of Language. The Theatre of Yussef El Guindi" (*American Studies Journal* 52 (2008).

Josef Früchtl is Chair in Philosophy of Art and Culture – Critical Cultural Theory at the University of Amsterdam. Head of the Department from 2007 to 2012. Research interests: aesthetics, ethics, critical theory, theory of modernity, philosophy of film. Publications include: *Das unverschämte Ich. Eine Heldengeschichte der Moderne* (2004)/ *The Impertinent Self. A Heroic History of Modernity* (2009); "Auf ein Neues: Ästhetik und Politik. Und dazwischen das Spiel. Angestoßen durch Jacques Rancière" (*Deutsche Zeitschrift für Philosophie* 55, 2007); "Vom Nutzen des Ästhetischen für eine demokratische Kultur. Ein Plädoyer in zehn Punkten" (*"Ästhetisierung,"* ed. Brombach et al., 2010); "On the Use of Aesthetics for a Democratic Culture. A Ten-Point Appeal" (*Esthetica online. Tijdschrift voor kunst en filosofie*, 2011); "Politik, Ästhetik oder Mystik des Zeigens. Benjamin, Deleuze und das Kino" (*Politik des Zeigens*, ed. van den Berg/Gumbrecht, 2010); "Exhibiting or Presenting? Politics, Aesthetics, and Mysticism in Benjamin's and Deleuze's Concepts of Cinema" (online proceedings of the 1st Congress of the European Society for Aesthetics, 2009); *Vertrauen in die Welt. Eine Philosophie des Films* (forthcoming 2013).

Andreas Hetzel teaches philosophy at the universities of Darmstadt and Innsbruck and media studies at Klagenfurt University. He studied philosophy and Germanic languages at the universities of Münster and Frankfurt/M. and obtained his PhD (1999) and his Habilitation (2009) at Darmstadt University (TU Darmstadt). His research interests include cultural studies, political philosophy, contemporary French theory, critical theory, German idealism, and ancient philosophy. He currently focuses on theories of rhetoric and philosophies of language and culture. Apart from co-editing eight books, he has published a book on the concept of culture: *Zwischen Poiesis und Praxis. Elemente einer kritischen Theorie der Kultur* (2001), and a book on the concept of language in classical rhetoric: *Die Wirksamkeit der Rede. Zur Aktualität klassischer Rhetorik für die moderne Sprachphilosophie* (2010).

Jon McKenzie is Director of DesignLab, a digital composition center, and Professor of English at the University of Wisconsin-Madison, where he teaches courses in performance theory and new media. He is the author of *Perform or Else: From Discipline to Performance* (2001) and such articles as "Global Feeling: (Almost) All You Need is Love" (2006); "Performance and Globalization" (2006); and "Towards a Sociopoetics of Interface Design" (2001). He is also co-editor of *Contesting Performance: Global Sites of Research* (2011). His work has been translated into a half-dozen languages. McKenzie has also produced a number of experimental video essays, including *The Revelations of Dr. Kx4l3ndjer* (2012) and *This Vile Display* (2006), and gives workshops on performative scholarship and smart media.

Dieter Mersch is Professor for Media Theory and Media Studies at the University of Potsdam and Head of the Department for Arts and Media. He studied mathematics and philosophy in Cologne and Bochum and received his PhD in philosophy from the Technical University Darmstadt. His main areas of interests are the philosophy of media, language, and art, as well as semiotics, picture-theory, hermeneutics and post-Structuralism. Publications include: *Was sich zeigt. Materialität, Präsenz, Ereignis* (2002); *Ereignis und Aura. Untersuchungen zu einer Ästhetik des Performativen* (2002); *Die Medien der Künste. Beiträge zur Theorie des Darstellens* (ed., 2003); *Performativität und Praxis* (ed. with Kertscher, 2003); *Logik des Bildlichen: Zur Kritik der ikonischen Vernunft* (ed. with Heßler, 2009); *Posthermeneutik* (2010); *Ikonizität: Medialität und Bildlichkeit* (forthcoming).

Chantal Mouffe is Professor of Political Theory at the Centre for the Study of Democracy at the University of Westminster in London. She has taught and researched at many universities in Europe, North America and South America, and is a corresponding member of the Collège International de Philosophie in Paris. She is the editor of *Gramsci and Marxist Theory* (1979); *Dimensions of Radical Democracy. Pluralism, Citizenship, Community* (1992); *Deconstruction and Pragmatism* (1996); and *The Challenge of Carl Schmitt* (1999); the co-author with Ernesto Laclau of *Hegemony and Socialist Strategy. Towards a Radical Democratic Politics* (1985); and the author of *The Return of the Political* (1993); *The Democratic Paradox* (2000); and *On the Political* (2005).

Maria Muhle is professor for aesthetic theory at Merz Akademie Stuttgart. Her research focuses on contemporary political and aesthetic theory, especially on biopolitics and the notion of "aesthetic realism" in the context of a political aesthetics. She is also the co-founder of August Verlag Berlin, a publishing house for theory at the crossroads of philosophy, politics and arts. Recent publications include: "Realism, disidentification and the image" (*Everything is in Everything: Between Intellectual Emancipation and Aesthetic Education*, ed. Smith/Weisser, 2011); "Reenactments der Macht. Überlegungen zu einer medialen Historiographie" (*Zeitschrift für Ästhetik und Allgemeine Kunstwissenschaft* 56.2, 2011); "Zweierlei Vitalismus" (*Gilles Deleuze: Philosophie und Nicht-Philosophie. Aktuelle Diskussionen*, ed. Balke/Rölli, 2011); "Ästhetischer Realismus: Strategien post-repräsentativer Darstellung anhand von *A bientôt j'espère* und *Classe de Lutte*" (*Das Streit-Bild*, ed. Hübel/Mattl/Robnik, 2010); and *Eine Genealogie der Biopolitik. Der Lebensbegriff bei Foucault und Canguilhem* (2008).

Nikolaus Müller-Schöll is Professor for Theatre Studies and Head of the MA Programme *Dramaturgie* at the Institute for Theatre, Film and Media Studies, Goethe University Frankfurt/M. His research focuses on the comical as a paradigm of modern experience (17th–20th century); (re)presentation "after Auschwitz"; theatre architecture as built ideology; questions between theatre, philosophy, politics, and literature, including topics of alterity, fictionizing the political and potentiality, as well as experimental forms of contemporary theatre and performance. His publications include *Das Theater des "konstruktiven Defaitismus". Walter Benjamin, Bertolt Brecht und Heiner Müller* (2002); *Ereignis* (ed. 2003), *Aisthesis* (co-ed. 2005); *Politik der Vorstellung. Theater und Theorie* (co-ed. 2006); *Performing Politics* (co-ed. 2012).

Stephan Packard is Junior Professor for Media Culture Studies at Freiburg University; previously, he was Assistant Professor for Comparative Literature in Munich, where he received his PhD. Interests focus on semiotic and psychoanalytic research into new and traditional media; the semiotics of affect; censorship and other forms of media control; as well as comics studies. He is an active member of the German Society for Comics Studies (ComFor), on the editing board of the journal *Medienobservationen*, and edits the new open access journal *Mediale Kontrolle unter Beobachtung* on censorship and media control. Publications include: *Anatomie des Comics. Psychosemiotische Medienanalyse* (2006); *Bilder des Comics* (ed., 2012); *Poetische Gerechtigkeit* (ed. with Donat/Lüdeke/Richter, 2012); *Abschied von 9/11* (ed. with Hennigfeld, forthcoming); and *Comics und Politik – Comics & Politics* (ed., forthcoming).

Wim Peeters is a literary scholar, currently working as lecturer and postdoctoral researcher at the German Department of the TU Dortmund. He is the author of a PhD thesis on chatter (*Recht auf Geschwätz. Geltung und Darstellung von Rede in der Moderne*, publ. 2012). Further publications focus on Robert Walser, the Sacrifice of Abraham, 9/11, "social exclusion" and affect in contemporary literature and film, politics of comment in modern literature, and the poetics of counsel. Publications include: *Kriegstheater. Zur Zukunft des Politischen III* (ed. with Oberender/Risthaus, 2006); *Mythos Abraham. Texte der Genesis bis Friedrich Chr. Delius* (ed. with Niehaus, 2009); 'Wenn kein Gebot, kein Soll herrschte in der Welt, ich würde sterben.' Jakob von Gunten als Glossator" (*Gesetz. Ironie*, ed. Campe/Niehaus, 2004); "9/11 und das Insistieren des Alltags. Pressefotografie und deutsche Gegenwartsliteratur" (*9/11 als kulturelle Zäsur*, ed. Poppe/Schüller/Seiler, 2009); "Deconstructing Wasted Identities in Contemporary German Literature" (*The Aesthetics of Trash: Objects and Obsolescence in Cultural Perspective*, ed. Pye/ Schroth, 2010).

Jacques Rancière is Professor Emeritus at the University of Paris VIII, where he taught philosophy from 1969 to 2000. He was a student of Louis Althusser at École Normal Supérieure in Paris. His work deals with emancipatory politics, aesthetics, and the relationship between aesthetics and politics. He also writes extensively on cinema. His translated works include: *The Nights of Labor* (1989); *The Ignorant Schoolmaster. Five Lessons in Intellectual Emancipation* (1991); *Disagreement: Politics and Philosophy* (1998); *The Politics of Aesthetics: The Distribution of the Sensible* (2004); *The Future of the Image* (2007); *Hatred of Democracy* (2007); and *The Emancipated Spectator* (2009).

Juliane Rebentisch is Professor of Philosophy and Aesthetics at the University of Arts and Design in Offenbach/Main. Her main research areas are aesthetics, ethics, and political philosophy. Publications include: *Ästhetik der Installation* (2003)/*Aesthetics of Installation Art* (2012); *Die Kunst der Freiheit. Zur Dialektik demokratischer Existenz* (2012); *Kreation und Depression. Freiheit im gegenwärtigen Kapitalismus* (ed. with Menke, 2010).

Gabriel Rockhill is Assistant Professor of Philosophy at Villanova University, Directeur de programme at the Collège International de Philosophie in Paris, and Chercheur associé at the Centre de Recherches sur les Arts et le Langage (CNRS/EHESS). He is the author of *Logique de l'histoire: Pour une analytique des pratiques philosophiques* (2010) and is currently completing *Radical History and the Politics of Art* (forthcoming 2013). He co-authored *Politics of Culture and the Spirit of Critique: Dialogues* (2011), and co-edited and contributed to *Jacques Rancière: History, Politics, Aesthetics* (2009) and *Technologies de contrôle dans la mondialisation: Enjeux politiques, éthiques et esthétiques* (2009). He is also the co-founder of the Machete Group, a collective of artists and intellectuals based in Philadelphia (http://machetegroup.wordpress.com/).

Frank Ruda is a researcher at SFB 626 at the Free University Berlin and Visiting Lecturer at the Institute of Philosophy at the Centre for Scientific Research, Slovenian Academy of Art and Sciences. He has published extensively in the fields of politics and philosophy, contemporary French thought and aesthetics. His most recent publications include: *Hegel's Rabble. An Investigation into Hegel's Philosophy of Right* (2011); *For Badiou. Idealism without Idealism* (2012); "Exiting the Woods. Cartesianism for the 21st Century" (*Monokl*, 2012).

Philipp Schulte studied Applied Theatre Studies at Bergen University (Norway) and Gießen University, where he graduated in 2005. He received his Ph.D. from Gießen University in 2011 with the completion of his thesis on *Identität als Experiment* (publ. 2011). Since 2007, he has worked as contributor at the Hessian Theater Academy in Frankfurt, as a freelance author, and as a dramaturge. Since 2009, he is a researcher at the Institute for Applied Theater Studies in Gießen. Further publications include: "Das Echte im Falschen. Die angebliche Rekonstruktion der Kriege im Libanon in den Arbeiten der Atlas Group" (*Echte Geschichte: Authentizitätsfiktionen in populären Geschichtskulturen*, ed. Pirker et al., 2010); *Die Kunst der Bühne. Positionen des zeitgenössischen Theaters* (ed. with Tiedtke, 2011).

Thinking Resistances
Current Perspectives on Politics and Communities in the Arts, Vol. 1

Gerald Siegmund, Stefan Hölscher (Hg.)
Dance, Politics & Co-Immunity

ISBN 978-3-03734-218-3
292 pages, € 26,95 / CHF 40,00

This volume is dedicated to the question of how dance, both in its historical and in its contemporary manifestations, is intricately linked to conceptualisations of the political. Whereas in this context the term "policy" means the reproduction of hegemonic power relations within already existing institutional structures, politics refers to those practices which question the space of policy as such by inscribing that into its surface which has had no place before. The art of choreography consists in distributing bodies and their relations in space. It is a distribution of parts that within the field of the visible and the sayable allocates positions to specific bodies. Yet in the confrontation between bodies and their relations, a deframing and dislocating of positions may take place. The essays included in this book are aimed at the multiple connections between politics, community, dance, and globalisation from the perspective of e.g. Dance and Theatre Studies, History, Philosophy, and Sociology.

With contributions by Ulas Aktas, Saša Asentić, Gabriele Brandstetter, Ramsay Burt, Bojana Cvejić, Mark Franko, Stefan Hölscher, Gabriele Klein, Bojana Kunst, André Lepecki, Isabell Lorey, Erin Manning, Randy Martin, Brian Massumi, Gerald Raunig, Petra Sabisch, Gerald Siegmund, Ana Vujanović.